Ephesians, Colossians, Philemon

New International Biblical Commentary

Ephesians, Colossians, Philemon

Arthur G. Patzia

New Testament Editor,
W. Ward Gasque

HENDRICKSON
PUBLISHERS
PEABODY, MASSACHUSETTS 01961-3473

Copyright © 1984, 1990 by Arthur G. Patzia
Hendrickson Publishers, Inc.
P.O. Box 3473
Peabody, Massachusetts 01961–3473
All rights reserved.
Printed in the United States of America

ISBN 0–943575–19–2

Library of Congress Cataloging-in-Publication Data

Patzia, Arthur G.
    Ephesians, Colossians, Philemon / Arthur G. Patzia.
        p. cm. — (New International biblical commentary; 10)
    Includes bibliographical references and indexes.
    ISBN 0–943575–19–2
    1. Bible. N.T. Ephesians—Commentaries.
    2. Bible. N.T. Colossians—Commentaries.
    3. Bible. N.T. Philemon—Commentaries.
    I. Title. II. Series.
    BS2695.3.P378   1990
    227—dc20   90-24092
                                                             CIP

Scripture taken from the HOLY BIBLE, NEW INTERNATIONAL
VERSION. Copyright © 1973, 1978, 1984 International Bible Society.
Used by permission of Zondervan Bible Publishers.

Dedicated to my wife
DOROTHY
who is a living expression
of God's love, grace, and forgiveness

Table of Contents

Foreword xi

Editor's Note xv

Abbreviations xvii

Colossians

Introduction: Colossians 3

§1   Paul's Greetings (Col. 1:1-2) 15
§2   Paul's Prayer of Thanksgiving (Col. 1:3-8) 17
§3   Paul's Prayer of Intercession (Col. 1:9-14) 21
§4   The Hymn to Christ (Col. 1:15-20) 27
§5   The Application of the Hymn to the Colossians
      (Col. 1:21-23) 36
§6   Paul's Personal Suffering (Col. 1:24) 39
§7   Paul's Proclamation of the Mystery (Col. 1:25-29) 43
§8   Paul's Concern for the Churches (Col. 2:1-5) 46
§9   A Summons to Steadfastness (Col. 2:6-7) 49
§10   Christian Versus Human Tradition (Col. 2:8-10) 51
§11   The True Circumcision and Its Effects (Col. 2:11-15) 55
§12   A Manifesto of Christian Liberty (Col. 2:16-23) 61
§13   The Ethical Dimensions of the Christian Life
      (Introduction to Col. 3:1-4:6) 68
§14   The Heavenly Life (Col. 3:1-4) 70
§15   The Vices of the Old Life (Col. 3:5-9) 72
§16   The Virtues of the New Life (Col. 3:10-15) 76
§17   The Expressions of True Worship (Col. 3:16-17) 81
§18   The Household Rules (Introduction to Col. 3:18-4:1) 83
§19   Wife-Husband Relationships (Col. 3:18-19) 88
§20   Child-Parent Relationships (Col. 3:20-21) 90

§21   Slave-Master Relationships (Col. 3:22–4:1)..............91
§22   Exhortations to Pray and Witness (Col. 4:2–6)...........96
§23   Final Greetings and Instructions (Col. 4:7–18)...........99

Philemon

Introduction: Philemon...................................105

§1   Paul's Greetings (Philem. 1–3)........................106
§2   Paul's Praise for Philemon (Philem. 4–7)...............108
§3   Paul's Request for Onesimus (Philem. 8–22)............110
§4   Paul's Final Greetings (Philem. 23–25).................117

Ephesians

Introduction: Ephesians..................................121

§1   The Opening Greeting (Eph. 1:1–2)...................145
§2   A Hymn of Praise (Eph. 1:3–14).....................148
§3   Prayer for Divine Enlightenment (Eph. 1:15–19)........163
§4   The Result of Christ's Enthronement (Eph. 1:20–23).....169
§5   Christ and the Salvation of Believers
      (Introduction to Eph. 2:1–10).......................175
§6   Salvation from Spiritual Death (Eph. 2:1–3)............177
§7   Salvation to Spiritual Life (Eph. 2:4–10)................179
§8   Christ and the Unity of Believers
      (Introduction to Eph. 2:11–22)......................187
§9   The Gentiles Apart from Christ (Eph. 2:11–12).........189
§10 The Gentiles in Christ (Eph. 2:13–18).................193
§11 The New Unity (Eph. 2:19–22).......................200
§12 Paul and the Mission to the Gentiles
      (Introduction to Eph. 3:1–21).......................205
§13 Presenting the Mystery of the Gospel (Eph. 3:1–13).....209
§14 Praying for Enlightenment (Eph. 3:14–19)..............220
§15 Praising Through Doxology (Eph. 3:20–21).............227
§16 The Appeal and Pattern for Unity (Eph. 4:1–6.)........228
§17 The Giving of Spiritual Gifts to the Body (Eph. 4:7–11)..235
§18 The Attainment of Unity (Eph. 4:12–16)...............243
§19 The Old and the New Life (Eph. 4:17–24)..............248

§20 Specific Ethical Directions (Eph. 4:25–5:2)..............252
§21 Living in the Light (Eph. 5:3–21).....................256
§22 Wives and Husbands (Eph. 5:22–33)..................266
§23 Children and Parents (Eph. 6:1–4)....................277
§24 Slaves and Masters (Eph. 6:5–9)......................280
§25 The Christian's Armor (Eph. 6:10–20).................283
§26 Final Greetings (Eph. 6:21–22).......................293
§27 Closing Benediction (Eph. 6:23–24)...................294

For Further Reading......................................295

Subject Index...299

Scripture Index...305

Foreword
New International Biblical Commentary

Although it does not appear on the standard best-seller lists, the Bible continues to outsell all other books. And in spite of growing secularism in the West, there are no signs that interest in its message is abating. Quite to the contrary, more and more men and women are turning to its pages for insight and guidance in the midst of the ever-increasing complexity of modern life.

This renewed interest in Scripture is found both outside and inside the church. It is found among people in Asia and Africa as well as in Europe and North America; indeed, as one moves outside of the traditionally Christian countries, interest in the Bible seems to quicken. Believers associated with the traditional Catholic and Protestant churches manifest the same eagerness for the Word that is found in the newer evangelical churches and fellowships.

We wish to encourage and, indeed, strengthen this world-wide movement of lay Bible study by offering this new commentary series. Although we hope that pastors and teachers will find these volumes helpful in both understanding and communicating the Word of God, we do not write primarily for them. Our aim is to provide for the benefit of every Bible reader reliable guides to the books of the Bible—representing the best of contemporary scholarship presented in a form that does not require formal theological education to understand.

The conviction of editor and authors alike is that the Bible belongs to the people and not merely to the academy. The message of the Bible is too important to be locked up in erudite and esoteric essays and monographs written only for the eyes of theological specialists. Although exact scholarship has its place in the service of Christ, those who share in the teaching office of the church have a responsibility to make the results of their research accessible to the Christian community at large. Thus, the Bible scholars who join in the presentation of this series write with these broader concerns in view.

A wide range of modern translations is available to the contemporary Bible student. Most of them are very good and much to be preferred—for understanding, if not always for beauty—to the older King James Version (the so-called Authorized Version of the Bible). The Revised Standard Version has become the standard English translation in many seminaries and colleges and represents the best of modern Protestant scholarship. It is also available in a slightly altered "common Bible" edition with the Catholic imprimatur, and a third revised edition is due out shortly. In addition, the New American Bible is a fresh translation that represents the best of post-Vatican II Roman Catholic biblical scholarship and is in a more contemporary idiom than that of the RSV.

The New Jerusalem Bible, based on the work of French Catholic scholars but vividly rendered into English by a team of British translators, is perhaps the most literary of the recent translations, while the New English Bible is a monument to modern British Protestant research. The Good News Bible is probably the most accessible translation for the person who has little exposure to the Christian tradition or who speaks and reads English as a second language. Each of these is, in its own way, excellent and will be consulted with profit by the serious student of Scripture. Perhaps most will wish to have several versions to read, both for variety and for clarity of understanding—though it should be pointed out that no one of them is by any means flawless or to be received as the last word on any given point. Otherwise, there would be no need for a commentary series like this one!

We have chosen to use the New International Version as the basis for this series, not because it is necessarily the best translation available but because it is becoming increasingly used by lay Bible students and pastors. It is the product of an international team of "evangelical" Bible scholars who have sought to translate the Hebrew and Greek documents of the original into "clear and natural English . . . idiomatic [and] . . . contemporary but not dated," suitable for "young and old, highly educated and less well educated, ministers and laymen [sic]." As the translators themselves confess in their preface, this version is not perfect. However, it is as good as any of the others mentioned above and more popular than most of them.

Each volume will contain an introductory chapter detailing the background of the book and its author, important themes, and other helpful information. Then, each section of the book will be expounded as a whole, accompanied by a series of notes on items in the text that need further clarification or more detailed explanation. Appended to the end of each volume will be a bibliographical guide for further study.

Our new series is offered with the prayer that it may be an instrument of authentic renewal and advancement in the worldwide Christian community and a means of commending the faith of the people who lived in biblical times and of those who seek to live by the Bible today.

W. WARD GASQUE
Provost
Eastern College
St. Davids, Pennsylvania

Editor's Note

Although the title of this volume is *Ephesians, Colossians, Philemon,* the three books are treated within the commentary in the order Colossians, Philemon, Ephesians. Titling the volume in this way was an editorial decision based on the canonical order of these epistles. The author has chosen, however, to discuss them in a different order for literary critical reasons. Many of the comments on the book of Ephesians, for example, are dependent upon comments made on the book of Colossians. It is hoped that this will not cause undue confusion.

Abbreviations

ATR	*Anglican Theological Review*
BibSac	*Bibliotheca Sacra*
BibTod	*Bible Today*
BJRL	*Bulletin of John Rylands Library*
BZNW	*Beiheft zur Zeitschrift für die neutestamentliche Wissenschaft*
CBQ	*Catholic Biblical Quarterly*
CTJ	*Calvin Theological Journal*
cf.	compare
disc.	discussion
EQ	*Evangelical Quarterly*
ExpT	*Expository Times*
ff.	following pages or verses
GNB	*Good News Bible*
IB	*Interpreter's Bible*
Interp	*Interpretation*
JBL	*Journal of Biblical Literature*
JETS	*Journal of the Evangelical Theological Society*
JSNT	*Journal for the Study of the New Testament*
JTS	*Journal of Theological Studies*
KJV	King James Version
n.	note
NASB	New American Standard Bible
NEB	New English Bible
NIV	New International Version
NovT	*Novum Testamentum*
NT	New Testament
NTS	*New Testament Studies*
OT	Old Testament
RB	*Revue Biblique*
RefThR	*Reformed Theological Review*
RevExp	*Review and Expositor*
RSV	Revised Standard Version
SBLDS	Society of Biblical Literature Dissertation Series

SBT	Studies in Biblical Theology
SJT	*Scottish Journal of Theology*
SNTSMS	Society for New Testament Monograph Series
ST	*Studia Theologica*
SWJTh	*Southwestern Journal of Theology*
TDNT	*Theological Dictionary of the New Testament*, edited by G. Kittel and G. Friedrich, and translated by G. W. Bromiley (1964–72)
TZ	*Theologische Zeitschrift*
v. (vv.)	verse(s)
ZNW	*Zeitschrift für die neutestamentliche Wissenschaft*

Colossians

Introduction: Colossians

The City of Colossae

Colossae was a major city situated near the Meander River in the Lycus Valley and thus along the main trade route that connected the cities of Phrygia in the east with Ephesus in the west. Historical records indicate that it enjoyed considerable wealth and prestige in ancient times (prior to 400 B.C.). Because of its commercial interests, Colossae had been a significant cosmopolitan city that included diverse religious and cultural elements. The Jewish population was due in part to Antiochus III, who settled about two thousand Jews from Mesopotamia and Babylon in that area around 200 B.C. G. L. Munn observes that "by 62 B.C. the Jews of the Lycus valley were so numerous that the Roman governor forbade the export of currency to pay the temple tax."[1] According to Cicero, there may have been as many as ten thousand Jews living in that area of Phrygia.[2]

Colossae diminished in importance as a city during the Hellenistic and Roman periods. By the time of the Apostle Paul, it was the least important city in the area. Historians record that it was severely devastated by an earthquake in A.D. 61, and unlike its neighboring cities of Laodicea (about ten miles west) and Hierapolis (about sixteen miles northwest), it was never rebuilt. The site was completely abandoned by the eighth century A.D., and to this day no major archaeological work has been carried out on its ruins.

The Church in Colossae

Very little is known about the founding of the Colossian church. The Book of Acts does not specifically record any visit to Colossae by Paul, although scholars such as Bo Reicke have suggested that Paul may have gone to Colossae and other cities in the Lycus Valley on his third missionary journey, when he passed through the "region of Galatia and Phrygia" (18:23) and "through the interior" on his way to Ephesus (19:1). Reicke takes this to mean the Lycus and Meander valleys, which would have

been accessible by the trade route that connected Colossae with
Pisidian Antioch.[3]

If this is true, then Paul could be considered the founder
of the church. He knows quite a few members of the congregation (4:7–17; Philemon), and those who do not know him personally (2:1) could be recent converts. The internal evidence of
the epistle leads one to conclude that the Colossians first heard
the Good News from Epaphras (1:7), who was from Colossae
(4:12) and who had become one of Paul's co-workers in the Lycus
Valley (4:13). Epaphras may have heard Paul teaching in Ephesus,
converted to Christianity, and returned home to start a church.
According to this reconstruction, Paul was connected with the
beginning of the church, but indirectly. The same would be true
of other churches that were started as a result of his ministry in
Ephesus ("so that all the Jews and Greeks who lived in the province of Asia heard the word of the Lord," Acts 19:10).

The False Teaching

The false teaching that was threatening the Colossian
church is best described as a syncretistic religious system, that
is, as a mixture of diverse religious and philosophical components coming from Oriental, Greek, Roman, and Jewish cultures.
Phrygia, the area in which Colossae was located, was the home
of Cybele, the great mother goddess of fertility. Some descriptions of the features of the Colossian heresy may refer to beliefs
and practices of this popular cult.[4]

Since Paul does not deal with the heresy in any systematic
way, we are left to reconstruct it on the basis of the words and
ideas he uses, as well as from our understanding of the religious
systems current in his day. His readers already knew the basic
tenets of this teaching, so it was not necessary for Paul to develop it in any detail. The complexity of the system may have led
the Christians at Colossae to believe that it was a better solution
for their religious hopes and fears than the simple gospel they
had heard from Epaphras.

The false teaching had several major components, all inter-
related in various ways:

Astrology. In the epistle, Paul warns his readers about the
"basic principles of this world" (*stoicheia tou kosmou*, 2:8), "powers

and authorities" (2:15), and "the worship of angels" (2:18). In ancient thought, the *stoicheia* were the basic or fundamental principles of knowledge and creation, thus making up the totality of the world. Under the influence of Hellenistic syncretism, including Pythagorean philosophy, these "first principles" were elevated to the status of "spirits," personified as cosmic rulers, and, along with all the other astral bodies in the universe, divinized.

One of the basic tenets of astrology is that there is a correspondence between the movements of the gods above and the alterations that take place on earth. People believed that their lives were controlled by these stellar divinities and thus sought to placate them through worship or to defuse their power through sorcery, rituals, magical rites, and so on. Some of the beliefs and practices that Paul exposes in the epistle are related to astrology. Even the worship of angels may come from the idea that these are powers that control one's destiny (fate) and need to be venerated. Lohse suggests that in some strands of Jewish speculation "the stars themselves were thought of as a distinct class of angels."[5]

Gnosticism. This component of Colossian heresy may explain such references as "hollow and deceptive philosophy" (2:8), "human tradition" (2:8), rules about "what you eat or drink" (2:16, 20–22), "his unspiritual mind puffs him up with idle notions" (2:18), "false humility" (2:23), and "harsh treatment of the body" (2:23).

Gnosticism is the name given to a complex syncretistic religious system in whose teaching knowledge (*gnōsis*) had a crucial place. Since Gnosticism existed in a variety of forms, there is no one unified movement that can properly be called Gnosticism. Much of the scholarly debate today centers around the dating and the doctrines of this heresy that confronted the church throughout its early history.[6]

Traces of Gnostic cosmology, soteriology (theories concerning salvation), and ethics can be found in Colossians. The Gnostics accepted the Greek idea of a radical dualism between spirit (God) and matter (the world). They taught that mankind was separated from God by a number of cosmic spheres (usually seven) inhabited and ruled by all sorts of spiritual rulers, principalities, and powers. These are the regions that one must penetrate if one wishes to gain access to heaven.

Salvation, which basically consists of the soul's ascent from earth to heaven, is made possible by *gnōsis*. This saving knowledge is available through such means as doctrinal instruction, ritual, prophecy, sacramental initiation, and self-discovery; it enables an individual to return to the realm of light where the soul becomes reunited with God.

The ethical life of the Gnostics took two major directions. Some moved toward a rigid asceticism. Because they believed that the world was evil, they separated themselves from "matter" in order to avoid further contamination. All the cravings of the body had to be severely restricted. Other Gnostics, however, practiced libertinism, reasoning that since the body already was evil, further indulgence in immoral practices would not have any serious consequences. Besides, they felt that they had supernatural *gnōsis* of their "true" nature, so it really did not matter how they lived.

The false teachers in Colossae held to a rigid system of rules and regulations that they felt were necessary to control their behavior. These rules, combined with some forms of Jewish legalism, account for Paul's "manifesto of Christian liberty" in 2:16–23. Basically, he teaches that such dogmas are transitory (2:17), divisive (2:18), enslaving (2:20), temporary (2:22), and useless (2:23). For Paul, these are "human commands and teachings" (2:22) and have nothing to do with the true gospel that comes from Christ (2:8).

Mystery Religions. The term *mystery religion* is the name given to a number of beliefs and practices that existed anytime from the eighth century B.C. to the fourth century A.D. They are called mysteries because so much of their teaching and ritual activity was carried on in secrecy.[7]

In Colossians, there may be an allusion to the mysteries in the phrases "the fullness of the Deity" (2:9), "false humility," and "a person goes into great detail about what he has seen" (2:18). Initiates of the mysteries would receive special knowledge and visions of the secrets of the universe. This, in turn, would set them apart from the uninitiated, creating divisions within the society.

Hellenistic Judaism. References to circumcision (2:11), holy days, the new moon festival, the Sabbath (2:16), and the worship of angels (2:18) are definitely Jewish. This is not, however, the orthodox Judaism of Palestine; rather, it is a Judaism that has been thoroughly Hellenized. As such, it forms part of the syncretistic "philosophy" (2:8) that was threatening the Christians at Colossae. Paul does not single out this Jewish element but attacks it along with the entire system.

His solution to the Colossian heresy is found in the application of the Christ hymn (1:15–20), which establishes the preeminence of Christ in the universe (cosmically) and in the church (ecclesiastically). Since Christ is superior to every other power in the cosmos (1:15–17; 2:10) and has, in fact, defeated these powers on the cross (2:15), why should believers go on living as if they were still subject to them? They have been set free from these powers by virtue of their union with Christ in baptism (2:20).

Much the same applies to the believers' spiritual life. The path to growth, maturity, and fullness for members within the body comes from their relationship to Christ, the head (2:19), not a return to the enslaving, legalistic rules and regulations that Christ set aside through his death (2:14). The purpose of the exhortations in 3:1 and the following verses is to remind these believers that they need to live out ethically what is theirs theologically because they are members of the body of Christ.

The Purpose of the Letter

If the reason for the writing of Colossians is connected with Epaphras' report to Paul about the false teaching that was threatening the church, then it follows that its purpose is to warn the readers about this heresy and to remind them of the truth of the gospel that they have already received and in which they now live (1:5). Basically, Paul is telling them that Christ has defeated the evil powers by his death on the cross (2:15). This means that the false teaching and enslaving regulations that come from human wisdom and from the ruling spirits of the universe (2:8) have no authority over the believer (2:10); their previous hold over a person's life in the form of an unpaid debt has been canceled (2:14). Paul wants his readers to realize this truth and so reminds them to walk in the light of the traditions that they have received about Christ and the gospel.

This fact accounts for the many references to the truth of the gospel (1:5, 6, 25–27; 2:8, 9, 12, 13) and the admonitions to understand and to live out their hope accordingly (1:9, 10, 12, 23,

28; 2:2, 3, 5–7). The ethical exhortations (3:1ff.) are a further reminder that the Colossians live in union with Christ and under the authority of the exalted Lord.

In Paul's understanding of the gospel there is no room for any kind of exclusivism. His concept of the "mystery" that he has been called to proclaim is that Jews *and* Gentiles, as well as the entire universe, are included in God's plan of redemption (1:20, 25–29). Thus he rejoices that "all over the world this gospel is bearing fruit and growing" (1:6, 23). Paul's wish is that during—and possibly after—his imprisonment, he may able to continue his proclamation of the mystery (4:3, 4).

One of the dangers of false teaching in any congregation is that it thwarts God's plan of inclusivism. Those following the "traditions of men" would set themselves up as the enlightened or spiritually elite, believing that their wisdom and legalism make them different from other members in the body of Christ. In opposition to this exclusivism, Paul is inspired to write that believers have already been circumcised in union with Christ (2:11, 12), and as a result of that union, "there is no Greek or Jew" (3:11; note GNB "there is no longer any distinction between Gentiles and Jews").[8]

Authorship

Apparently, the Pauline authorship of Colossians was universally accepted until the German scholar E. Meyerhoff questioned it in 1893, largely because of its close dependence upon Ephesians. He was followed by F. C. Baur, who claimed that the heresy described in Colossians could belong only to the second century. Since that time, a number of scholars either hold Colossians to be Pauline or designate it as one of the deutero-Pauline epistles, that is, an epistle written by an author using Paul's name.[9]

The questions of authorship center around the usual categories of vocabulary, style, and theology. Colossians has an unusually high number of *hapax legomena*, that is, it contains thirty-four words that do not appear elsewhere in the NT. In addition, there are twenty-eight words that appear in the NT but not in Paul's writings. A number of scholars question whether these could appear unless Colossians were the work of another author.[10]

The style in which the epistle is written is somewhat different from letters that are indisputably Paul's. Scholars have noted that Paul usually deals with theological problems in a vigorous or polemical manner (cf. Galatians, Corinthians, Philippians). In Colossians, the approach is more subdued and less argumentative. The style has a hymnic and liturgical quality about it, and the entire epistle uses a considerable amount of traditional material, that is, Christian teaching that was common in the early church and used by Paul and other writers of the NT.

In spite of the differences in vocabulary and style, however, nearly all scholars agree that these factors alone cannot decide the question of authorship. Some feel that the "special circumstances of the background and purpose of this letter" account for the differences; others claim that because of the high percentage of non-Pauline, that is, traditional, material in the epistle, it is impossible to make any reliable comparisons with Paul's other letters.[11]

E. Lohse, who firmly believes that Colossians is deutero-Pauline, acknowledges that studies of language and style do not settle the matter. For him, it is its theological teaching that sets Colossians apart from Paul and leads to the conclusion that this epistle is the work of a Pauline school using Paul's letters to address a new challenge in the church.

In his detailed and helpful excursus entitled "The Letter to the Colossians and Pauline Theology," Lohse examines the Christology (teaching of Christ), ecclesiology (teaching of the church), eschatology (teaching of the end times), and sacramentalism (teaching related to baptism as a sacrament) of Colossians and concludes that in all these areas there are substantial differences with Paul's theology as reflected in his genuine epistles. True, the historical situation necessitated some new theological formulations, but the differences are too divergent, according to Lohse, for Pauline authorship to be supported.[12]

Not all scholars, however, are convinced that the theology of Colossians is non-Pauline. Some believe that the threat of the false teaching required that Paul state and apply his gospel in different ways but deny that he changed or contradicted it. G. Cannon faults Lohse for neglecting the interrelatedness of these theological categories and failing to see that many of the ideas that he labels deutero-Pauline can be found in Paul's chief letters and in the theological affirmations of the traditional material that Colossians uses.[13]

Another argument in favor of Pauline authorship is the close connection between Colossians and Philemon. Since the Pauline authorship of Philemon is rarely questioned, it would follow that Colossians comes from Paul as well. Both epistles contain Timothy's name (Col. 1:1; Philem. 1) and include greetings from the same people (Col. 4:10–14; Philem. 23, 24). Also, Onesimus, the subject of the letter of Philemon, is mentioned as being a member of the group in Colossae (4:9).

Although all contrary evidence needs to be evaluated carefully, it seems reasonable to conclude with G. Cannon "that the author of Colossians was Paul the apostle and that he wrote to the churches of the Lycus Valley to warn them about a teaching which advocated practices which would put them in a pre-Christian situation and which contradicted the teachings which they had received about Christ in the gospel and in baptismal instruction."[14]

Origin

If Colossians was not written by Paul, then it must be the product of the Pauline school that probably was connected with Ephesus.[15] However, if Paul is the author, then it belongs to one of the "captivity epistles." There are three places of origin that normally are proposed—Rome, Caesarea, and Ephesus.

Rome. The traditional view reconstructed from the Book of Acts is that Paul wrote his captivity epistles while in prison in Rome (Acts 28:16–31; see also Eusebius' *Ecclesiastical History* 11.22.1, which identifies the place of Paul's imprisonment in Col. 4:10 as Rome). The relative freedom that Paul enjoyed in prison and the fellowship of his co-workers make Rome a likely place. Also, it is quite possible that Onesimus, the runaway slave, would have sought anonymity in a large city like Rome.

There are some factors, however, that mitigate against a hasty acceptance of a Roman origin for Colossians. For one thing, the distance between Colossae and Rome is about twelve hundred miles. Would Onesimus have attempted such a long journey with its increased risk of being caught? Also, according to Philemon 22, Paul expects to be released and to visit Colossae. His request that a room be prepared for him gives the impression that he is close enough for this to happen within a very short time. R. P. Martin also notes that a trip from Rome eastward to Colossae would entail a shift in Paul's missionary strategy, which, according to Romans 15:28, meant going west to Spain.[16]

Caesarea. After Paul was arrested in Jerusalem (Acts 21:27ff.), he spent two years in prison in Caesarea before he was taken to Rome (Acts 23:33–26:32). Bo Reicke, who is one of the main proponents for this view, argues that Caesarea is the most likely place for Colossians to have been written.[17]

There are a number of supporting arguments: First, a number of the friends who accompanied Paul to Jerusalem and who are with him at prison are from Asia (Acts 20:4; 24:23; cf. Col. 4:7–14 and Philem. 23, 24); second, the missionary activity that Paul envisioned when he wrote Colossians and Philemon and the dispatching of these letters to Colossae with Tychicus make sense if from Caesarea; third, Onesimus would have come to Caesarea because he had friends from that area and would then have returned to Colossae with Tychicus. These, together with other considerations, lead Bo Reicke to conclude that "Philemon and Colossians were sent from Caesarea to Colossae ca. A.D. 59."[18]

Ephesus. The arguments for an Ephesian imprisonment of Paul that could have made the writing of epistles such as Colossians possible are largely arguments from silence. Acts does not record any imprisonment in Ephesus. All that one can say is that the struggles that Paul had in Ephesus (Acts 19:23–41) may be reflected in his correspondence with the Corinthians (1 Cor. 4:9–13; 2 Cor. 1:8–10; 4:4–12; 6:4, 5; 11:23–25). The reference to fighting with "wild beasts" in Ephesus (1 Cor. 15:32) could be a metaphorical expression to indicate verbal confrontation with his opponents rather than a physical struggle with animals as in the gladiatorial arena. For Bo Reicke, "It is pure imagination to speak of any captivity in Ephesus."[19]

In spite of the lack of direct evidence, a surprisingly large number of scholars favor an Ephesian imprisonment and origin for Colossians. The proximity of Ephesus to Colossae, the likelihood of Paul's co-workers mentioned in Colossians and Philemon being with the apostle in Ephesus, and the gravity of the riot occasioned by Paul's preaching are mentioned as factors that merit consideration. R. P. Martin, for one, has examined most of the current theories and concludes that the Epistle to the Colossians "belongs to that tumultuous period of Paul's life, represented in Acts 19–20, when for a brief space his missionary labours were interrupted by an enforced spell as a *détenu* [prisoner] near Ephesus."[20]

Though all these suggestions about the origin of Colossians have strengths and weaknesses, there does not appear to be any *decisive* evidence for departing from the traditional view, Rome. The inconclusiveness about an Ephesian imprisonment, together with the advanced cosmic Christology of Colossians, makes it most likely that the epistle originated during a later period of Paul's life (ca. A.D. 60) and from a setting like Rome.[21]

Notes

1. G. L. Munn, "Introduction to Colossians," *SWJTh* 16 (1973), p. 10.

2. Schweizer, *Colossians*, p. 14, quotes Cicero's *Pro Flacco* 28.

3. B. Reicke, "The Historical Setting of Colossians," *RevExp* 70 (1973), pp. 429–33.

4. For additional information on the nature of the false teaching and some of the difficult problems of interpretation, see the commentary text and additional notes on 2:8–23.

5. Lohse, *Colossians and Philemon*, p. 98.

6. For some helpful sources on Gnosticism see R. M. Grant, *Gnosticism and Early Christianity* (New York: Harper Torchbooks, 1959); H. Jonas, *The Gnostic Religion* (Boston: Beacon Press, 1958); R. McL. Wilson, *Gnosis and the New Testament* (Philadelphia: Fortress, 1968); E. Yamauchi, *Pre-Christian Gnosticism*, 2nd ed. (Grand Rapids: Baker, 1973).

7. F. Cumont, *Oriental Religion in Roman Paganism* (New York: Dover, 1956).

8. For further insights into inclusivism in Colossians, see G. Cannon, *The Use of Traditional Materials in Colossians* (Macon, Georgia: Mercer University Press, 1983), pp. 217–29.

9. On the question of Pauline and non-Pauline authorship, see A. Patzia, "The Deutero-Pauline Hypothesis: An Attempt at Clarification," *EQ* 52 (1980), pp. 27–42; also see disc. in the Introduction to Ephesians.

10. For a detailed listing and analysis of the vocabulary, cf. Lohse's excursus: "The Language and Style of Colossians," in *Colossians and Philemon*, pp. 84–91. Further parallels between Colossians and Ephesians are discussed in J. B. Polhill, "The Relationship between Ephesians and Colossians," *RevExp* 70 (1973), pp. 439–57; and J. Coutts, "The Relationship of Ephesians and Colossians," *NTS* 3–4 (1956–58), pp. 201–7.

11. Martin, *Colossians and Philemon*, p. 40; Cannon, p. 175.

12. Lohse, *Colossians and Philemon*, p. 177–83.

13. Cannon, pp. 196–203.

14. Ibid., p. 14. Schweizer makes an appropriate comment on this issue when he writes: "Whether the voice of the apostle comes to us directly or through the mouth of his fellow-worker, it is the message that is essential, not the way in which it reaches us" ("Christ in the Letter to the Colossians," *RevExp* 70 [1973], p. 467); in his *Colossians*, Schweizer has some good practical applications as he addresses the topic, "The Epistle to the Colossians Today," pp. 298–302.

15. See n. 9.

16. Martin, *Colossians and Philemon*, p. 26.

17. Reicke, "Caesarea, Rome and the Captivity Epistles," in *Apostolic History of the Gospel*, ed. W. W. Gasque and R. P. Martin (Grand Rapids: Eerdmans, 1970), pp. 277–82; Reicke, "The Historical Setting of Colossians, " pp. 429–38.

18. Reicke, "The Historical Setting of Colossians," p. 435. For some decisive arguments against this theory, consult Martin, *Colossians and Philemon*, p. 25.

19. Reicke, "The Historical Setting of Colossians," p. 435.

20. Martin, *Colossians and Philemon*, p. 30. For supporters of the Ephesian origin of Colossians, cf. G. S. Duncan, *St. Paul's Ephesian Ministry* (New York: Scribner, 1930); idem, "Were Paul's Imprisonment Epistles Written from Ephesus?" *ExpT* 67 (1955–56), pp. 163–66; B. W. Robinson, "An Ephesian Ministry of Paul," *JBL* 29 (1920), pp. 181–89; D. T. Rowlingson, "Paul's Ephesian Ministry: An Evaluation of the Evidence," *ATR* 32 (1950), pp. 1–7; Schweizer, *Colossians*, pp. 25–26.

21. A variety of views on the authorship, origin, and nature of Colossians can be found in all of the major "introductions" to the New Testament. Cf. also F. F. Bruce, "St. Paul in Rome. 3. The Epistle to the Colossians," *BJRL* 48 (1966), pp. 268–85.

Note: A list of the abbreviations used in the commentary is found at the front of the book (see p. xvii). See also "For Further Reading" (p. 295); full bibliographical references for works referred to in short-form notes within the commentary are supplied there.

§1 Paul's Greetings (Col. 1:1–2)

The opening greeting in this epistle is typical of the way in which Paul has addressed other churches to whom he has written (1 Cor. 1:1–3; 2 Cor. 1:1–2; Phil. 1:1–2; 1 Thess. 1:1–2; 2 Thess. 1:1–2; cf. Eph. 1:1–2). Although the form of these salutations is quite similar to contemporary Greek models, the content is distinctly Christian and, in the case of Colossians, sets forth statements that are important to the body of the letter.

1:1 / Paul links Timothy with the writing of this letter (**and Timothy our brother**). This beloved co-worker had won a respected place in Paul's heart and had become a vital cog in all that Paul was attempting to do for Christ (1 Cor. 4:17; 2 Cor. 1:1; Phil. 1:1; 2:19–24; 1 Thess. 1:1; 3:1ff.; Philem. 1). By including Timothy in this greeting, Paul communicates to the Colossians that he is not alone in his imprisonment and that someone whom they know from his ministry in Asia Minor joins him in this epistle.

Paul uses a phrase that helps to convey the authority of his message: He is an apostle of Christ Jesus **by the will of God**. An apostle is one who is regarded as possessing power and authority. Although there is no indication that the Colossians were questioning Paul's apostolic authority, the content of the letter reveals that they were in danger of falling away from the truth of the gospel by turning to false teachings (2:1–8). Consequently, they needed to hear a strong and authoritative message from one of God's messengers.

1:2 / The Colossians are identified in two ways: First, they are **holy** (lit., "saints," *hagioi*). It was not uncommon for Paul to call Christians saints (1 Cor. 1:2; Phil. 1:1; Eph. 1:1), referring to their status in Christ and not to the degree of holiness that they may have attained (cf. 1:4). As saints, they are a distinct class of people who are called out and separated from their former way of life in order to live in and for Christ (1:21ff.).

Second, they are **faithful brothers in Christ**. Here there is
some uncertainty whether Paul's use of **faithful** carries the sense
of "reliability," or of "belief," that is, is the apostle referring to
those who are faithful to the gospel, or is he referring to those
who have been joined together by their faith in Christ and who
now form a believing community? Given that many of Paul's greetings and thanksgivings foreshadow later pastoral concerns, it is
quite possible that he has the readers' steadfastness or faithfulness in mind (1:10, 23; 2:6, 7).

The greeting ends with an appeal for **grace and peace**,
which have their source in God the Father. This serves to draw
attention to the favor that God freely bestows upon his undeserving people and to the healthy or peaceable condition of life that
they enjoy because of it.

§2 *Paul's Prayer of Thanksgiving (Col. 1:3–8)*

After the greeting, Paul offers a prayer of thanksgiving for his readers. Even though he has not ministered to them personally (1:6–8; 2:1), he feels that they are very much a part of his pastoral care and concern. Although Paul certainly is genuine in what he says, it does become apparent that his thanksgivings anticipate some of the problems he will deal with later. Thus, for example, he commends them for their "faith," "hope," and "love," (1:5) and yet strongly encourages them to be filled with the knowledge of God's will and to walk worthy of the Lord (1:9); he praises them for the spread and growth of the gospel in their lives (1:6) but nevertheless prays that they will "bear fruit" and "grow" in the knowledge of God (1:10; 2:6). The entire section 1:3–14 is a beautiful example of how Paul combines praise, thanksgiving, and prayer for his readers.

1:3 / Though the use of the plural **we** may mean that Timothy is a part of the prayer, it is more likely an example of the style that Paul employs on other occasions when he freely alternates between "I" and "we" (cf. 2 Cor. 13:7ff.; 1 Thess. 1:2; 2:13; 3:9; 2 Thess. 1:3; 2:13). The prayer is to **God, the Father of our Lord Jesus Christ.**

In this expanded version of his prayer (cf. shorter forms in Rom. 1:8; 1 Cor. 1:4; Phil. 1:2; 1 Thess. 1:2–3), Paul draws attention not only to God as Father—a distinctly Christian insight— but to the **Lord** [*kyrios*] **Jesus Christ**. This emphasis upon Christ's exalted status as Lord certainly would reinforce the idea that Christ is not an inferior deity but one in whom God himself is found (1:15–20).

1:4 / The next two verses introduce the familiar triad of faith, love, and hope. The numerous references to these concepts in the NT (Rom. 5:1–5; 1 Cor. 13:13; Gal. 5:5, 6; Eph. 1:15–18; 4:2–5; 1 Thess. 1:3; 5:8; Heb. 6:10–12; 10:22–24; 1 Pet. 1:3–8, 21, 22) reveal that they were a significant part of early Christian tradi-

tion. Here, Paul is not listing them haphazardly but is intention-
ally developing and applying them for his readers. He has heard
of their faith in Christ Jesus from Epaphras, the most likely
founder of the Colossian church (1:7).

Whereas Christ certainly is the content and object of faith,
Paul has in mind the realm or the sphere in which their faith
operates; that is, they not only *believe* in Christ but they *live* in
him as well (later, in 2:11, 12, and in other passages, such as Rom.
6:1–11; 1 Cor. 12:13, and Gal. 3:26–27, the apostle shows how believers have been baptized into [*eis*] Christ and incorporated into
his body). The result of a life *in* Christ is a life *for* Christ. Consequently, Paul can compliment the Colossians on their **love . . .
for all the saints**. Their faith in Christ was being demonstrated
in a love that had spilled over from their immediate congregation to other churches in the surrounding area, such as Laodicea
and Hierapolis.

1:5 / **Hope** is the third member of the triad and is introduced as the basis of **faith and love (the faith and love that spring
from the hope)**. This message of hope, which is such a vital component of the Christian life, came through the preaching of the
gospel. Here Paul is emphasizing that the original **word of truth**
that they received included a word of hope. It is a possession that
they had from the beginning and not something that only the
false teachers could offer (2:4, 8).

In this verse, Paul combines the *present* and *future* dimensions of hope. It is normal to think of hope only as something
to be realized at the end time when Christ shall appear (3:4). True,
hope is a possession given by God and **stored up for you in
heaven**. Scripture does teach that believers will inherit or possess God's promises at some future time (Rom. 8:24, 25). But here
Paul is placing a much-needed emphasis on the present aspect
of hope. He wants to show his readers that hope belongs to the
preaching that they originally heard and that they already possess by virtue of being in Christ ("this hope . . . that you have
already heard about in the word of truth, the gospel that has come
to you"). Hope is the basis of their love and faith and thus assures them of the adequacy of the gospel they have received. This
should preclude any desire to supplement the gospel with additional speculation from the false teachers.

1:6 / Here the emphasis continues to be on the truthfulness of the gospel. In 1:5 it was linked with hope; here the association is with the grace of God. From this, one could conclude that Paul is concerned to show that the message of the gospel is true with respect to hope and grace. But more likely he has the entire message in mind. This gospel, in contrast to the false teachings to which the Colossians have been exposed, is a true message.

The truthfulness and power of the gospel have practical dimensions as well. First of all, the gospel is universal in scope, that is, **growing** throughout the entire Roman Empire. The gospel of Christ is for everyone (inclusive) and not for a select few (exclusive) as the heretics are teaching (2:8–15). Second, the gospel is bringing blessings (lit., **bearing fruit**) to the whole world, even as it is to the Christians in Colossae. The true word of God is something that reproduces and grows (cf. the parable of the sower in Mark 4:1–20 and parallels); it does not sprout and then die out quickly (1 Pet. 1:23–25) as the false teaching was prone to do (2:14–15, 19).

Paul is establishing criteria by which the Colossians can counter the claims of the false teachers. With a concern much like the Apostle John, who wrote, "test the spirits to see whether they are of God" (1 John 4:1), Paul wants his readers to test the claims of these heretics against the claims of the gospel. Is it God's truth? Is it universal? Does it bear fruit in people's lives? If not, then it cannot be the gospel that they have received. The gospel needs to bear fruit in order for it to be the gospel!

1:7 / Another test is to consider the messenger. Although Paul did not bring the gospel to Colossae himself, he reminds his readers that they **learned it from Epaphras**, one of their own members whom Paul commends as **a faithful minister of Christ** (cf. 4:12). This brother, who also shared Paul's imprisonment (Philem. 23), is singled out in 4:13 for his faithfulness and diligence on behalf of the Colossian church.

1:8 / Epaphras has brought the news of the situation in Colossae back to Paul. True, they had some major problems and were in danger of falling into heresy, but Epaphras also told Paul of their **love in the Spirit**. In other words, their conduct in the community is marked by a love that has its source in **the Spirit** (cf. Rom. 15:30; Gal. 5:22).

Additional Notes §2

1:3 / For helpful insights on the Pauline thanksgivings, see P. Schubert, *Form and Function of the Pauline Thanksgivings*, BZNW 20 (Berlin: Alfred Töpelmann, 1939); J. L. White, *Form and Function of the Greek Letter: A Study of the Letter Body in the Non-Literary Papyri and in Paul the Apostle*, SBLDS 2 (Missoula, Mont.: Scholars Press, 1972).

1:6 / There is some ambiguity regarding the translation of this verse and the meaning of **truth**. Does the "it" refer to **God's grace** or to **this gospel**, i.e., did the Colossians come to know the gospel, or God's grace, **in all its truth** (*en alētheia*; cf. RSV, "grace of God in truth") From the Greek it appears that **truth** in 1:6 should keep its identification with **this gospel**, as in 1:5 (*en tō logō tēs alētheias tou euangeliou*). The important point, however, is that Paul's message is based on God's truth and is, therefore, correct teaching. For the phrase "truth of the gospel," see Gal. 2:5, 14.

The concept of **truth** that is employed here is not something that is gained by logical analysis or empirical observation, as in Greek or Western thought. Rather, it conveys the idea of *reliability* in what it claims (Schweizer, p. 35). Thus the Colossians, in addition to hearing the truth, came to recognize it **in all its truth**. Paul places emphasis upon *hearing* and *knowing* the gospel.

§3 Paul's Prayer of Intercession (Col. 1:9–14)

Following the words of thanksgiving (1:3–8), Paul turns to intercession (1:9–11) and lays a foundation for the Christ hymn (1:15–20). As we have noted (§2), Paul typically prays specifically for the things that he has mentioned in his thanksgivings (note the **for this reason**). Both the thanksgiving and the intercession are good examples of Paul's continued pastoral concern for this congregation (**we have not stopped praying for you**) even though he does not know most of them personally.

Although 1:9 forms one of the requests, it stands as a heading for the petitions that follow. Paul begins by asking that his readers be filled with the knowledge of God's will, **through all spiritual wisdom and understanding**. This is foundational for the apostle because in biblical thought there is a close relationship between the *knowledge of* and the *doing of* God's will. Those who are being filled in this way will (*a*) have a worthy walk (1:10a), (*b*) have a fruitful life (1:10b), (*c*) experience growth in the knowledge of God (1:10c), and (*d*) be made strong to endure with patience (1:11).

1:9 / The request that God **fill** (lit., "that you might be filled, *plērōthēte*), suggests that there is some spiritual vacuum that needs to be corrected. It is the same idea expressed in 4:12 with reference to Epaphras, whose concern for the Colossians was that they stand firm, "mature" (*peplērophorēmenoi*) and fully convinced, in complete obedience to God's will.

The filling is to be with the knowledge of God's will and not some type of speculative or intellectual *gnōsis* ("knowledge") so characteristic of the false teachers. **Wisdom** (*sophia*) and **understanding** (*synesis*) likewise are not some abstract intellectual concepts from the Greek world but attributes that God's Spirit gives. As spiritual gifts from God, they enable God's people to live abundant, fruitful, and obedient lives in accordance with his will. Paul's readers need spiritual wisdom to determine God's will for their lives; they need spiritual understanding to apply God's will to specific situations in life.

1:10 / This verse begins with a construction in Greek (an infinitive of purpose) that expresses the result of being filled with the knowledge of God's will. Hence the NIV's **in order that you may live a life worthy of the Lord** (cf. NASB "so that you may walk in a manner worthy of the Lord"). The first consequence of knowing God's will is to live as the Lord wants. The main idea is that a Christian's *profession* is to correspond with his or her *confession*.

Second, the believer is to please the Lord fully in all things. Although the Greek word *areskia* has a negative connotation in secular contexts, here it does not mean seeking favor with someone out of selfish interests or for personal advantage. A life that is lived worthy *of* the Lord will be a life worthy *to* the Lord. Thus a constant goal for a Christian is to please the Lord in every way, that is, in all areas of life.

The third result that the apostle envisions is fruitfulness in good works *and* growth in (by?) the knowledge of God. Although some commentators believe that this sentence expresses two separate petitions (fruitfulness *and* growth), it is better to keep the two Greek participles (*karpophorountes* and *auxanomenoi*) together. In 1:6, the apostle stated that the gospel was "bearing fruit" and "growing" throughout the whole world. Here he is showing that what is true of the gospel in the world should also be true in the lives of the Colossians.

One of the unfortunate distortions in some forms of Christianity is the misunderstanding of the relationship between theology and ethics, that is, between faith and action. Paul has been presenting a concept of wisdom and knowledge that has moral and practical dimensions. The readers need to be preserved from a barren orthodoxy. The faith that they heard and that transformed their lives is to manifest itself in good works that, in turn, will result in fruitfulness and personal growth (for similar concepts, cf. Rom. 7:4; 2 Cor. 9:8; Gal. 5:6; Eph. 2:10; 4:15; 2 Thess. 2:17; 1 Pet. 2:2; 2 Pet. 3:18). A Christian needs to be active in order to grow spiritually; otherwise, stagnation and regression will set in.

The NIV **growing in the knowledge of God** gives the impression that the growth consists in understanding more and more of God—hence similar to "the knowledge of his will" in 1:9.

But the Greek lacks the personal pronoun "your" (cf. GNB), and since the dative case in Greek expresses means or instrumentality as well as reference, it may be better to translate this phrase with the word "by" or "through." Paul does not mean, therefore, that their growth is *in* the knowledge of God; rather, it is the *result* of their knowledge of God. Moral and spiritual growth comes from knowing and doing the will of God. God requires (**live a life worthy of the Lord**) and enables each believer to live a worthy and fruitful life.

1:11–12 / This new life is made possible by the power of God. The repetition of the synonyms **strengthened, power, might,** shows how difficult it is to express the fullness of God's power in words. The expressions that Paul uses here are common in early Christian doxologies that praise God for his glory and power (1 Pet. 4:11; 5:11; Jude 25; Rev. 1:6; 5:13). He knows that his readers are going to need perseverance and steadfastness to continue in the will of God and to accomplish all the things for which he has prayed. Only the divine resources of God's mighty and glorious power can fortify them for this task.

The verb **strengthened** is a present participle (*dynamoumenoi*), indicating that this is a continuous activity of God in the believer and not a once-and-for-all experience. Endurance (*hypomonē*) is that lasting quality that enables one to continue toward a goal. It describes the athlete in Hebrews 12:1 who runs the race to completion or the Christian who patiently bears fruit (Luke 8:15). The Greek word *makrothymia*, often translated as "patience" or "long-suffering," is that quality of self-restraint that enables a person to withstand opposition without retaliation.

Giving thanks to the Father: Commentators have had some difficulty with the placement of the word **joyfully**. In the Greek text **joyfully** (*meta charas*) is part of 1:11. Hence the idea would be for believers to endure **joyfully**—a thought similar to Jesus' words in Matthew 5:11–12. Endurance, patience, and joy belong to the fruit of the Spirit (Gal. 5:22–23), and Paul may be calling upon the Colossians to manifest these specific graces in their lives.

The alternative is to connect **joyfully** with **giving thanks** (as in GNB; for a similar joining of these two concepts, cf. Phil. 1:4; 4:4–6; 1 Thess. 5:16–18; 1 Pet. 1:8; 4:13). Paul is developing a hymn of thanksgiving (1:12–20) and consequently directs his readers to express thanks **joyfully . . . to the Father**.

The concepts Paul mentions in the following verses are especially appropriate to the situation at Colossae. This church was
in danger of turning away from the truth of the gospel (1:5) to
"human tradition . . . rather than . . . Christ" (2:8). Since so much
of this teaching falsified and depreciated the person and work
of Christ, Paul sets out to correct their Christology and does so
in the form of a thanksgiving (1:12–14) and a hymn to Christ
(1:15–20).

There are several reasons why Paul's readers can rejoice with
thanksgiving: First of all, they have an inheritance. The imagery
behind this verse probably comes from God's dealing with the
people of Israel when he led them out of bondage in Egypt into
a portion of their inheritance in the promised land of Canaan
(Exod. 6:8). But the new Israel—the church—also has received an
inheritance. The reading **qualified you to share in the inheritance
of the saints** translates an awkward Greek phrase that literally
reads "unto the portion/share which consists in the lot/in-
heritance" (grammatically, a genitive of apposition that identifies
the noun and the word it modifies as the same thing).

Since God has provided the **inheritance**, he also qualifies
or authorizes (*hikanōsanti*) those who obtain it. And all this has
already happened to these believers. God has prepared them for
their **inheritance**; they already are **saints in the kingdom of light**.

Saints is a translation of *hagioi* (lit., "the separated ones").
The unusual phrase **kingdom of light** is somewhat ambiguous
and has received a variety of interpretations. Some commentators take **light** as the *means* by which a Christian qualifies for the
inheritance. Others base their understanding on such NT passages
as 2 Corinthians 4:6, Ephesians 5:8, and 1 Peter 2:9, where light
is used as a metaphor for new life. And a few believe that **light**
is analogous in meaning to the "in heaven" of 1:5 or that the
author is making a contrast to the "dominion of darkness" of 1:13
that he anticipates. The saints have been delivered from darkness and live in the domain of light.

E. Lohse draws upon passages from the Dead Sea Scrolls
that describe the human "lot" in terms of darkness or light. In
this literature, however, the "holy ones" (saints) are the angels
and not the people of God. It is possible that in this context Paul
may be thinking of some of the heretical teaching that included
the worship of angels (2:18) and the veneration of angelic powers

(2:8, 20). If so, his message to the Colossians is that they are joint heirs with the angels (saints) in the realm of light. There is no need to strive for something that they already possess.

1:13 / The second reason for thanksgiving is their deliverance from darkness and their transference to the kingdom of Christ. Darkness, in the NT, is a metaphor for evil, and those in darkness are without God and live under the rule of Satan, the evil one (Matt. 6:13). Paul, as a messenger of the gospel, was himself told: "I am sending you to them to open their [the Gentiles'] eyes and turn them from darkness to light, and from the power of Satan to God, so that they may receive forgiveness of sins and a place among those who are sanctified by faith in me" (Acts 26:17–18). Christians are described as those who at one time lived in darkness but in Christ have become people of light (Eph. 5:8; 1 Pet. 2:9; 1 John 1:5–7). In Colossians, Paul reminds his readers that they have been rescued from **the dominion of darkness**.

The positive side of God's action is that **he brought us** (lit., "transferred") **into the kingdom of the Son he loves**. The idea expressed by **kingdom** is that of a "rule" and is used as a counterpart to **dominion**. In other words, as the realm of darkness had a certain power, the transference is to the rule (power, authority) of **the Son** God **loves** (lit., "Beloved Son," as used at the baptism and transfiguration, Mark 1:11; 9:7, and parallels; cf. also Eph. 1:6). The Colossians have been rescued from the sphere of darkness dominated by evil powers and transferred into the realm of the victorious Son of God.

The phrase **kingdom of the Son he loves** or the "kingdom of Christ," is not common in the NT. Perhaps the apostle uses this expression to emphasize the *present* reality and sphere of their possession in Christ rather than the more common "kingdom of God," which has a connotation of the future (1 Cor. 6:9; 15:50; Gal. 5:21; 2 Tim. 4:1, 18). Or, Paul simply may be preparing the way for the Christ hymn that follows. At any rate, it serves to remind the readers that they are no longer subject to evil forces; they have been delivered from these powers and are reminded to live victoriously in the power of Christ (3:1–4).

1:14 / The third reason for rejoicing is the forgiveness of sins. Here the subject of the actions is no longer God, as in 1:12–13, but Christ. He is the agent of redemption and the means by

which **we have . . . the forgiveness of sins**. The GNB "by whom
we are set free" beautifully captures the essential meaning of
redemption as liberation, that is, freedom from the bondage of
the evil powers of darkness. The forgiveness of sins is an accom-
panying result of redemption and not a separate act of Christ as
may have been taught by the false teachers.

It would be natural for the Colossians to ask Paul when or
where all of this took place in their lives. When has God acted
so decisively for us by forgiving our sins and making us children
of light? The answer, according to the NT, is in baptism (see note
on 1:14).

Additional Notes §3

1:9 / Lohse (p. 24) has a detailed listing of the words and phrases
in 1:3–8 that recur in 1:9–11. He provides some excellent background material to this passage, particularly from the OT and the Dead Sea Scrolls,
where the idea is developed that "the will of God demands an obedience that is visible in one's actions" (p. 25). Wisdom and knowledge are
gifts of God received through the Spirit. The same is true in the NT,
which teaches that to *know* God's will is to *do* God's will (Matt. 7:21; Luke
12:47; 2 Tim. 2:15; Heb. 10:36).

1:10 / On knowledge (*epignōsis*), see Robinson's extended note
in his commentary *St. Paul's Epistle to the Ephesians*, pp. 248–54.

1:12 / See H. Foerster, "*klēroō,*" *TDNT*, vol. 3, pp. 758–85. For
Lohse's comment on angels, see pp. 35–36 of his commentary. Schweizer
thinks that "angels" is unlikely, because *hagioi* is used to describe members of the community (1:2, 4, 26; 3:12).

1:14 / The baptismal language and teaching of Colossians and
Ephesians will be brought out in the course of the commentary. On the
baptismal motifs of Col. 1:12–14, consult Cannon, pp. 16–19. Cannon's
conclusion on these verses is that their confessional nature strongly suggests that Paul was using traditional material connected with the sacrament of baptism.

§4 The Hymn to Christ (Col. 1:15–20)

Scholars are virtually unanimous in their opinion that verses 15–20 constitute a hymn. Since the existence of hymns in the early church was common (Phil. 2:5–11; Col. 3:16; Eph. 5:19), it is not difficult to believe that this is a carefully written poem intended to convey a specific self-contained message about Christ to the readers at Colossae.

Paul has already alluded to the work of Christ with respect to deliverance and the forgiveness of sins (1:13, 14). In the hymn he continues to draw attention to the person and work of Christ in cosmic and soteriological (pertaining to salvation) terms. Later, in 1:21–23, he shows the readers that they were reconciled to lead a moral and obedient life under the lordship of Jesus Christ.

Whereas most scholars agree on the hymnic nature of these verses, there is less unanimity surrounding such issues as the structure, author, source, and meaning and purpose of the passage.

The Structure of the Hymn

These verses have been arranged poetically in a number of ways. According to some reconstructions of the Greek text, the NIV translation would read as follows:

Strophe I

1:15—He is the image of the invisible God,
    the firstborn over all creation.
1:16—For by him all things were created: things in heaven and on earth (visible and invisible,
    whether thrones or powers or rulers or authorities;
    all things were created by him and for him).

Strophe II

1:17—He is before all things,
    and in him all things hold together.
1:18a—And he is the head of the body (the church);

Strophe III
1:18b–He is the beginning
   and the firstborn from among the dead
   (so that in everything he might have the supremacy).
1:19—For God was pleased
   to have all his fullness dwell in him,
1:20—and through him to reconcile
   to himself all things,
   whether things on earth or things in heaven
   (by making peace through his blood, shed on the cross).

The Author of the Hymn

If Paul is considered to be the author of the epistle, then
why are there so many questions about the authorship of this
specific hymn? The reasons for this are varied and complex, but
they center around the fact that (*a*) the passage contains many
words and phrases not found elsewhere in Paul's writings, and
(*b*) it was not uncommon for Paul to incorporate previously existing traditional material into his letters. Normally, this included
hymns, confessions, creeds, and liturgical materials used by the
early church. Where this occurs, Paul could be regarded more as
an editor than as the original author.

Most of the Christ hymn in Colossians has come to be regarded as a pre-Pauline composition. Though scholars may dis-
agree on its precise origin, they are quite certain that Paul, in
adopting the hymn, modified it in order to apply it to the specific situation at Colossae. (The phrases in parentheses in the reconstruction just given reflect the additions, i.e., interpolations,
that Paul *may* have made from the original hymn. The meaning
and purpose of these interpolations will be dealt with later.)

The Source of the Hymn

A number of sources for the hymn have been suggested.
Some scholars have analyzed the content of the hymn in light
of the OT and think that it has its origin in some type of rabbinical
Judaism. Others have come to appreciate its Gnostic background
and thus reconstruct its meaning based upon ideas and language
familiar to the teachings of Gnosticism at the time of Paul. Another group of interpreters sees the hymn originating from the

circles of Hellenistic Judaism, which, by the first century, had become very syncretistic in its beliefs and practices. Thus it is not uncommon for these authors to draw from Stoic, Gnostic, Hellenistic, and Jewish sources.

The hymn may have had several stages of development: first, as a non-Christian hymn created in the milieu of Greek philosophy and used by groups such as the Stoics and Gnostics; second, as a Christian hymn celebrating the cosmic role of Christ in Hellenistic-Jewish terminology; third, as a Pauline hymn that contains specific additions to correct the erroneous ideas of the false teachers in Colossae.

The Purpose and Meaning of the Hymn

It has been mentioned earlier that Paul's motives for adopting and applying this hymn center around his concern that the Colossians maintain a correct understanding of the person and work of Christ against the false teachings that they have been receiving. They were in danger of falling away from the truth of the gospel to man-made traditions. Paul wants them to remember to follow the gospel as they learned it from Epaphras: "So then, just as you received Christ Jesus as Lord, continue to live in him, rooted and built up in him, strengthened in the faith as you were taught" (2:6, 7).

The primary purpose of the hymn is to establish the superiority or the preeminence of Christ in all things (1:18).

Outline of the Hymn: The preeminence of Christ
   A. Christ's preeminence in the cosmos (1:15–17)
      1. The image of the Creator (1:15a)
      2. The agent of creation
         a. Of the visible world (1:15b)
         b. Of the invisible world (1:16)
      3. The means of cohesion (1:17)
   B. Christ's preeminence in the church (1:18–20)
      1. As its Head (1:18a)
      2. As its Lord (1:18b, 19)
      3. As its Reconciler (1:20)

1:15 / **He is the image of the invisible God.** By **image**, Paul does not mean mere resemblance or similarity, because the Greek word used is *eikōn*. This communicates the idea that Christ participates in and with the nature of God, not merely copying, but visibly manifesting and perfectly revealing God in human form (in 2 Cor. 4:4 Paul talks about "the glory of Christ, who is the image of God").

The result of the Incarnation is that the invisible God has become visible in the God-man, Jesus Christ. The Apostle John, in a different context, records statements that Christ made: "I and the Father are one" (10:30), and "Anyone who has seen me has seen the Father" (14:9). Such a claim could not be made for any angel or spiritual power. Christ's sovereignty is attested to by his personal and unique relationship to God.

By bearing the image of God in this way, Christ stands apart from the created order as **the firstborn over all creation**. The phrase **firstborn** (*prōtotokos*) has often been taken in a temporal sense implying that Christ is the first one to be created and thus belongs to the created order. Apparently the false teachers at Colossae had relegated Christ to the status of a created being. This heresy has a long history, for it was championed by the Arians in the fourth century A.D. and continues to be perpetuated by the Jehovah's Witnesses today.

Paul does not mean that Christ belongs to creation in a temporal way. The issue here is primacy of function, not priority in time. Since Christ participates in the act of creation, he stands over and beyond the created world as the agent by which everything came into existence.

1:16 / After establishing Christ's superiority in the created order, Paul moves on to the invisible world of heavenly and earthly beings. The "all creation" (1:15) is expanded by the phrase that **by him all things were created: things in heaven and on earth**. The Greek uses two prepositions that aid in the understanding of the action intended: God created the whole universe **by** (*dia*) and **for** (*eis*) **him**. In other words, Christ is both the *agent* and the *goal* of creation. He must not be relegated to the same inferior position as other spiritual powers. All of creation finds its goal in Christ alone. The use of the perfect tense of "created" (*ektisthē*) shows that what has taken place in God's creative activity continues to be effective into the present.

One gets the impression that Paul is taking great pains to avoid any misunderstanding on this matter. He already has emphasized that **all things** (used twice in this verse) were created by Christ. Now he amplifies this by the terms **heaven** and **earth** and **visible and invisible**. This includes all spiritual forces, **whether thrones or powers or rulers or authorities**.

These terms represent a view and classification of spiritual powers that were current in the first century. People believed that the world was inhabited by all sorts of alien powers that were a threat to human beings (Rom. 8:38; 1 Cor. 15:24; Eph. 1:21; 6:12; 1 Pet. 3:22). The fact that the reference to these powers is a probable interpolation by Paul into the hymn suggests that these powers were given undue prominence by the false teachers. Paul's point is that these powers are subject to Christ's superiority since they were created **by** and **for** him. He is Lord over all these powers (2:10, 15).

1:17 / The phrase **he is before all things** reaffirms some of the things that Paul has already said about Christ. But the new thought is that, **in him all things hold together**. The Greek word *synestēken* here connotes preservation or coherence. Thus the Lord who creates the universe also sustains it.

1:18 / From cosmic sovereignty, Paul turns to discuss Christ's preeminence in the church by using the head-body imagery. He has convincingly established Christ's lordship over the world; now he establishes Christ's lordship in the church.

If **the church** can be regarded as a Pauline interpolation, then an earlier version of the hymn must have proclaimed Christ as head of the body only. There is much speculation as to the source of the head-body metaphor in Paul's writings. Some scholars are attracted to the idea of "corporate personality" in which all of humanity is considered to be "in Adam." The counterpart in the NT is that, since all Christians are "in Christ"—that is, the church—they can be regarded as the body of Christ. Most scholars, however, believe that the idea comes from Hellenistic conceptions of the cosmic body.

In several Greek sources, including the writings of Plato, the Stoics, and the Alexandrian Jew Philo, there are numerous mythological conceptions of the universe as a body that is governed by a "head." Here, the cosmos is filled by the deity and consequently viewed as the body of the deity over which there is "Wisdom" or "Logos" as its head. The common belief was that, just as a person's physical body needs direction and guidance from the head, so the body of the cosmos needs a head such as Logos or Wisdom as a unifying principle.

What the Greeks attributed to Wisdom or Logos for headship, the early church attributed to Christ. He, in other words, is the divine Logos (cf. John's prologue in 1:1–3) who governs the body (*sōma*) of the cosmos. It is quite possible that a Christian version of this hymn initially celebrated Christ's headship over the cosmos. The new development in Colossians is that Paul interprets **body** not as cosmos but as **church**. In other words, although Christ is **head** of the whole world, only the **church** is his **body**.

The identification of **the church** as the **body** of Christ over which Christ is the head in Colossians (1:18, 24) and Ephesians (1:22, 23; 4:15, 16) is not the same as the description of the "body" in Romans and 1 Corinthians. In those two epistles (Rom. 12:1–8; 1 Cor. 12:4–31), Paul uses the concept of the church as the body of Christ and emphasizes the mutual relationships and obligations that exist among its members by virtue of their spiritual gifts. There the "head" is simply mentioned along with the other members of the body (1 Cor. 12:14–26). Only in Colossians and Ephesians is Christ designated as **head** over **the church**. The reason for this surely lies in Paul's intention to proclaim the lordship of Christ over all things. He wants the Colossians to know that the church is the place where Christ exercises his sovereignty over the cosmos.

This Lord is the **beginning** of the body's life, vitalizing and energizing it by virtue of his resurrection. Paul utilizes the phrase **firstborn** for the second time (cf. 1:15) in order to re-emphasize the priority of Christ. The final result of this is Christ's absolute preeminence (**so that in everything he might have the supremacy**).

1:19 / Paul goes on to say that **God was pleased to have all his fullness dwell in him**. There are two significant problems connected with the translation and interpretation of this verse.

The first problem is with the meaning of **fullness** (*plērōma*). In 2:9, *plērōma* is equated with all of God's nature as it dwells in Christ ("for in Christ all the fullness of the Deity lives in bodily form"). On this basis one is justified in giving it the same meaning as in 1:19 rather than seeing it in some Gnostic way in which *plērōma* is regarded as the totality or fullness of aeons emanating from God and filling the space between heaven and earth. Nevertheless, one aspect of the false teaching in Colossae was that it gave undue prominence to those supernatural powers that filled the universe by regarding them as intermediaries between God and the world. Paul corrects this by affirming that the full nature of God dwells in Christ exclusively.

The second issue centers around the subject of **pleased**. The Greek literally reads "because in him (Christ) was pleased all the fullness to dwell." At least three possibilities have been suggested: (*a*) to make Christ the subject, thus giving the meaning that he (Christ) was pleased that all the fullness of God should dwell in him; (*b*) to make *plērōma* the subject, resulting in a translation adopted by the RSV ("for in him all the fulness was pleased to dwell"); and (*c*) to regard God as the subject. Hence the NIV: **For God was pleased to have all his fullness dwell in him**).

The main argument against this third view is the introduction of God as the subject in a hymn that concentrates on Christ (God has not been mentioned since 1:15). But the Greek text does permit it, and the meaning has support elsewhere in Scripture (cf. Christ's baptism and transfiguration). These technicalities, however, should not detract from the essential truth that Paul wishes to stress, namely, that Christ is the dwelling place (*katoikēsai*, "to take up residence") of God. As such, another factor of Christ's sovereignty is established.

1:20 / A final tribute is given to Christ as the agent of reconciliation. God was pleased that his fullness should dwell in his Son (1:19). Now, God was also pleased **through him** [the Son] **to reconcile to himself all things**. Reconciliation implies an existing estrangement or hostility that needed to be corrected (1:12, 22; Eph. 2:16). The **all things** that are reconciled are clarified by the phrase **whether things on earth or things in heaven.** In other words, it is not just the church (humanity) that has been reconciled; the reconciliation wrought by Christ extends to the entire cosmic order. By doing this, Paul shows the Colossians that every part of the universe is included in the reconciling work of Christ. His love has no limits!

One needs to be careful not to push this language to the extreme. Some have understood it very broadly and believe that humanity and all spiritual powers—including the evil angels—are at peace with God. But such a teaching needs to be interpreted in the light of everything Paul, and indeed the entire NT, say about such doctrines as reconciliation and salvation. The main point Paul makes is that everything has been brought into har mony *through* Christ.

The third Pauline interpolation in this hymn includes the phrase **by making peace through his blood, shed on the cross** (cf. Rom. 5:1ff.). This locates reconciliation in a historical act, accomplished by the shedding of Christ's blood on the cross. Paul will have no part of some cosmic drama that may have been perpetuated by the false teachers.

There is a question regarding **himself.** The RSV and NIV are ambiguous enough that one may take it to mean either God *or* Christ. The same construction (*eis auton*) is used in 1:16, where Christ is the object. The GNB is probably correct in interpreting the verse to mean that reconciliation is to God ("God . . . brought back to himself all things"). Thus reconciliation is *through* Christ but *to* God!

Additional Notes §4

1:15 / See H. Kleinknecht, *"eikōn,"* TDNT, vol. 2, pp. 389–90.

1:16 / See W. Michaelis, *"prōtos,"* TDNT, vol. 6, pp. 865–82; Schweizer, *Colossians,* has a good section on the history of interpretation of this problem, pp. 250–52.

1:18 / "The [Greeks] all thought that the universe was something like a giant body ruled by the gods or, as more and more pagan Greeks would express it in the time of the New Testament, by a god or a supreme power or a universal spirit. There are some who had already used the figure of God as the head of the body, the universe. A Jewish philosopher and contemporary of Jesus, Philo of Alexandria, had already spoken of the logos (which means word and/or mind and/or spirit of God) being the head of the universe. Thus, everybody understood that Christ could be the head of the world" (Schweizer, "Christ in the Letter to the Colossians," p. 460).

On "body," see Schweizer, *"sōma,"* TDNT, vol. 7, pp. 1024–94; Barth, "Head, Body, Fulness," *Eph. 1–3,* pp. 183–210; Bruce discounts a Greek influence on Paul's theology with respect to these concepts (pp. 200–205).

1:19 / On "fullness," G. Delling, *"plērēs, pleroō,"* TDNT, vol. 6, pp. 283–311; Lohse, pp. 52–59; P. D. Overfield, " 'Pleroma': A Study in

Content and Context," *NTS* 25 (1979), pp. 384–96; Robinson, *Ephesians,* pp. 87–89.

1:20 / Barclay lists four different theories on the interpretation of "reconciliation" in this verse: (1) the angels needed reconciliation and redemption because they were under sin; (2) according to Origen, even the devil and his angels would be reconciled in the end; (3) the phrase just emphasizes completeness; and (4) the angels were reconciled to God but not to humanity (*The Letters to Philippians, Colossians, Thessalonians,* pp. 148–49).

§5 The Application of the Hymn to the Colossians (Col. 1:21-23)

1:21 / In the verses following the Christ hymn (1:21-23), Paul resumes the same kind of pastoral concern so evident in his thanksgiving and prayer (1:3-19). He reminds his readers that the cosmic and ecclesiastical reconciliation that he has just described in the hymn is true for them as well (**once you . . . but now he has reconciled you**). They have been made acceptable to God and now are challenged to continue in the truth that they have been taught.

One way to appreciate what God has done is to remember what one was before God's grace was experienced personally (cf. 1:26; 3:7; Rom. 6:22; 11:30; 1 Cor. 6:11). Hence Paul reminds them that in their pre-Christian state they were **alienated from God**, and as such, they were God's **enemies**. This enmity manifested itself in an evil manner of life and thought. This stands as quite a contrast to their Christian walk (described in 1:10).

1:22 / But a great change has taken place in their lives because God has acted decisively in Christ. Paul picks up the key word *reconciliation* from the hymn (1:20) and reminds them that God reconciled them **by Christ's physical body through death**. Both the hymn and this verse emphasize the personal and historical act of Christ. Perhaps the false teachers had either denied or minimized the reality of Christ's incarnation and death. The emphasis on Christ's physical death may also be a polemic against those teachers who included the angels in the work of reconciliation but who, in contrast to Christ, do not have a body.

Reconciliation has a moral aspect as well. The CNB captures the Greek *parastēsai*, which expresses purpose (**to present you holy in his sight, without blemish and free from accusation**). Some commentators believe that the terminology used here has a sacrificial or cultic meaning (cf. Heb. 9:14; 1 Pet. 1:19). However, the main idea appears to be judicial, that is, those who have been reconciled to God are acquitted of all charges; they are holy, pure, and faultless when they stand before him (Eph. 5:27; Jude 24).

The message for the Colossians is that all of this is true for them *now*. This *is* their standing before God because it is his gift to them through Christ. Nevertheless, there is a future aspect in all of this because the "already" and the "not yet" are so characteristic of Paul's writings. What Christians possess now they will have in full at the final Parousia of Christ.

1:23 / Lest his readers entertain any idea that their status in Christ can be treated with indifference, Paul emphatically reminds them of an important condition that needs to be kept in mind: **if you continue in your faith, established and firm.** Salvation, although a free gift from God, must be kept. Thus those who have received Christ are admonished to abide or to persevere in Christ (John 8:31; 15:4–7; Acts 14:22; Rom. 11:22; 2 John 9).

To counter the threat of their eroding faith and shifting hope, Paul draws upon building metaphors that, as elsewhere in Scripture, portray strength, endurance, and security (Matt. 7:24–27; 1 Cor. 3:10–15; Eph. 2:19–22; 1 Pet. 2:4–10). The recipients can only have such a foundation, **established and firm**, by following in the **faith** and **hope** of the gospel that initially was proclaimed to them as well as to the whole world.

With these themes of faith, hope, and the universality of the gospel, Paul returns full circle to ideas expressed in his opening thanksgiving (1:3–8). There, his concern was that the Colossians see this as evidence for the truth of the gospel; here, he admonishes them to apply this truth to their lives continually.

Paul closes this section by stating that he is related personally to this gospel as a servant (*diakonos*). By doing this, he shows his commitment to the message that the Colossians have heard as well as his identity with his co-workers Epaphras and Tychicus, who likewise are servants of the gospel (1:7; 4:7). The statement also serves as a transition to the following verses where Paul outlines his ministry to the church.

Additional Notes §5

Schweizer summarizes the hymnic nature of this passage rather well when he writes: "It is no longer a matter for dispute that we have in these verses a hymn which has been taken over by the author. The prerequisites for this are present, as far as form is concerned; there is a certain rhythm in the construction both as a whole and in detail. There is also a portrayal of Christ, self-contained and surpassing anything that might be expected in the context; and again, there is the customary opening by means of the relative pronoun. More importantly, the distinctive characteristics of the style of the author of the Epistle are not found here, although they otherwise appear throughout the letter, while a plethora of unusual concepts also appear. Above all, however, one cannot help but notice the theological difference between the hymn itself and the commentary which the author of the Epistle provides" (pp. 55–56).

On the reconstruction of the strophic divisions of the hymn as presented by E. Norden, J. M. Robinson, and Schweizer, see Cannon, pp. 19–23. Martin divides the passage into three parts: Strophe I (1:15–16); Strophe II (1:17–18a); Strophe III (1:18b–20), pp. 55–56. See also Martin's *Reconciliation*, pp. 111–26.

For a recent presentation of the hymnic material in the NT, see Cannon, pp. 6–9, esp. n. 17, for bibliographical sources. For Cannon's discussion of 1:15–20, see pp. 19–37. Lohse lists twenty-three significant studies on the hymn (pp. 41–46). Other helpful sources include W. McCown, "The Hymnic Structure of Colossians 1:15–20," *EQ* 51 (1979), pp. 156–62; Schweizer, pp. 55–88; idem, "The Church as the Missionary Body of Christ," *NTS* 8 (1961), pp. 1–11; idem, "Christ in the Letter to the Colossians," pp. 455–62. On the baptismal nature of the hymn, E. Käsemann, "A Primitive Christian Baptismal Liturgy," in *Essays on New Testament Themes*, SBT 41 (London: SCM, 1964), pp. 154–59.

1:21 / The Greek word *apallotrioō* (**alienated**, "estranged") occurs only here and in Eph. 2:12; 4:18. The use of the perfect tense (*apēllotriōmenous*) emphasizes that their alienation (**you were alienated**) was a continuous state of being.

1:22 / Anyone using the Greek text will discover a number of variant readings on the idea of reconciliation, showing the struggle that translators have had with this verse. The NIV, along with other English translations, accepts the active "he reconciled" rather than the passive "you (plural) were reconciled."

1:23 / The phrase **proclaimed to every creature under heaven** (cf. 1:6) is not to be taken literally unless it refers to the Roman Empire. Rather, this is a polemical statement to show the inclusiveness of the gospel as opposed to the exclusivism of the false teaching.

1:24 / Paul begins his discussion by referring to his physical sufferings (**in my flesh**) on behalf of the Colossian church. The fact that he is in prison may be uppermost in his mind (4:18), although there may be a general reference to other afflictions that he has experienced throughout his ministry as an apostle of Jesus Christ (2 Cor. 1:4, 6, 8; 2:4; 6:4; 7:4; 8:2; Phil. 1:17). The "rejoicing" does not come because Paul is undergoing trial or persecution. Paul is happy because his **sufferings** are for the believers at Colossae. In this, as well as in passages such as Romans 5:3, 8:38ff., the apostle captures the spirit of Jesus' words in Matthew 5:10–12, where happiness and persecution are linked together (cf. 1 Pet. 4:13).

In other passages, Paul indicates that his **afflictions** can be understood in a number of ways: They are a consequence of the Christian life and further the gospel (2 Cor. 6:4; Phil. 1:17, 18, 24; 3:10); they enable one to comfort others who are experiencing distress (2 Cor. 1:4, 5), they keep one humble (2 Cor. 12:10), and they are a preparation for future glory (2 Cor. 4:17). The apostle Peter indicates that trials act as a refining process for faith (1 Pet. 1:6, 7), and James mentions that they produce steadfastness (1:3, 4).

The major difficulty in this verse is interpreting Paul's statement that **I fill up in my flesh what is still lacking in regard to Christ's afflictions, for the sake of his body, which is the church**. This is different from suffering *for* Christ (Phil. 1:29) or even sharing *in* Christ's suffering (Phil. 3:10). Paul understands that his suffering somehow *completes* what is lacking in Christ's afflictions for the church.

A number of interpretations have been suggested for this verse: One view sees a certain deficiency in Christ's suffering for the redemption of the church and believes that Paul's sufferings, as well as the suffering of saints and martyrs, can supplement or complete what was lacking in Christ.

But this view has come under attack for several reasons. Scripture simply does not support the idea that Christ's suffering on behalf of the church, that is, his reconciling work through the atonement, is incomplete in any way. He is the perfect sacrifice for sins, and no one can add to his finished work. Indeed, it would be foolish and contradictory for Paul to imply such an interpretation in a context in which he has just finished emphasizing the sovereignty of Christ in all things. Besides, the Greek word used here for suffering (*thlipsis*) is not used in the NT with reference to Christ's atoning death.

A second interpretation acknowledges the perfection and completion of Christ's death and concedes that no amount of human suffering can add anything to that. Emphasis, therefore, is given to the edificatory nature of the sufferings that Christians endure for the building up of the church, the body of Christ. In other words, the church is built up by the sacrifices, afflictions, or sufferings of Christians everywhere. Certainly there is some truth to this, and it may imply what Paul means by suffering for Christ's sake (Phil. 1:29). However, this hardly does justice to the idea of completing what still remains of **Christ's afflictions, for the sake of his body**.

A third and rather detailed interpretation looks for a solution in Jewish and early Christian apocalyptic literature. E. Lohse, for example, believes that the phrase "what is lacking in Christ's afflictions" is equivalent to the concept of "a definite measure for the last days." Here it was believed (cf. also Matt. 24; Mark 13:5–27) that the return of God's anointed, the Messiah, would be preceded by a period of time when God's people would be called upon to suffer the "woes of the Messiah." Some commentators suggest that Paul sees himself as a martyr whose sufferings contribute to completing this period that awaits the return of the Messiah. Paul, therefore, suffers as a servant of the gospel and on behalf of Christ's body, the church.

It is quite possible that Jewish apocalyptic thought serves as a background for Paul's ideas on suffering. But whereas the Jews continued to wait for the messianic kingdom, the early Christians believed that the eschatological kingdom was inaugurated in the life and ministry of Jesus who suffered vicariously for his people.

A fourth view places Paul's statement within the context of the mystical union that the apostle has with Christ. Here reference is made to Paul's communion (fellowship) in Christ's death and resurrection (Rom. 6:3–11; 2 Cor. 4:10–14; Phil. 3:10) or to Acts 9:4, where Paul's persecution of the church is equivalent to persecuting Christ himself ("Saul, Saul, why do you persecute me?"). Paul's sufferings for the church, therefore, could be viewed as the sufferings of Christ himself, but through a member of his mystical body.

Some writers employ the term *the corporate Christ,* by which they mean that the sufferings of the church, or individual members of it, are one with the sufferings of Christ. In other words, the afflictions of the church are also Christ's afflictions. Paul's suffering for the church completes Christ's personal suffering.

After the death, resurrection, and exaltation of Jesus, members of the Christian community believed that they were called upon to suffer just like their Lord, although their suffering had no redemptive efficacy. Scripture is full of references that show that they were to expect various trials, tribulations, and persecutions (Matt. 5:10–12; 20:23; John 15:20; Acts 9:16; Rom. 8:17; 2 Cor. 6:4; Phil. 1:29; 2 Tim. 1:12; 4:5; James 1:2; 1 Pet. 1:6; 2:21; 3:14; 4:1, 13, 16; 5:10; Rev. 2:10).

With the development of Paul's mysticism, that is, his teaching of incorporation into Christ through baptism (Rom. 6:1–10; Col. 2:11, 12; Gal. 3:26–28), the followers of Christ came to believe that their sufferings and the sufferings of Christ were one. It could be that by the statement in 1:24 Paul sees the afflictions that he is suffering in his flesh as the afflictions of Christ (cf. 2 Cor. 1:5; 4:10; Phil. 3:10; 1 Pet. 4:13, for helpful parallels). Paul believes that he is helping to complete what the Messiah began for the church but will not be completed until his return.

One other interpretation understands the phrase "what is lacking in Christ's afflictions" (RSV) to refer to a deficiency *in Paul* and not in Christ. Paul realizes that his desire to share in Christ's sufferings and to become like his Lord in death is a continuing process (Phil. 3:10). He sees his suffering as a means by which he personally is enabled to reproduce more and more of Christ's Passion in his life. The suffering that the church endures is, therefore, for *its* completion and not toward anything lacking in Christ (see note).

Additional Notes §6

1:24 / For additional material on some of these interpretations, see R. Yates, "Notes on Colossians 1:24," *EQ* 42 (1970), pp. 88–102; on suffering, H. Schlier, *"thlibō," TDNT,* vol. 3, pp. 139–48. Schweizer, p. 98, lists a number of German sources on the suffering of Paul. Also helpful is F. Hauck's article *"koinos"* ("fellowship"), *TDNT,* vol. 3, pp. 789–809, esp. pp. 806–7, where he discusses the fellowship that the believer enjoys with Christ.

Lohse's view on the "woes of the Messiah" is discussed in his commentary, pp. 69–72. Martin adopts this interpretation of 1:24 when he states: "Paul takes over this notion and bends it to his purpose. In his life of service to the Gentile churches he is called upon to represent his people as a martyr figure and to perform a vicarious ministry (2 Cor. 1:6); and in this way he completes the still deficient tally of sufferings which God's new Israel had to endure before the end of the age" (p. 70).

The last interpretation suggested has the support of a number of authors. As early as 1958, E. Hoskyns and N. Davey stated: "This does not mean that there was something lacking in Christ's suffering, but that there was something lacking in St. Paul's. He desires that his body may be, as it were, the arena where the obedience to God may be as wholly displayed as it had been in the passion of Jesus Christ" (*The Riddle of the New Testament* [London: Faber & Faber, [1958], p. 158).

Similar statements are made by L. P. Trudinger, "Further Brief Note on Colossians 1:24," *EQ* 45 (1973), pp. 36–38; and W. F. Flemington, "On the Interpretation of Colossians 1:24," in *Suffering and Martyrdom in the New Testament* (Cambridge: Cambridge University Press, 1981), pp. 84–90. Flemington's ideas are clearly summarized in this quotation: "The defect that St. Paul is contemplating lies not in the afflictions of Christ as such, but rather in the afflictions of Christ as they are reflected and reproduced in the life and behavior of Paul his apostle. St. Paul strives continually to live *en Christō*, but he knows that in his life there is, as it were, an unpaid balance that needs to be made up before the reproduction of Christ's sufferings in Paul's person is complete. Paul rejoices because in all that he is suffering on behalf of the Colossians he is reducing his unpaid balance, he is making the reproduction a little more like the perfect original" (pp. 87–88).

§7 Paul's Proclamation of the Mystery (Col. 1:25–29)

1:25 / In this verse Paul continues to affirm his personal role in the events that he is describing: first, "I" became a servant of the gospel (1:23); then "I" am happy about my suffering for you (1:24); now **I have become its** [the church's] **servant** on your behalf (1:25). **Commission** is a translation of the Greek word *oikonomia*, which has the meaning of "management, stewardship, or commission to an office" (1 Cor. 9:17). Paul reminds his readers that his **commission** is by divine appointment and that they are included in his ministry, which is the task of fully proclaiming the gospel.

In its fullness should not be taken to imply that the previous proclamation of the gospel from Epaphras was somehow deficient or incomplete. Paul probably has the scope of the gospel in mind (Rom. 15:19). He already has alluded to the universality and the growth of the gospel (1:6); now he claims that God has appointed him to share in that task as well. The word of God will be fulfilled when it has been preached "to every creature under heaven" (1:23). However, given the situation at Colossae, it is not impossible that Paul is thinking of the content of the gospel. Both the NIV **(to present you the word of God in its fullness)** and the NEB ("to deliver [God's] message in full") understand it this way.

1:26 / The word of God that Paul has been called to proclaim is identified as **the mystery** that God has **kept hidden for ages and generations**. The word **mystery** is a translation of *mystērion*, which is used in Greek literature to convey the idea of something secret, mysterious, and unknown. The Greek "mystery religions," for example, were given their name because they performed secret rites on those who were initiates (the *mystēs*).

This term **mystery** is used rather extensively in the NT (twenty-seven times in all, twenty of which occur in Paul), and

so its meaning must be determined by the context. Here, as in
2:2, Ephesians 1:9; 3:3, 4, 9; 6:19, and Romans 16:25–26, it refers
to an aspect of the gospel that had previously been hidden but
now, according to the good pleasure of God, has been **disclosed
to the saints**.

1:27 / Paul leaves his readers in some suspense before dis-
closing the content of this mystery. **God has chosen**, he begins,
**to make known among the Gentiles the glorious riches of this
mystery**. And that **mystery**, he goes on to clarify, is that by virtue
of their incorporation into Christ his readers will share in the glory
of God. The gospel, in other words, initiates a process that moves
toward a goal that is yet to be fully realized. The content of the
mystery is expanded in Ephesians, where the author shows that
God's plan was to include the Gentiles in his plan of salvation
so that they, along with the Jews, are members of his body (Eph.
2:11–22; 3:2–12).

It is possible to translate the Greek *en* to read Christ *among*
you rather than **Christ in you**. If so, the emphasis is upon the
preaching of Christ in their midst rather than Christ dwelling
within their hearts. But though this may fit the context, it is
also true that the Colossians personally share in this mystery
by virtue of the indwelling Christ. The mystery is that Christ
is both in and among them. They are members of Christ's body
here and now; nevertheless, there is an eschatological ring to
this concept because their hope is directed toward the glorious
future.

1:28 / Now that the nature of the mystery is revealed, Paul
adds some specifics to his own commission. By changing the "I"
(1:23, 24, 25) to **we**, he accomplishes two things: First, he includes
his co-workers, particularly Epaphras and Tychicus, who served
the Colossian church; second, he sets the true messengers of the
mystery apart from the false ones who have been invading the
church with a different gospel.

Paul's task included the proclamation of Christ to **everyone**. Since this follows so closely after the clarification of the
mystery, Paul must mean that his message is the content of the
mystery, that is, Christ is in you, the hope of glory. To proclaim
Christ is equivalent to proclaiming the gospel (1 Cor. 9:14) or the
word of God (Acts 13:5; 17:13).

Besides proclamation, there is instruction: **admonishing and teaching everyone with all wisdom**. *Nouthetountes* is a pedagogical term used for training, disciplining, and warning (Rom. 15:14; 1 Thess. 5:12, 14). Paul must have found it necessary to protect the community from drifting away from the truth. The teaching is with all possible wisdom, implying, as in 1:9, a practical application to his instruction and not some speculative or esoteric knowledge.

The wisdom that Paul shares with his readers has a definite practical and ethical direction (cf. 1:6, 9); its goal is to **present everyone perfect in Christ** (cf. 4:12). Two important truths stand out in contrast to the teaching of the false teachers. First, the gospel is for **everyone**; it is a universal message available to all, not only to a special group of initiates. Second, the goal is maturity in Christ (**perfect** [i.e., mature] **in Christ**). The Gnostics stressed the perfection (*teleios*) of those who claimed to be filled with some special wisdom or power. Paul's goal, however, in preaching, admonishing, and teaching was to lead his readers into a mature spiritual life in Christ (cf. Eph. 4:13, 14).

1:29 / Even though Paul was not personally responsible for bringing the gospel to Colossae, he stresses that he labors for this Christian community. **This end**, that is, proclaiming the mystery, demands intense desire and hard work (**I labor**, [*kopiaō*] **struggling** [*agōnizomenos*]). Devoting such intensity to his task would be impossible without the enabling strength that Christ provides.

Additional Notes §7

1:26, 27 / Some helpful information on **mystery** can be found in G. Bornkamm, *"mystērion,"* *TDNT*, vol. 4, pp. 802–28; W. P. Bowers, "A Note on Colossians 1:27a," in G. Hawthorne, ed., *Current Issues in Biblical Patristic Interpretation* (Grand Rapids: Eerdmans, 1975), pp. 110–14; Lohse, pp. 74–75. For additional discussion, see §§ 12–15 on Ephesians.

2:1 / In the following verses (2:1–5) Paul elaborates upon his ministry as a servant of Christ. With the exception of 1:24, the previous section (1:24–29) describes a more general or universal situation: Paul suffers on behalf of the entire church; he is a servant of God who proclaims the "mystery" to all peoples; and he teaches in order that everyone may become a mature person in Jesus Christ. But the toil and agony that characterized his ministry to all the Gentiles is particularly evident in his relationship to the Colossians and the other congregations in the Lycus Valley.

Paul has worked as hard—literally, agonized (1:29)—for those whom he has never seen as for those to whom he has personally ministered. But he does not develop an inflated ego; nor does he sink into self-pity. He simply ties his labor in with the specific goals that he has sought to accomplish.

2:2 / Paul's ultimate goal is to encourage his readers (**that they may be encouraged in heart**). **Encouraged in heart** is a good translation of the Greek *paraklēsis* because Paul desires that they be strengthened or fortified inwardly in order to face the threat of false teaching. This encouragement comes, according to Paul, from that fact that they are **united in love** (*symbibasthentes en agapē*). The RSV makes this even more specific in its translation "that their hearts may be encouraged as they are knit together in love . . . "). In other words, love is the principle that unites this congregation as the people of God and encourages them to oppose the false teachers. The result will be the conviction of truth (**the full riches**—*plērophoria*—**of complete understanding**) as it relates to **the mystery of God, namely Christ**. The thoughts that Paul develops here are very similar to Ephesians 3:16–21, which mention inner strengthening, love, understanding, and maturity.

2:3 / This verse is the bottom line to the thoughts that Paul has been developing about the mystery. The mystery ("secret") is Christ (2:2), **in whom** (ultimately) **are hidden all the treasures of wisdom and knowledge.** Paul already has established the preeminence of Christ by showing that he is the supreme and complete revelation of God (1:15–20). It is not surprising, therefore, that Christ embodies *all* God's wisdom and knowledge as well. There is no need for the Colossians to look beyond Christ; there is no purpose in pursuing other systems of thought; there is no value in secret initiations. Christ is all and in him are all things!

2:4 / Up to this point it has been suggested that most of Paul's language and thoughts need to be interpreted within the context of the heresy that is threatening the church. Here, however, there is the first direct reference to the activity of these false teachers, who, apparently, were quite skilled with words. The Greek uses two colorful words to describe their devious methods: first, they use persuasive language (*pithanologia*, lit., "pithy speech"); second, they have the ability to deceive, delude, or seductively charm (*paralogizomai*) their victims. This necessitates Paul's strong warning to the Colossians: **I tell you this so that no one may deceive you by fine-sounding arguments.**

2:5 / Paul, although personally unknown by and physically separated from the church, is with them **in spirit.** By **spirit** he probably means more than his nonphysical parts such as thoughts, heart, or mind. He is with them because of their common faith in Christ; to be in Christ is to be in the Spirit—the Spirit of God (Rom. 8:9ff.).

The spiritual presence of Paul with this congregation is so real that he actually speaks of seeing them. And what Paul sees causes him to rejoice, for they have not yet succumbed to the false teaching. His prayers and his labor have not been in vain; the Colossians stand firmly together in their faith in Christ.

Additional Notes §8

2:2 / An alternate interpretation, with considerable merit, is suggested by O'Brien, *Colossians, Philemon*. O'Brien takes *symbibazō* in a didactic sense to mean "instruct," "make known," or "teach." The meaning then would be that Paul has instructed the readers in love in order that they become "enlightened in their faith over against heretical teachings and practices . . . " (p. 93).

2:3 / Schweizer points out that knowing Christ is never finished once and for all: "Revelation can only occur when one hears again and again afresh. Indeed, the point thus articulated is that Christ is sufficient, and that there are no other mysteries important for salvation besides or in addition to him. On the one hand, it is the case, then, that the whole revelation of God takes place once and for all in Christ, and one need no longer seek knowledge anywhere else, as some of those in Colossae were obviously trying to do. On the other hand, however, one can never appropriate such knowledge once and for all; rather, one must discover it again and again afresh, by allowing it to be given by Christ" (p. 118).

2:6 / The Greek text begins with "therefore," indicating that what the apostle is about to say is linked with his preceding discussion on the content of the mystery which is *Christ himself*. As someone has said, "Whenever you see a *therefore* in Scripture, go back to see what it is there for!"

To stand firm does not mean to stand still. Paul is aware that the best defense is a good offense. Consequently, he admonishes his readers to continue in their faith. By receiving the gospel they have **received Christ Jesus as Lord**. But that past event has an abiding significance upon their lives because they are to live in union with him—literally, to "walk with Christ." By stating this, Paul reinforces a theme common in his writings, namely, the relation between theology and ethics (3:1ff.; Eph. 4–5). Those who have **received Christ** are to **live in** Christ; or, those who are in Christ (the indicative of the Christian life) are to become what they are (the imperative of the Christian life).

2:7 / Paul amplifies what it means to live in union with Christ by utilizing the images of planting and building. The NIV **rooted . . . in him**—or any English translation for that matter—does not quite capture the significance of the Greek tenses that are employed. For **rooted**, Paul uses the perfect tense, which, in Greek, describes a present state that is the result of some past action. Here the meaning that the perfect passive conveys is equivalent to "having been rooted."

For the building metaphor, Paul uses the present tense, which describes continuous action. The building up of their life in Christ (*epoikodomoumenoi*) and the establishing (*bebaioumenoi*) of their faith are ongoing processes that are possible only because they are already rooted in the Lord. Hence the imperative tone in the NIV: **Continue to . . . [be] built up in him, strengthened in the faith**.

Some commentators suggest that the reference to **the faith** should be understood as "by your faith" (an instrumental dative) or "with respect to your faith" (a dative of reference). If the former, then the idea is that they are being built up by means of their faith—faith is the instrument of their growth. If the latter, then Paul desires that the Colossians grow in their faith (so NIV, RSV, GNB). Perhaps it may be wrong to make such a fine distinction, because as one grows in Christ one is established both *in* and *by* faith.

As you were taught is a specific reference to the gospel that the Colossians heard and had come to know as the truth of God (1:6). Paul is on the verge of exposing the heresy, and he wants his readers to know that their growth in Christ depends upon following the gospel as originally delivered to them (1:5–8; 2:6), not some secondary traditions of the false teachers (2:8).

And overflowing with thankfulness: Paul has already mentioned thanksgiving (1:3, 12) and will do so again in 3:15 and 4:2. This phrase surely ties in with his previous admonition to walk in the Lord (2:6). In other words, the Christian life is to be characterized by gratitude to God.

§10 Christian Versus Human Tradition (Col. 2:8-10)

2:8 / Earlier, the readers were cautioned about some of the methods employed by the false teachers (2:4). Now, in a stern warning (**see to it**), he exposes this heresy even further. First, its effect is to enslave its victims. The word *sylagōgeō* describes the action of one kidnapping or plundering and then making off with the catch as a prize. It is an appropriate way of portraying the malicious and seductive nature of the heresy.

Second, it is **hollow and deceptive philosophy** (RSV: "philosophy and empty deceit"; GNB: "worthless deceit of human wisdom "). This is the only time that the word *philosophia* occurs in the NT, so it must have been a special feature of this heresy. Paul is not objecting to the study of philosophy (lit., "one who loves wisdom"), because in the Hellenistic world religious communities offered their teaching as philosophy. His concern is with those who have turned the pursuit of wisdom into a "philosophistry" characterized by empty and deceitful practices. This teaching is **hollow** because it does not contain the truth; it is **deceptive** because it captivates people and prevents them from seeing the truth.

Third, these teachings are human and not divine in origin. The teaching according to Christ is Paul's reference to the word of truth, the gospel, which came to the Colossians directly through Epaphras (1:5-7) and indirectly through Paul as God's appointed servant (1:23, 25). The false teachers cannot make such a claim, because their doctrines come from human sources and from **the basic principles of this world** (*stoicheia tou kosmou*, lit., "elements of the universe"). Most English translations add the word "spirits" or **principles** to the phrase and come out with "elemental spirits of the universe" (RSV), "elementary principles of the world" (NASB), or "ruling spirits of the universe" (GNB). In Heb. 5:12, the NEB translates the phrase as "the ABC of God's oracles."

As the additional notes will show, there is a wide variety
of scholarly opinion as to the meaning of these concepts in the
NT (Col. 2:8, 20; Gal. 4:3). The term *stoicheion* indicates something
basic or rudimentary, such as the fundamental principles of learning (the ABCs), or the elements from which the world was created
(earth, air, fire, and water). These **principles** may have been elevated to the level of spirits or angels in the Hellenistic world.

Stoicheion also designates the heavenly bodies that in some
cases were personified and worshiped. The control that these elemental spirits had over human beings (fate) could only be broken
by correct knowledge (*gnōsis*) and/or ritual, usually in the form
of magic or ascetic practices (cf. 2:20–23). But these *stoicheia* could
also be the source of wisdom or knowledge and in this way provided the substance of the false message that Paul deals with in
the subsequent verses (2:16–19) and exposes as being contrary to
the gospel of Christ.

2:9 / In this verse Paul returns to a theme already developed in the Christ hymn (1:15–20) and reemphasizes that the
Colossians do not need any additional source of revelation or authority for their spiritual life. Christ is not simply another of the
spiritual forces that make up the fullness (*plērōma*) of the universe (cf. 1:19). He is superior to all others because he alone is
God incarnate and the whole fullness of deity is found in him.

2:10 / But there is more to this wonderful message: The
one who is the fullness of the Godhead is likewise the fullness
of each believer. The community is fulfilled in him. The Colossians do not need to look beyond Christ for their understanding
of the universe; nor do they need to supplement him in their personal lives, because those who are "in Christ" participate in his
fullness *now* (the Greek present tense *este*, "you are"). In other
words, there is nothing lacking in their relationship to God. Paul
ends by reasserting (cf. 1:15–20) Christ's preeminence over all alien
powers (**who is the head over every power and authority**). There
is no need, therefore, to pay homage to them!

Additional Notes   §10

2:8 / For some comments on the false teaching at Colossae see the Introduction. Nearly every major commentary has a discussion on the heresy as well as on the meaning of *stoicheia tou kosmou*: for example, Lohse, "The Elements of the Universe" (pp. 96–99), and "The Teaching of the Philosophy" (pp. 127–31); Martin, pp. 80–100; Schweizer, "Excursus: The Colossian Philosophy (2:8)," in his commentary, pp. 125–70.

Additional and more technical studies include "*stoicheia,*" in W. F. Arndt and F. W. Gingrich, *A Greek-English Lexicon of the New Testament,* 2d ed. (Chicago: University of Chicago Press, 1979), pp. 768–69; A. J. Bandstra, *The Law and the Elements of the World: An Exegetical Study in Aspects of Paul's Teaching* (Kampen: J. H. Kok, 1964); G. R. Beasley-Murray, "The Second Chapter of Colossians," *RevExp* 70 (1973), pp. 469–79; E. Burton, "The Elements of the Universe," in his *Critical and Exegetical Commentary on the Epistle to the Galatians* (Edinburgh: T. & T. Clark, 1921), pp. 510–18; G. Delling, "*stoicheō*" *TDNT* vol. 7, pp. 666–87; C. A. Evans, "The Colossian Mystics," *Biblica* 63 (1982), pp. 188–205. A volume listed in For Further Reading, F. Francis and W. Meeks, eds., *Conflict at Colossae,* contains the following articles: "The Colossian Heresy," by J. B. Lightfoot; "The Isis Initiation in Apuleius and Related Initiatory Rites," by M. Dibelius; "The Heresy of Colossians," by G. Bornkamm; "Paul's Adversaries in Colossae," by S. Lyonnet; "Humility and Angelic Worship in Col. 2:18," by F. O. Francis; and "The Background of *EMBATEUEIN* (Col. 2:18) in Legal Papyri and Oracle Inscriptions," by F. O. Francis. Cf. also M. D. Hooker, "Were There False Teachers in Colossae?" in *Christ and the Spirit in the New Testament,* ed. B. Lindars and S. S. Smalley (Cambridge: Cambridge University Press, 1973), pp. 315–31; Schweizer, "Christ in the Letter to the Colossians," esp. pp. 451–55; for other contributions by Schweizer, as well as additional foreign sources, see his *Colossians,* pp. 121, 311. A unique but helpful interpretation of the *stoicheia* is provided by W. Wink in "The Elements of the Universe in Biblical and Scientific Perspective," *Zygon* 13 (1978), pp. 225–48.

There continues to be debate whether *stoicheia tou kosmou* should be translated as "elements of the universe" or "elemental *spirits* of the universe." According to Schweizer, the designation "elements" does not include the stars and astrological spirits "until the second century A.D. Further, these elements are never adduced in the New Testament lists of powers and authorities, not even in Colossians (1:16; 2:10). Our starting point must be the fact that there is no contemporary evidence for the meaning of 'elemental spirits' or 'stars.' The power which they wield, by binding men to the "world" through ascetic "regulations" (vv. 20f.), is, then, probably comparable to the power belonging to the commandments of the law, which are certainly not demons either" (p. 128).

W. Wink goes through the history of research on the *stoicheia* but concludes that prior to the third century A.D. there is no evidence that they were regarded as personal beings or fallen angels or that they were divinized in any form. The meaning of the term can only be determined from the context, which varies in the NT, for example, the constituent elements of the physical universe (2 Pet. 3:10, 12), philosophical presuppositions (Col. 2:8), religious laws and practices (Col. 2:20; Gal. 4:3, 9), or the rudimentary or first principles (Heb. 5:12).

§11 The True Circumcision and Its Effects (Col. 2:11–15)

2:11 / It already has been noted that the doctrine of baptism has a significant place in this epistle (see note on 1:14). In this section (2:11–15), Paul turns to baptism as a way of explaining the means and the results of the believers' union with Christ. With the exception of the language of circumcision, the thoughts are similar to those developed in Romans 6:1–11 and Galatians 3:27–28. It is quite possible that the peculiar beliefs and practices of the Colossian false teachers necessitated this clarification on circumcision and its relation to new life in Christ through baptism.

By insisting that the Colossians already have been circumcised, Paul diffuses any claim for the continuation of this rite in the community. But their circumcision, he clarifies, is **not with a circumcision done by the hands of men**, literally, "not from human hands." As Gentiles, they have no need to undergo a cultic rite that was practiced by the Jewish people as a sign of membership in the covenant. Nor should they subject themselves to any initiation rites of the false teachers that degrade the body and the flesh.

Believers are circumcised **with the circumcision done by Christ**. This had nothing to do with the circumcision of Jesus as a Jewish boy (Luke 2:21). Rather, Paul is referring to a circumcision that belongs to Christ and that Christ performs when believers are united to him in baptism. Paul's main point is to contrast physical (outer) and spiritual (inner) circumcision. To experience the circumcision of Christ is nothing other than being buried and raised with him in baptism through faith.

The essence of this spiritual circumcision consists of **the putting off of the sinful nature** (lit., "the body of flesh"). Christ, in other words, liberates individuals from their unregenerate nature ("body of sin," Rom. 6:6; "body of death," Rom. 7:24). Paul develops similar ideas when he talks about the "old man" that is "put off" in baptism (Rom. 6:6; Eph. 4:22; Col. 3:9, 10) or the crucifixion of fleshly passions and desires (Gal. 2:19; 5:24).

What a tremendous message of liberation and victory this is for a congregation being seduced by a group of false teachers still enslaved to cosmic powers and authorities and seeking to free themselves through useless rituals and ascetic practices (2:16–23)! The Colossians needed to remember that Christ defeated (*apekdysis*, "putting off," "stripping," "disarming") these spiritual rulers in his death and triumphed over them in his resurrection (2:15). This victory, Paul reminds his readers, is theirs because they have been circumcised with **the circumcision done by Christ**, for by union with him in baptism by faith he frees humanity from the powers of evil.

2:12 / Since the "circumcision of Christ" is baptism, then this verse should be viewed as an elaboration of that truth rather than as an introduction of some new ideas. The Greek text begins with the passive participle *syntaphentes*, which is translated **having been buried**. The NIV correctly implies this continuity of thought in its translation. The RSV "and you were buried" may give the wrong impression that burial with Christ in baptism is a different experience.

The similarity of ideas in Colossians 2:11–15, Romans 6:1–11, Galatians 3:26–27, and Ephesians 2:1–10 suggests that these passages were part of standard baptismal instruction in the early church. There are, to be sure, some different nuances and applications necessitated by the context of each epistle. But basically, they teach (*a*) that baptism is a faith-baptism, that is, it is for believers who put their faith in Christ, (*b*) that it is a participation in Christ's death and resurrection, and (*c*) that it has ethical implications because in it the believer receives new life from Christ.

The imagery of burial (death) and resurrection (new life) comes from the NT practice of immersion—the believer was literally lowered into the water. Burial symbolized death to the old life, and the emergence from the water symbolized the new or resurrected life in Christ. Thus, in a very profound way, baptism outwardly symbolizes or dramatizes the inner experience of the forgiveness of sins.

All this should not lead to the conclusion that baptism is only a *symbol* of some prior experience such as repentance or conversion. Since the baptism of the NT is a faith-baptism, it is not uncommon to find forgiveness, regeneration, and justification linked with this rite (John 3:5; Acts 2:38; 22:16; 1 Cor. 6:11; Titus 3:5; 1 Pet. 3:18–21). In other words, baptism, when accompanied by faith, has a sacramental as well as a symbolical function. God, by his Spirit, has chosen to make something happen in baptism. Baptism is both the expression (symbol) *and* the vehicle (means, conveyance) of God's grace. It declares as well as effects one's union with Christ's death and resurrection (cf. Rom. 6:1–10); it is an initiation into Christ's body, the church (1 Cor. 12:13); it is God's way of stamping the believer with his seal of ownership (Eph. 1:13; 4:30).

The believers in Colossae who were **buried with him in baptism** were also **raised with him**. The most logical inference is that this "raising" is part of the baptismal event (from the Greek text *en hō* = in whom/which. Thus the RSV "in which [i.e., baptism] you were also raised with him through faith" and the GNB "in baptism you were also raised with Christ through your faith . . . "). Paul also presents Christ's resurrection as the supreme manifestation of God's power. This final thought is not unlike Eph. 1:19 where God's power is demonstrated in the resurrection of Christ from the dead.

It is significant that the action described in verses 11–12 is in the past tense (the Greek aorist): "you were circumcised" *perietmēthēte*); "having been buried" (*syntaphentes*); "having been . . . raised" (*synēgerthēte*). In other words, these are realities that these believers already possess by virtue of their union with Christ in baptism. There is no need to look for any additional spiritual experience to supplement their faith. The false teaching has nothing to offer that is not already theirs in Christ.

2:13 / The new life that these believers now possess in Christ is contrasted to what they were before their baptism. Basically, they were spiritually dead (cf. Eph. 2:1). This spiritual death manifested itself morally by their **sins** (*paraptōma*— or "trespass"). Thus, by way of a contrast, there is a connection with verse 11, where Paul talked about their "spiritual circumcision" (cf. Eph. 2:11, 12). The continuity with verse 13 is shown in the fact that **God made you alive with Christ**. As Christ was raised from the dead by the power of God, the believer, who is in Christ through baptism, has been raised (2:12) and brought to life (2:13).

The Greek text also illustrates how carefully Paul wishes to emphasize their union with Christ. The word for life (*zōē*) is prefixed with the preposition *syn* (*synezōopoiēsen*). This preposition is repeated with the pronoun "him" (*syn autō*), leaving no doubt that their resurrection and quickening to new life is God's action in Christ alone.

This new life in Christ has resulted in a radical change in their moral life. Before, they were **dead in** their **sins**; now, they are spiritually alive (God **forgave us all our sins**). The change from **you** to **us** probably indicates that Paul is using traditional material familiar to the early church (note Matt. 6:12 in the Lord's Prayer: "Forgive us our debts"). This "forgiveness" also has taken place in the past (the Greek aorist tense). Hence, there is no need to look beyond their experience with Christ to other alternatives.

2:14–15 / Here Paul begins his elaboration upon the meaning of forgiveness in terms that are particularly applicable to the situation. His main point is that forgiveness of sins means victory over alien powers and freedom from legalistic practices. Again, all the action is described in the aorist (past) tense: He "forgave" (*charisamenos*), "canceled" (*exaleipsas*), "nailed" (*prosēlōsas*), "freed" (*apekdysamenos*), and he "triumphed" (*thriambeusas*) over these **powers and authorities**.

In discussing the nature of forgiveness, Paul refers to a hand-written certificate of indebtedness, similar to a bond or I.O.U. (Greek, *cheirographon*). Scholars are divided on the meaning of this term and the proper interpretation of the entire phrase, **the written code, with its regulations, that was against us**. Some of the suggestions include (*a*) the law of Moses, (*b*) the covenant between Adam and the devil, (*c*) a certificate of debt, such as an I.O.U., from mankind to God, (*d*) a heavenly book on which God recorded human sins, or (*e*) Christ himself.

A significant number of interpreters understand this either to be a reference to the Jewish law—thus God's regulations—or to the man-made traditions of the false teachers that resulted in transgressions. In either case, human beings were unable to keep to these precepts, so these stood as a **written code** against humanity until Christ canceled it by his death.

Either interpretation makes good sense for a number of reasons: first, there are examples in contemporary Judaism in which the law was applied this way; second, it fits the context of this passage in which Paul is dealing with specific legalistic practices that worked against individuals unless they were kept; third, it helps to explain the occurrence of other terms in the verse, such as **having canceled** and the **regulations** (*tois dogmasin*). Although the exact meaning of Paul's phrases cannot be traced with certainty, it is clear that his main point is to emphasize the decisive and complete way Christ's death on the cross took care of humankind's indebtedness to God.

The negative aspect of Christ's work on the cross is the cancellation of the bond of indebtedness; the positive side is Christ's triumph over the evil powers. Here, on the cross, Christ **disarmed the powers and authorities**.

Paul enlarges this conquest in imagery of a victorious general leading his captives home in a victory procession in which their defeat would be proclaimed publicly. Christ's defeat of these evil powers has meant that they have been **made a public spectacle** by **triumphing over them by the cross**. The crucifixion and resurrection (verse 12) are the supreme historical (**public**) events of Christ's victory over evil.

Verse 15 also repeats an emphasis that has been seen throughout the epistle, namely, that in Christ alone, by virtue of his work on the cross, the evil rulers no longer have control over the believer. The readers would remember 1:13, where Paul said that they have been rescued from the power of darkness and brought safely into the kingdom of his dear Son. All those who have been baptized into Christ and made alive with him (2:12) participate in his victory over evil.

Additional Notes §11

2:11 / Beasley-Murray carried this imagery of circumcision even further: "In this context 'putting (or stripping) off the body of flesh' is most plausibly contrasted with the minor operation in circumcision: bluntly it appears to say that instead of stripping off a little piece of flesh, as in circumcision, the Christian has stripped off his whole body of flesh, and this happened because Christ was 'circumcised,' that is, killed on the cross, the Christian shares so completely in that event, it is as if he himself had suffered that appalling bloody death" ("The Second Chapter of Colossians," *RevExp* 70 [1973], p. 474).

2:12 / Beasley-Murray's comment on the symbolic sacramental nature of baptism in the early church speaks to this point: "In such a setting baptism is less a testimony to a faith previously received than a declaration of a faith here and now embraced, an embodiment of conversion to Christ, and a submission to him who is able to save. In such a milieu it is not surprising that the spiritual realities of conversion and baptism are merged together, for in that context they do fall together" ("The Second Chapter of Colossians," p. 476).

On Paul's emphasis on resurrection in baptism, it should be noted that, in Romans, the resurrection is spoken of as future ("we shall be one with him by being raised to life as he was," 6:5). This (cf. also 2 Cor. 4:14; 2 Tim. 2:11) could be a correction to a certain element in the Gentile church that thought that the resurrection was completed in baptism (2 Tim. 2:18). In Colossians, Paul's emphasis is upon the present reality of the resurrected life in Christ because the false teachers were claiming that the soul was still in the process of ascending to heaven (Schweizer, pp. 144-45).

2:14 / A good description of some of these views is provided by W. Carr in his article, "Two Notes on Colossians (1. Col. 2:14; 2. Col. 2:18)," *JTS* 24 (1973), pp. 492-500. Carr's conclusion is that the dogmas (**regulations**) are not God's rules but "those decisions of men which issue in transgressions" or "the autograph of our self-condemnation in all its detail" (p. 496).

For reference with respect to Jewish and Hellenistic literature, see Lohse, pp. 108-9; Martin, *Colossians and Philemon*, pp. 83-85. Martin is attracted to a view that takes the *cheirographon* as a book of works kept by God in which all of humanity's sins are recorded. Although the record is used by the evil spirits to accuse men and women of their fleshly and unspiritual condition, it ceases to be binding, because Christ has destroyed its effectiveness by his death on the cross. It appears, however, that such a view may concede too much. Would Paul not fall into the heretic's trap by acknowledging the existence of something so preposterous as such a list? For another view, cf. O. A. Blanchette, "Does the Cheirographon of Col. 2:14 Represent Christ Himself?" *CBQ* 23 (1961), pp. 306-12.

2:15 / The verb *apekdysamenos* is an aorist middle participle. As a deponent verb, however (*apekdyomai*), it is active in meaning and makes God the subject. Thus, "God stripped the evil powers of their dignity and authority" (see Lohse, pp. 111-12; Martin, pp. 86-88; Bruce, pp. 239-40; Abbott, pp. 258-61).

§12 A Manifesto of Christian Liberty (Col. 2:16–23)

2:16 / Christ's defeat of these evil powers forms the basis for Paul's polemic in this section. **Therefore** refers back to the work of Christ and his victory over those spiritual rulers and authorities that were thought to exercise power over the Christian. Christ has freed these believers, and they must guard that freedom by resisting all attempts from the false teachers to subject them to another set of legalistic rules and regulations.

This entire passage is somewhat difficult to interpret. First, Paul uses slogans and phrases that were employed by the false teachers. Though these would have been familiar to the Colossians, they are difficult for the modern reader to understand. Second, in spite of such specific references to the beliefs and practices of the false teachers, it is impossible to identify the heresy with any precision. Some of the things that Paul says look Jewish; others appear more pagan and Hellenistic. A third alternative, and one that attracts the most attention, is that the heresy represents a form of syncretism that combined elements from a number of religious sources (see discussion in the introduction).

Identifying the heresy is not essential for understanding Paul's basic message. He wants to reassure his readers that, by virtue of the person and work of Christ, they have no need to surrender their freedom to legalism (**do not let anyone judge you**). The **anyone** refers to the person(s) attempting to set up as a judge over members of the congregation who do not follow certain laws with respect to food and the observance of religious festivals.

These regulations go far beyond the requirements of the OT, since the food laws that governed the people of the old covenant were set aside by Christ (Mark 7:19) and declared nonbinding upon the Gentiles (Acts 10:9–16; 15:19–29). One gets the distinct impression that the regulations threatening the Colossians were all man-made traditions. People in the ancient world would abstain from certain foods for a variety of reasons (cf. Rom. 14:17, 21; 1 Tim. 4:3).

The Colossians are not to be bound by rules with respect to food (**what you eat or drink**) or the religious calendar (**a religious festival, a New Moon celebration or a Sabbath day**). It is quite possible that these "special days" governed what a person might or might not eat as well. At any rate, Paul declares freedom from all regulations imposed by the false teachers. By submitting to such regulations, the Colossians would be acknowledging the continuing authority of the evil powers over them. They need to remember that in Christ they have been set free from such tyranny (2:20).

2:17 / All these dogmas are **a shadow of the things that were to come**. At one time such rules may have served as a transitory "type" or **shadow** of something more permanent in the future. But since the age of fulfillment has come in Christ, these rules have no further intrinsic value. Their function in foreshadowing has been surpassed by Christ: He is the **reality** (cf. RSV: "the substance belongs to Christ"; GNB: "the reality is Christ"; NIV: **the reality, however, is found in Christ**).

The word used to express **reality** is *sōma*. On the one hand, it may simply distinguish true **reality** (substance) from appearance (**shadow**). But *sōma* is the same word that Paul uses for the church as the body (*sōma*) of Christ (1:18; 2:19). This fact, along with the corporate identity that exists between Christ and the believer, makes one wonder whether Paul actually has the church as Christ's body in mind. If so, he would be saying that the reality that exists in Christ is likewise shared by members of his body, the church.

2:18 / One of the devastating effects of all false teaching is the division that it creates within the Christian community (cf. 1 Cor. 1–3; 1 John 2:7–11). When certain individuals, for example, set themselves up as the spiritual elite by claiming special access to visions, revelations, tongues, prophecies, and so forth (1 Cor. 14), they ignore others who cannot make such claims. At Colossae, this took the form of judgment or condemnation: **Do not let anyone who delights in false humility and the worship of angels disqualify you for the prize**. Quite possibly this heresy had some affinity to the mystery religions, in which such visions were received when the initiate performed certain rites or entered (*embateuō*) into the innermost part of the pagan sanctuary.

The reference to the **worship of angels** goes far beyond anything found in Scripture. True, angels were regarded as celestial beings, intercessors, messengers, agents of God, and so forth, but they were never worshiped as a class of spiritual beings. The elevation of them to cosmic powers and the veneration of them as objects of worship must, therefore, belong to this syncretistic heresy. The angels may, in fact, be the principalities, powers, and authorities that Paul mentions throughout the epistle. If so, they would be worshiped for their power as well as for their control over human beings.

The Greek word used for **humility** is *tapeinophrosynē*, which, on other occasions, is a positive and commendable disposition of character (3:12; Eph. 4:2; Phil. 2:3; 1 Pet. 5:5). Here the context shows that the heretics were guilty of a **false humility** in connection with their worship of angels. The RSV translates it as "self-abasement," indicating the inward and selfish nature of their cultic conduct.

Paul continues his scathing indictment of these perpetrators of deceit: They claim to be spiritually superior because of their visions and cultic practices, but there is no substance to their claim (**such a person . . . his unspiritual mind puffs him up with idle notions**). It is all vanity and without purpose.

The source of this vanity lies in an **unspiritual mind**. The false teachers may have thought that they were in communion with God; they may have believed that they were inspired by the Spirit. But their thoughts and actions were of human rather than divine origin. Thus they remain under the control of the flesh (*sarx*). Paul does not mean to imply that the flesh, in itself, is evil; verses 18 and 19 together show that the problem is in putting one's trust or self-confidence in the flesh rather than in Christ.

2:19 / The false teachers have fallen into error because they have stopped holding on to **the Head, from whom the whole body . . . grows**. Paul already has discussed the headship of Christ as it relates to the cosmos and the church (1:15–20; 2:10). Here he applies that concept to the problems facing the church by using the analogy of the human body (cf. 1 Cor. 12:12–31; Eph. 4:15–16). Because these false teachers have detached themselves from

Christ, they have deprived themselves of the true source of nourishment and unity.

Christ himself is the only true source of life for the church, for under his control the entire body is **supported** (*epichorēgoumenon*). This is a present participle, indicating that the process of support or nourishment is a continuing one. The same continuing action applies to the unity of the body as well (*symbibazomenon*): Under Christ's control the whole body is **held together by its ligaments and sinews** (cf. Eph. 4:16). These anatomical features provide the necessary cohesion for the body. But they can do so only if they remain joined to the head.

Under the headship of Christ, the body grows according to God's plan. Literally, the Greek translates into an awkward phrase "it (the church) grows (unto?) the growth of God." The basic meaning, however, is that God provides the pattern for the church's growth; he also is the source of that growth, which is mediated through Christ, the head.

All of what Paul has been saying adds to his indictment of the false teachers for being vain and carnal (2:18). Since they have cut themselves off from the source of nourishment, unity, and growth, it follows that they are undernourished, fragmented, and stagnant. In fact, the imagery can be carried even further, for it leads to this inescapable truth: The one who separates himself from Christ, the head of the church, is cut off from the church, the body of Christ; the one who separates himself from the church is cut off from Christ, the head.

2:20 / One cannot help but notice the repetition of Paul's earlier thoughts in 2:6–23. First, he applies the truths of the Christ hymn to the situation at Colossae (2:6–10); then he explains the effect of the believer's union with Christ in baptism, culminating in victory over all spiritual rulers and authorities (2:11–15). The heretics, however, did not claim that victory in Christ, because they continued to live in bondage to these spiritual powers—a bondage that manifested itself in cultic practices and angel worship.

Now, in verses 20–23, Paul resumes his indictment of the heresy by exposing its nature even further. Anyone practicing this false religion, he claims, is still enslaved to the cosmic powers. They do not live out the fact that at the time of their baptism (2:11, 12) they died with Christ and were set free from the power of the ruling spirits of the universe.

The tragedy is that the false teachers are not living in the victory and freedom that is theirs in Christ. Since you **died** to the powers **of this world, why**, asks Paul, **as though you still belonged to it, do you submit to its rules?** The Greek word (*dogmatizesthe*) was used in 2:14 and translated as "regulations." Here, it occurs in the verbal middle form, which carries the idea "why do you *subject yourselves* to dogmas . . . ?" **why . . . do you submit to its rules?**

2:21 / The first characteristic of such rules and regulations is that they are enslaving (**"Do not handle! Do not taste! Do not touch!"**). Such prohibitions can make people paranoid and paralyze them in their conduct for fear of sinning. Apparently this heresy had a long list of foods that were religiously unacceptable, that is, unclean (cf. 1 Cor. 8:1; 1 Tim. 4:3). There does not appear to be any deliberate gradation in this list, although "to handle" (*haptō*) can imply taking hold for the purpose of possessing.

2:22 / Second, these rules and taboos are temporary (**these are all destined to perish with use**). Literally translated, the Greek reads: "which things are all for corruption in the using." Without exception these taboos are subject to dissolution (decay). Why, then, stake so much of your life on things that have no enduring consequence, no eternal reality, no lasting effect?

Third, they are human precepts (**human commands and teachings**). No doubt this is an allusion back to such passages as 2:8 and 2:17-18, where Paul already has discussed human traditions and regulations. The idea here is similar to a reference Jesus makes to the Pharisees: "You hypocrites! Isaiah was right when he prophesied about you: 'These people honor me with their lips, but their hearts are far from me. They worship me in vain; their teachings are but rules taught by men' " (Matt. 15:7-9; cf. Mark 7:7). A similar concern occurs in Titus 1:13-14, where Paul appeals to them to be "sound in the faith" and to "pay no attention to Jewish myths or to the commands of those who reject the truth." The church of Jesus Christ continually needs to be on guard lest human traditions rob its members of their freedom in Christ.

2:23 / Fourth, they are deceptive and useless: The thoughts in this verse are quite similar to those in 2:18, where Paul talked about visions, false humility, and worship of angels.

Here, he adds that the rules and regulations **have an appearance of wisdom, with their self-imposed worship, their false humility and their harsh treatment of the body.** At best, however, all of these requirements are counterfeit, for they can deliver only appearances and impressions. The wisdom, worship, and humility do not bring them closer to God; the ascetic practices have no effect in preventing sins of the flesh. Basically, all such human attempts at religion are worthless—**they lack any value in restraining sensual indulgence.**

Additional Notes §12

2:17 / The grammatical problems of the phrase *to de sōma tou Christou* are discussed by Schweizer, pp. 157–58. Perhaps a nominative (*ton*) originally stood in place of the genitive, thus meaning that in contrast to "shadow," "the body *is* Christ"; or, to supply words to produce the meaning, that "the body belongs to Christ" or "the body, however, is the body of Christ." In spite of this, "The only point that is not altogether certain is whether it is Christ or the church that is set as reality in contrast to the shadow" (p. 158).

2:18 / The word *embateuō* has been discussed by a number of scholars: Carr, "Two Notes on Colossians," pp. 492–500, gives it the meaning of entering into the sanctuary "of the mind" rather than a sanctuary connected with initiation into one of the mysteries. Consequently, the translation of the verse reads: "Let no one judge you unfit to be a Christian with his personal wishes about religious excess and his haunting the courts of heaven at worship with angels, his so-called visions, puffed up by his private earthly imagination" (p. 499). This view comes close to that of Schweizer, who talks about a kind of "religious meditation" in which an individual would receive a vision of God ("Christ in the Letter to the Colossians," p. 454).

For other comments, see Francis, "The Background of *EMBATEUEIN* (Col. 2:18) in Legal Papyri and Oracle Inscriptions," in *Conflict at Colossae*, pp. 197–207. Francis concludes that *embateuein* does not confirm a type of mystery religion, but in the context of Colossians is used as a word for entering into heaven; H. Preisker, *"embateuō," TDNT,* vol. 2, pp. 535–36. In the commentaries, Bruce, pp. 248–49, esp. n. 93; Martin, pp. 94–95.

The problem of angel worship is explored by Francis, "Humility and Angelic Worship in Col. 2:18," in *Conflict at Colossae*, pp. 163–95. He takes the phrase "worship of angels" as a subjective genitive, meaning that it is the angels who worship and not people who worship the angels, as is commonly thought. See also A. R. R. Sheppard, "Pagan Cults of Angels in Roman Asia Minor," *Talanta* 12/13 (1980–82), pp. 77–101.

2:20 / The choice, as Schweizer points out, "is between the 'world' and its elements on the one hand and 'heaven' and the sovereignty of God on the other" (p. 166). Much of Schweizer's understanding of the false teaching relates to Gnostic ideas of the soul's ascent to heaven. Consequently, he understands Paul's polemic in this verse accordingly: "Since the Colossians are anxious that they may not, after their death, be able to ascend to that region above, the author stresses the other side of the matter: they have actually been transposed into that region above already, even if this fact is not yet clearly evident. They must therefore no longer allow regulations to be made as though they were still living in the world" (p. 166).

2:23 / The translation and exposition here do not indicate the difficulties commentators have with a text that many describe as "hopelessly obscure." For attempts to clarify its meaning, see B. Hollenback, "Col. 2:23: Which Things Lead to the Fulfillment of the Flesh," *NTS* 25 (1979), pp. 254–61; Houlden, *Paul's Letters from Prison*, pp. 199–200; Lohse, p. 124–26; Martin, pp. 98–100; Schweizer comments that "the verse is almost impossible to translate" (p. 168).

§13 The Ethical Dimensions of the Christian Life (Introduction to Col. 3:1–4:6)

Chapter three begins what normally is called the "ethical section" of the epistle. This follows a general trend in Paul's epistles in which he first deals with the theological issues and then builds his ethics upon that foundation (cf. Rom. 12:1ff.; Gal. 5:1ff.; Eph. 4:1ff.; Phil. 4:1ff.).

It is quite common to discuss this characteristic as the *indicative* and the *imperative* of Paul's theology. Basically, it is the "you are" and the "you ought" of the Christian life. In some ways this concept comes across as a paradox in Paul's thought. On the one hand, he can say that, by virtue of his or her position in Christ, the believer *is* "dead to sin," "light in the Lord," "a new creature," and so forth. But then on the other hand, Paul says, "Now become what you are," that is, live as if you were dead to sin, light in the Lord, new creatures.

This tension between the indicative and the imperative, of belonging spiritually to the age to come but living temporally in this present age, is a striking feature of Paul's theology (cf. Rom. 6:1–4, 11, 12, 13; 8:9–17; 13:14; 1 Cor. 6:8–11, 19, 20; 2 Cor. 5:17–21; Gal. 5:24, 25; Eph. 4:1–6; 4:22–5:20; Col. 1:9–15; 3:1–4). This third chapter of Colossians illustrates this principle by stating that the believers "have been raised with Christ" but then are summoned to set their hearts "on things above" (3:1); they have died with Christ (2:20; 3:3) but are subsequently told to "put to death" certain vices (3:5). The language of "putting off" (3:9; cf. Eph. 4:22) and "putting on" (3:10; Eph. 4:24) carries a similar message.

This relationship between theology and ethics, or the indicative and the imperative, often is developed around the sacrament of baptism (cf. disc. on 2:11–15). This truth becomes obvious when one considers the consequences of dying and rising with Christ. Since baptism is the founding of a new existence, the Christian life must manifest that change by a corresponding ethical life. The true meaning of baptism, in other words, needs to be lived out in the life of each believer.

This close relationship between baptism and ethics accounts for the numerous associations of the ethical exhortations in Colossians and Ephesians with the baptismal event. It also is quite natural to find baptismal and ethical language in close proximity, because baptism was the occasion for ethical instruction.

The preceding discussion provides a context for understanding 3:1ff., because Paul uses the baptismal event as a means of developing an ethical pattern for his readers. From his previous discussion (2:11–15), they would know that he had baptism in mind when he says "you died" (2:20; 3:3) and "you have been raised with Christ" (2:12; 3:1).

Paul discusses the believer's ethical life in a series of relationships that include Christ (3:1–8); the local church (3:9–17); the family (3:18–21); one's vocation (3:22–4:1); and society in general (4:2–6). Although these sections contain no specific references to the false teaching in the community, there can be no doubt that an understanding of and obedience to these ethical admonitions will fortify the congregation against the false teachings they have heard and assist them to fulfill their mission before God.

Additional Notes §13

For a helpful discussion of this concept, see W. D. Dennison, "Indicative and Imperative: The Basic Structure of Pauline Ethics," *CTJ* 14 (1979), pp. 55–78.

Although general divisions between the theological and the practical nature of the epistles may be helpful, they are somewhat superficial, because Paul frequently combines theological and ethical truths throughout his epistles. V. P. Furnish, for example, has shown that the ethical instruction in Paul's letters is not restricted to the closing sections (*Theology and Ethics in Paul* [Nashville: Abingdon, 1968]).

3:1 / As with a number of other "ethical" sections (cf. 3:5; Rom. 12:1; Eph 4:1), Paul begins with the word "therefore" (*oun*). The NIV **since, then,** has the similar effect of tying Paul's ethical instruction and theological thought together. These believers **have been raised with Christ**. On the basis of that fact they are to set their hearts on the **things above**. The verb **set** is a strong imperative and is a good translation of *zēteō*, which means to seek, examine, or search something out with the desire to possess. Those **things above**, both here and in 3:2, are not identified. They may be the virtues of the Christian life that Paul commends in 3:12–16 in contrast to the "earthly" things mentioned in 2:20–23 and 3:5–9 (cf. Phil. 3:19).

Above (i.e., heaven, cf. GNB), **where Christ is seated at the right hand**, should not be understood as some geographic place in the cosmos. The language here, as elsewhere (Matt. 6:20; Eph. 1:3; 2:6; 3:10), is figurative rather than literal; it designates a quality of existence, not a place of being. By **above**, Paul means that unseen realm of spiritual reality, the eternal world in contrast to a world that is earthly and transitory.

Through baptism into Christ, the believer participates in that spiritual and eternal realm in which Christ has been exalted and enthroned (Eph. 1:20; Phil. 2:9–11). This reminds the Colossians that they already share this exaltation with Christ. It is not merely a future inheritance, because "God raised us up with Christ and seated us with him in the heavenly realms in Christ Jesus" (Eph. 2:6).

3:2–4 / In addition to setting their hearts they are to **set** their **minds** on heavenly things. To keep one's mind fixed is to be intent and determined to do something (the RSV has "seek" at 3:1 and "set" at 3:2; the NIV uses **set** in both verses). Basically, the message is that, since the Colossians have **set** their minds on heavenly things, they are to keep holding on to that perspective and not to the things to which they have already died. Since the resemblance to 2:20 is so striking, Paul obviously has those legalistic rituals in mind (2:21-23) as well as the vices enumerated in 3:5-9. This, too, is a good example of the indicative and imperative in Colossians. In 2:20 Paul stated: "you died with Christ to the basic principles of this world"; in 3:3-4, there is a similar development of thought in that something that was hidden is revealed. The new life that the believer receives in Christ is **hidden**, that is, it is a mystery that one cannot fully explain or physically display. But the true nature of that **life** will not remain a secret, because it is indissolubly bound to Christ and will be revealed at his return. This interpretation, which takes **life** in the sense of quality or essence, is preferred to the view that looks to the return of Christ as the time when those who are saved and thus belong to God will be identified.

Additional Notes §14

3:1 / For a helpful discussion on this section, see C. F. D. Moule, "The New Life in Colossians," *RevExp* 70 (1973), pp. 481-93.

3:2 / If Colossians addresses a Gnostic view of the universe, then "heaven" or "the things above" would be understood in a literal or topographical way. In the ascent of the soul the Gnostics hoped to leave behind all earthly or material things in order to return to an existence in heaven (see Schweizer, p. 175).

§15 The Vices of the Old Life (Col. 3:5–9)

3:5 / The imperative tone that characterized 3:1–2 ("set," "keep") is picked up again in 3:5, but this time in a negative way: **Put to death, therefore. . . .** This list of prohibitions belongs to a category of vices that are scattered throughout the NT (cf. Matt. 15:19; Mark 7:21, 22; Rom. 1:24, 26, 29–32; 13:13; 1 Cor. 5:10–13; 6:9–10; 2 Cor. 12:20; Gal. 5:19–21; Eph. 4:31; 5:3–5; Col. 3:5, 8; 1 Tim. 1:9, 10; 6:4–5; 2 Tim. 3:2–5; Titus 3:3; 1 Pet. 2:1; 4:3, 4; Jude 8, 16; Rev. 9:20, 21; 21:8; 22:15). Later, in 3:12, Paul mentions a list of virtues that a Christian is to "put on." This, too, belongs to a catalog—of virtue (Matt. 5:3–11; 2 Cor. 6:6, 7; Gal. 5:22, 23; Eph. 6:14–17; Phil. 4:8; Col. 3:12; 1 Tim. 3:2, 3; 6:11; Titus 1:7, 8; James 3:17; 2 Pet. 1:5–7).

Of all the lists of vices and virtues in the NT, the lists in Colossians, Ephesians, and 1 Peter are the most similar. Scholars who have researched these "catalogs" have concluded that the lists that appear in these three epistles belong to a traditional body of instructional material of the early church and would have been passed on to new Christians on the occasion of their baptism. But even though Colossians, Ephesians, and 1 Peter contain a significant amount of baptismal language and theology, they probably were not written solely for that occasion and should not be regarded as baptismal tracts.

The command (imperative) **put to death** is a clear reference to the "death" that these believers have already experienced in baptism. They now are called upon to appropriate that death by removing all earthly desires from their life. The Greek uses the term "earthly members" (*ta melē ta epi tēs gēs*) because it was believed that such vices were located in certain parts of the body. In Romans 6:13 Paul uses the same word when he says: "Do not offer the parts [*ta melē*] of your body to sin, as instruments of wickedness, but rather offer yourselves to God, as those who have been brought from death to life; and offer the parts of your body [*ta melē*] to him as instruments of righteousness."

The list in this verse includes five vices that are related to sexual sins. As such, they are manifestations of evil desires and are harmful to other people. **Sexual immorality** (*porneia*) includes all kinds of unlawful sexual behavior, including deviations (1 Cor. 5:1, 10; 6:9; 2 Cor. 12:21; Gal. 5:19; Eph. 5:3; 1 Thess. 4:3; 1 Tim. 1:9, 10) such as prostitution and fornication. **Impurity** (*akatharsia*) is almost synonymous with *porneia* and is used in the NT to describe immoral intent as well as the practice of sexual vices.

Lust (*pathos*), in this context, probably implies some kind of sexual passion, that is, passion or lust that leads to sexual sin. Its counterpart, **evil desires** (*epithymian kakēn*), is used for the desire of something that is forbidden but is pursued in order to satisfy one's desires. Galatians 5:16, for example, says "Live by the Spirit, and you will not gratify the desires [*epithymia*] of the sinful nature."

The last vice to be mentioned is **greed** (*pleonexia*), or covetousness (RSV), literally, a desire to have more, to appropriate another's possessions. Since the NT has many warnings against this sin (cf. Mark 7:22; Rom. 1:29; 1 Cor. 6:10; Eph. 5:3), it is not clear whether its occurrence here is linked with sexual immorality or with all areas of life. Both ideas could be in the apostle's mind. The parenthetical **which is idolatry**, paralleled in Ephesians 5:5, underscores the idea that greed, along with the other vices, is an illicit evil desire (1 Cor. 5:10, 11; 6:9; Gal. 5:20). Greed is idolatry because it leads one to focus attention and affection on things other than God. This can happen in sexual life as well as with material things. The solution to such idolatry has already been given: "Set your hearts . . . set your minds" on heavenly things! In other words, give Christ preeminence in your ethical life as well.

3:6 / Lest anyone minimize the seriousness of these vices, Paul reminds his readers of **the wrath of God** (cf. the footnote: The NIV rightly omits "those who are disobedient" because of poor textual evidence. Its inclusion probably is due to Eph. 5:6.). God's judgment upon these sins is widely attested throughout Scripture (Rom. 1:18–32; 1 Cor. 5:10, 11; 6:9, 10; 1 Thess. 4:3–6).

3:7 / Before the Colossians became Christians their lives were characterized by such evil passions. They already have been reminded that at that time they were "spiritually dead" in their sins (2:13) and lived as though they belonged to the world (2:20; cf. Eph. 2:1-3). Their whole pagan way of life had been one of enslavement to evil *powers* as well as to evil *passions*. Fortunately, a wonderful change has taken place in them in Christ (the indicative); as a result, they are called upon to demonstrate this new life ethically (the imperative).

3:8 / Paul exhorts those who have been raised with Christ to manifest a new attitude toward sin. What was true of sexual sins applies equally to sins of speech: **But now,** that is, as Christians (cf. the "once you were" and the "now you are" in Eph. 2:3, 11-19), **you must rid yourselves of all such things as these.** The word *apothesthe,* "rid yourselves of" (RSV, "put off, away"), is part of the clothing imagery that Paul uses in connection with the old and the new life. One's sins are like an old garment that is taken off and discarded so that a new one can be put on (2:11; 3:10, 12; Eph. 4:22, 24). Such language accounts for a custom in many churches when candidates for baptism by immersion "put off" their old, ordinary clothes and "put on" white robes to symbolize their new or resurrected life in Christ.

The sins that affect social relationships can be divided into two categories: **Anger** (*orgē*), **rage** (*thymos*), and **malice** (*kakios*) are sins that can be internalized; they may or may not be expressed in overt action, although either way they clearly are wrong (Matt. 5:22-30). The other sins are those that are verbalized: No **slander** (*blasphēmia*) **and filthy language** (*aischrologia*) **from your lips.**

3:9 / Lying, although it may not belong to the list of the other five vices, certainly fits the context as a verbal sin as well as causing grievous damage to personal relationships, particularly within the body of Christ. Here, as in 3:5-8, Paul reminds them that this sin also belonged to their former way of life and has been put off in baptism (cf. Rom. 13:12-14; Gal. 3:27, 28).

Additional Notes §15

3:5 / One of the most recent discussions on the vices and virtues in the NT, particularly in their application to Colossians, is by Cannon, pp. 51–94. Other helpful studies include B. S. Easton, "New Testament Ethical Lists," *JBL* 51 (1932), pp. 1–12; Schweizer, "Traditional Ethical Patterns in the Pauline and Post-Pauline Letters and Their Development (Lists of vices and the Housetables)," in *Text and Interpretation: Studies in the New Testament Presented to Matthew Black*, ed. E. Best and R. McL. Wilson (Cambridge: Cambridge University Press, 1979), pp. 195–209.

3:10 / The NIV clarifies that the **new self** is the new being **which is being renewed in knowledge in the image of its Creator**. Behind this verse one can anticipate a serious question that the Colossians must have had concerning their new life in Christ: "How can I live out ethically for Christ what I have become sacramentally in Christ?" Paul himself was well aware of the tension between the indicative and the imperative, between his status in Christ and the process still to be accomplished (Rom. 7). He knew that in this life the believer is continually being called upon to become *in reality* what he or she is *in fact*.

But how, one may ask, is this seemingly impossible task to be accomplished? How can a person make the right choices? Who will give this new self the necessary ability and strength? The answer, says Paul, lies in the activity of God: **the new self . . . is being renewed in knowledge in the image of its Creator** (cf. Rom. 8:29). These words recall Genesis 1:27, which states that originally human beings were created in the image—that is, moral and spiritual likeness—of God and at that point had the ability to choose between good and evil. In the Fall, however, that image was destroyed. But the good news of the gospel is that now, in Christ, God is at work restoring that lost image. This restoration or re-creation is not mankind's work at all; it is not a process of giving up some vices and accepting a few virtues. This **new self** is God's doing! To express this process the Greek uses a present passive participle (*anakainoumenon*) to indicate that renewal is continuous (the present) and that it has an outside source (the passive, **the new self which is being renewed**).

In light of Paul's christological teaching in the epistle, one may have expected him to refer to a renewal in Christ's image, or to the second Adam, as he does elsewhere in his writings (Rom. 5:12–21; 8:29; 1 Cor. 15:45–49; 2 Cor. 3:18). Perhaps they are one and the same for Paul, since earlier he referred to Christ as "the image of the invisible God" (1:15). The purpose of this renewal, he adds, is to bring you to a full knowledge of himself. The believers need to become aware of God in order to do his will (cf. 1:9); God's presence in Christ will enable them to make the right moral decisions.

3:11 / At first glance the thoughts in this verse do not appear to fit the context of the ethical life that Paul has been describing. However, the NIV preserves the continuity of thought by translating the Greek particle *hopou*, which commonly denotes place ("where") as **here**—that is, within a new or renewed humankind. In other words, the consequence of being in Christ, of putting off the sins that exploit and divide humanity, of being renewed after the image of God, is the obliteration of all racial (**Greek or Jew**), religious (**circumcised or uncircumcised**), cultural (**barbarian, Scythian**), and social (**slave or free**) distinctions.

The creation of a new humanity (the church as the body of Christ) is one of the wonderful truths of the gospel. Ephesians 2:11–22 is the most extensive commentary on how Christ broke down the "wall" that separated Jews and Gentiles (cf. also Rom. 2:25–29; 4:9–12; Gal. 5:6). Even the maligned slave and the most primitive pagan (Scythian) are unified in Christ. At the foot of the cross the ground is level!

Though Paul is stating a general theological truth in this verse, there is no doubt that he has the church in Colossae in mind. What is true universally is true locally as well. That congregation probably was a mixture of all kinds and classes of people. However, those distinctions no longer have any significance when it is realized that Christ is everything and that he dwells in all people (**Christ is all and is in all**). Paul had a similar message for the Corinthians (1 Cor. 12:13) and the Galatians (3:26–28).

3:12 / Verses 12–17 are a continuation of Paul's discussion of those who are baptized. He already has dealt with the negative side by showing that those who have died to their old life are to put off those vices that characterized them as pagans. In this section, Paul turns to the positive side by listing a number of virtues that are to characterize their new or resurrected life. The **therefore** indicates that what follows is linked to the previous ideas on the new self (3:10, 11).

There are several features of this list of virtues that are worth noting: First, as already explained, this list is part of a body of traditional material that was transmitted in the early church (cf. disc. on 3:5). The language "put on" (**clothe yourselves**) shows that this belongs to the context of baptismal instructions. Second, these virtues are very similar to the "fruit of the Spirit" mentioned in Galatians 5:22, 23. Three of the "fruit" (**compassion, kindness, humility**) are directly in the list, while "love" and "peace" are picked up in 3:14 and 3:15 respectively.

A third characteristic of these virtues is that they are "godly qualities," which are used to describe either God or Christ. Many references in the NT, for example, talk about the mercy or **compassion** (Rom. 12:1; 2 Cor. 1:3), **kindness** (Rom. 2:4; 11:22; Eph. 2:7), **humility** (Phil. 2:5–11), meekness (2 Cor. 10:1), and long-suffering (Rom. 2:4; 9:22) of God and Jesus. The application of these virtues to the Christian would follow naturally from the call to imitation, union, or likeness with Christ. Believers are to act toward one another as God and Jesus act toward them.

Fourth, these virtues are social in nature, that is, they describe attitudes and actions that are important for healthy personal relationships. As the Christian has emptied (put off) his or her life of harmful and selfish vices, he or she now is instructed to fill (put on) that void with virtues that have the well-being of others as their prime goal. These virtues are lived out in the context of the local church (body, 3:15) where the Colossians are members with each other (3:13, 16). Their relationships with each other, including worship (3:16, 17), should bear witness that they are new people in Christ.

In verse 12, the believers are identified as **God's chosen people**, literally, the *hagioi*, "saints," "holy ones" (1:2). This was made possible, Paul tells his readers, because of God's love and election. Their status had nothing to do with their own striving; it was God's choosing. All three concepts (saints, love, election) are reminiscent of OT descriptions of Israel but are taken over and applied to the new Israel, the church (cf. 1 Pet. 2:9).

The Colossians are instructed to put on a number of virtues: **Compassion** is a translation of two Greek words, *splanchna* and *oiktirmos*, literally translated as "bowels of mercy" (KJV) because the bowels, or inner viscera, of a person were regarded as the seat of emotions. As such, the term denoted compassion that comes authentically from the heart and that is translated into corresponding action toward another person.

Kindness (*chrēstotēs*), with such corresponding concepts as goodness, generosity, or courtesy, describes an individual whose life and relationship with others are gracious and empathetic—genuinely concerned for the feelings of others. **Humility** (*tapeinophrosynē*), when properly directed (i.e., not false humility), is a spirit of modesty and disregard for status. It is that quality of Christ that best describes his willingness to become incarnate and suffer for humanity (Phil. 2:5–11).

Gentleness (*prautēs*), which appears in the RSV as "meekness," sometimes has been taken as a sign of weakness, particularly by the Greeks. In the NT, however, it is a disposition characterized by gentleness, consideration, and submissiveness—just the opposite of arrogance, rebellion, and violence. **Patience** (*makrothymia*) is a passive virtue, amplified by additional concepts such as endurance (cf. 1:11), forbearance, and steadfastness. In personal relationships, it is the grace of one who may have the right to retaliate but who chooses to exercise patience instead.

3:13 / There are bound to be conflicts (**grievances**) within the church. When this occurs, says Paul, **bear with each other forgive . . . one another**. Tolerance and forgiveness should not be regarded as two additional virtues but rather as explanations of how gentleness and patience are to be exercised in the body. To be tolerant is to be patiently forbearing of others with the idea of forgiving them. Paul appeals to his readers' experience of forgiveness in Christ. They are to forgive because of and according to the example of the Lord.

3:14 / **And over all these virtues put on love**. Paul still has the list of virtues in mind that the Christian is to "put on." Love is the crown of all these virtues; it is the final outer garment **which binds them all together in perfect unity** (lit., "the bond of perfectness"). The idea here is similar to Ephesians 4:2–3 and 15–16, where love is the manifestation of new life in Christ and what leads to maturity and unity in his body. Such love removes all feelings of anger, hatred, or an unforgiving spirit (cf. Rom. 13:8–10; Gal. 5:14).

3:15 / The peace of Christ has a twofold application. Since it comes from him, it provides an inner peace for each believer; it is to **rule** (lit., *brabyein* means "to arbitrate," "to control"), to guide in the decisions that he or she makes. Those at peace with themselves will be at peace with others; it enables individuals to be united into a single body. The "grievances" (3:13) that members have against each other are settled when Christ's peace rules in their midst. In the context of the indicative and the imperative, the meaning of Paul's admonition could be stated this way: By virtue of being reconciled to God by Christ you *are* at peace (the indicative; cf. Rom. 5:1; Eph. 2:14; Col. 1:20); now live out that peace (the imperative) in your personal and corporate life.

And be thankful: Thanksgiving (cf. 1:12; 2:7), which is basically a response to the grace of God, is mentioned three times in verses 15–17. Thus, rather than a final admonition in the preceding list of virtues, it serves as a summons to articulate that response in corporate worship and everyday living.

§17   The Expressions of True Worship
(Col. 3:16–17)

3:16 / Here is a verse loaded with important truths. Paul has just spoken about the peace of Christ that is to rule in the believers' hearts (3:15). Now he turns to another aspect of Christ, namely, **the word of Christ**. This phrase, taken as an objective genitive in Greek, means the words about Christ, that is, the gospel.

The word of Christ is to dwell within the believer and can do so either richly or feebly. Although the gospel certainly is "rich" in meaning, content, and so on, the Greek adverb **richly** definitely is intended to characterize the manner in which Christ's message is to inhabit the believer: **Let the word of Christ dwell in you richly.**

The indwelling word will manifest itself in two ways: First, the Colossians are exhorted to **teach and admonish one another with all wisdom**. This is a pedagogical process (cf. 1:28) in which all members share responsibility. In light of Paul's ministry as a teacher and Epaphras' as a transmitter of tradition, this verse should not be taken to imply a deficiency in these church leaders.

The second manifestation of the word of Christ is in worship. Considerable research has gone into analyzing the different components mentioned, so it is not unusual for commentators to suggest that **psalms** (*psalmois*) may have their heritage in the Old Testament; **hymns** (*hymnois*) could include psalms but may be more Christian songs of praise to God or Christ; **spiritual songs** (*ōdais*) may be musical compositions originating from ecstatic utterances under the inspiration of the Holy Spirit (cf. 1 Cor. 14:16).

On the basis of this passage and a similar one in Ephesians 5:19, it is not possible to establish distinctions with any precision, even though there is a certain diversity about the three. It does help one to appreciate both the richness of Christian hymnody even at this early stage of the church's life and the function of music within the context of worship. When such music is grounded in the word of God (i.e., doctrinal in content), it definitely serves a teaching and instructional function within the body.

Singing is to be expressed in a spirit of **gratitude**. Music may edify the members of a congregation, but its primary function is to render thanks to God. The word translated **gratitude** is *charis*, not the more common *eucharistia*. *Charis* can also mean "grace," and with the inclusion of the article (*en tē chariti*), Paul may be referring to the grace of God. When Christians sing "in the grace," they sing by virtue of the grace of God which is theirs. (The NIV rightly uses **God** rather than "Lord," which has weaker manuscript evidence and probably represents an attempt to harmonize it with Eph. 5:19.)

3:17 / Although this verse follows Paul's thoughts on corporate worship, it is intended to be universal in scope. The apostle has been listing a number of virtues and suggesting patterns of conduct that are to regulate life within the community. But it is obvious that he cannot make a detailed list of vices and virtues to cover every aspect of life. To do so would mean reverting to the type of Pharisaism that Jesus so vehemently condemned in the Gospels, or patterning his gospel after the heretics at Colossae, with all their rules and regulations (2:8–23).

Rather than a directory of rules, Paul leaves an important principle with his readers: Everything they **do, whether in word or deed, do it all in the name of the Lord Jesus**. They were baptized into that name and thus stand under the authority of Christ. Their ethical life—in word or deed—is to manifest that fact. In other words, the best testimony of a meaningful baptism is an obedient life.

Finally, **do it . . . giving thanks to God the Father through him**. The Christian lives out his or her obedience to Christ, not under compulsion as a duty, but in freedom with thanksgiving. What a striking contrast to the enslaving rules and regulations of the false teachers! The Christian's praise is offered to God through Christ. Once again, Paul reminds his readers that Christ is the only mediator to God.

§18 The Household Rules (Introduction to Col. 3:18–4:1)

The NIV entitles this section "Rules for Christian Households." Here Paul sets forth a series of reciprocal admonitions that are to govern the relationships between wives and husbands, children and parents, and slaves and masters. This list forms what has come to be known in academic circles as the *Haustafeln*, a German term meaning a list of rules or duties for members of a household. Similar lists to the one in Colossians are found in Ephesians 5:21–6:9 and 1 Peter 2:18–25, 3:1-7. The Pastoral Epistles (1 Tim. 2:8–15; 6:1–10; Titus 2:1–10) deal with the same classes of people but in a less structured and unified way.

The appearance of these "household rules" in so many NT epistles indicates that such instruction was necessary in the early church. People needed to know how their new life in Christ affected their personal relationships in the household as well as in the larger body of Christ. The similarity of these exhortations, particularly in Colossians, Ephesians, and 1 Peter, indicates that they were part of a body of traditional material that was developed and passed on in the churches. The instructions on slavery, for example, are much longer and serve a different function in 1 Peter than in Colossians or Ephesians; 1 Peter has no instruction for masters, whereas in Colossians and Ephesians it is an important part of a reciprocal relationship. The fact that wives and slaves are found in all lists indicates a concern that needed particular clarification.

Since it is obvious that other cultures and societies, such as the Jewish, Greek, and Roman, had rules and regulations governing social and personal relationships, there has been considerable conjecture in scholarly circles regarding the source of these *Haustafeln* in the NT. Some writers are attracted to ideas in Greek philosophy, particularly in the ethics of Stoicism, where there are significant parallels to the NT. Others suppose Jewish influence, drawing attention to ethical patterns and social concerns in Palestinian and Hellenistic Judaism. A few scholars argue for a distinctly Christian origin, believing that these rules can be traced back to the teachings of Jesus, Paul, and other apostles. There is, however, no easy solution to the question of sources, transmission, and final composition. Suffice it to say that by the time of their appearance in the NT they are regarded as authentic and authoritative instructions.

What does all of this mean as far as Colossians is concerned? First, it would be fair to say that Paul is using a body of traditional material dealing with personal relationships and applying them to the church at Colossae. Second, they must serve a specific function within this letter. As an isolated unit (3:18–4:1) they may simply have a domestic or sociological function. But their location in the epistle is not without significance.

At first glance, this section appears to interrupt Paul's ideas on worship (3:16, 17)—a theme that is continued in 4:2–4 with an emphasis on prayer and thanksgiving. However, by placing the *Haustafeln* in the context of worship, Paul wishes to emphasize the need for *order* in the church, particularly among women and slaves. The primary function of these domestic rules, therefore, is ecclesiological (for the church) rather than merely sociological (for society).

The need for "order" at Colossae, as well as in such congregations as Corinth and Ephesus, has to be seen within the cultural and religious context of the first century. First, there were concerns that arose because of the delay of the return of the Lord. The followers of Jesus expected him to return within their lifetime (Mark 9:1; 13:30, and parallels); Paul, likewise, believed that the coming of the Lord was imminent (1 Cor. 15:51–58). When this did not occur, and problems arose in the church because of it, he offered some correctives (2 Thess. 2:1–12; cf. also 1 Thess. 4:13–5:11). The Second Epistle of Peter may be one of the best documents in the NT cautioning against an expectation of the Lord's early return. With the Lord, writes Peter, "a day is like a thousand years, and a thousand years are like a day" (3:8).

When it was believed that the Lord's return was imminent, there was no reason to be concerned about rules governing church order. The early church was basically charismatic in nature, that is, it exercised considerable freedom of the Spirit in its life and worship. This provides a backdrop for much of Paul's concern for the disorder in the Corinthian church, where spiritual gifts were overemphasized and the congregation became fragmented and competitive (1 Cor. 11–14). This manifestation of religious enthusiasm may have been inspired by the prophetic fulfillment of Joel 2:28ff. (cf. Acts 2:17–21) and influenced by pagan cults in which ecstasy and spiritual excesses abounded. At any rate, the church service is not the place for everyone to do as he or she pleases; things need to be done in an orderly manner, and the welfare of the entire body must be considered.

With the delay of the Lord's return, the need for order in the church became more obvious. The teaching ministry that initially belonged to the twelve apostles and to charismatic leaders such as prophets and teachers (cf. Acts) was enlarged to include appropriately appointed leaders like Paul, as well as bishops (*episkopos*, 1 Tim. 3:1–7; Titus 1:7), deacons (*diakonos*, 1 Tim. 3:8–13), and elders (*presbyteros*, Titus 1:5), who were to teach and care for the church of God. There needed to be order in the church with respect to what was said (received tradition) and how things were done (proper offices).

The delay of the Lord also raised questions about the relationship of Christians to society. What is God's will for believers in the world? How are those who are "in the Lord" to walk before those who are not in the body of Christ? These household rules were created as patterns of instruction to answer such questions and to regulate personal relationships within the home, the church, and society. This concern was extended to include instruction regarding relationships to political authorities as well (Rom. 13:1–7; 1 Pet. 2:13–17).

A second factor at work in this section centers around the growing sense of freedom of women and slaves during Paul's time. Unfortunately, more is known about the subjection of women and slaves than about their emancipation. In Jewish culture, for example, women were relegated to a position inferior to that of men. They were denied certain functions in worship; their court in the temple area was outside of the "court of Israel." According to one rabbinic tradition, Jewish men repeated this blessing every morning. "I thank the Lord that he did not make me a Gentile . . . a woman . . . a boor."

Slaves suffered a similar fate in Greek and Roman society. Much secular literature of that period speaks of slaves in derogatory and demeaning terms. A slave was a living tool and, with the exception of the ability to speak, was considered no better than a beast. Their masters had powers of life and death over them, and they could be abandoned when their usefulness was gone. Many were killed at the slightest provocation.

At the same time, there are many examples of humanitarianism and manumission by slave owners. In some cases, slaves were part of the household and had responsible personal and financial positions. Many of them were treated kindly and honorably. However, the existence of the admonitions to the masters in these codes indicates that this relationship needed to be clarified for Christian slaves and masters.

The emancipation of women was more pronounced in the Gentile than in the Jewish culture, which basically was a patriarchal society. Greek and Roman women had rights and privileges that were denied their Jewish counterparts. Undoubtedly there are exceptions, for one can find conflicting reports in secular literature. Attitudes toward the status and role of women varied at different periods and geographical areas—not unlike today. In worship, however, Gentile women had an advantage over Jewish women. Many of the Greek and Roman deities were female (e.g., Isis and Diana), and most religious cults freely admitted women as participants and leaders.

This kind of religious freedom may have contributed to the problems faced in some of the Gentile churches, such as Corinth. Women—as well as men—who had been converted to Christianity would bring some of their previous religious practices into their new faith. But the ecstasy, glossolalia, prophecy, enthusiasm, and so forth sanctioned in some of the pagan cults was not welcomed in Christianity; it did not produce the kind of reverence and order that was necessary for building up the body of Christ.

This background assists one to place into a proper context other statements by Paul concerning women and worship. Paul's responses often are drawn from his Jewish background, in which the role of males was still dominant. Thus his attitude toward women is determined by the order of creation (1 Cor. 11:3–8; 1 Tim. 2:13), the sin of Eve (1 Tim. 2:14), and subjection as symbolized by the woman's covered head (1 Cor. 11:5–8). Women in the church during Paul's time are instructed to follow these admonitions and not to do anything that will disturb church order or hinder their witness to the world.

Undoubtedly, the most significant note of liberation for women and slaves was sounded in the proclamation of the gospel itself, in which freedom and equality are essential ingredients to new life in Christ. It is in this spirit that Paul writes to the Galatians: "You are all sons of God through faith in Christ Jesus, for all of you who were baptized into Christ have clothed yourselves with Christ. There is neither Jew nor Greek, slave nor free, male nor female, for you are all one in Christ Jesus" (Gal. 3:26–28). In Christ, all racial, religious, cultural, and social barriers have been removed (cf. disc. on 3:11). How were the slaves and the women in Paul's day to understand and then translate their newly found freedom in Christ into daily life? The household rules are part of the apostolic response to such questions. By including them in his letter to the Colossians, Paul reminds his readers of the need to maintain religious and social order.

Additional Notes §18

There are many valuable studies on the origin, nature, and teaching of the "household rules" in the NT. In commentaries, see esp. Lohse, pp. 154–57; Schweizer's excursus, "The Household Rules," pp. 213–30. Other sources include: P. R. Coleman-Norton, "The Apostle Paul and the Roman Law of Slavery," in *Studies in Roman Economic and Social History,* ed. idem (Princeton: Princeton University Press, 1951), pp. 155–77; G. Hinson, "The Christian Household in Colossians 3:18–4:1," *RevExp* 70 (1973), pp. 495–506; W. Lillie, "The Pauline Housetables," *ExpT* 86 (1975), pp. 179–83; W. Munro, "Col. 3:18–4:1 and Eph. 5:21–6:9: Evidences of a Late Literary Stratum?" *NTS* 18 (1972), pp. 424–47; K. H. Rengstorf, *"doulos," TDNT,* vol. 2, pp. 261–80; E. Schweizer, "Traditional Ethical Patterns in the Pauline and post-Pauline Letters and Their Development (Lists of vices and house-tables")," pp. 195–209; T. Wiedemann, *Greek and Roman Slavery* (Baltimore: Johns Hopkins University Press, 1981). For a current bibliography on the literature dealing with the household codes, see Cannon, pp. 119–20, n. 2. Cannon's discussion of these codes and their application to Colossians includes pp. 95–131.

3:18 / There are two striking features about the following exhortations: First, according to the acceptable cultural patterns of that day, the first party addressed (wives, children, slaves) is subordinate to the second (husbands, parents, masters); second, in all cases, these are reciprocal admonitions—mutual love and mutual submission are the key elements in these relationships.

Wives are to submit themselves (Greek middle form) to their husbands. Obedience, or submission (*hypotassō*), is enjoined on the basis that it is the "Christian" thing to do, or **as is fitting in the Lord**. Either way, it means that Christian wives are to acknowledge what is socially acceptable or "proper" with respect to their husbands. Paul simply states this principle and does not debate the rightness of it or seek to interpret its meaning.

There is nothing in *this* verse to suggest that subordination is based on a hierarchical relationship, sometimes inferred from other Scriptures (cf. 1 Cor. 11:3; Eph. 5:23). *Hypotassō*, from which the word *taxis* ("order," as in taxonomy) is derived, is a common word to designate a relationship of mutual submission. Nothing harsh or demeaning is implied (cf. 1 Cor. 15:28 and disc. on Eph. 5:21ff.).

3:19 / Husbands are to love their wives and not be harsh with them. **Love** (*agapē*) and harshness stand in stark contrast to each other. Lest husbands interpret "obedience" incorrectly, Paul reminds them that theirs is a relationship to be governed by the highest of all loves—a love that avoids any bitterness, resentment, or tyranny, because its supreme aim is the well-being of the other person.

Additional Notes §19

3:19 / L. J. Baggott states it well when he writes that "the rule of love is always better than the love of rule" in *A New Approach to Colossians* (London: Mowbray, 1961), p. 121.

3:20 / Children are to **obey** their **parents in everything**. **In everything** indicates that this is to be a total obedience, governed, as in 3:18, by the fact that this is the right and acceptable thing to do. It is not known whether Paul had Christian parents in mind or what limits he would have placed on obedience contrary to the law of Christ. Since **pleases** (*euarestos*) is used elsewhere in Scripture as "that which is acceptable and pleasing to the Lord" (Rom. 12:1; 14:18; 2 Cor. 5:9; Eph. 5:10), the implication is that a child's obedience has the same effect.

3:21 / The obedience required of children does not give parents the freedom to abuse them. Hence, parents are not to **embitter** their children, that is, do anything that will provoke or tyrannize them (*erethizō*). The reason for this is to avoid the negative reaction of discouragement. Harsh and provoking treatment of children merely leads to exasperation and misunderstanding. Parents need to restrain their authority; they should deserve rather than demand obedience. As with wives, the subordinated party (the child) is exhorted to be submissive and respectful; as with husbands, the ruling party (the parent) is admonished to be loving and responsible.

Additional Notes §20

3:20 / According to Hinson, "The strong emphasis upon unqualified obedience of children reflects a Jewish attitude and perhaps indicates a synagogal origin" ("The Christian Household in Colossians 3:18–4:1," *RevExp* 70 [1973], p. 499).

§21 Slave-Master Relationships
(Col. 3:22–4:1)

Since many slaves became Christians, it should not come as a surprise that they are singled out for some specific instructions in the NT (cf. 1 Cor. 7:20–24; Eph. 6:5–8; 1 Tim. 6:1, 2; 1 Pet. 2:18–25). For the majority of them, membership in the church may have been the only time and place they could experience equality and brotherhood. But belonging to Christ did not remove them from the world or lead to their emancipation. Allegiance to the *heavenly* Lord did not mean freedom from their *earthly* lords. They, more than anyone else, needed clarification on the relation of their status in Christ to their lot on earth.

A quick reading of the passages directed to slaves reveals that the writers of the NT did not take a negative attitude toward the practice of slavery in the ancient world; nor did they attempt to abolish it. Several factors may lie behind their approach:

First, Christianity was not a revolutionary movement bent on destroying the existing world order. To do so would have been suicidal, for what effect would a small and powerless group of Christians have had upon the might of Rome? Any attempt at revolution would have been met with severe persecution and martyrdom.

One of the clear messages in the Book of Acts is that Christianity has not engaged in treasonous activity and should, therefore, be regarded as a legal religion within the Roman Empire (Acts 25:8). Believers are admonished to obey their rulers and accept the temporal order even though it may be unsatisfactory in many ways (Rom. 13:1–7; 1 Pet. 2:13–17).

Second, slavery in the ancient world was a necessary evil, although it was human beings who made the institution evil. Greek and Roman society was made up of masses of individuals without the ability or opportunity to work. The economic, social, and monetary systems that regulate modern society were unknown in the first century. Think of the social chaos that would have resulted from setting free millions of slaves. What would these people do, and how would they be fed? Slavery was a means of maintaining peace and order in the empire; the abolition of this institution would have led to political and economic chaos.

All this does not mean that Christianity merely adapted to its environment without a struggle or any concern for social justice. The ministry and teachings of Jesus (Matt. 25:35–40; Luke 4:18, 19), the life of the early church (Acts 6:1–6; 2 Cor. 8:1–4), and the suffering of Christians (1 Peter, Revelation) prove otherwise. Rather than exercise *revolutionary* power, Christians proclaimed a *transforming* power. By their life and message they set a process in motion that eventually culminated in the abolition of slavery, for once slaves and masters regarded themselves as brothers, equally precious in God's sight, such divisions could not continue.

The approach that the church took toward slavery was determined largely by its theology rather than motivated by its concern for safety. Christians believed that God had chosen them and given them an inheritance; they believed that Christ had brought them freedom and that this would be enjoyed fully when the Lord returned to judge the world and reward the saints. And since they had no mandate from God to overthrow the world, they lived peaceably in the assurance that the last days were near. God had promised them a new Spirit, not a new social order.

As confidence in an imminent return of the Lord waned, the slaves—as did most believers—became restless. They must have wondered when their equality and freedom in Christ would become a social reality. If the Lord was not going to come soon, how much longer were they expected to go on living as slaves? These slaves needed some direction for their lives; they needed a higher motive than maintaining the status quo to explain why they must continue in their lowly position in the social order.

These rules are attempts at guiding slaves and masters on sensitive and significant issues. The fact that Paul includes such a lengthy exhortation in Colossians indicates it was an issue that had to be emphasized to preserve order. He also may have had Philemon and Onesimus in mind, although the specifics of that case are not developed here (cf. Philemon).

What Paul does in this section is to place slavery within the scope of Christ's lordship—a thought not surprising, considering the development of the preeminence of Christ throughout the epistle. He who is Lord of the universe is Lord of the church (1:15–20); and that lordship extends to all its members, including the slaves. Under Christ's lordship, Paul mentions a number of significant changes that have taken place with respect to their status:

3:22 / First, slaves have a new *attitude*. At one time they were motivated by a need for recognition and praise from their master. The unusual word *ophthalmodoulia* is a compound of *ophthalmos* ("eye") and *doulos* ("service"). As non-Christians, their service was performed to gain human approval.

As believers, however, their labor is to spring inwardly from the **heart** rather than from outward considerations. They are to realize that their work ultimately is directed toward Christ, not individuals. "Fear" (*phobeomai*), or reverence for the Lord, becomes the motivating principle that enables slaves to perform their daily tasks.

3:23 / Second, slaves have a new *center of reference*. This is implied already in the last phrase of verse 22, which the thoughts of verse 23 amplify somewhat. Paul wants them to understand that, in spite of their position, they are serving Christ and not men. As a result of their relationship to Christ, they have been freed from viewing work as an obligation and performing it methodically and unenthusiastically for human approval. Thus Paul states that they are to work heartily, as though they were **working for the Lord, not for men**.

3:24 / Third, they have a new reward. Once again, Paul reminds them of their new center of reference—**It is the Lord Christ you are serving**. Undoubtedly there is an allusion here to wages—or rather the lack of them—and the resentment that may have been generated between slaves and masters. In monetary terms, slaves were poor and had little opportunity of receiving an inheritance or improving their lot. Ultimately, their compensation had to come from the Lord.

The **reward** is the same one referred to in 1:12 with respect to the believer's inheritance. This, however, is not something that the slave earns as a result of faithful service, because the believer's inheritance is a gift of God. The slave's motivation is not material gain but "seeking the things that are above," which, in this case, is service to Christ and the reward that he gives.

3:25 / The point of reference in this verse is not clear; does **anyone who does wrong** refer to the slave or to the slave owner? Since the masters are not addressed formally until the next verse (4:1), it would be easy to assume that they are not the intended target of this rebuke. But given the context of the preceding verse, with its teaching on reward, could it be that the wrongdoer is the master who has failed to compensate his slave adequately? Paul advised the slaves, therefore, to remember that God ultimately will judge all wrongdoing (**Anyone who does wrong will be repaid for his wrong, and there is no favoritism.**) If this verse is taken as a reference to masters, then it forms a beautiful link with 4:1, where the ideas of fairness and justice are raised.

There is a sense in which this verse can apply to the slave as well. They have been exhorted to obey in all things (3:22), to work heartily and sincerely (3:22, 23), and to maintain an eternal perspective (3:24). Could Paul mean that any slave who falls short of that ideal will be judged as a wrongdoer? Slaves who do their work faithfully will be rewarded by God; slaves who fail in their responsibility can expect God's judgment. God does not show favor to slaves just because of their low estate.

4:1 / Again, Paul does not demand the abolition of slavery. Christian slave owners are not required to terminate a culturally acceptable practice just because they have become Christians. Nevertheless, Christian **masters** are different people because of their relationship with the Lord. They, too, have a new center of reference and so are called upon to demonstrate fairness and justice toward those who serve them; they too have **a Master in heaven**.

Here the principle of reciprocity is at work: The same transforming power that enables a slave to perceive and to perform his or her tasks differently is at work in the master who no longer treats the slave as a tool but regards him or her as a person, even as a "brother in the Lord" (Philem. 16). When such a relationship exists between master and slave, there will be no problem of disorder in the church.

Additional Notes §21

Other helpful insights on slavery can be found in the sources listed in the note in § 18. See disc. and bibliography on Eph. 6:5–9.

3:22 / "Fear should certainly not be thought of as the opposite of trust; this is shown by the fact that in Ps. 33(32):18, for example, it is equated with hoping for God's grace. What fear really means is a way of living which is afraid of nothing except of losing this one Lord, in the same way that a person who is in love fears nothing so much as losing the affection of the beloved" (Schweizer, p. 225).

3:25 / It is interesting to note that the phrase **there is no favoritism** clearly is applied to masters in Ephesians 6:9, a point in favor of applying it to masters in Colossians as well, unless the author of Ephesians was trying to make a different point. But given the context of Colossians and the need for "order" in all things, it makes sense to see 3:25 as a reference to the slaves. Obedience is the governing principle in the *Haustafeln*, and here it applies to the slaves. Schweizer suggests that "perhaps the question of who is being addressed is deliberately left open because what is said is valid for everyone" (p. 227).

§22 Exhortations to Pray and Witness (Col. 4:2–6)

4:2 / The opening verse in this section continues the ideas on corporate worship that were developed in 3:16–18. The summons to **devote yourselves to prayer** is a theme that is repeated a number of times in the NT (Luke 18:1; Acts 1:14; 1:24; 6:4; Rom. 12:12; Eph. 6:18). This idea of persistence is emphasized by the additional exhortation to be **watchful** (*grēgoreō*) **and thankful.** Thus it is not just the importance of prayer but the manner in which it is offered that is stressed.

This exhortation may be a caution against casualness in prayer. The call to "watchfulness" formed one of the categories of the baptismal (catechetical) instruction that was given to new Christians (cf. Eph. 6:18–20: "Pray . . . be alert"; 1 Pet. 4:7; "clear minded . . . pray"; 5:8: "Be self-controlled and alert"). Its inclusion in Colossians is another example of traditional material that was taken over and applied to the situation at Colossae.

Prayer is to be offered in thanksgiving. This is the seventh time that thanksgiving is mentioned in the letter (1:3, 12; 2:7; 3:15, 16, 17). Both thanksgiving and prayer are appropriate responses of the Christian and should be exercised by the worshiping community as well as by the individual. It is the pattern that Paul followed in the letter as he thanked God for the Colossians (1:3–8) and then prayed specifically for them (1:9–14).

4:3–4 / From a general admonition on prayer, Paul turns to a personal and specific request that God will **open a door for our message. Door** comes from the Greek *thyra*, and is an expression used in Scripture as a metaphor for opportunities to witness (1 Cor. 16:9; 2 Cor. 2:12). The content of Paul's message is the unveiling of **the mystery of Christ**, something that he already has explained in 1:26 and 2:2 (cf. Eph. 3:3–6, 9).

Paul indicates that he is **in chains** (*dedemai*, a perfect passive of *deō*; cf. 4:18). His request for an opportunity to preach may imply a desire for personal release (cf. Philem. 22); but Paul often used his imprisonment to share the gospel as well (Acts 28:30) and felt that these circumstances "served to advance the gospel" (Phil. 1:12). This desire is not only for himself, since he includes his co-workers (the plural **us**) such as Timothy (1:1), Epaphras (1:7; 4:12), Tychicus (4:7), Onesimus (4:9), and others he mentions in his final greeting (4:7–18). The desire for clarity (**Pray that I may proclaim it clearly,** *phaneroō*) in his proclamation must not be taken as a second request, because this "purpose clause" is subordinated to the previous one: Paul simply wants an opportunity to preach the **mystery of Christ** clearly.

4:5–6 / In the next two verses Paul provides some guidelines for Christian relationships with unbelievers (cf. 1 Thess. 4:12). He would not sanction any movement of Christianity into private cliques or withdrawal from society. Rather, believers are to give visible (conduct) and verbal (speech) witness to their faith. The apostle seeks to encourage his readers to behave in a way that will authenticate their faith before **outsiders** (*tous exō*). The idea behind **opportunity** is the picturesque word *exagorazō*, which means to "buy" or to "redeem" (*agora*, "marketplace"). It is unclear whether Christians are to **make the most of every opportunity** because it was believed the Lord was near, or, in the light of Ephesians 5:16, "because the days are evil." Either way, the emphasis is upon using every available opportunity for Christian witness. This, however, is to be done wisely. Enthusiasm must be accompanied by common sense and tact. Witness without wisdom often produces ill-will and negative results.

Paul realizes that the witness of one's life must be accompanied by the spoken word. **Know how to answer everyone** may refer to answers required as the result of a personal presentation of the Good News (the Greek is "each one individually"), or Paul may envision a situation similar to 1 Peter: "always be prepared to give an answer to everyone who asks you to give the reason for the hope that you have" (3:15, 16a; cf. also Matt. 10:19; Mark 13:11; Luke 12:11, 12; 21:14).

Whatever the situation, two qualities of speech are essential: First, it must be **full of grace**. This is a translation of *en chariti*, literally, "in grace," thus "gracious speech" (RSV). The Christian who is in God's grace will demonstrate that fact by the nature of his or her speech. Second, it must be **seasoned with salt**, which suggests an image of speech that is wholesome, witty, and palatable, just the opposite of words that are insipid, that is, dull and flat.

With this section, the formal and theological aspects of Colossians come to a close. But what remains in the following verses (4:7–18) should not be regarded as mere addenda that have nothing to do with the content of the letter. These greetings and final instructions make two significant contributions to this epistle.

First, they continue to reveal the true personal interest and pastoral heart that Paul has for this congregation. Throughout the letter he has indicated his concern by way of thanksgiving, intercession, agony, and suffering. That spirit continues here: Paul wants the news of Tychicus to "encourage their hearts" (4:8), and he shows how Epaphras shares the goals that he himself has for this congregation—for their commitment, maturity, and obedience to the gospel.

Second, they provide valuable historical insight on Paul's co-workers and their relationship to the Colossian church. The personal kinship and support that Paul shows for these "fellow servants" is exemplary of his capacity to love people and to recognize the contribution that they make to his life and the Lord's work. These verses, along with Romans 16:1–24, are a helpful commentary on how God used a number of people for the proclamation of the Good News and the building of the church of Jesus Christ.

Additional Notes §22

Similar exhortations to pray and witness can be found in Gal. 5:26–6:6; Phil. 4:8–13; 1 Thess. 5:12–22.

4:6 / See W. Nauck, "Salt as a Metaphor in Instructions for Discipleship," *ST* 6 (1952), pp. 165–78.

§23 Final Greetings and Instructions (Col. 4:7–18)

4:7–8 / Two of the individuals mentioned in this list are personal emissaries of Paul to the Colossian church. Tychicus is singled out and commended as **a dear brother, a faithful minister and fellow servant**. Paul's association with him goes back to Ephesus (Acts 20:4), where it appears Tychicus may have spent some time as a church leader (2 Tim. 4:12; Titus 3:12).

Paul dispatches Tychicus to Colossae as a personal messenger and probably as the bearer of this letter and anticipates that his coming will encourage their hearts. The word for **encourage** is *parakaleō*, which conveys a sense of comfort in this context. As a "paraclete," Tychicus is a personal agent of the Holy Spirit to this congregation (John 14:16, 26; 16:7).

4:9 / **Onesimus**, who is another **faithful and dear brother**, accompanies Tychicus to Colossae for the same reason. For Onesimus, the return to his hometown must have included some mixed emotions, for he is the slave who ran away from his owner, Philemon. The details of this case, however, are dealt with in Paul's personal letter to Philemon.

4:10–11 / **Aristarchus** (Acts 19:29; 20:4; 27:2), **Mark** (Mark 14:51; Acts 12:12, 25; 13:13; 15:37, 39; 2 Tim. 4:11; Philem. 24), and **Justus** are identified by Paul as **the only Jews among my fellow workers for the kingdom of God**. One can almost detect a note of pathos in Paul's statement, since he must have expected a larger number of Jewish Christians to become his co-workers. Nevertheless, he is deeply appreciative for the personal assistance that they have given to him. **Comfort** (*parēgoria*) may best express the feeling of gratitude that Paul has for these three individuals.

The phrase **kingdom of God** appears to be another way to express the missionary preaching of Paul and his co-workers (cf. Acts 19:8; 28:30, 31), for their goal was to announce that the kingdom of God has come in Christ, the Messiah. Elsewhere, Paul identifies this "kingdom of God" as the domain of the righteous (1 Cor. 6:9; Gal. 5:21).

Although Aristarchus is identified as being a **fellow prisoner** with Paul, there is no way of knowing whether this (cf. Philem. 23) is to be taken literally or metaphorically (i.e, as a prisoner of the Lord or for Christ's sake, cf. Eph. 3:1; 4:1). The historical circumstances of Paul's imprisonment, the use of the term *synaichmalōtos* (**fellow prisoner**), and the absence of any qualifying phrases (such as "of the Lord") favor the literal meaning.

Of these three individuals, Mark was the least known to the Colossians. Thus he is identified as the **cousin of Barnabas**—someone with whom they must have been acquainted. Paul reminds the Colossians of previous instructions to receive Mark if he comes their way. Nothing beyond this reference is known about a previous contact with the church on Mark's behalf. Paul may have given the original instruction himself or he may now be simply endorsing an earlier recommendation by someone else.

4:12–13 / Epaphras, another **servant of Christ Jesus**, has been identified with the Colossian church from the beginning (1:7), and so the inclusion of his name comes as no surprise. Paul's commendation of this fellow prisoner (Philem. 23) comes out of a long personal relationship that the two have had. Epaphras must have come to Ephesus during Paul's stay in that city (Acts 19) and been converted under Paul's preaching. Paul's stay in Ephesus was rather lengthy (three years, according to Acts 20:31), and it included an extensive teaching ministry ("had discussions daily in the lecture hall of Tyrannus. This went on for two years, so that all the Jews and Greeks who lived in the province of Asia heard the word of the Lord," Acts 19:9, 10).

Epaphras must have been well schooled in Paul's theology and thus prepared to be a missionary and teacher in his own right. The gospel that he brought to his native town had given birth to the church in Colossae (1:7) as well as to those in the neighboring cities of Laodicea and Hierapolis. The importance of Epaphras as a missionary to the Gentiles should not be overlooked. Perhaps he had come to Rome to get some advice from Paul on how to deal with the heresy that was threatening the church (2:8).

Epaphras' concern for his congregation manifested itself in his prayer life: He did not give birth to the church and then abandon it; rather, states Paul, **He is always wrestling in prayer for you**. The concerns of his prayer are quite similar to those that Paul himself has expressed throughout the epistle (cf. 1:9, 11, 23, 28; 2:2, 5–7; 3:1, 2). The qualities of firmness, maturity, conviction, and obedience will enable the Colossians to deal effectively with the heresy that is threatening their faith.

4:14 / **Luke** and **Demas** also are included in the list of greetings. Luke's association with Paul remained intimate and strong (2 Tim. 4:11); Demas, however, chose a different fate at a later point in his life ("Demas, because he loved this world, has deserted me," 2 Tim. 4:10).

4:15–16 / These verses provide some interesting information about church life in the first century: First, it is another example of early Christians gathering in homes for their meetings (cf. Acts 12:12; 16:40; Rom. 16:5; 1 Cor. 16:19; Philem. 2). It was not until the late third century that Christians began to meet in places expressly set aside for worship. Paul sends his greeting to such a house congregation in Laodicea, which met in Nympha's home.

Second, it shows that the churches enjoyed fellowship with each other. It does not appear unusual for Paul to request that his greetings in the Colossian letter be conveyed to a neighboring congregation. The same applies to the exchange of correspondence between the congregations at Colossae and Laodicea. Since Paul's letters could not be duplicated and purchased by members, they were read aloud and, in this case, exchanged as well (cf. 1 Thess. 5:27).

No one has been able to identify this epistle from Laodicea. Some have suggested that it may be the Epistle to the Ephesians or even Philemon. The most obvious explanation is that it is a letter Paul wrote specifically to this congregation but that for some reason was not retained in the Pauline corpus and (apparently) did not survive. Perhaps it disappeared because the church to whom it was written became spiritually anemic ("lukewarm") and died (Rev. 3:14–22).

4:17 / **Archippus**, possibly another member in the Colossian church, is given a specific charge by Paul to finish the work that he was given **in the Lord**. Since **work** is a translation of *diakonia*, some commentators have wondered whether Archippus' ministry was that of a deacon. There is, however, no way of knowing whether a specific office is meant or just a specific task to be completed. It must have been a significant matter for Paul to single out Archippus in this way, especially since the letter would be read in public for all to hear.

4:18 / It was customary for such writers as Paul (cf. Rom. 16:22) and Peter (1 Pet. 5:12) to employ secretaries (amanuenses) for the composition of their letters. Paul, for example, may have dictated certain ideas or even written down a broad outline that a secretary would complete. The personal signature (**I, Paul, write this greeting in my own hand**) would have given the letter a sense of intimacy (cf. 1 Cor. 16:21; Gal. 6:11; 2 Thess. 3:17).

The concluding request is that the Colossians **remember my chains**. Earlier, he made a similar request for their prayers (4:3). One wonders whether the request comes from a lonely and discouraged apostle, or whether it is to be understood as an indirect affirmation of his entire ministry as a servant and prisoner for Jesus Christ. Since the normal word for prayer (*proseuchomai*) is not used, it seems likely that the phrase is an appeal to remember and respect Paul for who he is and for what he has written.

Finally, the benediction: **Grace be with you**. As the letter began (1:2), so it ends, with a prayer for grace. The Colossians needed more than a letter to sustain them in their Christian life. Only God's grace could fortify them against the false teaching and enable them to remain true to the gospel they had received.

Additional Notes §23

Apart from the major commentaries on this section see G. E. Ladd, "Paul's Friends in Colossians 4:7–16," *RevExp* 70 (1973), pp. 507–14.

4:15 / Although the NIV has decided (correctly so) that Nympha is a woman, it should be noted that there is a textual variant that has changed the gender to masculine, thus reading "Nymphas, *his* house." For suggestions on this verse, see C. P. Anderson, "Who Wrote 'The Epistle from Laodicea'?" *JBL* 85 (1966), pp. 436–40.

Philemon

Introduction: Philemon

This epistle of Paul's is a personal letter to Philemon, a member of the Colossian church and master of the slave Onesimus. Onesimus has run away from his master and made his way to where Paul is in prison. Here he has become Paul's friend and helper. But Paul realizes that Onesimus needs to correct his actions by going back to Philemon where he rightfully belongs. Paul's Letter to Philemon is an attempt to plead Onesimus' case before Philemon, whom he hopes will respond out of love and forgiveness and restore Onesimus not only as a slave but as a beloved brother in Christ.

From the discussion in Colossians, it already has become obvious that Paul's letter to the Colossians and his letter to Philemon have a number of things in common: First, they are written from the same place (see Introduction to Colossians); second, they are addressed to the same church, although Philemon is more a personal letter for one of the church members. Onesimus (Col. 4:9) and Archippus (Col. 4:17) belonged to the Colossian church, so it is fairly safe to assume that Philemon lived in Colossae as well; third, both epistles mention similar circumstances of Paul's imprisonment (Col. 4:3, 18; Philem. 1, 13); fourth, the list of personal greetings is almost identical; fifth, both Colossians (1:1) and Philemon (v. 1) name Timothy as cooperating with Paul in writing the letter; sixth, these letters probably were collected and kept as a single piece of Paul's correspondence. Unfortunately, the compilers of the NT did not keep Colossians and Philemon together in the text.

§1 Paul's Greetings (Philem. 1–3)

1 / Here is a letter from **Paul** who is **a prisoner of Christ Jesus** (cf. Col. 4:3, 18). On the basis of verses 9 and 10, this definitely is a physical confinement and not a way of speaking metaphorically. Paul's **brother** in Christ, **Timothy**, joins him in the sending of the letter (cf. Col. 1:1) to Philemon, a **dear friend and fellow worker**. Philemon is a **dear** (*agapētos*, "beloved") **friend** because he belongs to a community that is characterized by love; he is a **fellow worker** because he is actively involved in the work of the gospel in Colossae.

2 / One of the ways in which Philemon has demonstrated his love and concern for the gospel is by opening his house for church meetings. The fact that the greeting extends to **the church** and includes **Apphia** and **Archippus** makes this epistle more public than private. The content may primarily be directed to Philemon, but the entire matter surrounding Onesimus is a concern to the entire church. No special military significance should be attached to the term **fellow soldier** (*systratiōtēs*). This is another metaphor Paul uses to describe one of his colleagues in the ministry. In Philippians 2:25 the same word is used of Epaphroditus. In the case of Archippus, **fellow soldier** rather than "fellow worker" may be used because he has some special task to fulfill (Col. 4:17).

Not too much is known about **Apphia**, but since she is so closely linked with Philemon, it is possible that she is his wife. However, it does not necessarily follow that Archippus was their son, as some commentators have speculated. John Knox, for example, has attempted to show that Archippus, not Philemon, is the master of Onesimus and that the "work" that Archippus was to finish (Col. 4:17) refers to the way he was to handle Onesimus. The details of this task are outlined in Paul's Letter to Philemon, which, according to Knox, is the "letter from Laodicea" (Col. 4:16). There are too many difficulties, however, with this theory, and the identity of Archippus, beyond what is said in Colossians and Philemon, remains highly speculative.

3 / The closing of Paul's salutation is similar to Colossians 1:2 and the way in which Paul addresses other congregations as well. **Grace . . . and peace** are two of the greatest gifts of the Christian life.

Additional Notes §1

---

2 / John Knox, *Philemon Among the Letters of Paul*. For an evaluation of the ideas presented by Knox, see Lohse, pp. 186–87.

Two helpful English articles on Philemon are E. W. Koch, "Cameo of Koinonia," *Interp* 17 (1963), pp. 183–87; F. F. Church, "Rhetorical Structure and Design in Paul's Letter to Philemon," *HTR* 71 (1978), pp. 17–33.

§2 Paul's Praise for Philemon (Philem. 4–7)

4–5 / These verses draw attention to the individual Philemon in much the same way that Paul's thanksgiving and prayer in Colossians focused upon the congregation (Col. 1:3–14). Paul's gratitude for Philemon's love for God's people (v. 5) forms the basis of his request in verse 9; Paul affirms his fellowship with Philemon (v. 6) and, on that basis, requests Philemon to act kindly toward Onesimus (v. 17); as Philemon has cheered the hearts of all God's people (v. 7), Paul desires that his own heart be cheered through Philemon's love (v. 20). Here, too, remembrance becomes an occasion for thanksgiving and prayer: **I always thank my God as I remember you in my prayers**.

Paul is grateful because of the positive things that he has heard about Philemon's **love** (*agapē*) and **faith** (*pistis*) (the order of these two terms is reversed in NIV). Normally, Paul mentions faith first and then shows that Christian love springs from and is nourished by faith in the Lord (Col. 1:4; Eph. 1:15). Literally, the sentence in Greek reads: "I hear of your love and faith which you have to the Lord Jesus and to all the saints." From this, there is no way of knowing toward what **love** and **faith** are each directed.

In the NIV, the sentence is given this translation: **I hear about your faith in the Lord Jesus and your love for all the saints**. The translators arrive at this interpretation because they realize that the Greek sentence probably employs a grammatical structure known as chiasm. The term comes from the Greek letter *chi*, which is written like an *X*. In a sentence, words or phrases are arranged in inverted parallelism. Verse 5, for example, would read:

a **love**
  b **faith**
  b' **in the Lord Jesus**
a' **for all the saints**

Love (*a*) comes first because Paul is thinking of Philemon's love, both explicitly (vv. 7, 9) and implicitly (vv. 14, 16, 17, 20);

(*b*) **faith** is the source from which love is derived; (*b'*) faith has as its object **the Lord Jesus**; (*a'*) love is directed to (*eis*) **all the saints**. This explanation reflects the usual Pauline way of associating faith with the Lord and directing love to God's people.

6 / Since this is the most obscure verse in the epistle, it may help to compare several translations:

Greek—literally, "so as the fellowship (*koinōnia*) of your faith working may become in full knowledge of every good thing in us for Christ."

NIV—**I pray that you may be active in sharing your faith, so that you will have a full understanding of every good thing we have in Christ.**

RSV—"and I pray that the sharing of your faith may promote the knowledge of all the good that is ours in Christ."

GNB—"My prayer is that our fellowship with you as believers will bring about a deeper understanding of every blessing which we have in our life in union with Christ."

The best way to approximate what this verse means is to see it in the context of the letter as teaching these truths: All Christians share a common faith; faith should be an active faith because it promotes an understanding of the blessings believers have received; the response of faith is for Christ, that is, for his glory; Philemon's recognition of these blessings will cause him to respond appropriately with respect to Onesimus (v. 14).

7 / The theme of Philemon's love (v. 5) is repeated in this verse: **You . . . have refreshed the hearts of the saints**. Although there is no way of knowing specifically what Philemon has done, the result was a cheering or refreshing (*anapauō*) of their innermost feelings (**hearts**). Paul is not as eager to describe Philemon's actions as he is to accentuate his spirit; that same spirit of love will determine how he responds to Paul's request regarding Onesimus (cf. v. 20, where the same word is used). The relationship of Paul to Philemon is that of a **brother**. This is a status that Paul, Timothy, Philemon, and even Onesimus (v. 16) enjoy together.

Paul indicates that he personally has benefited from Philemon's love in a vicarious way. In Philemon's love for all God's people, Paul has experienced great **joy** (*charis*) **and encouragement** (*paraklēsis*). Paul had a similar feeling of identity with the Corinthian church when things were going well (cf. 2 Cor. 7:4, 7).

Now that Paul has sufficiently commended Philemon for his exemplary Christian life, he moves to the heart of his request regarding Onesimus. In one way, Paul gives the impression that he is "shadow boxing," that is, skirting around the real issue and not confronting Philemon directly. But Paul's strategy is determined by two factors: First, he needs to move very carefully and weigh every word. After all, a request to reinstate a runaway slave was quite unusual in the first century. According to Roman law, masters could demand the return of a slave and inflict punishment at their discretion.

Second, Paul wants to avoid any impression of legislating the decision that he wishes Philemon would make. Even if he has the authority to do so, he realizes that "a man convinced against his will is of the same opinion still." Thus Paul will suggest a course of action and appeal to Philemon's Christian standards but leave the ultimate choice to the slave owner.

8–9 / **Therefore** (*dio*) links the introductory matters of verses 4–7 with the request that follows. On the basis of Philemon's gracious and generous character, Paul feels that **in Christ** he has a certain relationship with Philemon that gives him the freedom to make this special appeal. In fact, Paul's language is rather strong, and in a sense, must be based upon his apostolic authority, when he claims that he could order Philemon to take the appropriate action. Paul believed that his office as an apostle of Jesus Christ gave him a certain power and required him to make important decisions (cf. 1 Cor. 5:3; 7:6; 9:1; 2 Cor. 12:12). He is **Paul—an old man and now also a prisoner of Christ Jesus**. Perhaps his authority is enhanced because he is also suffering imprisonment for Christ's sake.

There is some dispute regarding the translation of the Greek word *presbutēs*. KJV and NIV use "aged man" or **old man**, whereas GNB and RSV use "ambassador." The only difference between the Greek word for **old man** (*presbutēs*) and "ambassador" (*pres-beutēs*) is the letter *e*. Some text critics have suggested that the letter may have been left out inadvertently during the process of copying the letter; others have argued that *presbutēs* occasionally is used in nonbiblical material as "ambassador" or "envoy" and could, therefore, carry that meaning here. The choice of words is important in understanding the spirit of Paul's request.

If the proper word is **old man**, then Paul's appeal has an emotional overtone, that is, he appeals to Philemon as an old man and a prisoner of Christ Jesus. "Ambassador," on the other hand, continues to ring of the authority that he has alluded to in the previous verse. Here, the force of his statement is that, although he could decide for Philemon on the basis of his apostolic authority, he will waive that privilege just as he has before (v. 8). He wants Philemon to act out of conviction, not out of compulsion. But he also wants Philemon to know that his request comes from the heart and not the head only (**I appeal to you on the basis of love**).

10 / Finally, it appears that Paul is ready to state his request. But no such luck, for the reader is not informed of that until verse 17. All of Paul's comments prior to that show that he approaches Philemon gradually, tactfully, and in deep humility.

Paul calls Onesimus **my son** because he has become a member of God's family. Since Paul was instrumental in bringing Onesimus to Christ through his witness, he describes his relationship to Onesimus as that of a spiritual father. He uses this language of father and child on other occasions when he has been responsible for people having become Christians (cf. 1 Cor. 4:15, 17; Gal. 4:19).

By taking the Greek preposition *peri* as "I am asking **for** him," it is possible to believe that Paul desired to retain Onesimus for his own personal use in prison. But although Paul admits the temptation of such a possibility, one can see from verse 15 that his intention all along has been to return Onesimus. His appeal is "for the sake of," or "on behalf of" rather than **for** Onesimus.

11 / The expressions **useless to you** and **useful both to you and to me** are a play on the name Onesimus, which means "useful." (This was a common name for slaves in the ancient world because of that meaning.) The force of the pun (a play on words) is this: Before (**Formerly**) Onesimus was a useless slave to Philemon, perhaps even when he was in Philemon's possession, but more probably as a runaway slave; **but now**, that is, after his conversion to Christ, **he has become useful both to you and to me**. The irony is that Onesimus can remain useful to Paul only if he remains with him in prison and to Philemon only if he returns home to Colossae. But either way, he is a changed man. The contrast in his personal life is as dramatic as it was for the Gentiles whose former life of sin often is contrasted with their new life in Christ ("once . . . now": cf. Col. 3:7, 8; Eph. 2:11, 13; 5:8).

12 / Paul's relationship to Onesimus is so close (son and spiritual father) that Onesimus' departure is like losing part of himself. This is a beautiful example of a brotherhood in which social distinctions no longer matter. In Christ, a delinquent Phrygian slave could become a brother with the great apostle to the Gentiles. Nevertheless, Paul cannot let his heart decide for him, for he knows that the only right and legal thing for him to do is to see that Onesimus goes back to Philemon. This action is affirmed by Paul's resolve to send him back to his rightful owner. The Greek construction is epistolary aorist, which means that even though it is in the past tense the meaning is in the present—hence, **am sending** rather than "have sent."

13 / Once again, Paul indicates that his personal preference would be to keep Onesimus with him in prison. Somehow Paul envisions that, in spite of his imprisonment, Onesimus' service could promote the gospel in some way. **He could take your place in helping me** suggests that Paul is thinking of some kind of service from Philemon himself. Did Philemon owe Paul something? The only hint at some kind of debt comes in verse 19, where Paul may be reminding Philemon that it was through Paul's ministry that he became a Christian.

14 / Here Paul displays extreme caution in building up his case. He feels a certain right to retain Onesimus on Philemon's behalf, but he wants such a decision to come directly from Philemon (**I did not want to do anything without your consent**). The Greek literally reads "your good deed" (*agathon*), which recalls the same use of the word in verse 6, translated "good thing" in the NIV. But anything that Philemon chooses to do must be done willingly. Compulsion, constraint, coercion, necessity, and so forth are not the attitudes out of which a person is to serve Christ. God loves one who gives gladly, "not reluctantly or under compulsion" (2 Cor. 9:7). Philemon will best reveal his true Christian character when he acts voluntarily.

15 / Up to this point one could interpret the case of Onesimus as a tragedy. Here is a person who has wronged his master, who may have taken something that did not rightfully belong to him, and who capped that wrong by running away as a fugitive to be hunted down. This is how the situation is viewed on the human and earthly level.

Paul, however, sees it differently, for he perceives it from the viewpoint of eternity—in other words, from God's providential arrangement of events. Onesimus' action was deliberate; but his departure did not remove him from the sovereignty of God. True, Onesimus was away from Philemon **for a little while**; but the end result is that God so ordered Onesimus' life that Philemon was able to have him back **for good**. Human failures often become God's opportunities! Here is a case in which a temporary loss was turned into an eternal gain.

16 / The providential and eternal relationship that Paul envisioned in verse 15 is now elaborated in words that capture the very heart of the gospel itself. Now that Onesimus has become a Christian, he is not **a slave**. Onesimus comes no longer as a slave, **but better than a slave, as a dear brother**. This brotherhood is spiritual and results from the fact that Paul, Onesimus, and Philemon have been united as brothers in Christ. Although this relationship is meaningful to Paul personally, he rightly perceives that Onesimus' new status has a more meaningful application to Philemon, for whom Onesimus is *both a man* (i.e., someone "in" the flesh—*sarx*) and **a brother in the Lord**.

Here is more of that wonderful exchange Paul began talking about in verse 15. Onesimus leaves for a short time and returns forever; he leaves as a slave and returns **as a man** and **a brother**. Paul does not use this opportunity to denounce slavery, for Onesimus' spiritual position in Christ does not free him from his human obligations to Philemon. In this respect Paul is consistent with the principles that he laid out in Colossians 3:22–4:1. The new relationship that Philemon and Onesimus have to each other is one in which the human and the spiritual overlap.

17 / At long last, the request: **So** (lit., "therefore") . . . **welcome him as you would welcome me**. All along Paul has been appealing to Philemon on the force of certain statements, such as Philemon's Christian character (vv. 4–7), Paul's position as an apostle and prisoner (vv. 8–9), Onesimus' newly found faith and usefulness (vv. 10–13), the principle of voluntarism (v. 14), and Christian providence and brotherhood (vv. 15–16). But before the request comes, Paul lays out yet another incentive—namely, that of partnership. When two people are in *koinōnia* they have common interests, feelings, and goals (cf. v. 6). Paul and Philemon certainly had this by virtue of their common faith. Hence Paul is reasoning that, if Philemon really regards him as a partner, there will not be any problem in honoring the request.

But Paul goes one step further, for he identifies himself so closely with Onesimus that he wants Philemon to receive his slave as he would the apostle—**as you would welcome me**. Partnership in the Lord has broken down all barriers. Paul epitomizes in his life what he has verbalized in his letter.

18 / The **if** should not be taken as setting up a hypothetical case, since Paul knows full well that Onesimus has wronged his master by running away. Paul does not overlook this, for he believes that some compensation should be given to Philemon for the losses that he has suffered. Onesimus' debt has been taken by some to imply that Onesimus stole some money or personal possessions from Philemon before he fled. More probably, Paul has "time" in mind, since Onesimus' absence would have cost Philemon something. Paul is assuming Onesimus' debts because it was customary in those days for the outstanding debts and penalties of a slave to be assumed or paid for by a new owner. Paul, although he is not the new owner, is willing to repay Philemon for any losses—**charge it to me**.

19 / Paul reaffirms his intention by stating that he will take care of the outstanding debt. The effect of his personal signature is to "seal" what is like a promissory note—an I.O.U.— and to legally bind him to his newly assumed debt. But having done this, Paul effectively negates the force of it by a gentle reminder to Philemon that since he owes Paul so much he should not think of asking for or receiving any remuneration. It was through Paul that Philemon became a Christian, and in the spiritual realm there is no way that outstanding debts can be paid. Paul's statement reminds one of the parable of the unforgiving servant, in which the Lord faults a servant who was forgiven of a large debt by the king but who, in return, would not forgive a fellow servant a small debt (Matt. 18:21–35).

20 / The intimacy between Paul and Philemon is reinforced by the term **brother** (cf. v. 7). This enables Paul to state quite bluntly that Philemon should honor his request **in the Lord**—literally, "may I have joy, profit, or help from you in the Lord." The Greek word for **benefit** is *oninēmi*, which closely resembles **Onesimus**, the name of the slave. This similarity has led some interpreters to conclude that Paul is playing on these words for the purpose of requesting Onesimus for himself. If so, the thought that he is expressing could be either, "may I have Onesimus from you," or, "as Onesimus has been profitable to you, you be of benefit to me."

The phrase **refresh my heart** recalls a similar expression in verse 7, where Philemon's love "refreshed the hearts of the saints." Here Paul appeals to Philemon's love, but for a personal reason. The acceptance of Onesimus by Philemon would **refresh** his heart. But it is a joy that is unselfish because it is placed in the sphere of the Lord **(in Christ)**. Paul will rejoice because he knows that Philemon is responding from the new life that he has experienced in Christ.

21 / Since Paul knows Philemon so well, he is **confident of** his friend's **obedience** to his request to receive Onesimus. Paul speaks of a trust or confidence in Philemon's **obedience** (*hypakoē*)—an **obedience** based not on Roman law or apostolic command but on the principle of Christian love. Such love leaves Philemon with only one choice, namely, the highest good for his servant and for the apostle.

Paul is confident that Philemon **will do even more**. But what more could he do? Does Paul anticipate that Philemon will turn Onesimus over into Paul's custody, or does he hope that Philemon will grant his slave *complete freedom*? The final decision is left up to the master.

22 / Paul envisions one more exchange that may be possible within the providence of God. This time, it involves him-

self and the **hope** that he can exchange his imprisonment for freedom. Thus he prays he will **be restored to you in answer to your
prayers.** It is significant to note that the entire congregation (**you**
and **your** are plural in Greek) is interceding for Paul's release. Such
action binds him closer to this church and gives him hope that
God will make it possible for him to see all of them.

Paul is so confident about this that he makes a reservation
for a room. The early Christians placed considerable emphasis
upon hospitality (Rom. 12:13; 1 Tim. 3:2; Titus 1:8; Heb. 13:2; 1
Pet. 4:9), so Paul's request is not unusual. Since Philemon had
a home large enough to hold church services, there would be no
problem accommodating Paul if and when he returned to Colossae.

Additional Notes §3

---

8 / Although unusual, Paul's request is not without precedent.
Lohse quotes a personal letter from Pliny the Younger in which this Roman official writes to a certain slave master Sabinianus, interceding for
an errant but repentant slave (pp. 196–97).

15 / Paul uses what in Greek is called a passive verb: *echōpisthē*
literally means "he was separated from" you. On this, Martin refers to
the Hebrew; in that language, the divine passive "is a mode of expression to denote the hidden action of God as the agent responsible for what
is done" (p. 166).

§4 *Paul's Final Greetings (Philem. 23–25)*

23–25 / These final verses are almost identical to the closing section of Colossians. Paul ends this letter with words familiar from the opening salutation (v. 3). Here the phrase **the grace of the Lord Jesus Christ be with your spirit** serves more as a prayer of benediction than a greeting. Again **your** is plural; thus Paul intends that this letter be received by the entire congregation (cf. Gal. 6:18).

Additional Notes §4

On these greetings and the personalities mentioned, see disc. on Col. 4:7-17. These lists show the significance of Paul's co-workers for his ministry. Lohse has an excellent comparison of the names that occur in Colossians and Philemon in his commentary, pp. 175-77.

Ephesians

Introduction: Ephesians

The title and salutation in the NIV indicate that this is Paul's Letter to the Ephesians ("Paul . . . To the saints in Ephesus . . ."). From its earliest times, this epistle has been regarded as an authentic epistle of the Apostle Paul, written to the church in Ephesus where he spent about three years as a teacher (Acts 19:10; 20:31).

Since the epistle claims to have been written by Paul, it is not unusual to find a number of personal references to himself and the situation to which he is writing. Basically, he identifies himself as an apostle of Jesus Christ by the will of God on their behalf (1:1) who, although he is in prison (3:1; 4:1), appeals to his office as one entitled to proclaim the mystery of the gospel to the Gentiles (3:1-9) and to relate to his readers the essence of the Christian life (4:17ff.).

Although the epistle does not follow the epistolary form of Paul's letters completely (salutation—thanksgiving—prayer—body—ethical exhortations—greetings), it has many verbal, theological, and literary affinities with Paul's thought. At first glance, there appear to be no glaring differences in Ephesians from the picture that we get of Paul and his thought in other books of the NT. The epistle contains familiar Pauline themes such as God's sovereignty, resurrection, the Holy Spirit, ethics, and so forth; and even though there are some new theological emphases, they appear to be consistent with Paul's thought.

The external factors surrounding this epistle likewise suggest that its authenticity was not disputed in the early church. It is listed in Marcion's canon of the NT as the epistle to the "Laodiceans" (ca. A.D. 140) and is recognized in the Muratorian canon (A.D. 180) as Paul's work. This is supported by the testimony of the early church fathers of the second century, such as Irenaeus, Clement of Alexandria, and Tertullian. With a few minor exceptions, the consensus of scholarly opinion is that Ephesians was consistently regarded as a Pauline epistle until the age of critical scholarship in the eighteenth century.[1]

Identifying the *destination* of the epistle, however, has not been without debate. The phrase, "in Ephesus" (*en Ephesō*) is missing in the oldest and most reliable manuscripts. As in other

translations (RSV, GNB, NEB), the footnote in the NIV indicates that
there is a textual problem at this point. This reading is verified
by Origen, Tertullian, and Jerome, even though church tradition
has associated the letter with the city of Ephesus.

The reasons why the address was omitted—if it was ever
present—and why it became associated with Ephesus are varied
and complex. The most popular theory, in part suggested by the
general nature of the epistle, claims that it was a circular letter
that Paul intended to be read at more than one place. The original manuscript may have had a blank space, and each congregation could have read its own name into that blank.[2] For
various reasons—primarily because of Paul's long association with
that church and the importance of that congregation in Asia
Minor—it became attached to Ephesus.

With the rise of critical Bible scholarship in the eighteenth
century, the attitude toward Pauline authorship changed dramatically. By adopting a critical methodology and applying its principles to the external and internal study of the epistle, more and
more scholars concluded Ephesians was not authentically Pauline.
The end result is that there are two major positions regarding the
authorship of Ephesians today: either it is Pauline or non-Pauline.

Scholars who doubt the Pauline authorship of certain epistles
(generally 2 Thessalonians, Ephesians, Colossians, and the Pastorals) claim that they were written by a "second," that is,
"deutero," Paul. Basically, this necessitates envisioning an individual or a group of Paul's close co-workers who earnestly desired to communicate the message and authority of Paul to
succeeding generations. Many scholars see this as a plausible
solution to some of the questions related to authorship.

Several things about the deutero-Pauline hypothesis need
clarification. First, it is quite possible that the practice of pseudo-
nymity (writing in the name of someone else) in the first century
included some of the letters that make up the canon of the NT.
Unfortunately, a number of NT scholars look upon this in a negative way. They see it as constituting forgery or fraud and the
authors of such pseudonymous materials as nothing but charla-
tans, imposters, or deceivers. But such is not the case: Anyone
writing in Paul's name could have done so out of sincere motives
and believed that he or she would not dishonor God or the apostle
or deceive readers.

Second, a deutero-Paulinist would not be just a compiler, copier, and transmitter of genuine Pauline material. This would make the deutero-Pauline literature nothing more than a mosaic of passages from Paul's epistles. The one writing in Paul's name would have been a theologian in his or her own right. The author would be faithful to Paul but would find it necessary to modify and expand Paul's ideas and apply them to later developments in the church.

A number of Paul's close associates, such as Timothy, Tychicus, and Luke, would be capable of producing this kind of material. It is even possible that Paul may have led some kind of theological school "in the lecture hall of Tyrannus" while he was in Ephesus, where his ideas were presented and continued to be discussed even after his death (Acts 19:9). Some of his pupils could have felt responsible to interpret, reinterpret, and apply their master's theology to new situations in the post-apostolic period. Writing in Paul's name would have given their letters the stamp of apostolic authority, especially where false teaching was threatening the church.

If Ephesians fits into this hypothetical reconstruction, it could be regarded as a continuation of Paul's thought in another generation. It would be an attempt by the author to present a timely reaffirmation of Paul's understanding of "the mystery of Christ" to the Gentiles. Or, as C. L. Mitton puts it: "the author has presented us in Ephesians with a brilliant and comprehensive summary of Paul's main theological emphases, though he has, where necessary, adapted and interpreted them for the needs of a new situation. Published about a generation after Paul's death, it is, as it were, 'Paul's Message for Today.' "[3] R. P. Martin's suggestion that Luke wrote Ephesians is both intriguing and commendable.[4]

Of the factors that raise questions about the Pauline authorship of Ephesians, there is, first of all, the vocabulary of the epistle. About ninety words and phrases in Ephesians, including such things as "the devil," "in the heavenly realms," and "the One he loves" (as a title for Christ), are not used elsewhere in Paul's epistles.

In addition to vocabulary, there is the matter of the style in which the epistle is written. In contrast to the polemical tone and rapid movement in Paul's chief letters, Ephesians has a poetic or liturgical ring to it. This comes from a number of features, including its long and complex sentences, an extensive use of prepositions, and the joining of synonyms.

Although most scholars will agree that linguistic and stylistic differences alone do not disprove Pauline authorship, they do find it difficult to conceive of Paul writing Ephesians in this form. Proponents for its authenticity counter by claiming that the language and style can be accounted for by such considerations as Paul's versatility as a writer, changed historical circumstances, and the fact that the epistle is more reflective and liturgical in nature. "Could," writes A. S. Wood, "an imitator have given birth to anything at once so authentic and yet so original? If he rivaled Paul as a spiritual genius, it is strange that the primitive church knew nothing of him."[5]

A second set of questions about Pauline authorship relates to the repetition in Ephesians of Pauline words, phrases, and concepts, especially from Colossians. Approximately one fourth of the vocabulary and one third of the content of Ephesians are paralleled in Colossians, including some verbatim agreement (cf. Eph. 6:21ff. and Col. 4:7ff.). Numerous parallels to other Pauline epistles, as well as affinities with 1 Peter, Hebrews, Luke–Acts, and the Gospel of John have been observed, contributing further to the suspicion that the author of Ephesians was borrowing material from some of these letters for his composition rather than creating his own epistle. Some scholars have found more affinities to the writings of Qumran (the Dead Sea Scrolls) and Gnosticism than to the NT. Even more problematic is the claim that certain words and ideas are used differently or take on a different meaning in Ephesians than they have in Paul's genuine letters (church, stewardship, mystery, and fullness, to name a few).

To counter such conclusions, proponents of Pauline authorship believe that the close connection between Ephesians and other Pauline epistles, including Colossians, is accounted for better by Pauline than by non-Pauline authorship. They argue that the apparent differences in usage or meaning of terms do not warrant denying them to Paul. Here D. Guthrie speaks for a number of people when he writes that "the most natural conclusion from the abundance of parallel passages is that the same mind is reflected in Ephesians as in the other Pauline epistles."[6]

A third consideration related to Pauline authorship is that the historical circumstances surrounding the epistle are vague. It is difficult to believe that Paul would write to a congregation with whom he had spent three years and not include any personal greetings or refer to any local issues. The author writes as if he and the readers do not know each other (1:13, 15; 3:1; 4:21). Even if Ephesians were a circular letter, one would expect some allusions to personalities or circumstances associated with Paul's missionary activity in that part of Asia Minor. Barth's suggestion that the epistle was written to Gentile converts who came into the church after Paul's ministry in Ephesus is unconvincing.[7]

There are other problems beyond the impersonal nature of the epistle. Historically, the controversy related to Jews and Gentiles in the church that occupied so much of Paul's life appears to be over (cf. Acts 15; Gal. 2). Many scholars feel that Ephesians reflects the situation sometime after Paul when the church was being prepared to face the future and to guard itself against the threat of heresies like Gnosticism.

Unfortunately, the historical factors alone cannot decide the question of authorship. The problems between Jewish and Gentile Christians are difficult to document historically and may have varied from one area of the empire to another. Some authors place considerable emphasis upon the destruction of Jerusalem in A.D. 70, claiming that if the epistle had been written after this period there would have been some specific reference to that fact, especially in the context of 2:11–22.

Fourth, there are some theological issues that raise questions about Pauline authorship. For convenience, they can be discussed according to the following categories:

Cosmology. Ephesians, even more than Colossians, presents a cosmic picture of God's saving activity and the role of Christ. It gives increasing attention to the principalities and powers and their defeat by God.

Ecclesiology. One of the most significant and noticeable differences from letters that are undeniably Pauline is that the church in Ephesians is universal, not local. The author writes to embrace all believers everywhere, not only those in Ephesus. Here, as in Colossians, the church is defined as the body of Christ, and Christ is related to the body as the head. In Romans and Corinthians the head is not given such distinction but is recognized as another part of the body.

In Ephesians, the church takes on a cosmic function; through it, the angelic rulers and powers in the heavenly world might know God's wisdom, in all its different forms (3:10). This goes far beyond the local function that the church serves in Paul's undisputed epistles. Some, particularly the German scholar E. Käsemann, see Ephesians moving from Christ—which was the center for Paul—to the church as the center. For Käsemann, this is a sure sign of "early Catholicism."[8]

Part of the ecclesiology in Ephesians centers around the prominence and role of the apostles and prophets (2:20; 3:5) in the founding of the church. For some, the veneration of these offices, the structure and function of the ministry (4:11–16), and the acknowledgment of apostolic authority are signs of a post-Pauline church. These are matters that arose after Paul's lifetime.

Eschatology. In Paul's undisputed epistles one gets the impression that the Parousia is imminent, that is, Christ is about to return. Consequently, much of Paul's theology and ethical instruction is placed within the context of the end times. Ephesians lacks that eschatological urgency and presents more of a realized eschatology by emphasizing the believers' present experience with Christ. Resurrection and exaltation are already enjoyed by believers in Christ; more attention is given to life in the Spirit now and less to the future; and even though the church maintains a future hope (1:18), the directives in the epistle prepare the believers to live out that hope in the realities of daily life.

This change in eschatological perspective affects how the author prepares readers to face the future. Thus the mission of the church takes on a new significance: The church becomes the instrument for fulfilling God's purposes in the world, particularly in uniting Jews, Gentiles, and the cosmos (2:21; 3:10; 4:13, 16; 5:27). The ethical exhortations, household rules, and so on suggest that the church is to be as concerned about social and community relationships (socioethical) as it is with personal salvation or reconciliation.[9]

Christology. Some scholars feel that Ephesians omits crucial elements of Paul's Christology and presents a different understanding of the person and role of Christ. Missing is Paul's emphasis on Christ's death, the doctrine of justification, and the Parousia; prominent is the resurrected, exalted, and triumphant Christ. According to J. A. Allan, the "in Christ" formula in Ephesians lacks the mysticism that was so characteristic of Paul.[10] Also, reconciliation is not between humanity and God but socially between Jew and Gentile and cosmically with the spiritual principalities and powers. Acts that Paul attributes to God, such as reconciliation (Col. 1:21; 2:13, 14) and the appointment of church officials (1 Cor. 12:28), are, in Ephesians, presented as the work of Christ (2:16; 4:11).

The conclusion to which many scholars have come after analyzing the theological, historical, ecclesiological, and cosmological thought of Ephesians is that it is difficult—if not impossible—to maintain the Pauline authorship of this epistle. W. G. Kümmel probably represents most scholars who question Pauline authorship when he writes: "In view of this linguistic, literary and theological state of affairs, it cannot seriously be doubted that Ephesians does not come from Paul and is therefore a pseudonymous writing."[11]

The big question, of course, is whether such observations are true and capable of only one conclusion. Could it be that critics of Paul have misunderstood Ephesians and are guilty of utilizing false assumptions and methodologies—thus arriving at false solutions? That this is possible is certainly made evident by the host of serious scholars who believe that the external and internal evidence with respect to Ephesians confirms the traditional conclusion. For them, Ephesians will remain Pauline until it can definitely be proved that it is non-Pauline.

D. Guthrie represents such a conviction when he states: "To maintain that the Paulinist out of his sheer love for Paul and through his own self-effacement composed the letter, attributed it to Paul and found an astonishing and immediate readiness on the part of the Church to recognize it as such is considerably less credible than the simple alternative of regarding it as Paul's own work."[12]

The question of the authorship of Ephesians currently is at an impasse, with reputable scholars on both sides of the issue. Here it needs to be stressed that this matter should not divide scholarship into conservatives and liberals. Rather than looking at the problem as a case of right or wrong, one needs to appre-

ciate that though both sides are sincere in their approach, everybody possesses certain theological presuppositions that affect the
approach to an understanding of God's Word and, in this case,
the Epistle to the Ephesians.

Above all, one should avoid concluding that deutero-Pauline
authorship of Ephesians makes this a false document that, consequently, has no inspiration, validity, or authority for the church
today. Once the motives of a deutero-Paulinist are properly understood and appreciated, Ephesians can speak to the church with
the same authority as Paul himself. The church retained and
canonized the Epistle to the Hebrews, for example, even though
its author is anonymous.[13]

Although the matter of authorship has had a negative effect,
polarizing scholarship, there have been two striking positive
results with respect to studies in Ephesians: First, the detailed
linguistic, literary, and theological study of the epistle has led to
a new appreciation of its value to the church. A. M. Hunter includes several centuries of thought when he writes: "John Calvin
called it his favourite epistle; Coleridge pronounced it 'one of the
divinest compositions of man'; Dr John Mackay has said, 'To this
book I owe my life,' and C. H. Dodd has named it 'the crown
of Paulinism.' "[14]

Beyond such a eulogy, it is not unusual to discover other
accolades, namely, "The Queen of the Epistles," "the quintes-
sence of Paulinism," "The Epistle of the Ascension."[15] J. N.
Sanders considers this book Paul's spiritual testament to the
church, "the final summing up of the apostle's life, work and
thought."[16]

Second, new studies on the nature, purpose, and content
of the epistle have been produced. Of the more significant theories are those suggesting that it is a summary of Paul's theology,
a reminder and congratulation, an antiheretical tract, a liturgical
document, a discourse on the unity of the church.

A Summary of Paul's Theology

Though most of these insights do not depend upon Pauline
authorship and can be appreciated by everyone, one idea is that
Ephesians is a comprehensive summary of Paul's theology or a
commendation of Paul's theology to the church of another gen-

eration (Beare; Mitton). R. P. Martin, writing in the *Broadman Commentary*, sees the author "gathering a compendium of Paul's teaching on the theme of Christ-in-his-church; and added to this body of teaching a number of liturgical elements (prayers, hymns, and confessions of faith) drawn from the worshiping life of the apostolic communities with which he was himself familiar."[17]

One of the most ingenious and elaborate theories in this regard is by E. J. Goodspeed. Vexed by the internal and external problems of Ephesians, Goodspeed suggested that the epistle was written by Onesimus (former slave and later bishop of the Ephesian church) as a cover or introductory letter for the collection of Paul's epistles (corpus) that was made near the end of the first century after the publication of Acts had created a new interest in Paul. For Goodspeed, Ephesians is "a rhapsody on the worth of salvation," "a mosaic of Pauline material," "a Pauline anthology."[18] The strength of Goodspeed's hypothesis lies more in his understanding of the nature of Ephesians than its purpose.

Some of Goodspeed's insights on the linguistic and literary peculiarities in Ephesians paved the way for other studies. Consequently, it is not unusual for scholars to see the epistle as a summary of Paul's thought to a later generation even if it is not some kind of cover letter for the Pauline corpus. The key to the deutero-Pauline hypothesis, however, is that the author is more than just a collector of Pauline ideas from his genuine epistles; he is "an independently acting and judging theologian of Pauline stamp."[19]

A Reminder and Congratulation

The theory that it is a reminder and congratulation is largely promoted by N. A. Dahl, who understands Ephesians to be addressing the problem of disunity in the church. Consequently, the author appeals for unity by calling the churches back to their beginnings and reminding them that they too share in the privileges that God granted to the Jews. Based upon his understanding of the concepts of "once" and "now" in the epistle, Dahl suggests that Ephesians is "a letter of reminder and congratulation, i.e., not so much as some abstract doctrine on the church, but rather as simply reminding us that we do indeed belong to the church, the body of Christ, and asking us to dwell on all that that implies."[20]

The value of Ephesians for Dahl is that, although its original message had a definite historical context, it can be universalized to speak to the church in every generation: "For the letter to the Ephesians is a congratulation for and a reminder of the sum total of what has been given to us."[21]

As such, the letter presents the reader with both a privilege and responsibility: Believers are privileged to have received such a rich inheritance in Christ. This, however, should not lead to spiritual pride or Christian triumphalism, because believers are reminded of the "once you were" of their lives. The "now you are" is the ethical imperative to live out the new life responsibly.

An Antiheretical Tract

The view that it is an antiheretical tract includes a vast array of scholarly opinion on the nature and purpose of Ephesians. Some scholars, such as F. C. Baur, P. Pokorný, H. Schlier, E. Käsemann, H. Conzelmann, and F. Mussner, believe that the epistle can best be understood within the context of first-century Gnosticism.[22] They find Ephesians to contain a large number of Gnostic terms ("knowledge," "fullness," "mystery," "perfection," "body," "new man," "heavenly union," "revelation," "principalities and powers") and concepts (dualism, cosmology, and ethics). These scholars are not suggesting that the author is a Gnostic or that Ephesians is a Gnostic tract; rather, they believe that the author transfers Gnostic language and thought to the church in order to counter this heresy, which was threatening the church. His method is to provide a point of contact with the readers, but in the process he gives these words and concepts new meaning: "Ephesians turns Gnostic language against Gnosticism."[23]

In this process, scholars such as H. Schlier and F. Beare see the author developing a distinct Christian "*gnōsis*" (a theory of knowledge) that explained such things as a knowledge of God, humanity, and the world. Schlier went so far as to call Ephesians a meditation on the wisdom of the mystery of Christ—a "*Weisheitsrede* or *Sophiarede*."[24]

All this research has opened up another possibility for understanding the nature and purpose of Ephesians. Unfortunately, not enough is known about first-century Gnosticism to conclude whether the author was confronting this heresy directly or just utilizing the language and concepts of his day.[25]

Another group of scholars has sought to explain the origin of Ephesians on the basis of parallels to the language and theology of the Dead Sea Scrolls—that body of literature belonging to the Qumran community. So far, the most valuable contributions have come from individuals like K. G. Kuhn, J. Murphy-O'Connor, and F. Mussner.[26]

These scholars have made extensive comparisons between Ephesians and the Dead Sea Scrolls regarding the hymnic and paraenetic (exhortative material) structure; general concepts like cosmology, creation, dualism, evil; and specific parallels, such as the mystery, saints, temple of God, and so forth.[27] Most of these scholars hoped to establish direct literary influence by Qumran on Ephesians. Murphy-O'Connor went so far as to suggest that Ephesians was written by an amanuensis of Paul who had come from the ranks of the Essenes.[28]

Unfortunately, the evidence does not permit one to come to any definite conclusions regarding the literary connections between Ephesians and the Dead Sea Scrolls. The author of this epistle may simply be using expressions that were common in his day and that he and the writers of the scrolls used independently. For Barth, "Ephesians *in toto* is neither in form nor in substance any more closely related to Qumran than any other key passages in undisputed Pauline writings."[29]

This brief survey is intended to show that Gnostic and Qumran parallels have received considerable attention and serve as a framework out of which a number of scholars seek to explain the epistle. If the author is consciously combating Gnosticism, then Ephesians could be called an anti-Gnostic tract. With respect to the relationship between Ephesians and Qumran, however, it does not appear that the author is addressing a heretical threat to the church. In this case, he may simply belong to the same literary tradition as that of Qumran.

A Liturgical Document

An analysis of the stylistic features of Ephesians has led a number of scholars to propose that this is some kind of liturgical document rather than an epistle. Moffatt, for example, refers to

Ephesians as a "homily" rather than a letter.[30] And, on the basis of stylistic features such as the hymnic material, long sentences, and the piling up of synonyms, Martin calls this an exalted prose-poem, "a typical early Christian liturgy."[31] J. Kirby's work on Ephesians led him to conclude that the epistle is a prayer and a discourse cast into the form of a letter.[32]

Although some hymnic elements of Ephesians were identified quite early by scholars such as M. Dibelius, E. Lohmeyer, and T. Innitzer, the extensiveness and function of hymnic-catechetical-liturgical material in Ephesians had not been explored until recently.[33] Many scholars concur that the utilization of so much traditional material directs Ephesians toward a liturgical function in the church. But just what that function was varies from scholar to scholar.

Kirby, for example, claims that the author writes chapters 1–3 in the form of a Jewish *berakah* (blessing), possibly to be used at the celebration of the Eucharist. Beyond that, the epistle incorporates liturgical material from the church of Ephesus, particularly that which was used for the renewal of the covenant to celebrate Pentecost.[34] N. A. Dahl, in a number of his writings, has proposed that Ephesians is a baptismal letter.[35] This theory has found popular acceptance among a number of NT scholars who believe that the epistle can best be understood in a baptismal setting.

References to the baptismal nature of Ephesians will be made throughout the commentary. It is my opinion that even though Ephesians employs a significant amount of baptismal imagery, it was not written as a baptismal tract to be used in celebrating baptism or giving baptismal candidates catechetical instruction; rather, *baptismal language and theology are used to develop the author's theme of unity in the church.*

A number of scholars, among them C. L. Mitton, do not attempt to identify the purpose of Ephesians with any specific event such as baptism, the Eucharist, or Pentecost. The writer used this liturgical style, according to Mitton, because he has the worshiping congregation in mind; he knows that they will be reading this letter in the context of worship and prayer. Consequently, "he phrased what he wrote in a style suitable for the hearer and the worshipper rather than the private reader. This would lead him to use a declaratory style—what today is often called a liturgical style. It would not be surprising if he incorporated here and there snatches from a familiar hymn or a phrase from a creedal affirmation; but the liturgical style comes not so much from his borrowings as from his awareness of the context in which his writing would be used."[36]

A Discourse on the Unity of the Church

Anyone reading Ephesians will soon become aware that the church (*ekklēsia*) is given considerable attention:

a. It is mentioned nine times (Greek text, 1:22; 3:10, 21; 5:23, 24, 25, 27, 29, 32).

b. It is discussed by means of various metaphors: biological (the body of Christ: 1:22, 23; 2:16; 4:4, 12, 16; 5:23, 30), architectural (the holy temple: 2:20–22; 4:12, 16), and social (the bride: 5:21–33).

c. It has a universal rather than local meaning. Here "church" is the new creation and the universal society consisting of Jews and Gentiles, not the local congregation "in Ephesus." This also is demonstrated by the transcendental status that believers have in the church because of the realized eschatology in the epistle. "The church shared the heavenly life of its exalted Lord even now in this age (1:22; 2:6; 5:27)."[37] It has a message that is valid for all generations, including the principalities and powers (3:10).

d. The church (body) and Christ (head) are united and interdependent rather than the Head simply being one of many members, as in Romans 12:4, 5, and 1 Corinthians 12:12–26. These observations make one aware that the teaching of the church in Ephesians is both important and new. Basically, the creation of this "one new man" shows that God has acted historically to unite humankind and that the church is a witness to God's ultimate plan to unite all things in Christ (1:10, 22, 23; 2:14–16). The church is, as John Stott so perceptively entitled his book, *God's New Society.*

Since the unity of the church has received so much attention in Ephesians, one naturally wonders what historical and theological factors led to that emphasis. One suggestion relates this theme to the problem of Gnosticism, which essentially dehistoricized Christianity into timeless myths. Thus the author seeks to ground the Christian life in the verities of history and to show that the church is a historical witness of God's redemptive activity through Christ.

But the focus of scholarly speculation on the occasion and purpose of Ephesians centers more around the problem of Jewish-Gentile relations. Both Jews and Gentiles were becoming Christians, but there were some basic differences in their understanding of the gospel of Jesus Christ.

One opinion sees the theme of unity in Ephesians necessitated by the problem of *Jewish exclusivism* in the early church. Basically, this is the negative attitude on the part of Jewish believers toward the Gentiles who were becoming Christians. Given their adherence to some of the prescriptions in the law (Torah)—particularly circumcision and Jewish food laws—some Jewish believers felt that Gentiles had to obey these Jewish laws when they became Christians. This was a threat to the gospel that Paul preached and would have made Christianity a sect of Judaism.

This problem of Jewish exclusivism is described and dealt with at the Jerusalem council in Acts 15:1–35 and in Paul's epistles to the Romans and Galatians. The council decided that Paul could evangelize the Gentiles without requiring them to be circumcised or to adhere to Jewish dietary laws (cf. Acts 15:19–29; Gal. 2). The heart of Paul's gospel is marked by inclusivism rather than exclusivism; it is a gospel characterized by faith in Jesus Christ, not works of the law—that is, circumcision and food laws; both Jews and Gentiles participate in Jesus Christ, and in him there is "neither Jew nor Greek" (Gal. 3:28).

Though the guidelines for Paul's gospel were established at the Jerusalem council, Jewish exclusivism continued, making it necessary to apply these principles in Paul's churches. Consequently, a major theme in Romans is that the Gentiles had as much right to receive salvation from God as did the Jews; they have been grafted into the "olive tree," which, at one time, had been the exclusive right of the Jews (11:13–24).

In Galatians, Paul faces a similar problem of Jewish exclusivism. His answer to the Jews is that the Gentiles are justified before God by virtue of their "faith in Jesus Christ," not by "observing the law" (2:16). In other words, Gentiles are not required to "live Jewishly" by submitting to circumcision and observing Jewish food laws.[38]

Could it be that the problem of Jewish exclusivism lies behind the writing of Ephesians? Did the religious and social barriers that separated Jews and Gentiles and that led to Jewish
exclusivism continue to operate in spite of Paul's earlier clarification of the gospel? Is Ephesians a final attempt to destroy Jewish
bigotry by reaffirming Paul's universal vision and showing that
the essence of the "mystery" is that Jewish and Gentile believers
have been united in one body?

Most of the content of Ephesians could be interpreted as
a message to Gentile believers that they have no need to feel
excluded from God's people. True, at one time their lives were
characterized by disobedience and sin (2:1–3); they were called—
probably disparagingly—" 'uncircumcised' by those who call
themselves the 'circumcision' " (2:11); they were "foreigners" who
were "excluded from citizenship in Israel" and as such had no
part in the covenants, were without hope and without God (2:12).
But the central message of Ephesians is that this is no longer true
because in Christ they have been brought near (2:13), and "the
law with its commandments and regulations" (circumcision and
dietary restrictions) that separated Jews from Gentiles, has been
broken down (2:14, 15).

The end result of God's redemptive activity is the union
of Jew and Gentile in the church. This is more than the picture
of grafting provided by the imagery of the olive tree in Romans
11:13–24. The union between Jews and Gentiles is not effected
by Gentiles becoming Jews but by the creation of a "new man,"
the church, that includes both Jew and Gentile (2:15; 3:6). Ephesians clearly teaches that the Gentiles have every right to be considered members of the body of Christ.

Another and more popular approach is to look at Ephesians from the perspective of *Gentile exclusivism*. H. Chadwick has
suggested that the letter was written to correct a spiritual misunderstanding that had arisen within post-Pauline Christianity.[39]
Apparently, the Gentile congregations had divorced themselves
from the salvation-history of the Jewish Christians and considered
themselves a separate spiritual entity. According to Chadwick, Ephesians insists upon the continuity of Gentile Christianity with Judaism and teaches that Jew and Gentile have been united in Christ.

Chadwick's interpretation is similar to the view of E. Käsemann, who believes that the author of Ephesians needs to re-

mind the Gentile Christians of their roots and of the historical origin of the gospel because they were despising their Jewish fellow believers. In this respect, the epistle elaborates upon a theme that is briefly discussed by Paul in Romans 11, namely, the incorporation of Gentiles into Jewish Christianity.[40]

All this, however, does not provide any clue as to what occasioned such strained relations between Jewish and Gentile believers. W. Grundmann attempts to make a historical connection with the migration of Jewish Christians to Asia Minor after the Jewish war and argues that the influx of this Jewish-Christian circle into the predominantly Gentile-Christian churches of Asia Minor led to a split that a Pauline pupil sought to bridge in Ephesians with the application of Pauline thoughts about the unity of these two groups.[41]

A more recent theory by K. M. Fischer attempts to locate the problem of a Jewish and Gentile schism in the church within the context of the Roman Jewish war during the years preceding and following the destruction of Jerusalem in A.D. 70.[42] This war threatened the close relationship between Jewish (synagogue) and Gentile (church) believers because the Gentiles felt that they had to disassociate themselves from all forms of Jewish nationalism (the Zealots) so as not to raise suspicions and risk reprisals from the Roman authorities.

The author of Ephesians, according to Fischer, addresses this situation. Whereas Paul had argued for the inclusion of the Gentiles into the church without their becoming Jews (Rom. 9–11; Gal. 1–3), "the author of Ephesians uses Paul's name to argue for the inclusion of Jewish Christians in the community without assimilation to the views of the Gentile majority. When Paul had argued for the inclusion of *gentiles qua gentiles*, the author of Ephesians argued for the inclusion of *Jewish Christians qua Jewish Christians*."[43]

Unfortunately, all these views are highly conjectural, and one is forced to agree with W. G. Kümmel that the concrete situation that occasioned "this reworking of the Pauline message by emphasizing the unity of the church comprised of Gentiles and Jews cannot now be perceived."[44] All one can envision is some kind of spiritual crisis in post-Pauline Gentile Christianity that necessitated an emphasis upon the universal church consisting of Jews and Gentiles.

From the perspective of Gentile exclusivism, these Christians were reminded not to disregard their spiritual heritage with Israel. In their pagan state they were separated from the Jews and had no point of contact with God's covenant people (2:11ff.). But through Christ and in the church, they have become "fellow citizens with God's people and members of God's household" (2:19; 3:6). If the Jews had no right to exclude them from the church, then it was equally wrong for them to disregard the Jews!

Perhaps Ephesians has a dual message: A deutero-Paulinist could be extending Paul's vision of a universal and united church that includes the incorporation of the Gentiles while at the same time reminding them that they are part of God's history of salvation. "Ephesians," writes Barth, "more than any other New Testament epistle, will press the point that Gentiles receive no salvation other than the one they share with Israel and receive through the Messiah. It is the salvation first promised and given to this people alone: Israel."[45]

Failure to identify the concrete situation that occasioned the epistle does not, however, detract from the fact that *unity* is its dominant theme. Although some of this has already been mentioned, there are some specific characteristics of Ephesians that make this obvious and by which the author develops this theme:

a. The source of all unity is in the elective will and purpose of God (1:4, 5, 10; 3:11).

b. Christ is the agent by which or through whom this unity is accomplished. According to J. A. Allan, the phrase "in Christ," "in whom," and so on is used thirty-four times in Ephesians.

c. There are twelve occurrences of the word "one" (*hen*) in the Greek text ("the two one," 2:14; "one new man," 2:15; "one body," 2:16; 4:4; "one Spirit," 2:18; 4:4; "one hope," 4:4; "one Lord," 4:5; "one faith," 4:5; "one baptism," 4:5; "one God and Father," 4:6; "each one of us," 4:7; "each part," 4:16; "each one of you," 5:33); also, the force of *ana* in *anakephalaioō* (1:10) is "one by one," bringing separate items into a single whole.

d. The preposition *syn* ("with," "together with") is used with a number of verbs and nouns. In some cases, these words are used in connection with the believers' union with Christ, such as he "made us alive with Christ" (*synezōopoieō*, 2:5), "God raised us up with Christ" (*synegeirō*, 2:6), he seated us in the heavenlies (*synkathizō*, 2:6).

The *syn* nouns are also used to describe the fact that the Gentiles are "joined together" (*synarmologeō*, 2:21; 4:16), "held together," (*symbibazō*, 4:16), and "are being built together [*synoiko-domeō*] to become a dwelling in which God lives by his Spirit" (2:22). Consequently, they are "heirs together" (*synklēronomos*, 3:6), "members together of one body" (*syssōmos*, 3:6), and partners (*symmetochos*, 3:6). On two occasions there is a negative use of these compound words: The believers are not to become partners (*symmetochos*, 5:7) with immoral people or join together in fellowship (*synkoinōneō*, 5:11) with the heathen.

e. Considerable attention is given to the concept of peace. Apart from the standard greeting (1:2) and farewell (6:23), peace is central to the idea of reconciliation and unity between Jews and Gentiles (2:14, 15, 17) and is essential for maintaining the unity of the body (4:3). Finally, believers are to arm themselves with "the gospel of peace" (6:15).

f. The Greek word for "unity" (*enotēs*) occurs twice in Ephesians (4:3, 13) and nowhere else in the NT.

g. Apart from these specific examples, there are some general observations that appear to accentuate the need and the possibility for unity: The ethical exhortations are given to the church as a means of maintaining the unity and peace that was brought about by Christ (4:1–6); the gifts of the Spirit show that there can be unity and singleness of purpose in the midst of diversity; believers in the body of Christ "put away" those vices that harm interpersonal relationships (4:25); rather than promoting individualism, life in the church is a joyful sharing together in the common elements of worship (5:15–20); and finally, the principle of submission is given, so that the different members of the household can live together in unity, peace, and love (5:21–6:9).

The attention given to this theme has led H. von Soden to view Ephesians as a "hymn of unity."[46] One dimension of that theme is ecclesiological: Jew and Gentile have been brought together into one body, the church. The other dimension is cosmological: The church is a witness to the cosmic powers (3:10) that God's ultimate purpose of bringing all creation together is being accomplished (1:10, 22, 23).

Throughout the epistle the author uses the language and theology of baptism to develop the theme of unity. He considers baptism to be the rite by which one participates in Christ (2:5–

10) and thus partakes of all the blessings of God (1:3–14; 2:13ff.; 5:8ff.). Furthermore, the appearance of the *one baptism* in 4:5 as one of the foundational principles of the unity of the church demonstrates the importance of this sacrament for the author and his agreement with the tradition of the early church in considering baptism a sacrament of unity (1 Cor. 1:13ff.; 12:12, 13; Gal. 3:27, 28; Col. 3:10, 11).

The act of baptism is also used to describe the change of status from pagan to believer. The author accentuates this change by contrasting what his readers once were (2:1ff., 11ff.; 5:8a) and what they have now become in Christ (2:4ff., 13ff., 5:8bff.) This also is in keeping with the view of the early church that interpreted baptism as participation in the events of Christ (indicative) and the beginning of a new ethical life (imperative; cf. Rom. 6:1–11; 2 Cor. 5:17; Col. 3:3; Titus 3:5–7).

Ephesians contains a large amount of paraenetic material (4:1–3; 4:17–5:20; 5:21–6:9) that probably belonged to the common catechetical tradition of the early church. The author uses these exhortations to expound upon the nature of the new life in Christ and to show the unifying effect this ethical action is to have upon all human relationships in the church (4:3, 15, 16, 25–32; 5:31–33).

From the preceding discussion it becomes obvious that all questions about Ephesians are related to the question of authorship. If Ephesians is written by Paul, the following conclusions are possible:

Origin. Ephesians is one of the "captivity epistles," written while Paul was in prison. The NT records a brief imprisonment in Philippi (Acts 16:19–33), two years in Caesarea (Acts 23:23–26:32), and two years in Rome before the end of Paul's life (Acts 28:16–31).[47]

Although there is no specific mention of an Ephesian imprisonment, Paul's references to the suffering and affliction he experiences in Asia (2 Cor. 1:8–10), to other imprisonments (2 Cor. 6:5; 11:23), and his statement, "I fought wild beasts in Ephesus" (1 Cor. 15:32), have been taken to imply an Ephesian imprisonment of some duration. Though this theory has some appeal, it is basically an argument from silence and depends upon its association with Colossians (cf. Introduction to Colossians). The same can be said for an origin from Caesarea (cf. Introduction to Colossians). If it is seen as a Pauline epistle, there is precious little evidence to overthrow the traditional theory that it was written by Paul during his Roman imprisonment. The style and content make more sense if associated with the final years of Paul.

Date. A Roman origin would date the epistle somewhere between A.D. 62 and A.D. 64; if Ephesus, about A.D. 54–57; if Caesarea, about A.D. 59–61.

Destination. Given the problem regarding the phrase "in Ephesus," the best solution appears to take the epistle as some kind of circular letter that was intended for more than one church but that, in the course of events, became associated with Ephesus.

This identity with Ephesus could be the result of Paul's personal ministry there as well as the significance of that city as a religious center and capital city in Proconsular Asia. The NT references to Ephesus indicate that it held a strategic position for the missionary activity of the early church (Acts 19:10; 1 Tim. 1:3; 2 Tim. 1:18; 4:12; Rev. 1:11; 2:1–7).

While Paul was teaching in Ephesus (in the "hall of Tyrannus," Acts 19:9, 10), Epaphras heard the gospel and, as a result of his conversion to Christianity, went back to his home in Colossae and started a church there (Col. 1:7; 4:12). Much the same thing may have happened with the seven churches mentioned in Revelation 1–3 and other cities not mentioned in the NT. A. S. Wood observes that "Ephesus was surrounded by 230 independent communities within the Roman province of Asia. If the Christian faith were firmly established in the capital city, it could be spread from the hub to the rim."[48]

If Ephesians is the product of a deutero-Paulinist, then the following conclusions are possible:

Origin. The origin must remain highly conjectural. But given the significance of Ephesus as an evangelistic and teaching center for Paul and his "school," the epistle probably emerged from this location.

Date. The date must be somewhere after Paul's death (ca. A.D. 64) and before the end of the first century. Since there are some echoes of Ephesians in Clement's letter to the Corinthians (ca. A.D. 95), it must have been written no later than the early 90s.

Destination. Ephesians is a universal letter intended for a number of Gentile churches in Asia Minor, including the Ephesian congregation.

Conclusion

All the internal and external questions surrounding this epistle should not detract from its essential beauty, value, and complete authority for the church. It just happens that there is a uniqueness or elusiveness about it that makes it difficult to categorize or place within the context of Paul's life. And because it is capable of fitting into more than one historical context, it seems best to regard it as a development of Paul's vision for a universal and unified church consisting of Jewish and Gentile believers.

Notes

---

1. Barth, *Ephesians 1–3*, p. 37; Mitton, *Ephesians*, pp. 2–4. For a helpful article see J. B. Polhill, "An Introduction to Ephesians," *RevExp* 76 (1979), pp. 465–79.

2. For further details on the circular letter theory, see most introductory sections in the major commentaries and D. Guthrie's *New Testament Introduction* (Downers Grove, Ill.: InterVarsity Press, 1971), pp. 510f. (hereafter cited *Introduction*). Several specialized studies include R. Batey, "The Destination of Ephesians," *JBL* 82 (1963), p. 101. (Batey suggests that during the process of transmission the textual reading *ousin* replaced the original *Hasias.*) D. A. Black, "The Peculiarities of Ephesians and the Ephesian Address," *Grace Theological Journal* 2 (1981), pp. 59–73; M. Santer, "The Text of Ephesians I.1," *NTS* 15 (1969), pp. 247–48. Best gives a very thorough study of all the evidence in "Ephesians I.i," in *Text and Interpretation*, pp. 29–41.

3. Mitton, *Ephesians*, p. 11; cf. also *The Epistle to the Ephesians: Its Authorship, Origin and Purpose* (Oxford: Clarendon, 1951), pp. 243ff., for a more complete treatment of his views on the date of Ephesians. For clarification on this view of a later author, see A. Patzia, "The Deutero-Pauline Hypothesis," pp. 27–42.

4. R. P. Martin, "An Epistle in Search of a Life-Setting," *ExpT* 79 (1968), pp. 296–302. For comments on Martin's views, cf. D. J. Rowston, "Changes in Biblical Interpretation Today: The Example of Ephesians," *Biblical Theological Bulletin* 9 (1979), pp. 121–25.

5. Wood, "Ephesians," p. 7. For a defense of Pauline authorship on these grounds, see Guthrie, *Introduction*, pp. 491ff.; Barth, *Ephesians 1–3*, p. 6. The most thorough book in English dealing with all matters

of introductory problems in Ephesians is A. van Roon, *The Authenticity of Ephesians, Supplement to NovT,* vol. 39 (Leiden: Brill, 1974). Cf. also J. N. Sanders, "The Case for Pauline Authorship," in *Studies in Ephesians,* ed. F. L. Cross, pp. 9–20.

Much of the debate regarding authorship centers around the similarities between Ephesians, Colossians, and other NT epistles. Useful comparisons can be found in most commentaries; see Abbott, *Ephesians and Colossians,* pp. xxiii–xxix; Foulkes, *Ephesians,* pp. 20–30; Mitton, *Ephesians,* pp. 11–18; idem, *The Epistle to the Ephesians,* parts II and III and appendixes; Moule, *Ephesians,* pp. 29–32; Westcott, *Ephesians,* pp. xxv–lx. Two excellent articles are Coutts, "The Relationship of Ephesians and Colossians," pp. 201–7; Polhill, "The Relationship between Ephesians and Colossians," pp. 439–50.

6. Guthrie, *Introduction,* p. 497.

7. Barth, *Eph. 1–3,* pp. 3–4.

8. For an explanation of Käsemann's ideas on "Early Catholicism," see Patzia, "The Deutero-Pauline Hypothesis," pp. 30–31.

9. Barth, *Eph. 1–3,* p. 45.

10. J. A. Allan, "The 'In Christ' Formula in Ephesians," *NTS* 5 (1958–59), pp. 54–62.

11. W. G. Kümmel, *Introduction to the New Testament,* 17th ed. (Nashville: Abingdon, 1975), p. 361. See also D. E. Nineham, "The Case Against the Pauline Authorship," in Cross, *Studies in Ephesians,* pp. 21–35. All the issues surrounding the authorship, destination, purpose, and so forth of Ephesians can be frustrating to the reader. H. J. Cadbury recognized this a long time ago in his article, "The Dilemma of Ephesians," *NTS* 5 (1958–59), pp. 91–102.

12. Guthrie, *Introduction,* pp. 507, 508.

13. The value and authority of Ephesians as a deutero-Pauline epistle is discussed by Mitton in his *The Epistle to the Ephesians,* pp. 270–78. He believes that on the analogy of the authorship of the Epistle to the Hebrews an initial loss turns out to be a gain. As a deutero-Pauline letter, Ephesians reveals a new mind and an authoritative voice in the generation of believers that followed Paul.

14. A. M. Hunter, *Introducing the New Testament,* 2d ed. (Philadelphia: Westminster, 1957), p. 120. Other studies that express similar views include N. Alexander, "The Epistle for Today," in *Biblical Studies,* ed. R. J. McKay and J. F. Miller (Philadelphia: Westminster, 1976), pp. 99–118; W. B. Colbe, "The Queen of the Epistles," *SWJTh* 6 (1963), pp. 7–19.

15. Barclay, *The Letters to the Galatians and Ephesians,* p. 83; Bruce, *Ephesians,* p. 11; C. R. Erdman, *The Epistle of Paul to the Ephesians* (Philadelphia: Westminster, 1931), p. 14.

16. J. N. Sanders, "The Case for Pauline Authorship," p. 16.

17. Martin, "Ephesians," p. 126. See also M. Barth, "Traditions in Ephesians," *NTS* 30 (1984), pp. 3–25.

18. Goodspeed's ideas are presented in *The Meaning of Ephesians* (Chicago: University of Chicago Press, 1933) and *The Key to Ephesians* (Chicago: University of Chicago Press, 1956). For a critique of Goodspeed's hypothesis, see Guthrie, *Introduction*, pp. 512–14; Wood, "Ephesians," p. 112.

19. E. Lohse, "Pauline Theology in the Letter to the Colossians," *NTS* 15 (1969), pp. 211–20.

20. N. A. Dahl, "Interpreting Ephesians: Then and Now," *Theology Digest* 25 (1977), p. 314.

21. Ibid., p. 314.

22. For a long list of scholars with this persuasion, see Barth, *Ephesians 1–3*, pp. 12ff.

23. Dahl, "Interpreting Ephesians: Then and Now," p. 307.

24. H. Schlier, *Der Brief an die Epheser* (Düsseldorf: Patmos Verlag, 1962), p. 21. For Beare's comments, see his "Ephesians," pp. 674–75.

25. See Yamauchi, *Pre-Christian Gnosticism*.

26. Kuhn, "Der Epheserbrief im Lichte der Qumrantexte," *NTS* 7 (1960–61), pp. 334–46; Murphy-O'Connor, "Who Wrote Ephesians?" *BibTod* 18 (1965), pp. 1201–9; F. Mussner, "Beiträge aus Qumran zum Verständnis des Epheserbriefes," *Neutestamentliche Aufsätze* (Regensburg: Verlag Friedrich Pustet, 1963).

27. See Mitton's summary, *Ephesians*, pp. 18ff.

28. Murphy-O'Connor, "Who Wrote Ephesians?" "The sometime Essene, now a disciple of the man who wrote I Corinthians 13, had well assimilated the most profound lesson of his master" (p. 1209).

29. Barth, *Ephesians 1–3*, p. 21; cf. also R. A. Culpepper, "Ethical Dualism and Church Discipline: Ephesians 4:25–5:20," *RevExp* 76 (1979), pp. 529–39, for comparisons between Ephesians and Qumran.

30. J. Moffatt, *Introduction to the Literature of the New Testament*, 3d ed. (Edinburgh: T. & T. Clark, 1918), p. 388.

31. Martin, "Ephesians," p. 128. See also Martin, *Reconciliation*, p. 157.

32. Kirby, *Ephesians: Baptism and Pentecost*.

33. One example is J. T. Sanders, "Hymnic Elements in Ephesians 1–3," *ZNW* 56 (1965), pp. 214–32.

34. Kirby, *Ephesians: Baptism and Pentecost*, p. 170.

35. Dahl, "Adresse und Proömium des Epheserbriefes," *TZ* 7 (1951), pp. 241–64; "Bibelstudie über den Epheserbrief," in *Kurze Auslegung des Epheserbriefes* (Göttingen: Vandenhoeck & Ruprecht, 1965), pp. 7–83; "Anamnesis," *Studia Theologica* I (1948), pp. 69–95. For other studies on the liturgical/baptismal nature of Ephesians, see R. R. Williams, "The Pauline Catechesis," in *Studies in Ephesians*, ed. Cross, pp. 89–96; P. Car-

rington, *The Primitive Christian Catechism* (Cambridge: Cambridge University Press, 1940); E. G. Selwyn, *The First Epistle of St. Peter* (London: Macmillan, 1946); J. Coutts, "Ephesians I.3–14 and I Peter I.3–12," *NTS* 3 (1956–57), pp. 115–27.

36. Mitton, *Ephesians*, p. 30.

37. Martin, "Ephesians," p. 129.

38. See Cannon, pp. 183–96. For some helpful correctives to the usual interpretation of Paul's attitude toward the law, cf. K. Stendahl, *Paul Among Jews and Gentiles and Others Essays* (Philadelphia: Fortress, 1976); E. P. Sanders, *Paul and Palestinian Judaism: A Comparison of Patterns of Religion* (Philadelphia: Fortress, 1977).

39. H. Chadwick, "Die Absicht des Epheserbriefes," *ZNW* 51 (1960), pp. 145–53; also his "Ephesians," in *Peake's Commentary on the Bible*, ed. M. Black and H. H. Rowley (Edinburgh: Thomas Nelson, 1962), pp. 980ff.

40. E. Käsemann, "Ephesians and Acts," in *Studies in Luke-Acts*, ed. L. E. Keck and J. L. Martyn (Nashville: Abingdon, 1966), pp. 288–97.

41. W. Grundmann, "Die NEPIOI in der Paränese," *NTS* 5 (1958–59), pp. 188–205.

42. See K. M. Fischer, *Tendenz und Absicht des Epheserbriefes* (Göttingen: Vandenhoeck & Ruprecht, 1973).

43. Quoted from C. Roetzel, *The Letters of Paul—Conversations in Context*, 2d ed. (Atlanta: John Knox, 1982), p. 104.

44. Kümmel, *Introduction to the New Testament*, p. 364.

45. Barth, *Ephesians 1–3*, p. 66.

46. H. von Soden, quoted in Wood, "Ephesians," p. 18.

47. For a discussion on the origin of Colossians, see the "Introduction" to that epistle. Beyond the sources listed there, additional studies by Duncan on the origin of the captivity epistles can be found in *ExpT* 43 (1931), pp. 7–11; *ExpT* 46 (1935), pp. 293–98.

48. Wood, "Ephesians," p. 12.

§1 The Opening Greeting (Eph. 1:1–2)

1:1 / Except for the omission of Timothy, the opening of this greeting is quite similar to Colossians 1:1. The letter claims to be from Paul, **an apostle of Christ Jesus**. This term was one that Paul used frequently to indicate that he was "one who was sent" (*apostellō*, "to send") as a missionary or special envoy of God. It is used of the twelve disciples as well as for others who fulfill an apostolic function, such as Andronicus and Junias (Rom. 16:7). At times, it is applied to Christians who have a very vivid experience of Christ (Acts 1:21, 22; 1 Cor. 9:1). By the time Ephesians was written, it was used primarily for those who were the founders of the Christian church (2:20).

The statement that Paul's apostleship is **by the will of God** repeats a theme that Paul emphasizes throughout his epistles: At his commissioning, he and Barnabas are set apart to do the work to which God has called them (Acts 13:2); to the Romans he writes "called to be an apostle and set apart for the gospel of God" (1:1); to the Galatians he states in no uncertain terms that his call did not come from "men nor by man, but by Jesus Christ and God the Father" (1:1; cf. also 1:13–16); and though Paul may at times feel unworthy of his calling (1 Cor. 15:9), he affirms that God's grace has made him what he is (1 Cor. 15:10). This awareness of God's initiative in his call kept Paul from boasting about his position; it also legitimized his office as an apostle on occasions when his authority was questioned (cf. Galatians and Corinthians).

The readers are identified, first of all, as **saints**. As such, they are people who are consecrated to God by being separated from sin. Second, they are **the faithful in Christ Jesus**, i.e., those who are being faithful or trustworthy. The footnote in the NIV text indicates that the Greek *pistois* (**faithful**) could also be taken to mean "believers." Thus the greeting would read "to the saints and believers who are . . . " Both meanings, however, are expressed within the body of the letter: God's people are those who have put their faith in Christ (the indicative) and who live out that faith in obedience to the Lord (the imperative).

The text indicates that the letter is addressed to God's people who live **in Ephesus**, although the NIV footnote indicates that there is a textual question concerning the inclusion of the phrase **in Ephesus**. Most likely the destination was not present in the original manuscript because the epistle was intended to be a universal letter to be circulated among a number of churches (see Introduction).

1:2 / The greeting ends with Paul's usual mention of **grace and peace** (cf. Rom. 1:7; 1 Cor. 1:3; 2 Cor. 1:2; Gal. 1:3; Phil. 1:2; Col. 1:2; 1 Thess. 1:1; 2 Thess. 1:2; 1 Tim. 1:2; 2 Tim. 1:2; and Titus 1:4 include grace, mercy, and peace). *Chairein* ("Greetings") was a common word for greeting in the Greek world (Acts 15:23; 23:26; James 1:1). Paul uses *charis* ("grace"), which to believers has come to mean God's free and unmerited goodness upon humankind.

The Hebrews greeted each other with *šalôm*, a common term for "peace" as well as fullness or wholeness of life. The apostle, likewise, is doing more than just greeting his readers with these terms, because grace and peace are gifts of God given through Christ. By bringing these two gifts together, he is urging that his readers enjoy life because of the favor that God freely has bestowed upon them. Both concepts form an important part of the letter (peace: 2:14, 15, 17; 4:3; 6:15; grace: 2:5, 7, 8; 3:2, 7; 4:7).

One cannot help but notice the significant role attached to Christ in these opening verses. Paul is designated as an apostle of **Christ Jesus**; the believers live their life in **Christ Jesus**; and together with God the Father, the **Lord Jesus Christ** bestows the divine gifts of grace and peace upon his people.

In the following discussion it will be noted that Ephesians has a number of stylistic features similar to Colossians. First, Ephesians follows the pattern of praise, thanksgiving, and prayer. In Colossians, Paul began by thanking God for his readers (1:3–8) and then praying that God would accomplish certain things in their lives. In Ephesians, there is a similar structure: The epistle begins with a great hymn of praise or thanksgiving to God (1:3–14) and follows up with a long prayer (1:15–2:20) in which the apostle expresses the concern that his readers understand how God has blessed them through Christ.

A second similarity relates to the hymn and its place in the epistle. In Colossians, the ideas of the Christ hymn (1:15–20) were applied again and again throughout the letter. Much the same could be said of Ephesians, for this opening eulogy serves as an excellent preface to the remaining doctrinal section. The idea of redemption is prominent in the phrases dealing with the exaltation of Christ (1:15–22), salvation by faith (2:1–10), the unity between Jew and Gentile (2:11–22), and the revelation of the mystery of Christ (3:1–12).

Third, Ephesians may be divided conveniently into a doctrinal and a practical section, since we find the author providing a theological base (chapters 1–3) and then applying these truths to the Christian life (chapters 4–6). Such divisions, however, should not be taken too rigidly, for one finds ethical exhortations in the midst of doctrinal discussion (e.g., 1:4; 2:10) and doctrinal teaching continues throughout the last chapters (4:4–16; 5:21–6:9).

Many elevated words and phrases have been used to describe the beauty of this opening hymn that praises God for the spiritual blessings he has bestowed upon the believer in Christ. Stott, in his commentary (p. 32), quotes a number of authors who use such phrases as "a magnificent gateway," "a golden chain of links," "a kaleidoscope of dazzling lights and shifting colors," a "rhapsodic adoration," a "paean of praise."

Unfortunately, the English translations do not retain the hymnic nature and rhythmic pattern that is discernible in the original language. In the Greek, for example, the entire section of twelve verses is one long sentence. This helps one to appreciate how the author's thoughts keep moving to new heights. Having to divide the section into sentences (RSV and NIV, eight; NEB, eight; GNB, fifteen) destroys the continuity of both style and thought.

A number of proposals have been offered with respect to the origin of the hymn. Those who take the Ephesian letter to be genuinely Pauline naturally attribute these verses to the great apostle. Scholars who question Pauline authorship suggest that an author writing in Paul's name borrowed terms and phrases from Paul's other epistles and composed a hymn that resembles something that Paul would have written.

The search for origins and models has moved in a number of directions. J. Kirby believes that this passage is modeled after a Jewish *berakah* ("blessing") in which God is praised for his goodness. Others have noted the strong liturgical nature of the passage and have suggested that it belongs to the worshiping community. As such, either it could have a prior and independent existence apart from Ephesians or it could have been written by the author to provide a liturgical piece to be used for church worship and instruction (Mitton, pp. 22–24).

A number of scholars who have tried to explain the origin of Ephesians from a baptismal context have focused their attention on this particular hymnic section. In the hymn, the author utilizes baptismal terms and concepts such as sonship (1:5), redemption (1:7), and sealing (1:13). The most likely explanation for this is that the writer is drawing upon baptismal theology to thank God for all the blessings of redemption that he has provided through Christ to those who have believed. Since the passage is a hymn, it is quite possible to regard it as a baptismal hymn that may have been part of the worshiping tradition in the early church and that the author took over and incorporated into his redemptive doxology. The baptismal motifs in this hymn have been so convincing to some scholars that they have concluded that the entire epistle was written as a baptismal tract or at least connected with the celebration of baptism in the church.

From the baptismal nature of this opening hymn, however, it does not necessarily follow that the occasion of this epistle is to instruct the readers on the meaning of their baptism. If this were the purpose, one might expect baptism to be mentioned more explicitly, for as it stands, the word "baptism" occurs only once (4:5). Rather, the author finds the baptismal motifs and language appropriate to describe to his readers all the blessings that God has bestowed in Christ. The early church understood baptism to be the act in which the believer appropriates in faith the blessings of redemption in Christ. Thus it was sufficient for him to allude to baptism but not to define its meaning directly.

Another noticeable feature of the hymn is the place that it gives to all three members of the Trinity. In a broad sense, the work of the Father is described in verses 3–6; the Son, in verses 7–12; and the Holy Spirit, in verses 13–14. But all three persons permeate the entire passage. God is the *source* of all the spiritual blessings mentioned in the hymn; Christ is the *agent* in whom these blessings are realized for the believer. The name "Christ"— or some form of that name, or the personal pronoun "in him"— occurs thirteen times in this passage. All that God has purposed for the believer is fulfilled in Christ. The Holy Spirit is mentioned as the one who *seals* or marks the believer as belonging to Christ. And, since the blessings that are enumerated in this passage are "spiritual," they are given by the "Spirit."

1:3 / **Praise be**: The Greek word is *eulogētos*, which carries the meaning of speaking (*legō*) well or kindly (*eu*) of someone. In this context, the phrase could be expressed as "thanks be," "blessed be," as well as **praise be** to God. In the NT, the word is used exclusively for God, since he alone is worthy to be blessed; he is blessed because he is the author of all the blessings that he bestows upon the believer in Christ. Since such forms of blessings were common among the Jews, this passage may have a Jewish antecedent.

Praise is given to **the God and Father of our Lord Jesus Christ** (cf. 1:3; 2 Cor. 1:3; 1 Pet. 1:3). Grammatically, the phrase could read, "God who is the Father of our Lord Jesus Christ." As such, it indicates the unique relationship that God and Christ have to each other. In the context of the NT, believers call God "Father" because of the sonship that is received through Christ (cf. 1:5; Rom. 8:14–17; Gal. 4:6, 7).

Who has blessed us: It is important to note that this is in the past (Greek aorist) tense, meaning that the author is envisioning a time when God acted to provide these blessings rather than anticipating that God will do something in the future. These blessings became a reality for the believers **in Christ**—that is, in baptism.

The nature or essence of the blessing is **spiritual**. Although the word is singular (**every spiritual blessing**), it needs to be understood as a comprehensive phrase: God's blessings are unlimited, and he does not withhold anything from his people. The sphere of these blessings is **the heavenly realms**. Thus, the reference is not to material, physical, or temporal blessings: They are not part of one's treasure "where moth and rust destroy, and where thieves break in and steal" (Matt. 6:19). As spiritual gifts in the heavenly world, they are imperishable and belong to the eternal order "where moth and rust do not destroy, and where thieves do not break in and steal" (Matt. 6:20).

The phrase **in the heavenly realms** is a translation of the Greek "in the heavenlies" (*en tois epouraniois*). Since it is an adjective without a noun, English translations supply such terms as "world" (GNB), "places" (RSV), or **realms** (NIV). This clarification, however, should not lead one to conclude that Paul has a geographical place or cosmic location in mind somewhere in the universe above the earth. *Heavenlies* is a term signifying the spiritual world, that is, the unseen world of spiritual reality and activity. This is the sphere in which the believers are blessed. The other four occurrences of "heavenly realms" in the epistle (1:20; 2:6; 3:10; 6:12) help to express this idea more clearly.

In the ancient world, it was believed that there was a great cosmic struggle between the forces of good and the forces of evil. Generally, the heavens were considered to be the place where this battle between the evil rulers, principalities, powers, and ruling spirits of the universe (*stoicheia tou kosmou*) was being waged. A significant part of the message in Colossians is that these spiritual forces are inferior to Christ in the order of creation (Col. 1:16) as well as subject to Christ through his victory on the cross, where Christ "having disarmed the powers and authorities, . . . made a public spectacle of them, triumphing over them by the cross" (Col. 2:15). Ephesians continues these ideas by teaching that, because of Christ's victory over these evil powers, he is exalted to God's right hand "far above all rule and authority, powers and dominion" (1:20, 21). Furthermore, these powers are learning of God's wisdom through the witness of the church (3:10).

Ephesians teaches that believers are involved in a similar battle: "For our struggle is not against flesh and blood, but against the rulers, against the authorities, against the powers of this dark world and against the spiritual forces of evil in the heavenly realms" (6:12). But by virtue of their union with Christ, they share in Christ's victory and likewise rule with Christ in the heavenly world (2:6). In fact, all the blessings that are enumerated in this passage are either fulfilled in union with Christ or are mediated through the agency of Christ.

1:4 / The first specific blessing mentioned is what is known in theological circles as election or predestination. Basically, this doctrine affirms that God has taken the initiative in the "electing" or "choosing" process. In the OT, God chooses Israel from among all the nations of the earth to be his covenant people (Deut. 4:37; 7:6, 7; Isa. 44:1, 2); in the NT, God chooses people to become members of the new covenant, the church (John 15:16; Rom. 8:29; 9:11; Eph. 1:4, 5; 2 Thess. 2:13; 2 Tim. 1:9; 1 Pet. 1:2); and individuals such as Jeremiah (1:5) and Paul (1 Cor. 15:9–11) believed that even their vocation was destined by God.

Unfortunately, the Christian church has become polarized into theological camps over this doctrine. Some (namely, the Calvinists) have placed all the emphasis upon the sovereign grace of God in matters of salvation; others (namely, the Arminians) have emphasized human free will in the salvation process. Since the Bible does not attempt to harmonize this apparent paradox, it continues to remain one of the more divisive and speculative "mysteries" of the Christian faith.

When dealing with this issue, one should avoid the extremes in theory and practice that so often characterize adherents of one view or another. Election to salvation does not imply that God, therefore, predestines the rest of humanity to damnation; nor should election lead to spiritual pride among the elect. Election simply affirms that personal faith rests upon the prior work (grace) of God, so that, with respect to salvation, God has taken the initiative to claim a people for himself. An individual is free to choose God only because God has already decided for such a person from eternity. Likewise, election should not lead to spiritual complacency; it is a privilege and responsibility that is unto holiness of life and for good works (1:4; 2:10).

The author indicates that God's intention for the salvation of humanity precedes the creation of the world and the historical process (**for he chose us in him before the creation of the world**). When Paul, a member of the church and a chosen apostle to the Gentiles, reflects upon the doctrine of election, he may be reasoning in the following way: "How did I, a Pharisee and a former persecutor of Christians, get to be what I am? How is it that the Jews—and now the Gentiles—have become part of God's family? Surely it is not because of some national merit or personal attainment through faith or good works! This had to be God's doing. He knew from eternity how he would work in me and in the world; it was not a last-minute decision that the Gentiles were to become heirs of salvation" (3:6). When the apostle writes to the Corinthians about their new existence in Christ, for example, he states: "All this is from God, who reconciled us to himself through Christ" (2 Cor. 5:17–19).

Stott makes a helpful comment by drawing attention to the relationship of the three pronouns in the phrase **he chose us in him**. God chose us, even before we were created, to be redeemed through the work of Christ that had not yet taken place (Stott, p. 36). Such, however, is the marvel of God's elective grace toward the human race.

The goal of election is that the believer be **holy and blameless** before God. This phrase is similar to Colossians 1:22 and may be part of the OT sacrificial language that the NT uses on other occasions (cf. 5:27; Heb. 9:14; 1 Pet. 1:19; Jude 24). In some cases, the doctrine of predestination has led to moral license rather than personal holiness. Not a few believers have reasoned that since they are "eternally secure," their ethical life is no longer of concern to God or to other people. This reasoning, however, is unfortunate, because the believers' standing before God and election (the indicative) are demonstrated by the kind of life that they live ethically (the imperative).

1:5 / It is difficult to know what to do with the phrase **in love**. The NIV (as RSV, GNB) takes it to go with verse 5, thereby indicating that God's choosing was motivated by his love. On the basis of this love, God **predestined us to be adopted as his sons** and daughters **through Jesus Christ**. But the phrase could be taken with the action described in verse 4, as humanity's love to God rather than God's love for humanity. Thus the meaning would be that believers should be holy and without fault before him in love (*en agapē*). *Agapē* is used elsewhere in Ephesians for Christian love (3:17; 4:2, 15, 16; 5:2). Still, it is fitting to mention *God's* love so early in the epistle, and that this is what motivated him to decide (lit., "foreordain") to redeem humanity: **adopted as his sons** and daughters . . . **in accordance with his pleasure and will**.

Sonship—referring to being a child of God (i.e., eligible to inherit his promises)—is the second blessing listed in this passage, and this, too, is a gift mediated **through Jesus Christ**. Paul uses this term in Romans 8:15, 23, 29, and Galatians 4:5 to indicate the special relationship that believers have to God. Here sonship is tied in with God's elective purpose for humanity.

The language of this passage is similar to that in the accounts of Jesus' baptism (Matt. 3:13–17; Mark 1:9–11; Luke 3:21, 22) and transfiguration (Matt. 17:5; Mark 9:7; Luke 9:35). In these Gospel accounts of Christ's baptism, as in Ephesians 1:5 and 6, baptism and sonship are closely related and Christ is given the title "beloved" or **the One he loves** (1:6). This similarity of language and ideas (sonship, *huiothesia*; good pleasure, *eudokia*; and beloved, *agapētos*) leads one to infer that this reference to the election and sonship of the Christian may have some connection with the baptism of Jesus. Thus one could say that as Jesus was proclaimed Son at his baptism, baptism is the event whereby believers obtain their sonship. This thought is quite explicit in the baptismal passage in Galatians 3:26–27 that states that "You are all sons of God through faith in Christ Jesus, for all of you who were baptized into Christ have clothed yourselves with Christ."

1:6 / Theology is doxology! In other words, sonship (the indicative) is a summons to praise God for his glorious grace. Literally, from the Greek, the phrase reads, "to the praise of the glory of the grace of him of which he graced us in the beloved." This reading helps one to see how much emphasis the writer puts upon grace (cf. 1:2). He seems so enraptured by the thought of God's grace that he does not want to let it go. Also, it is a fitting way to end a section devoted to the work of the Father (1:3–6). That almost identical phrases are used in 1:12 and 1:14 ("the praise of his glory") confirms the hymnic nature of this entire section.

1:7 / There is a definite parallel here to Colossians 1:14, where **redemption** and **the forgiveness of sins** are closely connected. But in Ephesians, the means of **redemption** is amplified by the phrase **through his blood, the forgiveness of sins**. The emphasis here is upon forgiveness, which in turn is followed by the resounding response concerning the greatness of God's grace. Since sonship takes place through baptism, and since sonship and forgiveness are so closely linked in this passage, one wonders if the author still has the baptismal event in mind when he speaks of the forgiveness of sins.

1:8 / The magnitude of God's grace is amplified in this opening phrase, **that he lavished on us** (*eperisseusen*). The poetic nature of the Greek makes it difficult to know whether to attach the following words (**with all wisdom and understanding**) with verse 8 or verse 9. Is it *God's* wisdom and insight (GNB, RSV) or is it wisdom and insight that God, through his grace, has lavished upon believers so that they could understand God's will (NIV, NEB)? Given the parallel with Colossians 1:9 and the meaning of verse 9, it seems better to take wisdom and insight as coming from God's grace.

The two terms, **wisdom** (*sophia*) and **understanding** (*phronēsis*), though not consistently distinguished in Scripture, generally refer to the knowledge of something, followed by the ability to apply that knowledge or wisdom to a right course of action. God has provided the knowledge and ability to know and to do his will.

1:9 / God's gift of wisdom and insight enables the believer to understand **the mystery of his will** (cf. GNB: "secret plan"). In Colossians, that mystery meant that the Gentiles were recipients of the gospel and heirs of salvation (1:26, 27; 2:2; 4:3). Though this thought appears also in Ephesians (cf. 3:3-6), this epistle carries the concept somewhat further with its emphasis upon the church and the unity of mankind. The revelation is part of God's eternal plan **(his good pleasure which he purposed)** and is something that will be accomplished **in Christ**. As in verse 5, God's purpose includes his **good pleasure** as well (cf. *eudokia* in Luke 2:14; Gal. 1:15). It pleased God to make his plan or will known and to complete that plan in his Son.

1:10 / God's "good pleasure" is **put into effect** or administered by Christ (for the use of *oikonomia* as "management," "stewardship," or "administration," cf. Luke 16:2-4; 1 Cor. 9:17; 1 Pet. 4:10). He is the steward through whom God is working out his plan for the world—a plan that is in process and that will be culminated **when the times will have reached their fulfillment** (lit., "in the fullness of time").

God's ultimate plan is to unify all of creation under the headship of Christ. Elsewhere in the epistle, the author talks about bringing the Jews and Gentiles together into one body (2:11, 12; 3:6); here, however, he envisions a global unity. In many ways the words are reminiscent of the Christ hymn in Colossians, in which all things on earth and in heaven are reconciled in Christ (1:20).

It is difficult to know how far one should push this language or attempt to comprehend the scope of the author's ideas. Are **all things** (*ta panta*) and **heaven** and **earth** just metaphors for universality, or does he mean the unity of heavenly beings (i.e., angels, principalities, powers, spirits, etc.) with human beings? Is he thinking of a cosmic and earthly renewal characteristic of the end times (Matt. 19:28; Rom. 8:18-25; 2 Pet. 3:10-13)? Although one cannot be sure of the details, it is clear that this hymn praises God that ultimately all things will find their place and unity in Christ.

The difficult word *anakephalaiōsasthai* is translated appropriately in the NIV **to bring . . . together under one head, even Christ**. In secular terms, the word is used for the summation of things, such as adding up numbers in mathematics or concluding an argument in a debate. In today's language, people speak of "the bottom line" in much the same way. Paul uses the term in Romans 13:9 when he indicates that all of the commandments are being "summed up" in the one command of love.

In Ephesians, however, "addition" or "summation" does not quite express the author's thought adequately. To bring everything together **under one head, even Christ** suggests that all things (human beings, history, and the entire universe) find their focus in Christ. This, essentially, is the content of God's secret plan!

1:11–12 / Up to this point in the hymn (vv. 3–10), the personal pronouns "we" and "us" refer to all Christians, irrespective of ethnic origin. But an important change takes place in the concluding verses of the hymn, where a distinction is made between Jewish and Gentile Christians: In verses 11–12, the "us" with whom the author identifies himself is the Jewish Christians; in verse 13, the "you" definitely refers to the Gentile believers; then the "we" in verse 14 refers to all of God's people—both Jewish and Gentile believers. The distinctions mentioned here will receive further attention in chapter 2 of the epistle, where it is shown *how* Jews and Gentiles were brought together into one body in Christ.

When the author describes God's action upon the Jewish believers, he repeats many of his earlier words and ideas: **having been predestined** (1:4) **according to the plan** (cf. 1:5, 9) **of him who works out everything in conformity with the purpose of his will** (1:5). With respect to the Jewish Christians, he wants to emphasize that what has happened to them was not by chance or by human merit but is due entirely to the eternal and elective purposes of God in Christ. All is of God!

The NIV **In him we were also chosen** does not quite capture the essence of the Greek *eklērōthēmen*. The verb *klēroō* means "to choose," "to appoint by lot." The noun (*klēros*), therefore, would be "the lot," "share," or "portion" that was obtained by lot. The Greek word for "inheritance," "possession," or "property" is the cognate word *klēronomia* (cf 1:14).

Behind this language is the OT concept that Israel was God's "lot" or "chosen people" (Deut. 4:20; 9:29; 32:9; 1 Kings 8:51; Ps. 106:40; Jer. 10:16; Zech. 2:12). Given the context of verse 11 within a hymn that is celebrating God's elective purpose, it seems likely that the author is referring to the Jewish Christians as those whom God has chosen as his own people. Now, however, that possession is claimed by virtue of their union with Christ (**in him**).

While being God's people may result in praising God through prayer, worship, etc., the phrase **in order that we . . . might be for the praise of his glory** suggests that one's very being or existence is involved. These new people of God are summoned to be a praise to God in the same manner that Israel was called as a nation to declare God's glory in their life, witness, and worship (Isa. 43:21; Jer. 13:11).

Who are those who were **the first to hope in Christ?** Some commentators, by virtue of the Greek article with Christ, take the reference to be to the Jewish nation and their expectation of "the Christ," that is, the coming Messiah; others see the comment applying to those Jews who believed in Christ and became the first Christians. In priority of time, they preceded the Gentiles with their hope (and faith) in Christ. This latter view appears to fit this context where the contrast between Jewish (1:11–12) and Gentile believers (1:13) is being discussed.

1:13 / Here the author turns to the Gentiles and affirms that they, too, **were included in Christ.** He then proceeds to outline the steps that were involved in their coming to Christ:

First, they **heard the word of truth, the gospel of your salvation.** On some occasion these readers heard the message of the gospel, which resulted in their salvation. In this context, salvation probably signifies inner renewal and all the blessings and privileges available to believers because of their status in Christ (cf. 2:1ff.) rather than preservation from the wrath of God (cf. Rom. 5:9).

The phraseology of this opening statement is similar to Colossians 1:5 and to the ideas in Romans 10:14 and 17, which show that the proclamation *of* the gospel precedes faith *in* the gospel. A similar sequence takes place during Peter's sermon on the day of Pentecost when he summons those who heard the gospel to repent and be baptized (Acts 2:37ff.).

Second, they **believed** in Christ, literally, "in whom also having believed." Although the content of belief is not mentioned, it definitely must include the person of Christ ("If you confess with your mouth, 'Jesus is Lord,' and believe in your heart that God raised him from the dead, you will be saved," Rom. 10:9) or the gospel that bears witness to him.

Third, **you were marked in him with a seal, the promised Holy Spirit**. The imagery behind this phrase comes from the ancient custom of sealing (*sphragizō*), in which personal possessions (e.g., animals, household goods, slaves) received a mark or stamp of ownership in much the same way that things are branded or identified today. This act also confirmed or authenticated something as genuine. A seal on a letter or document, for example, declared that it was legally valid. People belonging to religious cults often were sealed with marks that bore the image of their god(s). The Book of Revelation talks about those who have or do not have "the seal of God on their foreheads" (Rev. 9:4; cf. also 7:2–8; 22:4; 2 Tim. 2:19).

In the NT, there are a number of references that indicate that the Holy Spirit is the Christian's seal: In Romans, Paul relates the inner witness of the Spirit to the believer's sonship (8:15, 16; cf. Gal. 4:6), thus affirming that the presence of the Holy Spirit in the believer is a sign that he or she belongs to God. The apostle is even more explicit in 2 Corinthians 1:22, "[God] set his seal of ownership on us, and put his Spirit in our hearts as a deposit, guaranteeing what is to come." Ephesians 1:13 confirms this by assuring the believer that the **seal** is the possession of the Holy Spirit. It is a visible attestation that one belongs to Christ.

Although Paul connects the giving of the Holy Spirit to the acts of "hearing" the gospel and "believing" in Christ, there are credible reasons to believe that verse 13 has the baptismal event in mind, even though the term is not mentioned explicitly. First, there is an inseparable connection between faith and baptism in the NT. Baptism is believers' baptism, and those who believed in Christ expressed their faith almost immediately in baptism (Acts 2:38, 41; 8:12, 35–38; 9:18; 10:47, 48; 19:5). Faith and baptism went so closely together that they were regarded as *one* act rather than two. Peter, for example, instructs his hearers to repent, that is, to have faith, believe, *and* to be baptized for the forgiveness of sins (2:38). When Paul becomes a Christian, he is told to "Get up, be baptized and wash your sins away, calling on his name" (Acts 22:16). Within the framework of the NT, one was not baptized unless one believed; nor did one believe without being baptized.

Second, the NT connects baptism with the reception of the Holy Spirit. Peter summons his audience to be baptized and receive "the gift of the Holy Spirit" (Acts 2:38). Paul associates baptism and the Holy Spirit on several occasions in his letters (1 Cor. 6:11; 12:13; Titus 3:5). And when Luke describes some of the major epochs in the life of the early Christian church, he includes faith, baptism, and the reception of the Holy Spirit as essential parts of becoming a Christian, that is, of Christian initiation (Acts 2:38ff.; 8:12–17; 19:1–6; cf. 10:44–48). There is no need for a "Spirit baptism" or a rite of confirmation apart from the reception of the Holy Spirit at the time of water baptism.

On the basis of these observations it appears legitimate to interpret 1:13 within the context of baptism. The aorist participles "having heard" (*akousantes*) and "having believed" *(pisteusantes)*, followed by the aorist passive ("you were sealed with the Holy Spirit of promise"), are reminiscent of the faith, baptism, Holy Spirit pattern noted above. The author does not envision a sequence of events separated by a long period of time.

Although the Holy Spirit is the seal (1:13; 4:30; 2 Cor. 1:22), and 1:13 is a strong allusion to baptism, it is by no means certain that sealing is used as a technical term for baptism in Ephesians. The first definite reference to the "seal of baptism" occurs in the second century (ca. A.D. 150) in the *Second Letter of Clement* (7.6; 8.6). From this time onward, *sphragis* is the seal received by all Christians at baptism and thus becomes a term for baptism itself.

The effect of the Holy Spirit is to mark the believer **with a seal**. As a seal, the Spirit marks one out as belonging to Christ. It is interesting to note that this is virtually the same effect that baptism "into Christ" has. To be baptized into the name or person of Christ is to become Christ's possession, to be placed under the Lord's authority and protection.

1:14 / In addition to ownership, the Holy Spirit is a **deposit guaranteeing** that believers will receive God's promises. Most commentators suggest that the idea of guarantee (*arrabōn*) came into the Greek world from the Phoenicians who, in matters of trade, often would make a deposit or an installment as earnest money with the balance to be paid in full at some later date. This act obliged both buyer and seller to complete the transaction. But "the deal" included a sense of "quality" as well, for the person receiving the down payment looked forward to receiving full payment with goods of the same quality (Mitton, pp. 62–63). In the Christian life, the Holy Spirit is a pledge that God will complete his promise to deliver **our inheritance**. The statement in 2 Corinthians 5:5 is more specific about this idea: "God . . . has given us the Spirit as a deposit, guaranteeing what is to come." One's present life *in* the Spirit is a foretaste of one's future and eternal life *with* the Spirit!

Beyond **guaranteeing** one's **inheritance**, the Holy Spirit assures believers of **the redemption of those who are God's possession**. Included in this translation are the two important theological concepts of **redemption** (*apolytrōsis*) and **possession** (*peripoiēsis*). Some commentators (cf. Abbott, p. 24) believe that the context (**our inheritance**) requires that possession likewise be "our possession." Thus, believers are redeemed, but await a future time when they will take full possession of their redemption. This view has led to the ambiguous and inadequate translation in the RSV, "which is the guarantee of our inheritance until we acquire possession of it, to the praise of his glory."

Most commentators—and as a result most English translations, like the NIV—think the verse is stressing that God is the agent of redemption and that believers are **God's possession** (NIV, NASB), "his own" (NEB), or "those who are his" (GNB). Although redemption is a present gift, the Holy Spirit assures the believer that ultimately God will redeem completely those who are his; he is a guarantee until the complete freedom (**redemption**) of God's own people (cf. 1 Pet. 2:9).

These thoughts recall the "already" and the "not yet" aspect of the Christian life. Believers have been given the Holy Spirit, enjoy new life in Christ, have been redeemed, but still await the fulfillment of these blessings at the second Advent. The sealing of the Holy Spirit has an eschatological function that points toward the final day, when their bodies will completely be freed (redeemed) from all the effects of sin. Ephesians 4:30 expands this concept more fully when it refers to "the Holy Spirit of God, with whom you were sealed for the day of redemption." A similar thought concerning redemption is expressed in Romans 8:23, where Paul discusses the future glory of God's people and God's creation: "We ourselves, who have the firstfruits of the Spirit, groan inwardly as we wait eagerly for our adoption as sons, the redemption of our bodies."

This great hymn of praise (vv. 3–14) ends with a note that has been sounded several times before with respect to God's elective purpose for humanity. Hence, election and sonship are **to the praise of his glorious grace** (v. 6); redemption, and all of its benefits (vv. 7–11), are to culminate in a life of praise (**that we . . . might be for the praise of his glory**—v. 12); finally, the pledge of the Holy Spirit is presented in relation to the unfolding plan of God. This, also, is **to the praise of his glory** (v. 14).

Additional Notes §2

On 1:3–14 cf. J. T. Sanders *"Hymnic Elements in Ephesians 1–3,"* ZNW 56 (1965), pp. 214–32. Other specialized studies include V. A. Bartling, "The Church of God's Eternal Plan: A Study of Ephesians 1:1–14," *Concordia Theological Monthly* 36 (1965), pp. 198–204; J. Coutts, "Ephesians I:3–14 and I Peter I:3–12," pp. 115–27; N. H. Keathley, "To the Praise of His Glory: Ephesians I," *RevExp* 76 (1979), pp. 485–93; P. T. O'Brien, "Ephesians I: An Unusual Introduction to a New Testament Letter," *NTS* 25 (1979), pp. 504–16. O'Brien notes that vv. 3–14 have a "didactic intent," a "paraenetic aim," and an "epistolary function."

The following phrases from vv. 3–14 in the NIV indicate the many variations of the "in Christ" statements:

in Christ (v. 3)
in him (*en autō*, i.e., Christ, v. 4)
through Jesus Christ (v. 5)
in the One he loves (v. 6)
in Christ (v. 9)
under one head, even Christ (v. 10)
in him (v. 11)
in Christ (v. 12)
in Christ (v. 13)
in him (v. 13)

1:3 / Some helpful material on "heavenlies" includes Caragounis, *The Ephesian Mysterion*, pp. 146–52; Robinson, *Ephesians*, pp. 20–22; A. T. Lincoln, "Re-Examination of 'The Heavenlies' in Ephesians," *NTS* 19 (1973), pp. 468–83. Lincoln gives a good history of interpretation as well as an examination of H. Odeburg's *The View of the Universe in the Epistle to the Ephesians* (Lund: C. W. K. Gleerup, 1934). He differs with Odeburg by concluding that 3:10 and 6:12 have a "local" rather than a "spiritual" meaning. "In Ephesians then it would not be surprising if *en tois epouraniois* were to have a reference to heaven as a distinct part of the created universe but one which retains its concealing relation to the spiritual world and to God himself, and thus also its aspect of incomprehensibility" (p. 480). See also Lincoln's *Paradise Now and Not Yet: Studies in the Role of the Heavenly Dimension in Paul's Thought with Special Reference to His Eschatology*, SNTSMS 43 (Cambridge: Cambridge University Press, 1981), esp. pp. 135–68.

1:7 / For the association between baptism and the forgiveness of sins in the NT, cf. Acts 2:38; 22:16; 1 Cor. 6:11; Titus 3:5; 1 Pet. 3:18–21 and the disc. on Col. 2:11–15.

1:10 / The ideas in this verse should not be used to promote a doctrine of "universalism" that teaches that all humanity ultimately will be saved (see Stott, *God's New Society*, pp. 42–45; Caragounis, *The Ephesian Mysterion*, pp. 143ff.; Hanson, on *anakephalaiosis*, in his *The Unity of the Church in the New Testament*, pp. 123–25).

1:11–12 / On "we" and "you," see D. Jayne, " 'We' and 'You' in Ephesians," *ExpT* 85 (1974), pp. 151–52; R. A. Wilson, " 'We' and 'You' in the Epistle to the Ephesians," *Studia Evangelica* 2 (1964), pp. 676–80.

1:13 / G. Fitzer, "*sphragis*," *TDNT*, vol. 8, pp. 939–53; P. W. Evans, "Sealing as a Term for Baptism," *The Baptist Quarterly* 16 (1955–56), pp. 171–75; J. Ysebaret, *Greek Baptismal Terminology* (Nijmegen: Dekker & Van de Vegt, 1962), pp. 182ff.

On water and Spirit baptism, see G. R. Beasley-Murray, *Baptism in the New Testament* (London: Macmillan, 1962); J. D. G. Dunn, *Baptism in the Holy Spirit* (London: SCM, 1970).

1:14 / On the "already" and the "not yet" in Paul's theology, cf. J. D. Hester, *Paul's Concept of Inheritance*. Scottish Journal of Theology Occasional Papers No. 14 (Edinburgh: Oliver & Boyd, 1968), esp. pp. 90–104; D. R. Denton, "Inheritance in Paul and Ephesians," *EQ* 54 (1982), pp. 157–62; P. L. Hammer, "Comparison of *klēronomia* in Paul and in Ephesians," *JBL* 79 (1960), pp. 267–72.

§3 *Prayer for Divine Enlightenment (Eph. 1:15–19)*

From the context of 1:15–2:10 it appears that these verses form the next major section of Ephesians. The apostle has just finished recalling the spiritual blessings that God, through Christ, has bestowed upon all believers. From this universal truth, he turns to something more specific: His thoughts move from doxology to prayer; he reminds his readers that he thanks God for them (vv. 15, 16) and that he prays specifically that they will have the necessary wisdom to understand these blessings in Christ (vv. 17–19).

When the apostle begins talking about Christ, however, he seems to abandon the form of prayer and move into an exposition of God's power as manifested in Christ's resurrection, exaltation, and headship over the church (1:20–23) and as manifested in the new life that he gives to the believer in Christ (2:1–10). It is possible to regard 1:20–3:13 as a long doctrinal parenthesis in which the apostle develops his ideas on the unity of Jew and Gentile in the church (2:11, 12) and expounds upon his personal role as a messenger of the gospel (3:1–13). In 3:14–21 he returns to the form of prayer found in 1:15.

1:15 / **For this reason** may refer to all that has been said in 1:3–14 about the blessings of God. But the apostle may have something more specific in mind, because he immediately mentions the faith and love of the readers. No doubt his thoughts and prayers go back to the fact that they, as Gentiles, heard the gospel and became God's people (1:13, 14).

The statement **ever since I heard about your faith in the Lord Jesus** speaks strongly against Ephesus as the destination of the letter, for it is unlikely that Paul would have been so vague and impersonal with people to whom he had ministered for three years (Acts 20:31). This is more what one would expect with Colossians; he does not know that congregation personally and only hears about the church through Epaphras' report (Col. 1:4, 7, 9). But it is remotely possible that he could be referring to a recent report—perhaps from someone like Epaphras—on the progress of their faith. All that he has heard is that God's people who are faithful (1:1) have their faith grounded **in the Lord Jesus**. Faith is given practical expression through their **love for all the saints** (cf. Col. 1:4); or to state it another way, love toward God's people is an outgrowth of their faith in Christ. Love, faith, and hope (1:12, 18) appear in Ephesians and in the Pauline epistles as basic Christian graces (cf. Col. 1:5).

1:16 / The report that the apostle has heard drives him to a prayer of thanksgiving for his readers (**I have not stopped giving thanks for you, remembering you in my prayers**). The combination of prayer and thanksgiving, as well as constancy in prayer, are characteristic of Paul (Rom. 1:8–10; Phil. 1:3, 4; 4:6; Eph. 5:19, 20; Col. 1:3; 3:15–17; 4:2; 1 Thess. 1:2; 5:18). In this prayer one notes that the petitions become more specific and relate to a deeper understanding and appropriation of the blessings that the readers already possess by virtue of being in Christ.

1:17 / Prayer is made to **the God of our Lord Jesus Christ, the glorious Father**. Basically, this is a variation of the title of God in 1:3. Christ not only addresses God as his "Father" Luke 10:21; John 17:1ff.; 20:17) but reveals him as such (John 14–17). Here that revelation is expanded by the phrase **the glorious Father**. This concept of God received considerable attention in the opening doxology (1:6, 12, 14) and beyond this verse is mentioned again in 1:18; 3:14, 16, 21. God not only is the Father of glory, "but he is the Father to whom all glory belongs." The glory of God is the full revelation of his attributes, including his majesty and power.

The first request in this prayer is that God will give believers **the Spirit of wisdom and revelation so that you may know him better** (lit., "in the knowledge of him [God]"). From the Greek, there is no way of knowing that the Holy Spirit is meant by "spirit" (*pneuma*). Normally, when "the Spirit" is intended, it is preceded by the article *the*. Without the article some manifestation or gift of the Spirit must be intended, such as the spirit of holiness (Rom. 1:4), gentleness (1 Cor. 4:21; Gal. 6:1), truth (John 14:17), or faith (2 Cor. 4:13; e.g., Westcott, p. 24). This accounts for the RSV reading of "spirit" with a small *s* (cf. NIV text note).

The readers already have received and been sealed in the Holy Spirit at the time of their baptism. This prayer, therefore, is not for the Holy Spirit itself, but for a spirit of **wisdom and revelation**, which is a special gift, manifestation, or application of the Holy Spirit. This giving of the Spirit will make the readers wise with respect to their understanding (*epignōsis*) of God. *Epignōsis*, as contrasted to *gnōsis*, which normally has a broad application, is "knowledge" limited to religious and moral things, hence directed toward God or the ways of God in some manner. The following verses reveal the spiritual direction of this request and how it is illustrated and developed. To know God is to "be enlightened" (1:18a); enlightenment leads to an understanding of the hope of God's call (1:18b), God's blessing (inheritance, 1:18c), and God's power (1:19), as demonstrated in Christ's resurrection (1:20) and exaltation (1:21–23).

1:18 / **I pray** should not be taken as a second request but as a continuation of the prayer that began in 1:17 (the Greek does not repeat the purpose clause): Enlightenment is the result of knowing God and his will more perfectly. Light and knowledge often are linked together in Scripture. Psalm 119:18, for example, is a form of a petition in which the author asks, "Open my eyes that I may see wondrous things in your law." In the NT, human beings are often depicted as living in darkness and needing the light of Christ or the light of the gospel to change their lives (cf. John 1:9; Acts 26:18; Eph. 5:8; 1 Pet. 2:9; 1 John 1:7; 2:8ff.).

This illumination takes place—literally—in **the eyes of your heart**. In biblical language, the "heart" is a comprehensive term used for the entire inward self or personality of an individual, including intellect, will, and emotions (Matt. 5:8; Rom. 10:8–10). Being enlightened by the light of God's truth affects one's *entire* inward being.

One of the problems in the interpretation of this verse is the meaning of "enlightenment." In the Greek, *pephōtismenous* is a perfect passive participle that denotes completed action, a present state that has resulted from past action. The tense of the verb here prohibits taking "enlightenment" in a progressive sense—that is, as becoming more and more enlightened. Such an observation leads to an obvious question: When has God acted upon the believer in such a way?

In the NT, the verb *phōtizein* ("to give light," "to illuminate") and the noun *phōtismos* ("enlightenment," "illumination") are used to express the results of spiritual encounter. Christ, for example, is the "true light that gives light to every man was coming into the world" (John 1:9). Second Corinthians 4:4 speaks of "the light of the gospel of the glory of Christ," and 4:6 says that "God . . . made [past tense] his light shine in our hearts to give us the light of the knowledge of the glory of God in the face of Christ." In 2 Timothy 1:10, the gospel is the means of bringing "life and immortality to light" (*phōtisantos*). Illumination, in other words, comes through the reception of the gospel.

On the basis of what has been said previously about the baptismal nature of Ephesians, is it possible that the author is thinking of baptism as the time when the believer was "enlightened"? It certainly is an appropriate term for baptism inasmuch as those who receive the light of God's word are baptized and in their baptism are given the Holy Spirit and its gift of wisdom and understanding (1:17).

Hebrews and 1 Peter provide some interesting insights on this point. In 1 Peter, an epistle that many scholars associate with baptism, the writer speaks of believers as "a people belonging to God" whom God called "out of darkness into his wonderful light" (2:9; cf. Eph. 5:8 and the disc. of 5:8–14 as a baptismal liturgy). On two occasions, Hebrews uses "enlightenment" in the past tense: In 6:4 it occurs in the context of teaching about "baptism" (cf. 6:2) and leads the author to state, "It is impossible for those who have once been enlightened [*phōtisthentas*], who have tasted the heavenly gift, who have shared in the Holy Spirit, . . . if they fall away, to be brought back to repentance." In 10:32 he summons his readers to "remember those earlier days after you had received the light [*phōtisthentas*], when you stood your ground in a great contest in the face of suffering."

Although the NT speaks of enlightenment in ways unconnected with baptism, Hebrews 6:4 and 10:32, 1 Peter 2:9, and Ephesians 5:8–14 provide some textual evidence to indicate that a connection was made and that "enlightenment" in Ephesians 1:18 could refer to baptism. In the second and third centuries, enlightenment definitely became a technical term for this Christian rite.

The prayer for enlightenment leads to a number of specific requests: first, that the readers will know the **hope** to which God has called them. Hope, here, is not some subjective feeling or personal aspiration such as "I hope that" or "I hope for" (cf. 1:12). Rather, it is an objective element that belongs to the believer. Elsewhere in Scripture, it is a deposit in heaven (Col. 1:5), Christ in the Christian (Col. 1:27), something "offered to" the believer (Heb. 6:18), and the second Advent (Titus 2:13). In this context, the author prays that his readers will have wisdom, understanding, and enlightenment to know the full meaning of their call from God (cf. 4:4) and the assurance that their life in Christ and sealing with the Holy Spirit brings.

A second request is that they will know **the riches of his glorious inheritance.** One way to understand this phrase is to see it as a clarification of the **hope** to which God has called his people—that is, that **hope** consists of the **inheritance** that God has granted to the believer (cf. 1:14 and Col. 1:12, which must be in the writer's mind). The Greek, however, indicates that this is *God's inheritance* (*tēs klēronomias autou*) and not something that the saints receive, as in 1:14 and Colossians 1:12. As such, the apostle is thinking of the church as God's people—God's inheritance. The prayer would then be for a deeper understanding of what it means to be God's possession. The focus is upon the "state" of the believers as God's people rather than on the details of the blessings that that inheritance includes.

1:19 / A third request is that believers know about the greatness of God's power within them. After the apostle has mentioned the hope of God's calling and the glory of God's inheritance, he is led to contemplate the power of God that makes all that possible. Stylistically, the sentences are highly poetic (liturgical language) in nature and in the Greek include such synonyms as **power** (*dynamis*), **working** (*energia*), and **mighty** (*kratos*) **strength** (*ischys*). By this, he simply wishes to emphasize that nothing is impossible for God. The power of God that is at work in the believer is the same power (**mighty strength**) that is manifested in the resurrection, exaltation, and universal dominion of Christ. The author returns to that power at the end of his prayer in 3:20.

Additional Notes §3

1:15 / The NIV does not indicate that some Greek manuscripts omit the word **love**. The result of this is the unusual and unprecedented expression that faith is toward (*eis*) God's people. The best explanation is that **love** belonged in the original text but was unintentionally omitted in the process of copying the manuscripts (see B. Metzger, *A Textual Commentary on the Greek New Testament* [New York: United Bible Society, 1971], p. 602; also, the explanation in Moule, *Ephesians*, p. 56). For comments on **saints**, cf. disc. on 1:1 and Col. 1:2.

1:17 / Westcott provides a helpful summary and explanation of "glory" in his *Ephesians*, pp. 187–89. On "knowledge" and **wisdom**, cf. disc. on Col. 1:9, 10, and the extended note on *epignōsis* in Robinson, pp. 249–54.

1:18 / The baptismal nature of 1 Peter is surveyed in R. P. Martin's "The Composition of I Peter in Recent Study," *Vox Evangelica*, 1 (1962), pp. 29–42. See also J. Coutts, "Ephesians I.3–14 and I Peter I.3–12," *NTS* 3 (1956–57), pp. 115–27; F. L. Cross, *I Peter: A Pascal Liturgy* (London: Mowbray, 1954); F. W. Beare, *The First Epistle of Peter*, 3d ed. (Oxford: Blackwell's, 1970). The reference for identifying enlightenment and baptism is in Justin's *Apology* I, 61, 65. Additional discussion is in Ysebaret, *Greek Baptismal Terminology*, pp. 157ff.

§4   The Result of Christ's Enthronement
(Eph. 1:20–23)

1:20 / The writers of the NT show that the early church was convinced that the Jesus of Nazareth, who died by crucifixion, also was raised by the power of God and exalted to a position of authority: "Christ Jesus, who died—more than that, who was raised to life—is at the right hand of God and is also interceding for us" (Rom. 8:34; cf. also Acts 2:32, 33; 3:15; 4:10; 5:30, 31; 10:40; Rom. 4:24; 8:11; 10:9; 1 Cor. 6:14; 15:15; 2 Cor. 4:14; Gal. 1:1; Col. 2:12; 1 Pet. 1:21). The early church also believed that he was very much alive in their midst through the Holy Spirit.

Although it is common to think of resurrection and exaltation as two separate events, it is helpful to consider them as two different ways of expressing the same theological truth, namely, the triumph of God over the forces of death. Paul illustrates God's power by stating that it was manifested when he raised Christ from death and seated him at his right side in the heavenly world (cf. also Acts 2:32, 33; Rom. 8:11; Phil. 2:9; 1 Tim. 3:16). Christ's post–resurrection appearances should be interpreted as periodic earthly visitations and manifestations of the resurrected and exalted Lord during a period of forty days. What Luke is saying in Acts 1:1–11 is that the ascension marked the end of that kind of appearance; henceforth, Christ will manifest himself through the Holy Spirit.

The phrases **seated him at his right hand** and **heavenly realms** come from Psalm 110:1ff.; all the honor, dignity, and authority of the enthroned king are now ascribed to Christ. These phrases are not to be interpreted literally but understood as metaphorical language expressing Christ's presence with his Father in the invisible world, the sphere of eternal reality. Later, in 2:1–10, the author will apply these statements to the believer as well. The reality of Christ's resurrection and exaltation becomes a sign and pledge of the triumph of the Christian (cf. Rom. 8:11; 2 Cor. 4:14; 1 Pet. 1:21).

1:21 / Christ's heavenly ascension and authority are expressed by stating that he rules there, **far above all rule and authority, power and dominion**. These categories are similar to the lists in Romans 8:38, 1 Corinthians 15:24, Colossians 1:16 and 2:15, and 1 Peter 3:22. Such concepts of "heavenly beings" belonged to the ancient world, were expanded during the intertestamental period in the apocryphal literature, and were employed by some authors of the NT to illustrate the spiritual struggle between the forces of good and evil or light and darkness. The exorcism of demons by Jesus, for example, is seen as a sign of his authority and power over demonic forces (cf. Mark's Gospel and disc. on Col. 1:16).

Part of the message of Colossians is that Christ is superior to all evil powers. In the Christ hymn (1:15–20), Paul affirms Christ's sovereignty by stating that these powers are created by Christ and thus are subject to his authority. Later, he shows that, by virtue of Christ's death on the cross, he has triumphed over them and leads them as a victorious captor (2:15). As a result of Christ's supremacy and victory, these evil forces are reduced to a state of impotence and inferiority; they no longer exert any power or influence over the believer who has identified with Christ.

Ephesians does not appear to direct any polemic against a false system that was elevating the importance of these spiritual powers. Although some interpreters have argued for a Gnostic background to the epistle (see Introduction), it certainly is not as obvious as it is for Colossians. The closest the author comes is to indicate that the Christian's spiritual battle is "against the rulers, against the authorities, against the powers of this dark world and against the spiritual forces of evil in the heavenly realms" (6:12).

In 1:21, these powers are mentioned only in the context of Christ's exaltation. In fact, the verse states that he is also seated **above . . . every title that can be given** (lit., "above every name that is being named"; cf. Phil. 2:9). Furthermore, this supremacy is so expansive or all-encompassing that it spans both the present and future ages. J. A. Robinson puts these great thoughts together succinctly when he writes: "Above all that anywhere is, anywhere can be—above all grades of dignity, real or imagined, good or evil, present or to come—the mighty power of God has exalted and enthroned the Christ" (p. 41).

1:22 / The apostle presses on with thoughts of Christ's supremacy, using images characteristic of a royal court, where the defeated foes pay homage to their victor: **God placed all things under his feet.** This appears to be an obvious quotation from Psalm 110:1 and, as applied to Christ, illustrates his conquest of all spiritual enemies and his authority over them.

Sometimes the readers of the NT find it difficult to interpret and apply this principle of Christ's sovereignty because it uses ancient cosmological concepts and is stated in mythic and poetic language unfamiliar to modern people. The tendency is either to dismiss the language as irrelevant and nonsensical or to demythologize it.

M. Barth has made an attempt to understand the apostle's thoughts by probing into the history, essence, and function of these spiritual powers. From his study, he concludes that "Paul means by principalities and powers those institutions and structures by which earthly matters and invisible realms are administered, and without which no human life is possible" (*Eph. 1–3*, p. 174). Barth includes categories such as kings, procurators, senators, judges, and high priests, who function in political, financial, juridical, and ecclesiastical offices. C. L. Mitton carries this even further and wonders about substituting for principalities and powers the "evil powers in our contemporary world [such] as racism, nationalism, hate, fear, uncurbed sexual desire, drug addiction, alcoholism, etc. As with 'principalities and powers,' before these the individual feels helpless even though he recognizes their power to destroy the best things in human life" (p. 72).

1:23 / From the ideal of sovereignty the apostle moves to the concept of vital union, which he expresses by the head-body metaphor of the church: **which is his body.** This idea is unique to the teaching of Ephesians (1:23; 5:23) and Colossians (1:18, 24; 2:19) and goes beyond Paul's idea on the church in Romans and Corinthians, where "head" is mentioned along with other members of the body (1 Cor. 12:14–26). Christ is not a part of the body (e.g., the head or the foot), but rather the whole of which the various members are parts (1 Cor. 12:12). In Romans and Corinthians, Christ equals the body; but in Ephesians and Colossians, the church equals the body, and Christ is the head.

In Colossians, the head-body metaphor was used to combat heretical ideas that limited Christ's unique position of authority in the universe and in the church. Paul's concern there is to restore Christ to his rightful place of preeminence in all things—including his headship over the church (cf. disc. on Col. 1:18). In Ephesians, there is no direct polemic against false teachers. The idea of Christ's headship over the church is introduced to illustrate another dimension of Christ's exaltation.

In some ways, Christ's lordship over the church is similar to his lordship over all things. As Lord, he rules, guides, inspires. However, Christ's lordship over the church is of a different nature, because the church is his body, and he is its head. As such, it is in vital union with Christ; it belongs to him and derives its meaning in union with him; it is **the fullness of him who fills everything in every way**. Thus, in some mysterious way, the church is necessary to Christ's completeness, and he imparts to it his fullness.

Up to this point in the text the author has indicated that God has put "all things under his feet" and made him Lord over all things, including the church. Now he enlarges on this by indicating that Christ **fills everything in every way**, literally, "all (things) in all (things)"! Perhaps these ideas are an expansion of 1:10, which states that it is God's plan "to bring all things in heaven and on earth together under one head, even Christ." Does he envision that this is being done through the church (cf. 3:10)?

The concept of Christ's **fullness** or completion is brought out several times in Colossians, where it is stated that the full nature of God dwells in the Son (1:19; 2:9). The believer, in turn, comes to fullness of life through union with Christ in baptism. Ephesians presents the same thought on two different occasions: The apostle prays that his readers may "be filled to the measure of all the fullness of God" (3:19) and exhorts them to reach "to the whole measure (lit., "stature") of the fullness of Christ" (4:13).

Scholars continue to struggle over the difficult theological concept and the grammatical construction translated **the fullness** [*plērōma*] of him. Some interpreters understand the church as somehow "completing" or "filling up" Christ. However, most take the phrase to mean that the Christ who fills **everything** also fills the church so that it (the church) is described as **the fullness of him**. One may wisely heed the caution of C. L. Mitton, who concludes: "It must be frankly confessed that the meaning of these concluding words in verse 23 is quite uncertain, and, therefore, they cannot legitimately be used to support any item of doctrine about Christ or his Church" (p. 79).

Additional Notes §4

1:20 / A useful discussion of Christ's post-resurrection appearances in relation to the ascension can be found in F. F. Bruce, *The Book of Acts* (Grand Rapids: Eerdmans, 1979), pp. 30ff.

1:21–22 / The many books and articles dealing with such concepts as principalities, powers, etc. in the NT is an indication of the difficulty there is in understanding them. Some helpful resources include G. B. Caird, *Principalities and Powers: A Study in Pauline Theology* (Oxford: Clarendon, 1956); W. Carr, *Angels and Principalities: The Background, Meaning and Development of the Pauline Phrase "hai archai kai hai exousiai,"* SNTSMS, vol. 42 (Cambridge: Cambridge University Press, 1981), esp. pp. 47–85 on Colossians and pp. 93–111 on Ephesians; G. H. C. Mac-Gregor, "Principalities and Powers: The Cosmic Background of Paul's Thought," *NTS* 1 (1954), pp. 17–28; R. Yates, "The Powers of Evil in the New Testament," *EQ* 52–53 (1980–81), pp. 97–111; idem, "Principalities and Powers in Ephesians," *New Blackfriar* 58 (1977), pp. 516–21; J. Y. Lee, "Interpreting the Demonic Powers in Pauline Thought," *NovT* 12 (1970), pp. 54–69.

P. T. O'Brien has written a helpful article entitled "Principalities and Powers and Their Relationship to Structures," *RefThR* 40 (1981), pp. 1–10, in which he reviews a number of scholars (namely, Barth, Berkhof, Caird, Rupp, Sider, Yoder) who interpret principalities and powers as sociopolitical structures, tradition, law, authority, religion, etc. For additional disc. on this topic in Ephesians, see disc. and notes on 3:10 and 6:12.

1:23 / The linguistic, syntactical, and exegetical technicalities go beyond the scope of this commentary. For an important and helpful discussion, cf. notes on Col. 1:18; also, G. Howard, "The Head/Body Metaphors of Ephesians," *NTS* 20 (1974), pp. 350–56. Valuable information on *plērōma* and the technicalities of this verse can be found in the commentaries of Barth (*Eph. 1–3*), pp. 200–10; Mitton, pp. 76–79; Robinson, pp. 42–45, 87–89; Stott, *God's New Society*, pp. 62–65. More specialized studies include P. Benoit, "Body, Head and *Plērōma* in the Epistles of the Captivity," *RB* 63 (1956), pp. 5–44; A. R. McGlashan, "Ephesians 1:23," *ExpT* 76 (1965), pp. 132–33. This last article led to a reply from R. Fowler, "Ephesians 1:23," *ExpT* 76 (1965), p. 294. R. Yates provides a more thorough examination of the problem in his "A Re-examination of Ephesians 1:23," *ExpT* 83 (1972), pp. 146–51. Yates's conclusions produce the following translation (p. 154): "And he (God) has brought all things into subjection under his (Christ's) feet, and he (God) gave him (Christ) to be head over all things to the Church, which is his Body, the fulness (that which completes) of him (Christ) who all in all (completely) is being fulfilled (i.e., made complete as men and women are being reconciled to God through Christ's work and incorporated into him through his Body, the Church)."

§5 Christ and the Salvation of Believers (Introduction to Eph. 2:1–10)

Chapter 1 of Ephesians is dominated by the theme of praise and thanksgiving. In verses 3–14 the apostle utilizes a redemptive eulogy to praise God for all the spiritual blessings that he has bestowed upon the believer. These blessings are mediated through the Son and are confirmed in the believer through the inner witness of the Holy Spirit. The use of baptismal themes suggests that the hymn may have been connected with the celebration of baptism in the early church.

From doxology, he turns to a prayer in which he expresses the wish that his readers personally understand and appropriate the blessings that he has just enumerated. Consequently, there are many verbal and doctrinal similarities between these two sections. In the prayer, the apostle asks that the believers might increasingly know the hope to which God has called them (1:18a) and the richness of God's blessing (1:18b) and that they will see God's power as manifested in Christ's resurrection, exaltation, and headship over all things, including the church (1:19–23).

The context makes it apparent that the mention of Christ's resurrection and exaltation provides the background for the thoughts that he develops in 2:1–10 and in 2:11–22. The apostle wants to demonstrate that the mighty power of God that was at work in Christ is also at work in the believer; what is true of Christ is also true for each believer in Christ. Unfortunately, this flow of thought is broken by the division of the text into chapters and verses. The Greek text permits one to appreciate the hymnic (liturgical) nature of this section because verses 1–7 form one sentence, and the first main verb does not occur until verse 5 (he **made us alive**).

In chapter 2, the apostle develops two specific themes that he has already mentioned: In 2:1–10, he picks up redemption and forgiveness (1:7) and applies it to the reconciliation of sinful humanity kind by God; in 2:11–22, he applies the principle of unity from 1:10 to the specific case of Jews and Gentiles and shows how they have been brought together into one body.

Chapter 2:1–10 contains a number of contrasting features: First, there are the people who are mentioned. The author begins by referring to the Gentiles specifically (2:1), but then in 2:3 he expands his audience to include the Jews as well. By this, he shows that all of humanity was alienated from God and became recipients of his grace (2:3–7). And even though he returns to "you" (second person plural) in 2:8, one gets the impression that he still has both groups in mind until he addresses the Gentiles directly in 2:11.

Second, there is the contrast between their former pagan way of life (2:1–3) and their new life in Christ (2:4–10). At one time they were spiritually dead, and because of their sinful nature, they lived sinful lives, walked in the evil ways of the world, and disobeyed God; but now, as a result of God's grace and mercy upon their lives, they have been made spiritually alive and share in Christ's resurrection and exaltation. Their new creation is a manifestation of "good works" (2:10) rather than a life of disobedience and evil.

Third, these two ways of life reflect the contrasting forces that confront mankind: On the one side, there is the world ("the ways of this world"), Satan ("the ruler of the kingdom of the air, the spirit who is now at work in those who are disobedient"), and the flesh ("the cravings of our sinful nature"); offsetting these are God's mercy, love, and grace, which make life, resurrection, and enthronement with Christ possible.

§6 Salvation from Spiritual Death (Eph. 2:1–3)

2:1 / The main contrast that the apostle makes in this section is between "death" and "life." He begins by reminding his readers of their past condition and then proceeds to describe the causes and effects of their spiritual death. One has to wait until verse 5 to pick up the contrasting idea of life (he "made us alive with Christ") and the features that characterize existence in Christ.

Those who live without Christ are described as being spiritually **dead**. In such a condition there is no desire to relate one's life to God, because such a life is characterized by disobedience (lit., "trespasses," *paraptōma*, and **sins**, *hamartia*). Many attempts have been made to distinguish these two terms and to define trespass as "false step," "deviation from a prescribed path," and so on, and sin as "missing the mark" or "falling short of a standard." However, the usage of these terms in the NT varies and does not permit refined distinctions. In this context it is better to take them as all-encompassing phrases that describe the lives of those who are spiritually dead.

2:2 / Before they became Christians these Gentiles **followed the ways of this world**. The word **followed** in Greek is "walked" (*peripateō*) and expresses one's way of life or manner of moral conduct. The Gospels talk about an open gate or one "way" that leads to life and another to death (Matt. 7:13, 14). Jesus is designated as "the way" (John 14:6), and his disciples are followers of "the Way" (Acts 9:2), "the way of the Lord" (Acts 18:25), and "the way of God" (Acts 18:26).

This "walk" or "way of life" is described by the following statements: First, it is **the ways of this world**. In other words, it is a pattern of life characterized by the world, which, in this context, means what is contrary to and apart from God. First John 2:15–17 aptly comments on this concept by defining "world" as "the cravings of sinful man, the lust of his eyes and the boasting of what he has and does." Paul admonishes believers not to "conform any longer to the pattern of this world, but be transformed by the renewing of your mind" (Rom. 12:2).

Second, it is obedience to **the ruler of the kingdom of the air**. The apostle already has spoken about Christ's exaltation over such spiritual powers (1:21), and he will go on to indicate that believers, likewise, are engaged in a vicious struggle against demonic forces (6:11, 12). Before one becomes a Christian, however, one virtually gives spiritual allegiance to these evil forces, particularly to the **ruler**, who is envisioned as Satan, or the devil (6:11). That ruler is defined further as **the spirit who is now at work in those who are disobedient**. The apostle envisioned that people in their pre–Christian state obeyed Satan and were under the controlling power of evil spirits that led them to disobey God (cf. Luke 11:14–26; John 13:2; Acts 5:3; 2 Thess. 2:9).

2:3 / This dreadful condition of life also applied to Paul and his fellow believers before they became Christians. What was true of the Gentiles was true of all humanity, for "all have sinned and fall short of the glory of God" (Rom. 3:23): **All of us also lived among them**. To live as the Gentiles is to live according to **the cravings of our sinful nature**. This does not appear to be a reference to the doctrine of original sin as taught elsewhere in Scripture (Rom. 1–3; 5:12–14). The phrase is more suggestive of a pattern of life that emerges when one is left to follow one's natural desires.

In such a condition, people do whatever suits the **desires and thoughts** of their **sinful nature**. Literally, the phrase is "lusts of the flesh" (*sarx*). The word *sarx* does not imply that the body is intrinsically evil but refers rather to the sinful principles, passions, or physical appetites that dominate one's life (Gal. 5:19–21). **Thoughts** includes one's intellectual and reasoning ability (cf. Col. 1:21). The consequence of such evil and ungodly action is to become **objects of wrath**. Thus, by following their natural desires, people became subject to the dreadful judgment of God ("we were by nature children of wrath," RSV).

Additional Notes §6

2:1 / On spiritual death, see E. Best, "Dead in Trespasses and Sins (Eph. 2:1)," *JSNT* 13 (1981), pp. 9–25.

2:4–5 / From the perversity of humanity as disobedient sinners deserving God's wrath, the apostle turns, in sharp contrast, to the mercy and love of God. God's mercy proceeds from his love and is his way of reaching out to those totally undeserving. **We were**, he claims, **dead in transgressions**. However, the good news of the gospel is that God has acted decisively in Christ to correct that situation. And finally, in 2:5, one finds the verb that has kept the reader in suspense since the beginning of 2:1: Those who were spiritually dead (2:1) have become the recipients of God's mercy and love in that he **made us alive with Christ**.

This action of God is the first of three experiences that the believer has in union with Christ. Literally, it reads that God's love and mercy have "made us alive together with Christ" (*synezōopoiēsen*), stressing the intimate union believers have with the Lord. All three verbs—"brought us to life," "raised us up," and "to rule with him"—are compound verbs prefixed with the Greek preposition *syn*, which means "together with." These terms express that the believer shares these experiences with Christ and thus with everyone else in the body of Christ. Believers who "die" or are "buried" with Christ (Rom. 6:4, 6, 8; Gal. 2:20; Phil. 3:10; Col. 2:12), also are made alive (Eph. 2:5), raised (Rom. 6:4; Eph. 2:6; Col. 2:12) and enthroned (Eph. 2:6; Col. 3:1).

There is no significant theological distinction between being "made alive" and "raised" with Christ. Both terms vividly contrast with the state of spiritual death that was mentioned earlier. In the Greek text (cf. RSV, NIV) the phrase **it is by grace you have been saved** appears as a parenthesis and receives no further explanation until 2:8. Grace is God's unmerited favor to humanity, and reference to it here is a sharp reminder that the change from death to life is due entirely to God's initiative and not human action. **Saved**, apparently, is equivalent to being brought to life with Christ. It appears in the perfect passive form as **you have been saved** (*sesōsmenoi*)—the tense in Greek that describes a present state that has resulted from a past action. Salvation, therefore, is an accomplished fact (*fait accompli*), and its effects are continuous upon the believer.

2:6 / In addition to life and resurrection, the believer also is exalted (*synēgeiren*) with Christ **and seated . . . with him in the heavenly realms**. Earlier, the apostle had talked about the believer's blessings "in the heavenly realms" (1:3); then he mentioned Christ's exaltation in the "heavenly realms" (1:20); and now the believer, by virtue of his union with Christ, is likewise enthroned in the invisible world of spiritual reality where Christ reigns supreme. The thought resembles Colossians 3:1, where believers are exhorted to set their mind on heavenly things because they have been raised to new life with Christ.

This teaching of the believer's participation in Christ is similar to the thoughts that occur in the baptismal texts of Romans 6:1–11 and Colossians 2:11–13 and 3:1–4. Ephesians, however, makes no mention of the believer's death or burial with Christ in the way in which it is presented in Romans or Colossians. The death of which Ephesians speaks is not the mystical participation in Christ's death but the natural state of humanity as being dead in trespasses and sins. But even though the reference is to people who are "spiritually dead," it is through union with Christ that they have been made alive.

On the basis of the baptismal nature and teaching of Romans and Colossians, it is not unreasonable to assume that the author of Ephesians has the baptismal event in mind when he speaks of the Christian's participation in Christ. Although he does not explicitly mention the rite, his readers would recognize that the language of life, resurrection, and exaltation with Christ alluded to baptism. The new feature in Ephesians is that it places the believer in the heavenlies along with the exalted Lord. By doing this, the author shows that the fullness of life "in Christ" includes all that has happened to Christ himself, including enthronement (1:20). As such, believers already share in Christ's heavenly rule.

The idea of enthronement or exaltation with Christ is difficult to grasp because there is a tendency among believers to think of this as something to be realized in the future—that is, at the end of this present age. Jesus, for example, tells his disciples this: "at the renewal of all things, when the Son of Man sits on his glorious throne, you who have followed me will also sit on twelve thrones, judging the twelve tribes of Israel" (Matt. 19:28; Luke 22:30). And some of the apocalyptic imagery in the NT speaks of a future time when the saints will be resurrected and reign with the Lord (1 Cor. 15:51–54; 1 Thess. 4:17; 2 Tim. 2:12; Rev. 3:21; 20:4; 22:5).

C. L. Mitton has noted in his commentary that some scholars go to great lengths to give a future meaning to the verbs in 2:5 and 6 even though they are in the past tense. They propose that the believer's resurrection can be referred to in the past tense because the future resurrection has already been guaranteed; or, the future state of believers with Christ is so secure that they already have a place in heaven assigned to them (pp. 89–90). These arguments have a certain kinship with the "prophetic future" wherein a coming event is so certain of being fulfilled that it is described as already having taken place.

Such interpretations, however, do not do justice to the thoughts in Ephesians, where the resurrection and exaltation of the believer are described as events that *have taken place* in union with Christ. In a number of cases, such views reflect attempts to make the eschatology of Ephesians—and Colossians—conform to the same pattern developed in the undisputed Pauline epistles.

One of the most significant aspects of Paul's understanding of eschatology is that he conceived of the eschatological process as having begun in the life, death, and resurrection of Christ. For him, these events represented God's breaking into the world and inaugurating his reign on earth. In Christ, therefore, the eschatological promises were already in the process of being fulfilled.

That there is an "inauguration" of the eschatological process does not, however, eliminate the futuristic element. Paul retains the conviction that the eschatological process now begun is moving forward toward a final day of consummation. This has a significant bearing upon Paul's theology because it places the individual in tension between the two aeons—the one begun with the coming of Christ and the one yet to come at his Parousia. The Christian occupies a position between the times because the Kingdom has come and is yet to come. One could characterize this position as the "now" and the "not yet" of Christian existence—one of the great paradoxes of the Christian faith.

Various phases of this paradox are brought out in the Pauline letters. Christ has come (1 Cor. 15:3ff.), yet he will come again (1 Thess. 4:16); the Christian has died to sin (Rom. 6:6), yet he or she is still in the flesh (1 Cor. 3:3); believers are citizens of heaven (Phil. 3:20a), yet eagerly await the Savior to come from heaven (Phil. 3:20b); Christians are new beings—a new creation (2 Cor. 5:17)—yet are to become new people at every moment of their lives (Rom. 12:1–2); believers have the first fruits of the Spirit (Rom. 8:23a), yet groan within themselves as they "wait eagerly for our adoption as sons, the redemption of our bodies" (Rom. 8:23b); here believers receive all of Christ's abundant wealth (Phil. 4:19), yet there is a glory to be revealed (Rom. 8:18).

To a certain extent, Ephesians and Colossians retain a belief in the Parousia as the hope of God's people. In Colossians, the Christian has died with Christ (3:3a), but this new life is hidden with Christ in God, that is, its fullness will be revealed at the Parousia (3:3b); believers are resurrected with Christ (2:12; 3:1) but are, nevertheless, admonished to set their hearts on the things that are in heaven, "where Christ is seated at the right hand of God" (3:1). In Ephesians, the baptized possess the Spirit as a first installment, a guarantee of a future inheritance (4:30). The church has been redeemed but still awaits its final glorification (5:27); the believer has been delivered from evil powers (2:1–5), but finds it necessary to be armed against principalities, powers, and so forth (6:12).

Even in Colossians and Ephesians humankind stands between the times—between promise and fulfillment. In one sense, the new "life" in Christ can be regarded as complete as "death" in Christ. Yet since human beings exist in a real world, Ephesians, as well as Romans and Colossians, lays great stress upon one's ethical life. Those baptized into Christ are to "live a new life" (Rom. 6:4) or are admonished to "set" and to "keep" their minds on things that are in heaven (Col. 3:2). In Ephesians, the author is no less explicit about the Christian's walk. Those baptized into Christ are created to "do good works" (2:10) and are exhorted to "live a life worthy of the calling you received" (4:1).

2:7 / When the apostle spoke about the resurrection and exaltation of Christ, he indicated that this was a demonstration of God's "power" (1:19, 20). But he speaks of the believer's resurrection and exaltation with Christ as a demonstration of **the in-**

comparable riches of [God's] **grace, expressed in his kindness to us in Christ Jesus**.

God already has demonstrated this grace in the present by blessing the believer so richly in Christ. To this, one naturally responds with comments such as "how wonderful," "how marvelous." This, however, is just a foretaste of the ongoing activity of God's grace **in the coming ages**. The reference here is not to the final coming age (cf. previous discussion on 1:21: **in the one** [age] **to come**) but **in the coming ages**. The author's use of the plural (*en tois aiōsin*) probably signifies that he envisions a series of "ages" (?generations) in which the **riches of his** [Christ's] **grace** are extended toward humankind through the church (3:10) until the inauguration of the final age.

2:8–9 / These verses often have been called the heart of Paul's gospel because they capture and summarize the essence of some of the great thoughts that he develops in Romans and Galatians. In this context, grace and faith are mentioned as the key elements in the believer's union with Christ. The apostle dispels any idea that their change in status from spiritual death to life and exaltation with Christ is due to any human effort. He concludes by stating that salvation is a call to a life of good works.

Grace can be defined as favor, graciousness, goodwill, and so on. When it is applied to God, it signifies that action of God by which he moved graciously upon undeserving humanity. The essence of grace is that it is God's (**for it is by grace**) and that it is free; otherwise, it would not be grace.

With respect to salvation, God always is the source of grace. When Scripture speaks about the "grace of our Lord Jesus Christ," it does so to indicate that Christ is the agent of God's grace—that is, he is the means by which God's grace is made known to humanity. Although the agency of Christ is not mentioned here, it definitely is affirmed in the preceding verses, where the parenthetical reference to God's grace (2:5) comes in the context of discussion about life in Christ.

Grace and faith are listed as the two essential elements in salvation. Basically, faith is the means by which God's grace for salvation is appropriated. One popular way of discussing the nature of faith is to develop, in the form of an acrostic, the letters that spell out the word: Forsaking—All—I—Take—Him! One side of faith is *passive*: it is "forsaking all." As such, it implies surrender before God, a willingness on the part of an individual to be open and receptive to God's grace. This, in a sense, also is a gift from God, because one's natural tendency is to be closed and unreceptive to God.

The other side of faith is *active*: "Forsaking all," *I take him.* Those who are willing to receive God's grace must respond personally in order to appropriate it. Faith is personal trust and confidence in God and the reception of the message of salvation that is offered in the gospel. In the NT, Christians are described as believers—that is, as those who have faith (*hoi pisteuontes*, Rom. 1:16; 3:22; 4:11; 1 Cor. 1:21) because they turned to God in faith (*pisteuein*, 1 Cor. 15:2, 11). Faith includes a willingness to surrender as well as a commitment to obey (cf. 2:10).

For it is by grace you have been saved, through faith. As in 2:5, the word for "salvation" occurs in the Greek perfect passive tense, thus reaffirming to the readers that their present and continuing state of salvation is the result of some action in the past when God's grace and their faith came together— undoubtedly when they were baptized into Christ as believers. In the framework of the NT, believers' baptism is a personal response to the proclamation of the gospel (Acts 2:38, 41, etc.).

Some commentators question this occurrence of "salvation" because Paul normally uses the word in the future tense as "you are being saved" (see Mitton, p. 94). Others wonder about the absence of the great Pauline themes of justification and reconciliation. However, believers need to recognize that the NT uses a number of different words and concepts when it talks about salvation or the process whereby one becomes a Christian. When, for example, one wants to know how to receive salvation, Scripture states that salvation is through *faith* (Mark 16:16; Acts 16:30, 31; Rom. 5:1; Eph. 2:8, 9), *repentance* (2 Cor. 7:10; 2 Pet. 3:9), *confession* (Acts 19:18; Rom. 10:9), *regeneration* (Titus 3:5), and *baptism* (Acts 22:16; 1 Cor. 6:11; 1 Pet. 3:21).

Since grace and to some extent faith are gifts of God, the readers are reminded that their salvation is not due to human effort and cannot, therefore, lead to spiritual pride. The principle of grace prohibits boasting (Rom. 3:27). The NIV is a bit ambiguous at this point with respect to the word **this** (*touto*). Because **this** follows immediately after **faith** (**you have been saved through faith—and this not from yourselves, it is the gift of God**, many have taken it to refer to **faith** rather than **grace**, thus emphasizing faith as a gift. But even though the idea is true theologically, the Greek sentence does not permit such an identification, because the two words differ grammatically.

The apostle has more than the gift of faith in mind, for **this** refers to the entire process of salvation of which faith is but a part. And since salvation is all God's doing, one cannot work for it or boast about it. **Not by works** is not the "works of the law" to which Paul referred when he wrote to the Romans (3:20) and to the Galatians (3:10). To these Gentile readers, **works** would be any human efforts directed toward obtaining salvation. If successful, such efforts would lead only to boasting and self-aggrandizement.

2:10 / This verse continues to emphasize God's activity and neatly sums up themes developed earlier in the epistle. First, **we are God's workmanship** (*poiēma*). This idea echoes the entire aspect of rebirth or re-creation that took place **in Christ Jesus** (2:4–6; cf. 2 Cor. 5:17, where Paul writes that "if anyone is in Christ, he is a new creation"). All of this is God's doing and eliminates any sense of pride that would come if this were a "self-creation."

Second, God has **created** us **in Christ Jesus to do good works** (cf. 1:4, 6, 12, 14, 15). The whole context, which emphasizes God's gift of grace and faith, as well as the stress upon being God's creation in Christ, prohibits one from taking **good works** in any meritorious way, even though they are an essential ingredient of one's new life in Christ. The expression means that believers are created with a view *toward* good works; believers are saved *for* or *unto* good works, not *by* or *because of* them. Good works are the outcome, not the cause, of salvation.

The contrast here is between the spiritually dead who once walked (*peripateō*) in disobedience and sin (2:1, 2) and those newly created in Christ to a life (*peripateō*) of good works. Such a life belongs to one's calling as a believer because faith is a call to obedience. And all of this is part of God's will from the beginning. As he chose us "to be holy and blameless in his sight" (1:4), he also determined that faith would issue forth in deeds **which God prepared in advance for us to do**.

This verse stands as a vivid reminder that there is more to salvation than just "getting saved." Though faith in Christ is important and is the beginning of the Christian life (the indicative), believers must remember that they are called to **a life** of faith, a life in which faith is demonstrated in **good works** (the imperative). James, for example, is one of the writers of the NT who places a strong emphasis upon the relation between faith and works (1:22; 2:14–26). On many occasions Christians are called upon to be examples of good deeds before the world (1 Tim. 6:18; Titus 2:7; 1 Pet. 2:12). Jesus put it very clearly when he said "Not everyone who says to me, 'Lord, Lord,' will enter the kingdom of heaven, but only he who does the will of my Father who is in heaven" (Matt. 7:21). C. L. Mitton concludes his discussion on this verse with an appropriate comment: "This final phrase about our 'walking in them' reminds us that fine phrases or eloquent sermons about love are not what is required, but the actions, costly actions, which express in practical conduct the love which God's saving power has created in our hearts" (p. 99).

Additional Notes §7

2:6 / For further direction on Paul's eschatology, see Lohse, *Colossians and Philemon*, pp. 177–83; C. K. Barrett, "Jewish and Pauline Eschatology," *SJT* 6 (1953), pp. 136–55; W. G. Kümmel, *Promise and Fulfillment* (London: SCM, 1957).

2:7 / On the suggestion that the plural, **ages**, reinterprets Paul's eschatology, cf. Mitton, pp. 91–92.

§8 Christ and the Unity of Believers
(Introduction to Eph. 2:11–22)

The apostle is addressing Jewish and Gentile believers in 2:1–10. He begins by showing that both groups of people were living in disobedience and sin; both stood in need of God's mercy and love. The Good News in the passage is that a loving and gracious God acted to correct that through his Son. In union with Christ, believers become a new creation and are resurrected and exalted with their Lord. As such, they are lifted out of their former evil condition that they might share in Christ's victory over sin and live a life of good works.

Up to this point the emphasis is on the privileges that Jewish and Gentile believers enjoy in Christ. In 2:11–22, however, the author moves from their unity in Christ to discuss their unity in the church. In this passage he shows that the church no longer is to be perceived as a body of Jewish and Gentile believers; rather, it is a completely new creation ("one new man" or "people") in which all racial barriers and prejudices are obliterated. For the apostle, the church is a vivid example of how God is working out his plan to unite (1:10) and to complete (1:23) all things in Christ.

In some ways, this concept of a "new people" is a development of thoughts about the new creation in Christ that Paul has expressed in his epistles. In 2 Corinthians 5:16ff., he refers to the process of reconciliation and how *all* humanity is reconciled to God as new beings; in Galatians 6:15 he indicates that racial distinctions are insignificant to the real issue of being a new creation ("Neither circumcision nor uncircumcision means anything; what counts is a new creation"). The new thought in Ephesians is that these "new beings" in Christ now constitute a single new humanity as the body of Christ, the church.

In this section, the author describes the alienation in which the Gentiles found themselves before they became Christians (vv. 11, 12), indicates how Christ made a new people out of two distinct ethnic groups (vv. 13–18), and, by way of the imagery of the heavenly building, shows how the church grows together into a sacred temple in the Lord (vv. 19–22). The entire passage has many liturgical features, draws heavily upon the language of the OT, and is rich in baptismal theology.

Additional Notes   §8

Beyond the commentaries there are some helpful studies dealing with issues in this chapter: W. Barclay, "The One, New Man," in *Unity and Diversity in New Testament Theology*, ed. R. A. Guelich (Grand Rapids: Eerdmans, 1978), pp. 73–81. Barclay's main point is that "new" (*kainos*) means something new in quality and character; E. K. Lee, "Unity in Israel and Unity in Christ," in *Studies in Ephesians*, ed. F. L. Cross, pp. 36–50; Martin, "Reconciliation and Unity in Ephesians," in his *Reconciliation*, pp. 157–98. Martin offers a detailed literary and theological analysis of 2:19–21; W. Meeks, "In One Body: The Unity of Humankind in Colossians and Ephesians," in *God's Christ and His People*, ed. J. Jervell and W. Meeks (Oslo: Universitetsforlaget, 1977), pp. 209–21.

§9 The Gentiles Apart from Christ (Eph. 2:11–12)

The apostle begins by describing the condition of the Gentiles before they became Christians. Though he already has done this to some extent, the emphasis in 2:1–3 was upon their alienation from God as individuals. In that condition, they had many things in common with the Jews, and so the author speaks about all of humanity. He goes on in 2:4–10 to emphasize God's mercy, love, and grace and how God brought mankind into relationship with himself through Christ.

The concern in 2:11–22 is with the national and covenantal alienation between Jews and Gentiles rather than with the spiritual alienation between God and humanity in 2:1–10. Thus the emphasis here is upon those aspects of Christ's redemption that break down divisions and lead to a new people of God characterized by peace and unity. Their past life "separate from Christ" (2:12) and their present life "in Christ Jesus" (2:13) contain some vivid contrasts.

The Gentiles in the Past:	The Gentiles in the Present:
separate from Christ (v. 12)	in himself (v. 15)
far away (vv. 13, 17)	brought near through the blood of Christ (vv. 13, 17)
excluded from citizenship in Israel (v. 12)	fellow citizens with God's people (v. 19)
foreigners to the covenants of promise (v. 12)	no longer foreigners and aliens (v. 19)
without hope (v. 12)	
without God (v. 12)	

2:11 / The Greek text begins with the emphatic **therefore, remember**. On the basis of all that these Gentiles have experienced from God through Christ (1:3–2:10), they are summoned to remember what they were **formerly**. They are addressed as **Gentiles by birth**. The inclusion of the article (lit., "you the Gentiles") indicates that the author is addressing a special class of people. It may be his way of giving special emphasis to the fact that the church is made up of two classes of people. Earlier (2:1, 2), he used only the second person plural ("you") in his reference to them.

Those who were Gentiles **by birth** ("in the flesh") were referred to by the Jews (**the circumcision**) as the **uncircumcised**. Circumcision is a physical rite performed on the Jewish male as a sign of the covenant (Gen. 17:11). Although circumcision is used in a spiritual sense in Scripture as something that God performs upon the human heart—thus not made with hands (Deut. 10:16; Rom. 2:28, 29; 4:11; 1 Cor. 7:19; Phil. 3:3; Col. 2:11)—the emphasis here is upon the human rite because it is **that done in the body by the hands of men**. Apparently, then, the Gentiles were distinguished from the Jews both by birth and by the outward physical rite of circumcision. These two facts provide the basis for the conditions listed in the next verse.

2:12 / In the past (**at that time**) the Gentiles were **separate from Christ**. In one sense, this was their major deprivation, for to be without Christ himself is to be deprived of any of the blessings that he gives. Hence the author mentions Christ for this very reason: As they have been blessed spiritually in Christ (2:1–10), he reminds them that it is through union with Christ that they are made one with the Jews and partake of the blessings that were theirs as God's covenant people. To be **separate** from Christ stands in sharp contrast to being "in Christ Jesus" (2:13). Since the first reference is just to "Christ" (in contrast to Christ Jesus), it could be that a reference to "the Messiah" is intended.

You were . . . foreigners to the covenants. This means that as Gentiles they were strangers or foreigners to the covenants that God made with his people. These covenants include those made with Abraham (Gen. 15:8–21; 17:1–21) and Moses (Exod. 24:1–11) and the new and everlasting covenants about which the prophets spoke (cf. Isa. 55:3; Jer. 31:31–34; Ezek. 37:26).

The covenants that God made with Israel served both a present and future function in that they established Israel as God's special people and assured them of God's continued presence (they were **covenants of the promise**). The wording of the Greek text ("covenants of promise"), together with a possible reference to "the Messiah," suggests that the author may have those particular covenants in mind that promised the Messiah. But as Gentiles they were not entitled to any of the provisions that God had made for, or any of the promises he had made to, his chosen people.

Another aspect of their former estranged condition is that they were **excluded from citizenship in Israel**. The Greek uses the rather strong word *apallotrioō*, which conveys the ideas of estrangement or alienation (cf. RSV). Not belonging to Israel (lit., "commonwealth," "polity," *politeia*) meant that they had no rights of citizenship and no participation in the national or religious life of the Israelites. And since Israel was the only nation to whom God had revealed himself in a special way, the Gentiles had no access to the true God. Their life in **the world** was lived **without hope and without God**.

Given the context in which the word **hope** appears, it most naturally refers to the Gentiles' general state of hopelessness: they do not belong to God's people and do not, therefore, share in the hope of the coming Messiah. In Christianity, people **without hope** are those who have no certainty in the future events that pertain to the Lord's return and everlasting life (Acts 23:6; 1 Cor. 15:29, 32; Col. 1:5, 27; 1 Thess. 2:19; 4:13; 1 Pet. 1:3; 3:5).

J. A. Robinson makes an interesting observation about Jewish hope and Gentile hopelessness when he writes: "The Jew had a hope: the Gentile had none. The golden age of the Gentile was in the past: his poets told him of it, and how it was gone. The Jew's golden age was in the future; his prophets told him to look forward to its coming" (p. 57). For a short period of time the Greek mystery religions, with their doctrines of purification, immortality, brotherhood, and so forth, offered a ray of hope to the Greeks and Romans. This, however, never approximated the Jewish belief in the coming kingdom of God or the certainty of Christianity, which based its hope on the verities of Christ's life and resurrection.

The Gentile's life in this world was also **without God**. This appears as a rather strange characterization of a people who were noted for their idolatry and polytheism (many gods). When Paul visited Athens, for example, "he was greatly distressed to see that the city was full of idols" (Acts 17:16). The irony is that, though there were "many 'gods' and many 'lords' " (1 Cor. 8:5), they were, in effect, "no gods" (Acts 19:26; cf. 17:22–31; 1 Cor. 8:4, 6;

Gal. 4:8). By believing in idols or self-conceived deities, the Gentiles really had nothing—they were **without God**. The Greek word *atheos*, from which the word "atheist" comes, occurs only here in the NT. In Greek literature, it was used to describe people who either were without God's help, lived in a godless manner, or did not believe in God at all (see Abbott, p. 59).

2:13 / The Good News of the gospel is that Christ came into an alienated and hopeless world to reverse the misfortunes of the Gentiles: **But now in Christ Jesus you who once were far away have been brought near through the blood of Christ**. There is nothing in the previous two verses that corresponds with the ideas of **far away** and **near** other than the obvious distance between the privileged Jew and the deprived Gentile. The imagery here comes from Isaiah 57:19, where the prophet says: " 'Peace, peace to those far and near,' says the Lord. 'And I will heal them.' " These are the same words that Peter uses in his sermon on the day of Pentecost, when he is addressing a mixed audience (Acts 2:39; cf. also Rom. 10:15). According to Ephesians, nearness to God has been made possible **through the blood of Christ**.

2:14–15 / Since the author returns to the concepts of "far away" and "near" in 2:17, it appears that 2:14–16 is a rather long parenthesis on how Christ's death brought a divided humanity together. He already has given a number of reasons why the Jews and the Gentiles differed from each other (2:11, 12). These racial, social, and religious distinctions resulted in various expressions of hostility and enmity.

The apostle refers to the Jewish **law with its commandments and regulations** as the cause of the divisions that existed between Jews and Gentiles. The effect of that "law," he states, was like a wall that separated both races and kept them apart as enemies. However, through Christ's death the wall was broken down, a new humanity was created. Gentiles and Jews were reconciled to each other, and both were reconciled to God.

The phrase **for he himself is our peace** is much more emphatic than it appears in English. Though it is true that he is the source of peace and brings peace through his life, he *is* peace— he gives peace because *he himself is peace*. This peace came about because Jews and Gentiles were made one people. The concept is reminiscent of Galatians 3:28, where Paul states that "there is neither Jew nor Greek, . . . for you are all one in Christ Jesus."

Once again, the author turns to the role that Christ played in effecting this peace. In verse 13 he refers to the blood (i.e., death) of Christ; now he states that **in his flesh** he abolished **the law with its commandments and regulations** (the author may consciously be using **flesh** [*sarx*] in this context to refer to the Incarnation—cf. Rom. 8:3; Gal. 4:4; Heb. 2:14). The practical effect of this, however, was to abolish the barriers that separated Jews and Gentiles.

The image of **the dividing wall** that Christ **destroyed** must be understood in connection with the reference to the **law** that follows in 2:15. Basically, **the dividing wall** is a symbol of the divisions that the Mosaic law ("the law of the commandments in ordinances," KJV) created and that kept the two races from having social and religious intercourse.

There has been considerable speculation with respect to the **wall** that is mentioned. Most scholars tend to believe that the author is referring to the wall that separated the Gentiles and the Jews in the temple area. Josephus, a Jewish historian in the first century, describes this wall as a stone barrier about five feet high (*Antiquities* 15.11). Gentiles may have wanted to approach the temple out of curiosity or to offer gifts and sacrifices to the God of the Jews. Hence, warnings were posted at appropriate places to remind them of their limits and the severity of punishment that would follow if the barrier were crossed. One such warning, now in the Museum of Constantinople, was discovered by archaeologists in 1871. Translated from the Greek, it reads:

NO MAN OF ANOTHER NATION TO ENTER WITHIN THE FENCE AND ENCLOSURE ROUND THE TEMPLE. AND WHO-EVER IS CAUGHT WILL HAVE HIMSELF TO BLAME THAT HIS DEATH ENSUES (quoted in Robinson, p. 60).

The seriousness of this is portrayed in Acts 21:27ff., where Paul is accused of bringing Greeks ("Trophimus the Ephesian," no less) into the temple area and thus defiling "this holy place."

This wall, which so dramatically symbolized Jewish separatism, was broken down along with the temple when Jerusalem was destroyed by the Roman general Titus in A.D. 70. But the destruction of that physical wall hardly eliminated the internal barriers that the Jewish law had erected: That took place through the death of Christ when he abolished **the law with its commandments and regulations**. This meant the abolition of all distinctions that separated Jew and Gentile.

Other, but less common, views of the meaning of **wall** include (*a*) the curtain in the temple that separated the Holy Place from the Holy of Holies; (*b*) a rabbinic statement about building "a fence around the law"; (*c*) sin, which is a separation between God and humanity; or (*d*) a Gnostic concept of some kind of wall that divided the spheres of heaven and earth (see Barth, *Eph. 1–3*, pp. 283–87).

The **commandments and regulations** are a reference to the ceremonial laws, including dietary regulations, circumcision, rites of purification, sabbath and festival observances, sacrifices, and so forth. Colossians 2:8–23, which likewise mentions the abolition of rules and regulations, expands the list beyond Jewish ceremonial law because it is dealing with a number of man-made proscriptions that the false teachers had added ("Do not handle . . . taste . . . touch!"). There the emphasis is on the believers in Colossae not becoming enslaved to such legalism, because in Christ they have been freed from these powers. In Ephesians, the point is that the abolition of the law unites two previously alienated and hostile groups.

The breaking down of this ceremonial law, however, did not mean that all moral standards were abolished. The early Christians adopted many of the moral teachings of Judaism into their theology as long as they conformed to the standard that Christ taught or that he fulfilled in his life (cf. the Sermon on the Mount, esp., Matt. 5:17–48). Stott mentions that although Jesus did not abolish the moral law "as a standard of behavior," he did abolish it "as a way of salvation" (p. 101).

It took the early church considerable time to realize the implications of this truth and to effect what was true in principle. Theologically, it is a process begun by Stephen in Acts (chap. 7) and worked out by Paul in Romans and Galatians. Practically, some of the divisions never were abolished completely, because the Jewish Christians in Jerusalem and Palestine remained more Jewish in theology and practice than their brethren outside Palestine (the Diaspora).

The largest percentage of early Christians were Jewish believers (Acts 1–12) who never fully separated themselves from

Judaism. When the Gentile mission was inaugurated, some of these Jewish Christians, represented by the Jerusalem and Palestinian churches, felt that the Gentiles should either become Jews before they became Christians—that is, submit to circumcision and the law (the extreme view)—or at least be sensitive to Jewish food laws in cases of social fellowship. The account of Peter's vision at the home of Simon the Tanner recounts how God declared that all foods are clean (Acts 10:1–43). The details of this and their implications for the Gentile mission are discussed at the Jerusalem council (Acts 15:1–35) as well as in Galatians 2.

The Good News in Ephesians is that Christ's death abolished the legal distinctions that separated Jews and Gentiles: The former divisive effect of the law is annulled and has lost its power (cf. Col. 2:15). Instead of enmity between the two races there is **peace**; in place of two separate entities there is **one new man** (people).

The effect of Christ's work in breaking down the barrier is twofold: First, it resulted in the creation of a new humanity (**his purpose was to create in himself one new man out of the two**). There is more here than simply the union or the mixture of two groups. This is not a case of the Greeks conquering the Jews or the Jews converting the Greeks to their faith and way of life. Rather, it is a completely new creation (**one new man**) that Christ has effected in union with himself (Gal. 3:28; Col. 3:11). To a certain extent, the church is the sum total of individuals who have become "new creatures" in Christ (2 Cor. 5:17; Gal. 6:15; Col. 3:10); but the author is thinking of something more profound—namely, the church as a corporate entity.

2:16 / Second, there is the aspect of reconciliation, which, for the apostle, has two foci: On the one side, the church effected a reconciliation between Jew and Gentile. The broken barrier—accomplished **through the cross**—and the creation of the church ("one new people") meant that the enmity between these two races was replaced by peace. Here the author uses the phrase "having slain (*apokteinas*) the enmity." The imagery of the cross suggests that he who himself was slain (Heb. 2:14) is now the one who slays (destroys) the enmity. Peace is illustrated by the metaphor of the body, the church. Jews and Gentiles are reconciled to each other because they are united into **one body** by means of the cross. Thus the church is presented as a living organism, composed of diverse parts, but existing peacefully as one body (cf. 4:4; 1 Cor. 10:17; 12:13; Col. 3:15).

The other side of Christ's work is that he brought about reconciliation between humanity and God (**to reconcile both of them**—i.e., the two who have been united in one body—**to God**). Here there is no question of Jewish privilege or Greek ignorance, since both are equally represented as objects of reconciliation: Through Christ's work on the cross, God "reconciled us to himself" (2 Cor. 5:18; cf. also Rom. 5:10).

2:17 / Before the author develops this concept of access, he turns from Christ the reconciler to Christ the proclaimer: **He came and preached peace to you who were far away and peace to those who were near.** The idea of **peace** may be taken from Isaiah 57:19, which he used earlier (2:13), or he may be utilizing Isaiah 52:7, which announces: "How beautiful on the mountains are the feet of those who bring good news, who proclaim peace."

Most scholars take Christ's preaching as an act related to his death-resurrection-exaltation and not to his earthly pre-resurrection ministry. The context appears to favor the idea that the peace that he effected on the cross is itself a proclamation and his way of announcing to the world that peace has been made. This verse could be in reference to Christ's post-resurrection appearances, in which his first followers are told not to fear (Matt. 28:5, 10), or to his benediction of peace in John 14:27 ("Peace I leave with you; my peace I give you"). However, there is much to be said for the view that takes it as the preaching of the earthly Jesus himself or, at least, as the preaching of his disciples.

Jesus does adopt the words of Isaiah 61:1, 2, as his life's mission ("the Spirit of the Lord is on me, because he has anointed me to preach good news to the poor," Luke 4:18, 19), and he does become involved with a segment of society that could be considered "far away" (cf. Mitton, pp. 109–10). But regardless of what view one may take, the important point is that in the Christ event (life-death-resurrection-exaltation), peace was achieved and access to God was made possible. Thus the author reminds his readers that it is through Christ that Jews and Gentiles "both have access to the Father by one Spirit" (2:18).

2:18 / Perhaps there is an allusion here to the curtain in the inner temple that separated the people from God and through

which only the high priest had access on the Day of Atonement
(Heb. 9:1-14). The Good News of the gospel, however, is that
Christ opened up a way of access to God by removing the curtain through his death (Heb. 10:19ff.). The imagery suggested by
the idea of "access" (*prosagōgē*) is that of an Oriental court where
subjects were presented to their monarch by a *prosagōgos*.

In the church, it is Christ who has made the way into God's
presence possible ("in him and through faith in him we may approach God with freedom and confidence," Eph. 3:12). Access
to God is through the **one Spirit** because all Christians are united
by one Spirit in their baptism into Christ (1 Cor. 12:12, 13; Eph.
4:1-6). And as a church (the body of Christ), they now are a fellowship of the Holy Spirit. In addition to this verse, the role of
the Spirit in worship is mentioned in 3:18-20 and in a similar passage in Colossians (3:16, 17).

There are a number of things that suggest that the author
may have baptism in mind throughout this entire discussion
(2:11-18). First, baptism provides the best answer as to where and
when all this took place for the Jew and the Gentile—that is, when
the "far away" were brought near and, together with the "near,"
united with Christ and made members of one another in the body
of Christ. To be sure, Christ accomplished that at the time of his
death on the cross, but the believer makes that his or her own
through faith and baptism in Christ.

Second, there are many close parallels in this passage to
the two baptismal passages in Colossians: Ephesians 2:11 is remarkably similar to Colossians 2:11-13; and 2:11-18 may be an
adaptation of the Christ hymn in Colossians 1:15-20, which has
considerable support as a baptismal hymn (see disc. on Col.
1:15-20).

Third, and perhaps most convincing, are those baptismal
passages that specifically mention baptism into Christ as the
means of breaking down all barriers, including racial distinctions.
Thus Paul writes to the Galatians, "You . . . were baptized into
Christ. . . . There is neither Jew nor Greek" (3:27, 28). And in
Colossians the baptismal imagery of "putting off" and "putting
on" is utilized, with the result that baptism eliminates the differences between Gentiles and Jews (3:9-11). It could be said
that the author turns to baptismal language in Ephesians 2:11-18
to support his theological assertion of the unity between Jew

and Gentile as one new people in Christ. Furthermore, since baptism is mentioned in his famous section on unity (4:1–6), one could infer that he understood baptism as the sacrament of unity (1 Cor. 12:13).

Additional Notes §10

2:14–15 / M. S. Moore presents a detailed analysis of these verses in his "Ephesians 2:15–16: A History of Recent Interpretation," *EQ* 54 (1982), pp. 163–69. For understanding the nature of Jewish and Gentile Christianity in the early church, see L. Goppelt, *Apostolic and Post-Apostolic History* (New York: Harper Torchbooks, 1970), esp. chap. 3, pp. 61–107.

2:17 / A thorough discussion of the expressions **near** and **far** is given by D. C. Smith, "The Ephesian Heresy and the Origin of the Epistle to the Ephesians," *Ohio Journal of Religious Studies* 5 (1977), pp. 78–103. Smith's investigation leads him to conclude that it is not that Gentile Christianity was threatening to lose its connection with Jewish Christianity, but "rather the issue is that certain Gentile-'Jewish'-Christians, on the basis of traditions derived in large part from Hellenistic Judaism, are displaying contempt toward natural Jews who have become Christians. These opponents of the author of Ephesians, then, represent a fascinating synthesis of esoteric elements drawn from Judaism, Christianity, and Hellenistic religion in general" (p. 103).

These verses concerning the incorporation of the Gentiles into a sacred temple in the Lord conclude the section on Christian unity (2:11–22). **Consequently** has the effect of pointing back to what was said in the previous verses and linking it to what follows. The main thought is that, because the Gentiles are now in Christ and have access in one Spirit to the Father, they are no longer "foreigners and aliens, but fellow citizens with God's people and members of God's household." By virtue of their faith in Jesus Christ, the "cornerstone," they are like an edifice that is built upon the foundation of "apostles and prophets" and that "rises to become a holy temple in the Lord."

2:19 / Now that the apostle has discussed the effects that Christ's death had upon Jews and Gentiles (2:14–18), he returns to his discussion of the Gentiles to complete the contrasts that he began earlier. At one time they were foreigners who did not belong to God's people (2:12), but now they are no longer **foreigners** (*xenos*) or **aliens** (*paroikos*). **Foreigners** are people outside a country or community, with no special rights or privileges. The word for **aliens** (*paroikos*) often is translated as "sojourners," a term that accentuates the transient nature of the Gentiles. In that condition they were like aliens with an "immigrant visa," which granted them limited rights and privileges, but not full citizenship or permanent residency.

But the status of the Gentiles has changed remarkably: First, the author uses a political expression and affirms that they are now **fellow citizens** (*sympolitai*) **with God's people**, that is, they are on equal standing with the historic people of God. Second, he uses the imagery of a building (*oikos*) to affirm that they are **members of God's household**.

2:20 / From the concept of the **household** or "family" (*oikos*) of God, the author turns to discuss the building (*oikodomē*) of this family, utilizing an architectural metaphor. The language reemphasizes that the Gentiles are part of an ongoing process: You, too, are **built on the foundation of the apostles and prophets**.

If the Gentiles had been guilty of forgetting or even scorning their relationship to God's redemptive work in history, these words would serve as a significant reminder that they are not the first or only people in God's eternal plan. Rather, they have been built (the Greek aorist tense refers to something that has happened) upon a foundation that already had been laid.

Apostles and prophets form the foundation of the church. Though some commentators take **prophets** to mean those in the OT, the word order—**apostles and prophets**—makes it more likely that the author has the NT prophets in mind (cf. Acts 11:27ff.; 1 Cor. 12:28, 29; 14:1–5, 24ff.). Both offices are used again in Ephesians (3:5; 4:11) with a clear reference to the NT period. They are considered the foundation of the church because of their importance as messengers and interpreters of the gospel.

The thoughts that the author is developing differ slightly from the picture that Paul gives in Corinthians. In Corinth, he is dealing with a divided church—a church that has polarized around Paul, Peter, Christ, and Apollos. Paul seeks to dispel party strife by showing that the ministry is the cooperative effort of a number of individuals, all of whom are servants of God and partners with each other (1 Cor. 1:10–13; 3:5–9). To anyone seeking to be the foundation of God's building, Paul warns that "no one can lay any foundation other than the one already laid, which is Jesus Christ" (1 Cor. 3:11). In Ephesians, the **apostles and prophets** are **the foundation** and Jesus becomes the **chief cornerstone** (cf. 1 Pet. 2:4–8—quoting Isa. 28:16 and Ps. 118:22—where Christ is interpreted as the cornerstone).

The reasons for this apparent shift are not easy to discern. One author suggests that, by the time Ephesians was written, Christ's centrality in the church was guaranteed, but because of the heresies that threatened the church, it became necessary to establish an authentic line of tradition through the apostles and prophets (Houlden, p. 292). T. K. Abbott reasons that the cornerstone was more important to Orientals because of its function in connecting and bearing the weight of the building (p. 71). This view does have some appeal, because in the context of the passage the emphasis is upon the function of Christ in keeping this growing structure unified. The cornerstone would have provided the key around which the foundation and the superstructure were built (Stott, pp. 107–8).

Though it is natural to think of the cornerstone as being on the foundational level of a building, there is an attractive alternative to this concept that takes the phrase not as a foundation stone but as a "keystone" to be placed at the summit of a building to crown its completion. Some believe that this is a more fitting explanation of the thought in Ephesians, where Christ is the head of the body (1:22) and the church grows into him who is the head (4:15).

The variety of interpretations of the difficult imagery and syntax should not distract the reader from the central message of this passage. The apostle is showing that the church consists of three significant elements: (*a*) the Gentiles, who are now part of God's people, and the Jews; (*b*) the apostles and prophets; and (*c*) Jesus Christ. But this is more than just a random combination of parts: They are joined together by the principle of unity and growth.

2:21 / The construction of this verse in the Greek is ambiguous and has led to a variety of translations and interpretations. Literally, it reads, "in whom every structure (*pasa oikodomē*) is joined together" (*synarmologeō*). The big question is whether *pasa oikodomē* should be translated as "every structure" or "the whole structure" and whether the thoughts should be taken literally or metaphorically.

Those opting for the former believe that this "sacred temple in the Lord" is like the Jewish temple, in which many buildings, rooms, and parts (see Moule, p. 85; Westcott, p. 41) made up the "whole temple." Mitton accepts "every structure" as preferred grammatically but gives it a metaphorical rather than literal meaning. Hence, he follows a line of interpretation that takes the "parts" as the local congregations that make up the one universal or catholic church (p. 115).

From the context of the passage, however, one seriously wonders whether the apostle has local congregations in mind, because he has been so concerned about the unity of the entire body. Robinson, for one, admits that the words are ambiguous but, within the context of the passage, emphasizes the process of building and takes the phrase to mean "all that is builded," that is, whatever building is being done (pp. 70, 165). What is in the author's mind, therefore, is the entire operation of the building rather than single structures that make up the whole (cf. also Abbott, pp. 74, 75. Barth, *Eph. 1–3*, p. 272; Foulkes, p. 87). The NIV follows this line of interpretation in its translation, **in him the whole building is joined together.**

The concept of a building process is continued in the following phrase: Christ is the one in whom it **rises to become a holy temple in the Lord.** Though the imagery is that of a building, the next verse (2:22) makes it clear that the author has a spiritual "house" in mind where God's presence is manifested. The **holy temple** is the translation of *naon hagion—naos* being the inner part of the temple where God was believed to reside and meet his people. In early Christian theology, believers are referred to as God's sacred temple, not in a material sense, but as a "spiritual building" where God dwells and manifests himself. Christians are that **holy** (or "sacred") temple by virtue of being in the Lord.

2:22 / Once again, the apostle emphasizes that the Gentiles have a part in all of this: **In him you too are being** (present tense) **built together to become a dwelling in which God lives by his Spirit.** This concept is reminiscent of Paul's ideas in his Corinthian letters, where he reminds the congregation that they are God's building—temple—in whom the Spirit of God dwells (1 Cor. 3:9, 16ff.; 2 Cor. 6:16). To the Gentiles, all of this stands as a vivid contrast to the beginning of their lives, which was "in the body" (2:11).

This passage (2:19–22) contains a number of striking linguistic and conceptual parallels with the liturgical hymn in 1 Peter 2:4–10. Both epistles, for example, refer to Christ as the cornerstone and emphasize that Christians are part of a building process that is growing into a spiritual temple. First Peter speaks of the "stone" rejected by the builders but that has become the elected cornerstone in Zion to the believing Gentiles.

In Ephesians, there is confirmation that the Gentiles, who were at one time far off, distant from the commonwealth of Israel, have been brought near and have become one with the people of God. In 1 Peter 2:9, 10, those who have been called out of darkness into light have now become the people of God; in Ephesians, this idea of the Gentiles becoming God's people is emphasized throughout 2:11–22, although the imagery of darkness and light is not used until 5:8–14 (cf. Col. 1:12, 13).

These similarities between 2:19–22 and 1 Peter 2:4–10 suggest that there was a tradition in the early church that described the role of Christ, the new status of Gentile believers (the indicative), and their ultimate goal (the imperative) by utilizing building imagery. Given the liturgical nature of both passages, it is not unreasonable to infer that these texts were used by the Gentile churches to celebrate their incorporation into the family of God. Although the imagery is different, there is a remarkable similarity in thought between the believers' union with Christ and their incorporation into Christ's body at the time of baptism.

Additional Notes §11

2:20 / This idea of a "keystone" apparently was first initiated by J. Jeremias in his article *"akrogōnias," TDNT*, vol. 1, p. 792, and is championed by Barth in *Eph. 1–3*, pp. 317–19. Mitton lists a number of objections to this theory and sticks with the traditional view, which sees Jesus as the cornerstone of the building "from which the future building will be gauged" (p. 115). This view is also supported by R. J. McKelvey, "Christ the Cornerstone: Eph. 2.11–22," *NTS* 8 (1962), pp. 352–59. McKelvey concludes that "the interpretation which explains *akrogōniaios* of Eph. ii.20 as a topstone is to be abandoned in favor of the traditional understanding of *akrogōniaios* as a stone connected to the foundation of the building, which was located at one of the corners (probably the determinative corner) and bound together the walls and the foundation" (p. 359). For further comments, see F. F. Bruce, "New Wine in Old Wine Skins: III. The Corner Stone," *ExpT* 84 (1973), pp. 231–35.

§12 Paul and the Mission to the Gentiles (Introduction to Eph. 3:1–21)

When the apostle completed his section on the spiritual blessings in Christ (1:3–14), he proceeded to offer a prayer of thanksgiving and petition (1:15–23). After this theological discussion in 2:1–22, it appears that he is once again ready to turn to prayer because the statement, "For this reason" (3:1), refers to what he has just said; furthermore, the actual prayer in 3:14ff. appears to relate to this section and would be a fitting climax to the thoughts that he has developed. But instead of a prayer, the apostle's thought is diverted to another topic of discussion— one that is related to Paul's call and mission as a proclaimer of God's secret. After a rather lengthy presentation of this subject (3:2–13), he returns to his initial intention to pray and subsequently offers one of the most beautiful and comprehensive prayers in the NT.

At first glance, Ephesians 3:2–13 appears to be a rather lengthy parenthesis vindicating Paul's apostleship to the Gentiles. The author has been discussing the unity of Jews and Gentiles in Christ and how the Gentiles are legitimate heirs of God's salvation (2:11–22); but for some reason he finds it necessary to define more precisely God's secret and the human agent through whom it was revealed. His definition of the secret (3:6) also extends previous imagery. In 2:19–22 the Gentiles were considered fellow citizens who are joined and built together into a sacred temple. The theme of unity is reemphasized in 3:6 by a number of similar expressions: "Through the gospel the Gentiles are heirs together with Israel, members together of one body, and sharers together in the promise in Christ Jesus."

There are many close similarities between Ephesians 3:1–13 and Colossians 1:23–2:2:

Ephesians	*Colossians*
3:1—I, Paul, the prisoner of Christ Jesus	1:23—I, Paul, have become a servant
3:2—God's grace that was given to me for you	1:25—the commission God gave me to present to you the word of God
3:3—the mystery made known to me by revelation	1:27—God has chosen to make known among the Gentiles . . . this mystery
3:4—you will be able to understand my insight into the mystery of Christ	2:2—in order that they may know the mystery of God, namely, Christ
3:6—through the gospel the Gentiles are heirs together with Israel, members together of one body, and sharers together in the promise in Christ Jesus	1:27—this mystery, which is Christ in you, the hope of glory
3:8—Although I am . . . least . . . this grace was given to me: to preach to the Gentiles the unsearchable riches of Christ	1:27—God has chosen to make known among the Gentiles the glorious riches of this mystery
3:9—to make plain to everyone the administration of this mystery	1:26—the mystery . . . but . . . now disclosed to the saints
3:10—through the church the manifold wisdom of God should be made known	1:26—the mystery . . . hidden for ages and generations, but . . . now disclosed
3:13—[do not] be discouraged because of my sufferings for you	1:24—I rejoice in what was suffered for you

In both epistles, the author is in prison and is suffering; he is considered the minister to the Gentiles; the "mystery" has been hidden but is now revealed; this secret is identified as the inclusion of the Gentiles in God's plan of salvation; it is the message that Paul has been commissioned to preach.

There are, however, some notable differences between these two epistles as well. In Colossians, the call of Paul as a missionary to the Gentiles (1:25, 26) is not as specific as in Ephesians (3:8), where he definitely is identified as a prisoner of Christ Jesus for the sake of the *Gentiles*, to whom his preaching is directed (cf. Acts 21:17–34; 22:21–24; 26:12–23).

The goal of Paul's preaching varies slightly also: In Colossians, the proclamation is given "so that we may present everyone perfect in Christ" (1:28); in Ephesians, it is oriented specifically

toward the revelation of the "mystery" ("to make plain to everyone the administration of this mystery"). Ephesians does not
touch upon the aspect of Christian maturity until 4:13.

But the main difference centers upon the nature of this
"mystery" that Paul has been called to preach. The brief mention of this in Colossians 1:27 almost goes unnoticed and hardly
gives any indication of what the secret is all about. Ephesians,
however, definitely is concerned about defining the "mystery"
(3:6) and presenting Paul as its chief exponent.

In 3:14–19, the author begins his prayer for spiritual growth
and unity. The specific requests include strengthening of the
readers' inner selves by God's Spirit (3:16), the indwelling of
Christ in their hearts through faith (3:17a), a strong grounding
in love (3:17b), comprehending the love of Christ (3:18–19a), and
being filled with the perfect fullness of God (3:19b). In some ways,
these requests are not unlike his earlier mention of wisdom (1:17),
knowledge (1:17), and enlightenment for the readers (1:18).

There is no specific reference to the problem of the unity
of the church. Mention of the Fatherhood of God (3:14) and the
comprehension of Christ's love by all God's people (3:18) does,
nevertheless, remind the readers that their unity in Christ is to
result in a unified Christian fellowship. The writer uses the expression "the saints" (*hoi hagioi*) on a number of occasions in the
sense of belonging or togetherness (1:1, 15, 18; 2:19; 3:18; 6:18).

The concluding benediction (3:20, 21) points out that God
is able to do far more than is requested, because the power of
Christ is at work within the believer. The mention of the church
is significant, for it is the sphere of the outworking of God's
purpose on earth as well as in heaven (3:10). In stating this,
Ephesians extends the mission of the church beyond that taught
in Colossians.

The new features of this chapter center around the clarification of God's "mystery," the prominence of Paul as an exponent of that secret, and the cosmic mission of the church. Beyond
that, there is a definite repetition of the ideas used earlier in the
epistle, for example:

the mystery as made known by
  revelation   3:3   = 1:9
the role of apostles and prophets 3:5   = 2:20
the inheritance of the saints   3:6   = 1:14

the grace and power of God	3:7, 20	= 1:19
God's eternal plan	3:9	= 1:10; 2:7
the cosmic scope	3:10	= 1:3, 10
God's eternal purpose	3:11	= 1:4
access to God	3:12	= 2:12
God the Father	3:14, 15	= 1:17
the Son	3:11, 17	= 1:3, etc.
the Spirit	3:5, 16	= 1:13, 14; 2:22
the fullness of God	3:19	= 1:23

§13 Presenting the Mystery of the Gospel (Eph. 3:1–13)

3:1 / As indicated in the introduction, the phrase **for this reason** points back to the theological ideas that have been developed in the preceding section and that lead the apostle to prayer. **I, Paul,** is an emphatic expression designed to draw attention to the apostle and what he has to say (cf. 2 Cor. 10:1; Gal. 5:2; Col. 1:23; 1 Thess. 2:18). What is emphasized is that Paul is **the prisoner of Christ Jesus** for the sake of the Gentiles. The NIV rightly translates the article before prisoner as **the** rather than "a" prisoner (RSV). Thus Paul is represented, not as one prisoner among many, but as *the* prisoner of Christ Jesus, because of the significance of his ministry to the Gentiles (Acts 21:17–34; 22:21–24; 26:12–23). **Gentiles** is an inclusive term and, as in 2:11, refers not to any one specific congregation but to all Gentiles (**Gentiles** also is preceded by an article and should read **you the Gentiles**). Other references to Paul's imprisonment are found in 6:20, Philippians 1:7, Colossians 4:10, and Philemon 1 and 9.

3:2 / The NIV (and GNB) **surely you have heard** is a better translation than the RSV "assuming that you have heard," which implies some kind of doubt rather than verification (cf. 4:21; Col. 1:23). The phrase does raise a question about the Ephesian destination of the epistle, but fits the "circular letter theory," which would include a number of Gentile congregations.

In the process of developing Paul's role as the missionary to the Gentiles, the author mentions several important things: First, God gave Paul a commission (**the administration** [*oikonomia*] **of God's grace that was given to me for you**); second, God gave him **grace**. Though Paul does connect God's grace with his mission (3:7, 8; 4:7; Rom. 1:5; 12:3; 15:15–16), it is God's **grace** and not the work that is given in this context. This is slightly different from Colossians 1:25, where it is the office (*oikonomia*) that was given (cf. Mitton, pp. 125, 126).

3:3–4 / In the next ten verses the author concentrates upon the mystery and how God used Paul to reveal that plan to the Gentiles. He begins by referring to **the mystery made known to me by revelation**. This follows the connection between revelation and the **mystery** that was alluded to in 1:9 and 10, but affirms that this revelation is from God and not something that Paul concluded from his studies or received from tradition (cf. Gal. 1:12, 16; 2:2).

Before the meaning of this mystery is developed, the author reminds his readers that he already has **written briefly** about this. Though a few commentators see an allusion in this phrase to an earlier epistle(s) to a Gentile audience, most take it as a reference to the brief mention of the "mystery" in 1:9–10 and to the outworking of it through the Jews and the Gentiles in 2:11ff. With that as background material, they can go on and **understand** the apostle's **insight into the mystery of Christ**. The author is confident that as they read—probably in a public worship service and then in private meditation—they will be able to appreciate the significance of Paul as a servant of Christ with respect to the **mystery**. It is unlikely that it refers to a reading of the OT (see Foulkes, p. 92).

Concerning the use of **mystery**, a number of items should be noted: In Colossians (1:27) the mystery is the rather mystical concept of the indwelling Christ ("Christ in you, the hope of glory"); in Colossians 4:3, the "mystery of Christ" alludes to the fact that the Gentiles are recipients of the gospel (cf. Rom. 16:25, 26); in Ephesians 1:9, the mystery is God's plan to unite all creation through the agency of Christ; in Ephesians 3:4, along with 3:6, the mystery is the unity between Jew and Gentile. This has partially been explained in 1:9–10 and 2:11–22, but now is made more explicit. Ephesians takes the concept of "the mystery" from a revelation of a gospel that included the Gentiles (Colossians) and develops it into a doctrine on the unity between Jew and Gentile in the church (3:6).

3:5 / This verse closely resembles Colossians 1:26, which talks about the mystery that was hidden through all past ages from all humankind but that God has now revealed to his people. There are, however, notable differences: First, there is the nature of the mystery itself. In Colossians, it is the message of the gospel to the Gentiles; in Ephesians, it is the unity between Jews and Gentiles. Second, the revelation is **by the Spirit to God's holy apostles and prophets** rather than to "all people." This change is significant in Ephesians because it confirms the emphasis given in the epistle to church leaders and ecclesiastical authorities rather than to all the people. Initially (3:3) the author stated that Paul alone was the recipient of this revelation; now he broadens it to include other inspired leaders in the church (2:20; 4:11).

The opening phrase in this verse ([the mystery] **was not made known to men in other generations**) raises a question about how much of God's plan for the Gentiles was revealed before Paul came along. There are some glimpses of this in the OT where references to all the nations who come to the "light" or join the Lord surely includes the Gentiles (Gen. 12:1-3; Isa. 11:10; 42:6; 60:3; Jer. 16:19; Mic. 4:2; Zeph. 2:11). Paul himself uses Isaiah 49:6 to justify his call to the Gentiles when he disputes with the Jews (Acts 13:47). And in Romans 15:9-12, he enlists a series of OT passages to demonstrate that the Gentiles always had a future in God's plan.

Thus, in a broad sense, one could say that God's purpose for the Gentiles was made known. But this is far short of the development in Ephesians, which envisions a universal community in which Jew and Gentile have equal share in what is to become known as the church, the body of Christ (cf. Stott, p. 118). The new revelation was made possible **by the Spirit**, that is, he is the agent who brought the mystery to light.

3:6 / Up to this point the author has alluded to the mystery a number of times: now, however, he becomes specific and defines it in a way that will remove any doubt about its content. **This mystery is that through the gospel**, that is, by way of the proclamation of the word of truth that was believed and accepted (1:13), the Gentiles have been given a completely new status with all of the privileges pertaining thereto. The author describes this with a number of picturesque words prefixed with the preposition *syn*.

First, **the Gentiles are heirs together with Israel**. The Greek word *synklēronoma* is the same one Paul uses on occasions when he talks about believers becoming "heirs" of salvation and of the blessings of God (Rom. 8:17; Gal. 3:29; 4:7). Here the preposition *syn* gives it the force of "fellow heirs," indicating that the Gentiles share equally with the Jews all the privileges and blessings of sonship.

Second, they are **members together of one body**. Since there is no occurrence of this word (*syssōma*) anywhere in the NT, the Septuagint (the pre-Christian Greek translation of the OT), or classical literature, it becomes obvious that the author coined it in order to describe the intimate relation that Jews and Gentiles have to each other in the body of Christ, the church. Robinson notes that there is no English equivalent and, in order to capture its full meaning, offers this idea: "In relation to the Body the members are 'incorporate'; in relation to one another they are 'concorporate,' that is, sharers in the one body" (p. 78).

Third, the Gentiles are **sharers together in the promise in Christ Jesus**. Once again, the author uses a *syn* noun (*symmetochos*) to emphasize that the Gentiles participate equally with the Jews in the promises of God. Their entire relationship with the people of God is established by their incorporation in Christ as it came to them through the gospel. The gospel is the proclamation of all the privileges that Christ has made available to humanity, including the Gentiles. Earlier, the author indicated that God's ultimate plan was to bring all creation together (1:10). One gets the distinct impression that the unity between Jew and Gentile is but the first step in a broader cosmic unity that is going to include all of creation under the headship of Christ (cf. Rom. 8:19–21).

3:7 / Having stated the role of the gospel in bringing this unity about, the author reminds his readers once again that Paul **became a servant of this gospel by the gift of God's grace** (cf. 3:2). Paul's ministry was neither a self-chosen nor a self-appointed one but a **gift of God's grace**. The ability to carry out that mission came **through the working of his** (God's) **power** and not Paul's strength (Col. 1:29). Everything that Paul received and achieved was the result of God's gift of grace and power.

3:8 / Readers of the Pauline epistles will recall statements similar to the one made here: **I am less than the least of all God's people.** When Paul's apostleship was being questioned by the Corinthians, he remarked that "I am not in the least inferior to the 'super-apostles,' even though I am nothing" (2 Cor. 12:11). And on occasions when Paul is haunted by his former persecution of the church, he reminds himself of his unworthiness and inadequacy (cf. 1 Cor. 15:9; Gal. 1:13; 1 Tim. 1:12–14). In this context, it appears that Paul's feeling of inferiority comes from reflecting upon the grace of God and how it has worked in his life and among the Gentiles. He is overcome, not by a guilty conscience or questions about his authority, but by a heart that is overflowing with the marvels of God's grace.

The next phrase indicates that there is a double function to Paul's apostleship: First, there is his ministry of the proclamation of the gospel to the Gentiles (**this grace was given to me: to preach to the Gentiles the unsearchable riches of Christ**). Though Paul has commented on his mission to the Gentiles, he appears to be amazed—and thankful—that God's grace was rich enough to include them and that he was God's instrument in bringing the message of reconciliation to them. F. Beare draws attention to the article before **Christ**, thus indicating that "the Christ," or "the Messiah" who was promised to the Jews, is now proclaimed to the Gentiles as well (p. 669). This could be a conscious thought in the author's mind, given the context of a passage in which the incorporation of both Jews and Gentiles is stressed.

The translation **unsearchable** (*anexichniastos*) **riches** captures beautifully the idea behind this Greek word (cf. NEB, "unfathomable"). Stott lists ten different English equivalents that he has discovered in various translations and commentaries—all attempting to define the word without confining its meaning (p. 120). Basically, it means "not to be tracked out," "beyond comprehension," or "inscrutable." Paul expresses this idea when he writes to the Romans: "Oh, the depth of the riches of the wisdom and knowledge of God! How unsearchable his judgments, and his paths beyond tracing out!" (11:33). The same thoughts occur in Job 5:9 and 9:10 with respect to God's creation and providence: they lie beyond human comprehension and defy description.

A modern analogy may be found in the current attempt to conquer the cosmos. The present universe, as it is known, is accessible and "trackable." But as one reaches farther and farther into space, one discovers that there are many more universes and galaxies to explore—literally, an infinity in space. And so it is with the riches of Christ! They are **unsearchable** to the extent that the moment one discovers some of them a new door is opened to God's treasury, which in turn leads to a supply of riches that is endless and even beyond comprehension. These **unsearchable riches** are none other than Christ himself.

3:9 / The second aspect of Paul's mission is **to make plain to everyone the administration of this mystery**. Literally, the phrase reads "to enlighten" (*phōtisai*), or "to bring to light what is the stewardship (*oikonomia*) of the mystery." The Greek word for "all people" (*pantes*) is omitted in some manuscripts, so the emphasis is on bringing God's mystery plan to light. Although not stated, the intention appears to be that the revelation is to **everyone** (as the NIV).

The idea of "illuminating," or making all of humanity see how God's mystery plan is to be put into effect, suggests something more than proclamation; it conveys the idea that Paul was used specifically to show the world how God publicly disclosed what had been kept secret. Paul accomplished this by explaining the incorporation of the Jews and Gentiles into the body of Christ. Everything that has taken place is part of God's master plan (*oikonomia*). The reference to God as the one **who created all things** is somewhat enigmatic. Does it mean that this mystery/plan of God is part of his creative activity, or does it emphasize that his mystery was hidden from the time of creation and **for ages past was kept hidden in God**?

The parallel in Colossians 1:26, for example, mentions the mystery hidden "for ages and generations" but without reference to God as the Creator. Beare concludes that the mention of God's creative activity is "in keeping with the writer's consistent association of creation and redemption, and his emphasis on the cosmic aspect of the saving work of Christ" (p. 670). It does confirm that God **created all things**, including that which is momentarily concealed but which, in his eternal plan, is made **plain to everyone**.

3:10 / What had remained hidden "for ages past" (3:9) is **now** (*nyn*) made manifest. This verse makes one of the most inclusive statements about the church in the entire NT. Simply put, it announces that the church has a cosmic function in the plan of God.

With this verse, the author reaches the climax of his development on the "mystery/plan of God." C. L. Mitton calls this "God's master plan" and outlines the sequence by which this revelation took place: "It was made known first to Paul (3:3), then to the apostles and prophets (3:5), then to *all men* (3:9). Only then, as God's reconciling power in Christ became effective in his Church and produced a united fellowship out of elements which in the world had seemed irreconcilable, did the powers of evil realize what God was achieving" (p. 127). This unfolding of God's plan as presented in Ephesians may be diagrammed in the following way:

Paul (3:3)	Apostles and prophets (3:5)	All mankind (3:9)	Angelic powers and rulers in the heavenly world (3:10)

In this last stage God's plan comes full circle: What was alluded to in the opening hymn of praise (1:10) is now complete. The grand purpose of the church is that through its agency, **the manifold wisdom of God should be made known to the rulers and authorities in the heavenly realms**. These angelic rulers and powers are those beings mentioned in 1:21 and in 6:12. Colossians used similar expressions when it taught Christ's—and consequently the believer's—victory over these evil forces (Col. 1:16; 2:15, 20; cf. also Rom. 8:38; 1 Pet. 3:22).

In order to understand this verse it is necessary to realize that the author is assuming an ancient cosmological system. In pre-Copernican times, astronomers believed that the earth was the center of the universe and that it had no motion. The earth was surrounded by a series of spheres that contained celestial bodies, such as the sun, moon, stars, and planets, which revolved around the earth. Beyond these spheres (usually seven) was the highest heaven, where God made his abode. In time, it was believed that these spheres were inhabited by some kind of "heavenly beings," which acted as sovereign rulers within these spheres. These heavenly powers could be either good and friendly or evil and hostile.

With respect to salvation, some religious systems, such as that of the Gnostics, believed that the human soul had to pass through these spheres as it ascended to its permanent abode with God in the highest heaven. But as it moved upward, it was confronted by the rulers and authorities of these spheres, who, in most cases, were hostile and needed to be placated or appeased in some way so that safe passage through the spheres could be guaranteed. This developed into elaborate systems of magic, sorcery, and astrology, many of which were current during Paul's time.

The central message in the book of Colossians is that Christ has defeated these evil powers through his death on the cross. Consequently, they no longer have any control or authority over humankind; believers share in that victory by virtue of their faith in Christ and by virtue of their union with his death and resurrection in baptism (Col. 2:20).

Ephesians retains a similar cosmology: Christ is exalted and rules "far above all rule and authority, power and dominion, and every title that can be given" (1:21); the Christian is engaged in a battle "against the rulers, against the authorities, against the powers of this dark world and against the spiritual forces of evil in the heavenly realms" (6:12); and in 3:10, these forces exist as witnesses to what God has done and is doing through the church. Thus, all forms of life—whether on earth or in the far regions of the cosmos—know about God's eternal plan and purpose.

Scholarly interpretations vary greatly in their approach to the cosmology presented in Ephesians and Colossians. Some believe that the concepts are obsolete and need to be demythologized, that is, reinterpreted in terms that have meaning for the modern era. A good example is Barth, who understands these concepts as politicoeconomic structures of society rather than as cosmic intelligences (cf. notes on 1:21, 22). At the other extreme there is the position represented by Stott, who takes exception to the kind of interpretation given by Barth and others. Stott does not accept the view that Paul was referring to earthly social structures that are included in the redemptive activity of God. In his book *God's New Society*, he provides a short history of the study of the principalities and powers (pp. 267-75) and makes a passionate appeal that readers of the NT understand them as supernatural beings rather than as "structures, institutions and traditions" (p. 273).

It is unclear what effect this revelation of God's mystery through the church is to have upon these heavenly beings. All the text says is that **through the church** they might know **the manifold wisdom of God**. Are they objects of God's redemptive activity, or are they merely cosmic spectators to a drama that is being worked out on earth through the church? The rest of the NT is silent on this subject, and only a few verses allude to some kind of intelligent activity among the angels (cf. 1 Cor. 4:9; 1 Pet. 1:12).

The author describes the unity of the church as the manifestation of **the wisdom of God**—wisdom to the extent that God's divine purposes were being accomplished throughout all the "past ages" down to the present time. Only an all-wise God could bring hostile nations and powers together into a unified whole.

God's wisdom, the author continues, is **manifold**. This is a translation of the Greek *polypoikilos*, which basically means "many-sided" or "varied forms" (NEB). God's **manifold wisdom** is like looking through a kaleidoscope that reveals an amazing array of shapes and colors as one turns it gently; it is like beholding a marvelous tapestry that a designer has woven from a variety of different strands (Stott, p. 123). In this verse, the author has a magnificent vision of a triumphant and unified church that demonstrates the entire creative and redemptive purposes of God to all humanity (3:9) as well as to all cosmic powers (3:10).

3:11 / The recent disclosure of God's mystery was something that God had planned to do from eternity. In a way, the apostle is sharing a philosophy of history in which he sees each successive age as a further revelation of the eternal plan that God is working out for humanity. Many Christian writers have suggested that history be spelled *His-story* (cf. Stott, p. 127). The One who "chose us in him before the foundation of the world" (1:4, RSV) has now made that election possible **in Christ Jesus our Lord**.

As in the opening hymn, the author indicates that Christ is the agent through whom God accomplishes his purposes. Here he uses three specific titles for Christ: He is "the Christ," that is, the Messiah for whom the Jews hoped; he is **Jesus**, the one whom the early Christians believed was historically present with them in the Incarnation; he is the **Lord**, who through death and resurrection has been exalted to the Father's right hand.

When this verse states that God's eternal purpose was **accomplished in Christ Jesus our Lord**, it implies that everything Christ did and said was important. The apostle is drawing attention to the entire Christ-event (incarnation-life-death-resurrection-exaltation), for in this, God accomplished his redemptive purpose for humankind. Ephesians 2:1–10 serves as a good commentary on how the apostle views the work of Christ as applied to the believer; 2:11–22 performs a similar function in showing how Jews and Gentiles are united in Christ to form his body. The church is a living testimony to the redemptive and unifying power of God on earth (3:9) as well as to all heavenly beings (3:10).

3:12 / Lest the readers conclude that the God who worked out this eternal plan is somehow removed from the everyday affairs of mankind, the apostle turns to a practical concern and reminds them that their union with Christ grants them the privilege of communicating with God (**in him and through faith in him we may approach God with freedom and confidence**). The words in Greek are "boldness" (*parrēsia*), "access" (*prosagōgē*), and **confidence** (*pepoithēsis*). *Parrēsia* is used in the NT in the context of speaking, such as boldness in proclaiming the gospel (Acts 4:31; Eph. 6:20; Phil. 1:20) and confidence in approaching God (Heb. 4:16; 10:19).

Christians have that boldness in approaching God because their faith and union with Christ have given them **confidence**. In Christ, all barriers have been removed that would keep the believer from approaching God openly and confidently. Christ has revealed the Father as one who has forgiven his children and who loves them. B. F. Westcott aptly comments that "the right of address and the right of access are coupled together as parts of the right of personal communion with God" (p. 49).

3:13 / In this verse there appears to be an abrupt shift in the author's thought, and he returns to his previous mention of being a prisoner (3:1). By reading between the lines one could get the impression that the Gentile congregations had become discouraged (*enkakeō*, "become weary," "despair," "lose heart," "be afraid") because their great spokesman had been imprisoned. Undoubtedly, much prayer went up to God on Paul's behalf (Col. 4:18). It could be that his discussion on the revelation of God's mystery and the reminder of the believer's freedom in approaching God led him to encourage his readers not to become **discouraged** over the circumstances surrounding his imprisonment.

Most commentators draw attention to the fact that the Greek phrase is capable of a number of translations and meanings because the verb "do not be discouraged" (*mē enkakein*) does not have a subject. Consequently, it could read *(a)* "I ask that 'I' may not be discouraged," or *(b)* "I ask that 'you' not be discouraged." The context of the passage, together with Paul's positive attitude toward his sufferings (Rom. 5:3; 2 Cor. 12:10; Col. 1:24), suggests that the author's concern is with the members of the Gentile congregations who may have become disheartened over Paul's imprisonment. Consequently, they are once again reminded (cf. 3:1) that Paul is suffering on their behalf; but this time the author adds that it is for your benefit, literally, "for your glory" (*doxa*). The immediate benefit, or **glory**, is that through Paul's ministry and subsequent imprisonment, the Gentiles have become members of Christ's body. This, in turn, should prevent them from losing heart. It is doubtful that Ephesians is teaching that the sufferings of the martyrs are the glory of the church—a concept that developed in later centuries.

Additional Notes §13

3:2 / For an extended discussion of the "mystery," see R. E. Brown, *The Semitic Background of the Term "Mystery" in the New Testament* (Philadelphia: Fortress, 1968); A. E. Harvey, "The Use of Mystery Language in the Bible," *JTS* n.s. 31 (1980), pp. 320–36.

3:10 / There is additional discussion of these concepts in the commentary on Col. 1:16; 2:15, 20, and Eph. 1:21–22 and 6:12. See the bibliographies listed in notes on Eph. 1:21–22 and 6:12. Cf. also Caragounis, *The Ephesians Mysterion*, pp. 139–42; Beare, pp. 671–72; Stott, pp. 267–75.

This section follows the same structural pattern that the author established earlier in the epistle. He began with a great hymn of thanksgiving for all of the spiritual blessings that God provided in Christ (1:3–14) and followed this by a prayer for his readers to understand their hope and inheritance in the Lord (1:15–20). In 2:1–3:13, the author provides a lengthy exposition on the believer's position in Christ (2:1–10), the incorporation of Jews and Gentiles into one body, the church (2:11–22), and Paul's personal role in revealing God's eternal and secret plan (3:1–13); this, too, is followed by a prayer that the readers will understand the magnitude of God's plan and be filled with the perfect fullness of God (3:14–19). An appropriate benediction closes the main doctrinal section of the epistle (3:20–21).

These similarities, however, should not prevent one from seeing some of the significant differences in the prayer. One devotional writer put the distinction in the following way: In the first prayer, "the apostle petitions God for knowledge; and in the second, he prays for love. The first is a prayer for revelation; the second is for enablement. It is not enough merely to *know*; we must *be*. The fruit of divine knowledge is the expression of divine life" (Strauss, p. 160).

Two significant features of this prayer should be noted. First, it has many parallels to the praise and prayer in chapter 1. In a sense, 3:14–21 could be considered a further application of the ideas developed earlier: prayer is offered to the Father (1:17 = 3:14f.); prayer is for the Spirit (1:17 = 3:16); the sphere of God's action is in the mind (1:18) or the inner self (3:16); there is an aim for knowledge and fullness (1:18f. = 3:18f.); there is a linking of knowledge and power (1:19 = 3:19); and finally, praise and glory are offered to God (1:6, 12, 14 = 3:21).

Second, this prayer has a wonderful and ever-expanding progression to it. The author begins by listing three specific requests: He prays that his readers may *(a)* receive inner strength

from the Holy Spirit (3:16), *(b)* experience the abiding presence
of Christ in their hearts (3:17a), and *(c)* root and ground their lives
in love (3:17b). The author envisions two significant developments from this: first, a deeper understanding and appreciation
of the extent of God's love (3:18); second—the ultimate goal—
being "filled to the measure of all the fullness of God" (3:19).

3:14 / C. L. Mitton begins his exposition of this prayer
by rightfully noting that "this short paragraph is one of the gems
of the NT" (p. 129). The section opens with the same phrase (**for
this reason**) as 3:1, where it appears that the author initially
wanted to offer this prayer but was momentarily diverted. To
kneel is an expression of deep emotion and humility—prostration
in the spirit of submission (Rom. 11:4; 14:11; Phil. 2:10). Another
posture of prayer was to stand with one's face and hands lifted
up to God (Matt. 6:5; Mark 11:25). Either way, it is the motive
and inner attitude that is important, not the method. Once again,
God is the **Father** to whom the prayer is directed.

3:15 / In Greek, there is a play on words between
"Father" (*patros*) and **family** (*patria*) that is not obvious in the
English. The author indicates that God, as Father, is the one **from
whom his whole family in heaven and on earth derives its name**.
The meaning of the text is ambiguous and raises a number of
problems: First, *patria* means a family, clan, or tribe that descends
from a common ancestor. It cannot be translated as "fatherhood,"
although the idea of fatherhood is there and has led some commentators to think of God as the prototype or archetype of all
fatherhood. This is different from saying that God is the father
of all, which the passage is not teaching.

Second, the phrase **whole family** (*pasa patria*) presents a
problem analogous to "whole building" in 2:21. Some translations (as NIV) use **whole family**, but to do so requires an article
(*pasa hē patria*). The GNB "every family" is the correct translation.
But this does not clarify the meaning.

Given the context of the passage, which includes the unity
of all people and reference to "angels, rulers, and powers," it appears that the apostle understands that "every family," that is,
every human and divine fatherhood, derives its pattern and
meaning from God, the divine prototype. The family on earth
could be the Jews and the Gentiles that make up the church as

the family of God. By "every family" **in heaven**, either the apostle envisions some kind of heavenly community in which family structures are meaningful, or he is using it as an inclusive way of saying that all conceivable family patterns, whether on earth or in heaven, receive their **name** from the Father. Mitton's suggestion that the verse could mean "local congregations" (on the earth) and "a company of departed Christians" (in heaven) is intriguing though not entirely convincing (pp. 131–32).

3:16 / In this prayer, the apostle draws upon the vast reservoir of God's resources—**I pray that out of his glorious riches**. The glory of God is the essence of all that God is, and so there is no limit to his ability to give. Normally, one's prayers are limited by the inability to comprehend God's riches and ask accordingly (3:20; James 4:2, 3). Ephesians reminds believers that God gives **out of his glorious riches**!

The first request is for inner strength from the Holy Spirit. **Inner being** is an inclusive term that can mean the heart, mind, spirit, and so on—anything that stands in contrast to the outer person (cf. Rom. 7:22; 2 Cor. 4:16). This inner strengthening is to take place by means of the **power** (*dynamis*) imparted by the Holy **Spirit**. It is the means by which God works within the believer's life.

3:17 / Second, there is the abiding presence of Christ in one's heart (**that Christ may dwell in your hearts through faith**). Here is another way that God prepares the believer to fulfill his ultimate purpose. This statement reverses Paul's usual terminology concerning the believer's union with Christ by emphasizing that Christ dwells within the believer. This indwelling is to be perceived as Christ taking up residency in the believer's heart, that is, in his or her inmost being. Furthermore, it is a relationship granted **through faith**, a thought reminiscent of 2:1–10 and the baptismal passages that connect faith with the indwelling Christ (Rom. 6:1–11; Gal. 3:26, 27; Col. 2:11–13; cf. also Gal. 2:20). Faith is one's inner response to the action of God through his Spirit.

Although the requests for strength from the Holy Spirit and for the indwelling of Christ are two separate expressions, they conform to Paul's theology that equates the Spirit as the Spirit of Christ: To have Christ is to have the Spirit; to be in the Spirit is to be in Christ (Rom. 8:9ff.).

The third request is that the readers may be **rooted and established in love**. The tense of these verbs in Greek (perfect passive, *errizōmenoi, tethemeliōmenoi*) indicates this action already has taken place but is to continue as a reality in the believer's life (see Col. 1:23; 2:7, for similar exhortations toward stability). To illustrate the depth of life that he is after, the author uses a botanical and architectural metaphor. One sends its roots deep into the soil, whereas the other is grounded on a firm foundation. The NIV indicates that the soil or foundation is **love**.

This translation does not indicate a rather serious textual question at this point. In the Greek, it is permissible to take the phrase **in love** with rooted and grounded (as NIV) or to take it with the preceding phrase to read "that Christ may make his home in your hearts, through faith in love." Robinson, for one, takes it in this latter sense; by faith the Gentiles are partakers of Christ, but they are bound together in love (p. 175).

Most scholars, however, take love as the soil into which the roots grow or the foundation upon which a structure is built. Love is seen more as the result of Christ dwelling within the believer than as the sphere in which he dwells. The ultimate truth is that those who are strengthened by the Spirit and in whom Christ dwells will have their lives rooted and grounded in love. Since love is the possession of Jews and Gentiles, both can grow together in their understanding of Christ's love.

3:18 / After making these three specific requests, the apostle concludes by mentioning the *effect* that his prayer will have upon their understanding of God. He is still addressing the Gentiles and indicates that their reception of God's gifts is not something that they experience in isolation but **together with all the saints**.

These words are especially appropriate to people of a Greek background, with their tendency toward rationalism and love for knowledge (cf. 1 Cor. 1:22; 8:1–3; Col. 2:18, 23; 1 Tim. 1:4; 6:4). But even though the author has been developing a Christian philosophy of history with respect to God, humanity, and the world, the emphasis is upon love rather than knowledge. He would not condone a Gnostic system that elevates knowledge as the highest gift. The real test of one's spiritual maturity is whether or not one is rooted and grounded in love; love, not knowledge, leads to a deeper understanding of God.

With the emphasis upon love rather than knowledge, one cannot help but feel that the author is attacking some form of Gnosticism (cf. Introduction). Besides stressing knowledge (*gnōsis*) in itself, Gnosticism's emphasis on the attainment and possession of knowledge often led to a kind of spiritual elitism in the church. In Corinth, for example, this developed into a division between the "spiritual," that is, those who possessed a higher knowledge, and the "fleshly," those who were less enlightened (cf. 1 Corinthians). The Apostle John confronts a similar problem in his first epistle, where a manifestation of Gnosticism threatened to divide the church. This made it necessary for him to emphasize the close relationship between knowledge and love: "Whoever does not love does not know God, because God is love" (1 John 4:8; cf. also 2:9; 3:11–19; 4:13–21).

Knowledge, when grounded in love, will unify, not divide, God's people. Thus the apostle prays that the Gentiles will realize that spiritual insight and maturity are not uniquely theirs; they do not exist in isolation from the way that God has worked out his purposes historically, particularly among the Jews. And since they are members of the same body, fellow heirs, and so forth (3:6), they share a knowledge of Christ's love and the fullness of God **together with all the saints**.

This knowledge of God's truth is not the possession of a few privileged individuals; it is not a matter of secret doctrines for a small inner circle. Knowledge of God's mystery is given to individuals in and for the community of believers in the same way that all spiritual gifts are given for the welfare of the entire body (4:11–16; 1 Cor. 12:4–13; 14:12, 26). This is a timely message to Christians of any age when individualism tends to destroy the unity of the body of Christ.

The prayer includes the **power to grasp**—in other words, strength to comprehend or the complete ability to realize—**how wide and long and high and deep is the love of Christ**. This spatial imagery should be seen as the author's attempt to show the magnitude of Christ's love and should not leave the reader searching for objects that the author may have in mind. A number of interpretations of this passage refer to the shape of the cross, the church, the temple, the visible universe, and so forth. At best, however, such suggestions are "curiosities" (Stott, p. 137), or fanciful and ingenious interpretations (Mitton, p. 134).

When the author begins to reflect upon Christ's love, he quickly discovers that there is no tangible way to describe it, and so he resorts to these rhetorical expressions. Christ's love can be described only in spatial images. Paul had a similar experience when he dwelled upon God's love in Christ and exclaimed that absolutely nothing can separate the believer from the "love of God that is in Christ Jesus our Lord" (Rom. 8:31–9). Ephesians uses spatial imagery in a way analogous to the psalmist when he describes God's love (Ps. 103) or omnipresence (Ps. 139). Every part of the universe is suffused with the love of Christ.

3:19 / But even as the apostle summons his readers to understand Christ's love, he realizes that any effort to do so falls short of its intended goal. No matter how much power of comprehension one has, Christ's love **surpasses knowledge**; it exceeds one's "capacity of comprehension" (Beare, p. 679). What an indictment of those people who claimed such knowledge for themselves! Though it is legitimate and necessary to seek such comprehension, it is folly to claim full attainment of it. (For another discussion of love and its superiority to knowledge see 1 Cor. 8:1–3; 13:1–3.)

Although believers never fully understand Christ's love, it is a step toward being **filled to the measure of all the fullness of God**. This is the second result of his prayer envisioned by the apostle. He began by praying that the power of the Holy Spirit, the indwelling of Christ, and grounding in love would lead to an understanding of Christ's love. But the ultimate goal is that the believers attain the fullness that belongs to God, that is, all the riches and glory that belong to him. "God's fullness or perfection becomes the standard or level up to which we pray to be filled" (Stott, p. 138).

The concept of "fullness" (*plērōma*) in Colossians (1:19; 2:9, 10) and Ephesians (1:23; 3:19; 4:13) is another way by which the author describes the indicative and imperative or the "already" and the "not yet" of the Christian life. In union with Christ, believers have been granted this fullness; but their possession is a goal that remains to be fulfilled as they appropriate God's gifts and grow in their capacity to receive them (1:14; 4:30). The apostle seems to be emphasizing the reality of this within the context of the church and is not alluding to some kind of heavenly perfection that awaits God's people when this earthly pilgrimage is over.

Additional Notes §14

On 3:14–21, see W. E. Hull, *Love in Four Dimensions* (Nashville: Broadman, 1982).

3:15 / For further discussion on **whole family** in 3:15, see Abbott, pp. 93–94; Mitton, pp. 130–32.

3:18 / See N. A. Dahl, "Cosmic Dimensions and Religious Knowledge (Eph. 3:18)," in *Jesus und Paulus,* ed. E. E. Ellis and E. Grässer (Göttingen: Vandenhoeck & Ruprecht, 1975), pp. 57–75. Also Barth, *Eph. 1–3,* pp. 395–97; Moule, p. 100; Robinson, p. 176.

§15 Praising Through Doxology (Eph. 3:20–21)

3:20 / The apostle has prayed earnestly for certain things, but he realizes that even his requests fall far short of what God is able to do. Thus he concludes this doctrinal section with an appeal to the infinite wealth and understanding of God: **To him who is able to do immeasurably more than all we ask or imagine**. He has opened to his readers the marvels of God's secret and how they have been incorporated into the body of Christ. But in spite of this vast and eternal plan of God, he reminds them that God has the resources to do much more **according to his power that is at work within us**. "Our experience of his power, as it is brought to bear within us, is a limited but true index to the nature of the power that governs the universe and brings all things to their appointed end" (Beare, p. 680).

3:21 / Most of the doxologies in the NT connect the glory of God to Christ in some way (Rom. 11:36; 16:27; Gal. 1:5; 1 Tim. 1:17; 1 Pet. 4:11; Jude 24, 25); this is the only passage that refers to **glory in the church and in Christ Jesus**. Some commentators take this as part of the author's liturgical language, which should not be pressed for any kind of theological precision (see Houlden, p. 305). However, given the teaching about the church in Ephesians, the relationship of the church as the body to its head, Christ, and the occurrence of so much liturgical language, it seems more likely that this statement is chosen deliberately. Christ (head) and his church (body) form the entire sphere of God's glory as well as provide the means by which that glory is proclaimed to all humanity. This praising of God's glory is to go on **throughout all generations, for ever and ever! Amen**. This **amen** is a final liturgical declaration that everything the apostle has written may indeed be so.

§16 *The Appeal and Pattern for Unity (Eph. 4:1–6)*

Chapter 4 begins what often is referred to as the ethical or practical section of the epistle. If chapters 1–3 provide the *theological basis* for Christian unity, then chapters 4–6 contain the *practical instruction* for its maintenance. Unity has been established (the indicative); now it becomes the duty of the believers to strengthen and maintain unity in their fellowship (the imperative).

This generalization does not mean that chapters 4–6 are devoid of theological content. The division of the epistle into such broad categories is somewhat misleading, because, as in the case of Colossians, the apostle throughout his epistles frequently combines theological and ethical statements (cf. disc. on Col. 3:1ff.). In Ephesians, the moral teaching is based upon what has been said in the earlier chapters (1–3) but also grows out of new theological concerns of the author, particularly with respect to the unity of the church. The liturgical style that characterized much of the first half of the epistle is maintained throughout the second half as well.

It has been suggested that the main theme in Ephesians is unity—a unity that has been effected by the reconciling work of Christ who has united all things in heaven and earth (1:10) and who has brought Jews and Gentiles together into the church. The apostle now exhorts his readers to maintain that unity in their personal, domestic, social, and ecclesiastical lives.

In the opening exhortation (4:1–3), he immediately draws attention to his main concern: The readers need to manifest those virtues characterizing their new life in Christ that "keep the unity of the Spirit" (4:3). This admonition is followed by a list of all the unifying elements of the church (4:4–6), which, in turn, are given further application throughout the remaining chapters.

4:1 / **Then** ("therefore," RSV), **I urge you** refers to what has been said in chapters 1–3. As in 3:1, the apostle reminds his readers that his vocation is the reason for his captivity (**as a prisoner for the Lord**). The Greek preposition *en* also points to the sphere of his captivity: He is a prisoner "in the Lord."

The exhortation begins by calling the readers to **live a life worthy of the calling you have received**. The concept of *calling* is an important one in biblical thought. On a number of occasions the prophets remind the people of Israel that they have been "called" by God to fulfill a specific function (see Isa. 41:9; 42:6; 43:1; 44:2; 45:3, 4; Hos. 11:1). Christians, likewise, have a calling from God, as is evident in the Lord's disciples (Mark 1:20), the Apostle Paul (1 Cor. 1:1), and the Gentiles (Eph. 3:6).

In Ephesians, the Gentiles have been told that God has chosen them to be his children (1:4, 5), appointed them to praise God's glory (1:12), called them to a wonderful hope (1:18), and incorporated them into the body of Christ for a life of good works (2:10). Now they are admonished to demonstrate their calling and position in Christ by living a worthy ethical life.

To live a life is a translation of the Greek *peripateō*, which means "to walk." At one time their "walk" conformed to "the world's evil way" (2:2); now they are exhorted to "walk," to live out their new life in Christ and the unity that is theirs in the church. They are a part of God's grand design for the world, which includes the uniting of all things in heaven and on earth (1:10).

4:2 / This verse presents a list of personal attitudes essential for unity in the body of Christ. There is a striking similarity to the list in Colossians 3:12–15, but here the application is developed around the theme of unity. Stott refers to these virtues as the "five foundation stones of Christian unity" (p. 149). As was noted in Colossians, many of these virtues are related, and it is sometimes difficult to draw distinctions between them.

Humility (*tapeinophrosynē*) is that attitude of mind that enables one to see people other than oneself. The Greeks disdained the idea of a submissive or subservient attitude, but Christianity, by virtue of Christ's example in the Incarnation (Phil. 2:5–11), gave it new meaning. When Paul met with the Ephesian elders, he reminded them that his ministry among them was carried out "with great humility" (Acts 20:19). Humility is especially important in the body of Christ, where interpersonal relationships are so important. The Philippian church is a classic example of how pride, selfishness, and conceit produce a fractured fellowship (Phil. 2:1–4).

Gentleness (*prautēs*) is consideration toward others. A gentle person will not insist upon his or her personal rights or be assertive at the expense of others. Stott notes how humility and gentleness go together by drawing upon an insight from R. W. Dale: "For 'the meek man thinks as little of his personal claims, as the humble man of his personal merits' " (p. 149).

Patience (*makrothymia*) and **bearing with one another** (*anechō*, lit., "endure someone or something") form another single thought. Patience would be the willingness and the ability to deal with people in a deliberate but courteous way—in the manner that God deals patiently with his people (Rom. 2:4; 9:22; 1 Tim. 1:16; 1 Pet. 3:20; 2 Pet. 3:15); Christians are called upon to demonstrate this virtue in dealing with one another (1 Cor. 13:4; Gal. 5:22; 2 Tim. 4:2). Such mutual tolerance within the body will go a long way in maintaining a spirit of unity.

The fifth virtue is **love**. Though it could be argued that love is not a separate quality from patience but "an amplification of what patience means" (Mitton, p. 138), love could be taken as the crowning virtue that embraces all the rest. Love is emphasized a number of times throughout the epistle (1:4; 3:17; 4:15, 16). And although love may include being helpful to one another, the author realizes that all virtues need to be practiced if there is to be unity within the church.

4:3 / **Make every effort** (Gk. *spoudazō*, which means "to exert zealous effort," "to take pains") **to keep the unity**. The entire expression underscores the apostle's concern that his readers to guard carefully the unity that has been given to them. In principle, this unity already exists as something **the Spirit** gives; now God's people are admonished to preserve and manifest that unity.

Ephesians is the only epistle in the NT that uses the word **unity** (*enotēs*, 4:3, 13). Elsewhere unity is described by such concepts as "fellowship," "communion," "one man," "one body," and so on. The unity here is a gift of **the Spirit** and should thus manifest itself in the human spirit.

Peace is introduced as the quality or means that forges a **bond** holding believers together. This is different from Colossians 3:14, where love binds all things together in perfect unity. In Ephesians, **peace** was obtained when the hostilities that separated Jews and Gentiles were broken down and both races were united in one new man in Christ (2:14–16); here it is presented as the **bond** by which that unity is kept.

Now that the author has exhorted his readers to maintain their unity through proper conduct, he presents the theological base from which all unity arises. Verses 4–6 list seven "ones" that relate the unity of the church to the unity of Christ and God.

There are a number of theories about the origin of this passage. Scholars have found striking parallels with forms of Hellenistic Judaism and Stoic philosophy. Beare, for example, lists a number of non-Christian sources that bear witness to the concern that existed in the ancient world about the unity of the cosmos, God, Law, Truth, and all areas of life (pp. 685–86). The assumption is that the author of Ephesians adopted such formulas, gave them a specific Christian content, and incorporated them into his epistle.

Most commentators, however, take verses 4–6 to be a compilation of verses and ideas that Paul has used throughout his writings. The main difference between Paul's undisputed writings and the epistle to the Ephesians is not so much the content as the structure in which these formulations occur. Only Ephesians collects and arranges the thoughts into a pattern that resembles a liturgical hymn or a creedal confession.

Though the author may be indebted to such Pauline texts as 1 Corinthians 8:6 and 12:4–13, the application that he gives to the ideas found there conforms to his specific concern for unity within the body of Christ. In Corinthians, for example (1 Cor. 12:4–13), a local concern is dealt with regarding a misunderstanding of spiritual gifts and their application in the church's worship and corporate life. It is emphasized that all spiritual pride and disunity should disappear because such gifts come from the same Spirit. In Ephesians, Christ is the dispenser of spiritual gifts, and the unity that embraces all of society is based upon the "oneness" of God himself as the ultimate source of unity (see Houlden, p. 309).

Structurally, several features of this passage are worth noting: First, the author moves from the church ("body") to the Godhead. One may have expected him to proceed from the unity of God to the unity of the church, but his order appears to be determined by his concern for unity within the body. Verse 4 flows quite naturally from his exhortation in verse 3 calling for the church to preserve the unity that the Spirit gives; thus, "there is one body and one Spirit."

Second, there is an obvious emphasis on all the members of the Trinity and the believer's relationship to the Spirit, Son, and Father. Though there have been a number of ingenious attempts at outlining the apostle's thoughts, there does not appear to be any conscious symmetry or parallelism in his mind. Stott, for example, applies four of the expressions to different members of the Trinity: "First, the one Father creates the one family. Second, the one Lord Jesus creates the one faith, hope, and baptism. Third, the one Spirit creates the one body" (p. 151). Basically, however, the passage teaches that the unity of the Godhead is the foundation of the church's unity. "Its unity is of the same order as the unity of Christ and of God; as there cannot be other gods or other lords, so there cannot be other churches" (Beare, p. 686).

4:4 / There is one body and one Spirit: The union of body and Spirit is noticeable in 1 Corinthians 8:6; 12:4–6, 13. The emphasis in Ephesians undoubtedly is related to the concept that believers are members of the body by virtue of the work of the Holy Spirit (Rom. 8:9; 1 Cor. 12:13). There is only one body because there is one Spirit.

Besides being one in body and Spirit, they **were called to one hope. Hope** is the goal or inheritance toward which the body strives in the Spirit (1:14, 18; Col. 1:4, 5). All who have been called by God share in the hope that is common to all believers.

4:5 / From "the body," the apostle moves to "the Head" (Christ) and what unites the believer to him. **Lord** is the Greek *kyrios*, which is attributed to Christ on a number of occasions (1 Cor. 8:6; 12:3; Phil. 2:11). The church is established by its acknowledgment of Jesus as "the sovereign Lord."

Faith may be taken in two ways: First, it could signify "the faith," that is, that body of teaching that contains all the truths about Christ's life, work, and so forth. In the early church this became a common expression for the Christian message (Gal. 1:23; Phil. 1:27; 1 Tim. 3:9; 4:1, 6; Titus 1:4; Jude 3). But the absence of the article "the" in this passage makes it more likely that the author is thinking of one's belief in Jesus as Lord and thus the acceptance and acknowledgment of him as Lord.

Baptism refers to the rite of water baptism, because it is the visible expression of one's faith in the Lord and is the means by which one becomes a member of Christ's body, the church (Rom. 6:1–11; Gal. 3:26, 27; Col. 2:11–13). It is doubtful that **one baptism** carries the idea that baptism is unrepeatable or that it is a polemic against other baptismal practices current at the time. All that is implied is that the one proper, or correct, baptism is the baptism of faith into Christ. Baptism is a sacrament of unity because it expresses a common faith in the one Lord.

The idea of baptism as a sacrament of unity is not unique to Ephesians. Behind Paul's rather sarcastic remark to the Corinthians—"Were you baptized into the name of Paul?" (1 Cor. 1:13)—lies the implication that their baptism into Christ should unify rather than divide. This is even more forcefully expressed in 1 Corinthians 12:13, where there is a specific reference to baptism "by one Spirit into one body." The direct mention of Jews and Greeks in this Corinthians passage, as well as in Galatians 3:27, 28, and Colossians 3:10, 11, fits well into the theme of unity in Ephesians.

Though faith, Lord, body, and Spirit all belong to the baptismal event, there is no way of knowing whether these phrases contain a baptismal formula or confession. If one subscribes to the liturgical setting of Ephesians, then it would be possible to envision these verses as a confession that a baptismal candidate recited or that the witnessing congregation sang as a hymn. The opening admonition to live a life that coincides with God's call could be taken to refer to the new life that is received in baptism. However, the appearance of this formula in Ephesians does not necessarily mean that the epistle is a baptismal treatise or liturgy. Its application of baptismal imagery and theology simply conforms to the author's purpose in describing the unity of the church. But behind the formula lies the idea of baptism as the "sacrament of unity," the rite by which Jew and Gentile have been made members of the body of Christ. Both their faith and their baptism are in Jesus Christ as **Lord**.

4:6 / The writer's thoughts reach their climax in the unity of God (**one God and Father of all**). The Christian community shared the Jewish concept of monotheism (**one God**) and through their relationship with Christ, appreciated God as **Father** (Rom. 8:15; 1 Cor. 8:6; Gal. 4:6; Eph. 3:14) **of all, who is over all and**

through all and in all. The KJV "in you all" reflects a reading that lacks strong manuscript evidence and that has been abandoned in subsequent translations.

Given the context of the passage, it would appear that the author has the community of God's people in mind (Stott, p. 151), even though such thoughts can embrace the entire universe. The concepts express God's transcendence (**over all**), his omnipresence (**through all**) and his immanence (**in all**). One wonders if there is a veiled reference to the triune God, for in Christian thought, God's omnipresence and immanence are manifestations of the Son and the Spirit. The verse is similar to Paul's benediction in Romans 11:36, where he states: "For from him and through him and to him are all things."

§17 The Giving of Spiritual Gifts to the Body (Eph. 4:7–11)

4:7 / The apostle has been discussing the unity of the whole (4:1–6); now he turns to the individual parts and shows how diversity within the body contributes to its unity. The body is unified but it is not uniform; every person has a special gift that makes a contribution to the whole.

In the verses following, the apostle lists the various gifts necessary for the body to function properly and ultimately to attain its goal of maturity—"attaining to the whole measure of the fullness of Christ" (4:13). **But to each one of us grace has been given**. Christ's giving is always a matter of his grace, and just as the apostle has emphasized how he personally was the recipient of grace (3:2, 7, 8), he reminds the readers that each one of them has received the same privilege. Later, he will show how that privilege leads to responsibility (4:12–16).

The gift is **as Christ apportioned it**. Though grace suggests the unlimited favor of God, this phrase shows that, as it was given to **each** individual, it does have limitations. No one person has all the gifts required for the body; rather, the gifts of each member are supplemented by the gifts of all members. It is the working together of each part that produces unity and growth. Here it is the gift that **Christ apportioned**, not the gift of the Spirit, as in Corinthians (1 Cor. 12:7–13).

The continuity of this passage is interrupted by a parenthesis at 4:9–10. The writer has introduced Christ as the giver of spiritual gifts, but before he goes on to enumerate them (4:11), he pauses to reflect upon the "giver" and how Christ's dispensing of these gifts relates to the humiliation and exaltation of Christ. This so-called parenthesis (4:9–10) is one of the most difficult and controversial passages in the entire epistle: First, there is the translation of an OT quotation; second, there is the application of the quotation to Christ; and third, there is the meaning of these verses within the context of Ephesians.

4:8 / **This is why it says** indicates that the author is quoting from the OT. The problem, however, is that the quotation in Ephesians differs considerably from Psalm 68:18, which is the only likely source of the quotation.

Psalm 68:18	*Ephesians 4:8*
When you ascended on high,	**When he ascended on high**
you led captives in your train;	**he led captives in his train**
you received gifts from men,	
even from the rebellious.	**and gave gifts to men**.

The NIV translation indicates that there is a change from the second person (you) to the third person (he), and it shows that the author has changed the phrase "you received gifts from" to "he gave gifts to." Scholarly reaction to this has varied from accusations of deliberate alteration (see Houlden, p. 310), an "unintentional misquotation" (Mitton, p. 146), a piece of rabbinical exegesis (Beare, p. 688), to Stott's explanation "that the two renderings are only formally but not substantially contradictory" (p. 157).

Initially, the psalm celebrated an earthly triumph of the Israelites over their enemies and the return of the defeated foes with the spoils of war to the capital city. This serves also as a picture of God's victory over all his enemies during the exodus and his enthronement in the holy city. At a later period, the rabbis interpreted this passage as referring to Moses' ascension of Mount Sinai to receive the law (Exod. 19). The giving of the Torah (Law) became associated with the festival of Pentecost. In this usage of the psalm, the rabbis understood that Moses ascended the mountain to receive gifts, that is, the law, *for* people so that he, in turn, might *give* it to people (see Barth, *Eph. 4–6*, p. 472; Beare, p. 688). An ancient Targum (an Aramaic translation of the Hebrew) actually changes the wording of the original psalm to "he gave gifts to men."

When the author of Ephesians comes to discuss the spiritual gifts that Christ bestowed upon the church, he draws upon that psalm because he sees Christ's ascension to the Father as its prophetic fulfillment (**when he ascended on high**). As Moses was given the law for the people of Israel, Christ, as a second but greater Moses, gave the Spirit to the church, which, in turn, included the gifts mentioned in 4:11 (**he . . . gave gifts to men**).

Captives refers to the principalities and powers that he led captive (1:20–22; Col. 2:15).

Either commentators are troubled by the author's cavalier use of the OT (Houlden, p. 310) and disregard for the original meaning of the OT text, or they accept this as "a true testimony of the Spirit of Prophecy" (Moule, p. 107). Stott reconciles the problem by stressing that "receiving" was for the purpose of "giving" and finds this principle illustrated in Peter's sermon on the day of Pentecost (Acts 2:33), when he states: "He has been raised to the right side of God and received from him the Holy Spirit, as his Father had promised; and what you now see and hear is his gift that he has poured out on us" (pp. 158f.).

4:9 / The author leaves the quotation and expands (parenthetically in NIV) upon the meaning of ascend and descend: **What does "he ascended" mean except that he also descended**. The phrase **to the lower, earthly regions** raises the second major interpretative problem in this passage. Commentators are full of suggestions, including *(a)* the earth; *(b)* the region below the earth, such as Hell or Hades; *(c)* Christ's descent at the Incarnation; *(d)* Christ's humiliation on the cross and his subsequent death and burial; and *(e)* Christ's return at Pentecost to give his Spirit to the church.

Since the apostle does not clarify what he meant, one assumes that his readers must have known to what he was referring. Some may have thought of a tradition in the early church that spoke of Christ visiting the underground between the time of his death and resurrection (1 Pet. 3:19; 4:6). However, it could be just an expressive way of being as inclusive as possible. It thus serves to balance the phrase "higher than all the heavens" in 4:10.

4:10 / From descent the apostle turns to ascent and stresses that the same person is meant in both cases: **He who descended is the very one who ascended**. This must be a reference to an early heresy known as Docetism, which denied the reality and integrity of the Incarnation (cf. 1 John). What the author would be saying is that the same Jesus who became incarnate, who suffered and died, who descended to Hades (?), is the same person who was exalted to the right hand of the Father and who is the dispenser of spiritual gifts.

The ascension is **higher than all the heavens**. Ancient cosmology depicted at least seven heavens above the earth (see disc. on 3:10). Here again the apostle is saying that Christ has been exalted to "the highest honor and glory possible" (Foulkes, p. 116); his presence permeates everything between the deepest deep and the highest high ("all things in heaven and on earth," 1:10). Early Christian theology described Christ's ascension as an exaltation in, through, or beyond the heavens (1:20, 21; Heb. 4:14; 7:26).

The purpose of the ascension is that Christ will **fill the whole universe** (cf. 1:23). This could mean that Christ simply pervades everything with his presence or that, by doing so, he brings all things into subjection under his sovereignty. At any rate, the central truth about the ascension is that it makes Christ accessible "to all men everywhere at all time" (Mitton, p. 149). In the context of the gifts, this passage shows that the ascended Lord is the same person who descended to the earth in order to give these spiritual gifts to the church.

4:11 / After this brief commentary on Psalm 68:18, the apostle returns to his thoughts on the special gifts that Christ has given to the church (4:7). From his rendering of the psalm, he repeats—as if to reemphasize—that Christ is the giver: **It was he who gave some to be apostles, some to be prophets, some to be evangelists, and some to be pastors and teachers.**

Although this verse may look relatively simple on the surface, there are a number of issues that make its meaning difficult and even ambiguous: First, within the canon of the NT there is often an overlapping of functions attributed to an office. Deacons and elders, for example, perform a similar ministry, and few scholars agree on how presbyters, bishops, and elders are to be distinguished from each other.

Second, churches may have differed in their organizational structure from place to place. Thus, what was true for one specific congregation may not have applied to all the other churches. It is a fairly well accepted theory that the "charismatic" leadership of the early church was gradually replaced by regulated offices (e.g., elders, bishops, deacons). The Pastoral Epistles (1 and 2 Timothy, Titus), for example, stress the offices of the church rather than the variety of gifts mentioned in 1 Corinthians 12.

Third, there also is the question of authority in the early church. Initially, spiritual and ecclesiastical authority belonged to the early leaders—the apostles, prophets, elders, and so on. Gradually, however, this authority was replaced, or rather superseded, by the canon of Scripture. As the early church leaders died, the church was forced to look at the inspired writings that they had left behind as their source of authority. Thus Paul's apostolic authority could be maintained for succeeding generations through his letters to the churches.

A fourth problem about Ephesians is the intention of the author. What were his reasons for presenting the list that he does? Why does he omit the gifts mentioned in 1 Corinthians? Does his selection conform to his presentation of a universal rather than local church? Unfortunately, the answers to these questions are not always easy to determine.

Finally, any interpretation of these "gifts" runs the risk of imposing contemporary ideas upon ancient categories. Since the church today does not generally use the office of apostle, for example, the temptation is to find a modern counterpart in church leaders such as area superintendents and overseers (see Stott, p. 160). There may be a certain legitimacy to this, but it does not help to clarify the original meaning of an office and/or gift and to understand it in the context in which it is used. Here, it is not a case of putting new wine into old skins; the church has new skins into which it is trying to pour old wine.

There are several things that can be noted about Ephesians: First, **apostles**, **prophets**, and **teachers** are the only three categories that are taken over directly from 1 Corinthians 12:28: "And in the church God has appointed first of all apostles, second prophets, third teachers." The **apostles** and **prophets** have already been mentioned in the founding of the church (2:20; 3:5); the other offices (**evangelists, pastors/teachers**) occur for the first time.

Second, the office of evangelist occurs only two other times in the NT. Philip is an "evangelist" (Acts 21:8), and Timothy is exhorted by Paul to "do the work of an evangelist" (2 Tim. 4:5). There is no way of knowing whether the author thought of **evangelists** as foundational to the church in the same way as **apostles** and **prophets**. Certainly their function as proclaimers of the gospel could be considered in this way.

Third, it appears that attempts to separate these offices into foundational and continuing ministries, or those intended for the universal (**apostles, prophets, evangelists**) and local church (**pastors/teachers**) are arbitrary. Had the apostle intended to make distinctions, one would have expected him to mention presbyters, bishops, and deacons as well. What is certain, however, is that Christ **gave** (appointed) these offices to the church for the specific function of having the church attain its full maturity in him (4:12–16).

Apostles: This term comes from the verb *apostellō*, which means "to send out." An apostle is one who has been sent. In the NT it is used of the Twelve, of those who are associated with specific churches (2 Cor. 8:23; Phil. 2:25), and of Christians generally (John 13:16). In the early church, the qualifications of an apostle of Christ were to have seen Jesus (1 Cor. 9:1, 2) and been a witness to the resurrection (Acts 1:21–23). Apostles were sent out as messengers, probably upon the commission of a church (after the Lord's death), to exercise leadership in spiritual and organizational matters.

Prophets: In biblical literature, a prophet is a proclaimer (forthteller) as well as a predictor (foreteller). These individuals received a specific message from God, either directly or through his Word, and by way of divine utterances made the will of God known in specific situations. In most cases, it was the communication of a specific and immediate message of God to his people or to the church (see Stott, pp. 161–62).

Evangelists: The most obvious definition of an evangelist is "a preacher of the gospel" (2 Tim. 4:2, "Preach the Word"). In the early church there were itinerant individuals who would move about into unevangelized areas in order to proclaim the gospel. However, an evangelist may also have the gift of making the gospel understandable or of leading individuals to accept it as God's word for them (cf. 2 Tim. 4:5: "But you, keep your head in all situations, endure hardship, do the work of an evangelist, discharge all the duties of your ministry").

Pastors and teachers: A common debate at this point is whether the author intended to express two distinct offices or whether pastors and teachers are two functions of the same office. The absence of the article before teachers (*tous de poimenas kai didaskalous*) leads one to suspect that these words express two aspects of the same office—an office that has a pedagogical and pastoral ministry.

This is the only occasion in the NT where the noun *poimēn* occurs as a title for a church leader. Undoubtedly, it comes from the application of the shepherd imagery that characterized the Lord's relationship with his disciples. Jesus is the good shepherd (*ho poimēn ho kalos*, John 10:11–18; cf. also Matt. 18:12–14; Luke 15:3–7; Heb. 13:20; 1 Pet. 2:25; 5:4); on several occasions, leaders in the church are exhorted to "be shepherds of God's flock" (1 Pet. 5:2; Acts 20:28); church leaders are to pattern their "pastoral" (shepherding) ministry after the example of Christ.

If the primary function of a pastor is to *care* for the flock in a loving and pastoral way, then the main function of the teacher would be the *feeding* of the flock through instruction. It is difficult to separate the two, because pastoring and teaching are so closely related. To quote Stott: "Perhaps one should say that, although every pastor must be a teacher, gifted in the ministry of God's Word to people (whether a congregation or groups of individuals), yet not every Christian teacher is also a pastor since he may be teaching only in a school or college rather than in a local church" (pp. 163–64). Pastoring, which includes an element of teaching, implies a long-term responsibility for the spiritual needs of people.

Additional Notes §17

4:8 / R. Rubinkeiwicz examines the targumic version of the psalm in his article, "Ps LXVII 19 (= EPH IV 8): Another Textual Tradition or Targum?" *NovT* 17 (1975), pp. 219–24. See also G. V. Smith, "Paul's Use of Psalm 68:18 in Ephesians 4:8," *JETS* 18 (1975), pp. 181–89.

4:9 / For further explanation of these theories, see Abbott, pp. 114–16; Barth, *Eph. 4–6*, pp. 433–34; Beare, pp. 688–89; Mitton, pp. 146–49; Stott, *God's New Society*, pp. 156–59. On the theory of Christ's descent at Pentecost, cf. G. B. Caird, "The Descent of Christ in Ephesians 4, 7–11," in *Studia Evangelica*, vol. 2, ed., F. L. Cross (Berlin: Akademie Verlag, 1964), pp. 535–45.

4:11 / An old but valuable discussion can be found in J. B. Lightfoot, "The Christian Ministry," in *Philippians* (London: Macmillan, 1898), pp. 181–269. On the offices, cf. K. H. Rengstorf, *"apostolos,"* *TDNT,* vol. 1, pp. 407–47; G. Friedrich, *"prophētēs,"* *TDNT,* vol. 6, pp. 781–861; idem, *"euangelistēs,"* *TDNT,* vol. 2, pp. 736–37; J Jeremias, *"poimōn,"* *TDNT,* vol. 6, pp. 485–502; K. J. Rengstorf, *"didaskalos,"* *TDNT,* vol. 2, pp. 148–60.

4:12 / After listing the offices, the apostle now clarifies their function or purpose. In conformity with Corinthians, the gifts are given to the church for the good of the entire body (1 Cor. 12:7; 14:26, 31). The work and the results described fit the ministry entrusted to the pastors and the teachers.

The first and immediate function of church leaders is **to prepare God's people for works of service**. The NIV correctly combines preparation and ministry, thus avoiding the error of some earlier translations that made two coordinate clauses out of the sentence (cf. KJV; RSV, 1947 ed.). In the body, every member and not only the ministers must be taught to serve. The word *katartismos* ("training," "preparing," "equipping") conveys the idea of an harmonious development in which all parts are brought to a condition of being able to perform according to their created purpose (2 Tim. 3:17).

The second phrase, **so that the body of Christ may be built up**, expresses the ultimate goal of the gifts given to the church. Here building imagery indicates that the body is being built as God's people are prepared for doing the work of the ministry (*diakonia*). Every member must contribute to this process, or the body will be deficient in areas of its growth.

4:13 / From these two general statements, the author goes on to define more specifically the various aspects of Christian growth in the body of Christ. The building up of the body of Christ includes several important features: First, there is an intellectual component (**until we all reach unity in the faith and in the knowledge of the Son of God**). Here is a call for the Christian community to collectively work toward attaining the unity of the faith (*eis tēn enotēta tēs pisteōs*). Since Ephesians already has spoken about the unity inherent in the "faith" (4:5), one sees this as another reminder that the readers are to progressively appropriate what is theirs by possession. The emphasis here is upon the corporate attainment of this unity (**we all reach unity**) rather than upon individuals striving for spiritual growth apart from the body.

In addition to faith, **knowledge of the Son of God** is a second condition of unity. **Son of God** is another designation for Jesus (Rom. 1:4; Gal. 2:20), and there does not appear to be any specific reason why this term is used here. What is important is that the **Son of God** is essential to unity because he is the object of Christian faith and knowledge. The realization of unity, in other words, is to be found only in a personal relationship of faith and knowledge to the person of Jesus Christ.

A second feature of bodily growth includes personal maturity—we shall **become mature** (*eis andra teleion*). Although some scholars take this as a reference to individual or personal maturity (Mitton, p. 154) or to Christ as the "Perfect Man" (Barth, *Eph. 4–6*, pp. 484–96), the context shows that the author is still thinking about the corporate nature and unity of the church. As a body it is to grow up as mature people, a goal that, of course, can be attained only as each individual member grows in the unity of the faith and in the knowledge of the Son of God.

The third feature is something equivalent to Christ-likeness (Mitton, p. 154)—**attaining to the whole measure of the fullness of Christ**. This is the final prepositional phrase (*eis . . . eis . . . eis . . .*), and it represents the final stage of the church's maturity. Christian maturity, whether individual or corporate, is that quality of life that belongs to Christ. As the church attains Christ's full stature there is a reciprocal benefit in that Christ also finds his fullness in the church (1:23).

So far the apostle has been describing Christian unity as a goal to be attained. True, there is diversity within the body with respect to the spiritual gifts that Christ has given to the church, but that diversity is to promote the unity of the faith and to assist the body in reaching its ultimate goal. Believers are to grow out of their individualism into the corporate oneness of the person of Christ. In the following verses he describes some circumstances that hinder the attainment of unity, and then he provides some insights on bodily growth.

4:14 / Although unity is an ideal to be realized, the writer is aware that the church's pilgrimage toward that goal is characterized by immaturity and instability. Currently, the body of Christ acts very much like **infants**, a designation that implies immaturity, erratic temperament, individualism, self-assertion, and so on. When the church attains its goal, then it will no longer act in a childish way.

Children also are unstable, that is, they can be like a little boat, **tossed back and forth by the waves, and blown here and there by every wind of teaching and by the cunning and craftiness of men**. The church acts in an immature and unstable way when it permits false teachings and doctrines to distract it from attaining its maturity in Christ. There is no way of knowing whether the author has any specific heresy in mind (such as Gnosticism or Docetism, cf., Acts 19:26–35), or whether it is a general exhortation toward sound doctrine. Either way, the teaching of false doctrine promotes sectarianism and individualism rather than corporate unity within the body of Christ.

The apostle expands upon the deceitfulness of humankind by employing a metaphor that comes from a game of dice—**in their deceitful scheming**. The Greek *kybeia* basically means "dice playing" but ultimately developed into such concepts as craftiness, trickery, and deceit.

It appears that false teachers deliberately tried to mislead the church through crafty and deceitful teachings. "The people are being swept along by the prevailing crazes and new fashions of thought; but also they are being manipulated by unscrupulous and clever men who by every trick they know are trying to divert them from the main life of the Church into divisive and sectarian movements" (Mitton, p. 155). All these negative qualities will disappear (**then we will no longer be . . .**) when the body of Christ has attained its goal of unity and maturity in Christ.

4:15 / From the negative, the apostle returns to the positive direction that the church is to take. A divided church is characterized by rivalry, suspicion, hatred, pride, selfishness, lack of direction, and so forth (cf. Phil. 2:2–4). **Instead**, he pleads that the church should be characterized by the qualities of truth and love (**speaking the truth in love**). Literally, the phrase should be translated "truthing in love" because there is no verb in the Greek text for **speaking**, and the essential meaning is that truth needs to be conveyed in love and not by deceit and craftiness.

Truth and love form two essential components of the church's life. The significant teaching in this phrase is how these

two virtues belong together. Christian truth has a moral as well
as an intellectual side; it affects the entire person, not just the
brain And though the possession of truth is crucial to the life
of the church, it also is important how that truth is obtained and
maintained. Christian teachers clearly cannot resort to the kind
of trickery that characterizes the false teachers (4:14).

"Truthing in love" suggests the idea of living out the truth
in a spirit of love. Some congregations may have all "the truth,"
but no love; others may have considerable love, but no truth. What
is needed is a combination and balance between the two. Stott
makes a fitting and astute statement on this point when he writes:
"Truth becomes hard if it is not softened by love; love becomes
soft if it is not strengthened by truth. The apostle calls us to hold
the two together. . . . There is no other route than this to a fully
mature Christian unity" (p. 172).

As with the apostle's other exhortation, this one is directed
toward the corporate life of the church as well. The individual
must learn to live as a part of a greater whole—**we**, that is, the
entire body, **will in all things grow up into him who is the Head,
that is, Christ**. The church is a living body, capable of manifesting such growth because of its relationship to Christ, the Head.

4:16 / As the head of the body, Christ directs and con-
trols the growth that is to take place. Thus he is the source as
well as the goal of the church's growth. To illustrate, the author
employs a physiological metaphor similar to the one in Colossians 2:19. In Colossians, the emphasis is upon the nourishment
and cohesion that the Head gives the body; in Ephesians, the
head-body relationship remains, but emphasis is given to the
interdependence of individuals within the body in much the same
way that muscles, nerves, limbs, and so on are joined together
in the human organism. The *syn* verbs (*synarmologoumenon*, "to
fit or join together," and *symbibazomenon*, "to bring, unite, knit
together"), underscore this concern, and their present tense indicates an ongoing process within the body of Christ.

Again, the author draws attention to the importance of parts
in relation to the whole: **The whole body, joined and held together . . . grows and builds . . . as each part does its work**. It
is one thing for individual members to be related to the Head
(4:15); but it is equally significant that the growth of the body
depends upon the way these members relate to one another and

perform their appropriate function as members of the body. This building and growing process takes place **in love**. As the readers have been exhorted to demonstrate love to each other (4:2, 15), they are reminded again that **love** is the soil out of which such growth in unity takes place (cf. 3:17).

Up to this point in the epistle there have been only occasional references to the ethical life of the Christian (2:10; 4:1–3, 15). In 4:1 it appeared that the apostle was preparing a lengthy description of the new life in Christ, but this led, instead, into a further exposition of the unifying elements of the church (4:4–16).

At 4:17, however there is a clear break from the theological aspects of unity to an emphasis upon the ethics of unity and how that unity can be maintained within the church. This large section begins by admonishing the readers not to walk—that is, to live—ethically like the heathen and continues with a description of the new standards that are to govern their life. In contrast to Colossians, there does not appear to be any moral crisis that necessitated these exhortations; rather, they form an integral part of the author's overall theme of unity.

The large ethical section of 4:17–5:21 may be broken up into several smaller parts: First, 4:17–24 forms a general appeal for the readers to abandon their former way of life, on the principle that their new life in Christ has meant a radical change in their behavior. Second, 4:25–5:2 includes a selected list of vices and virtues essential for maintaining unity within the body. Third, the ethical life of the old and new life is contrasted by the imagery of light and darkness (5:3–14). Fourth, there is another appeal to the Christian's "walk" in 5:15–21, including some exhortations within the context of Christian worship.

4:17 / That the apostle feels his ethical exhortations are urgent, significant, and authoritative is implied by his reference to **the Lord** (lit., "this, therefore, I say and bear witness in the Lord"). His basic concern is that they break away from their former pagan (**as the Gentiles**) way of life. The description resembles closely the one in Romans 1:18–24.

The Gentile way of life includes **futility of . . . thinking;** the Greek word behind this (*mataiotēs*) expresses uselessness and even vanity. Their life apart from God has no meaning or value.

4:18 / The Gentiles also have darkened minds; deprived of the true source of light and the illumination that God gives to his children (1:18), they live in a state of intellectual darkness.

They live in alienation because of **ignorance** (*agnoia*) and **hardening of their hearts** (*dia tēn pōrōsin tēs kardias autōn*); they are separated from all life with God. The author does not explain how this came about. Paul indicates in Romans that God made himself known through natural revelation but that humanity rejected this revelation and turned to self- and idol worship instead (cf. Rom. 1:18–23). "Stubbornness" (GNB) is an apt translation of *pōrōsis* and is preferable to "blindness" (see note on 4:18).

4:19 / All this has had two further degrading effects upon their lives. Callousness (**having lost all sensitivity**); and vice, (**sensuality** or "licentiousness," RSV), is another way of describing all sorts of sexual license and perversion (*aselgeia*, "licentiousness," "debauchery," "indecent conduct"). And this indecent conduct was practiced **with a continual lust for more** ("without restraint," GNB). *Pleonexia* describes greedy individuals continually seeking to gratify their desires. In this context, the author's thought is that the pagan way of life is characterized by an increasing desire to participate in more and more forms of sexual immorality.

One can see the futility of paganism. By rejecting God's revelation the non-Christian becomes hardened in heart and conscience. This sad state of affairs leads to participation in immoral behavior. Ultimately, it becomes a vicious circle because new perversions must be sought to replace the old (Mitton, pp. 161–62).

4:20 / In contrast to their former pagan way of life, the apostle reminds them, they learned something quite different when they became Christians—**you . . . did not come to know Christ that way.** The Christian walk is the exact opposite of the way of life that he has just described. The references to learning, hearing, and being taught undoubtedly refer to the time when these Gentiles became Christians through the proclamation of the gospel about Jesus. This would include subsequent instruction in the Christian faith. The phraseology suggests the existence of

a "school" or at least catechetical instruction being passed on to
new converts.

4:21 / Although the NIV mentions that the believers
"came to know Christ," the Greek has no infinitive and literally
states that *they learned Christ (emathete ton Christon)*! The implication appears to be that the voice of Christ is actually heard
through the apostles who proclaimed the gospel (Mitton, p. 163;
Stott, p. 179). In addition to proclamation (*kerygma*) there is teaching (*didachē*), of which Christ is the object (**you . . . were taught
in him in accordance with the truth that is in Jesus**).

There does not appear to be any reason why the author
switches from "Christ" (4:20) to **Jesus** (4:21). A number of commentators feel that this may be a deliberate reference to the historic personality of the Lord, because some false teachings at that
time distinguished between Christ and Jesus. This, however, is
speculative, and it could be that the apostle simply wishes to remind his readers that truth is embodied in Jesus—who, of course,
is the Christ.

4:22–24 / In 4:22–24 the author refers to the kind of instruction that new believers would have received at the time of
their baptism (cf. Col. 3:8–12). The Greek text has no new sentence at the beginning of 4:22, so the exhortation to **put off your
old self** and **put on the new self** must be seen in the context of
baptismal instruction. This passage shows the close relationship
between baptism and ethics. Christian morality cannot be considered apart from Christian revelation. The point is quite clear
that what was begun at baptism must be continued in the experience of the Christian. Baptism is the beginning of a new
ethical way of life.

Three important verbs govern 4:22–24. **Put off** and **put on**
are both aorist infinitives and as such express a single act based
on a past experience. The readers have **put off** (*apothesthai*) the
old self and **put on** the new self at the time of their baptism. This
is the indicative of their Christian life and forms the basis for the
imperative to live out that life ethically. Thus the apostle reminds
his readers: **You were taught, with regard to your former way of
life, to put off your old self, which is being corrupted by its deceitful desires.** The **new self**, on the other hand, which the believers put on in baptism, is **created to be like God.**

In Colossians 3:10, Paul talks about this new life as being renewed in God's image. Undoubtedly, both Ephesians and Colossians allude to the restoration of the image of God in humanity that had been lost after the Fall (Gen. 1:27) but restored through incorporation into Christ. This new creation is **created to be like God in true righteousness and holiness.**

But coming between the reminder that the readers have put off the old self and put on the new is the exhortation for continual renewal of their hearts and minds (lit., "in the spirit of your mind"). *Ananeousthai* is a present infinitive, thus indicating that creation in God's likeness is a continuing process even though it is an established fact. Here is another reminder to believers that they must *become* what they *are!*

Additional Notes §19

4:17 / A helpful table of comparisons between Romans and Ephesians is provided by Mitton, p. 159, and by Stott, *God's New Society,* pp. 177–78.

4:18 / Robinson supports the translation "blindness." See his lengthy discussion on the word *pōrōsis* in his commentary, pp. 264–74.

4:20 / Barth, *Eph. 4–6,* has many helpful comments in his discussion "The School of the Messiah," pp. 529–33.

The moral exhortations in this section are especially appropriate for maintaining unity within the body of Christ. The vices mentioned are destructive to Christian fellowship; the virtues promote the corporate unity of believers. But though the apostle may consciously have selected these qualities to strengthen his central thesis, it should be noted that his teaching has a wider application and is appropriate for people outside the church as well.

Basically, this section includes the vices and virtues that belong to the old and the new life. Consequently, whenever the author lists a vice that is to be "put off," he substitutes a virtue that promotes human relationships: Lying is replaced by truth (4:25); anger is removed by reconciliation (4:26); a person who once robbed goes to work (4:27); harmful words give way to helpful ones (4:29); bitterness, passion, anger, and insults give way to tender-heartedness, forgiveness, and love (4:31–5:2).

4:25 / The exhortation that each one **must put off falsehood** uses the same word (*apotithēmi*) that was used in 4:22. Lying is to be put away because it does not belong in one's new life. Colossians 3:9, 10 is even more explicit when it states: "Do not lie to each other, since you have taken off your old self with its practices and have put on the new self." The Ephesians passage appears to be a quotation from Zechariah 8:16 ("speak the truth to each other"). The GNB translates *plēsion* (**neighbor**) as "fellow believer," thus accentuating that **we are all members of one body**. Although lying is wrong under any circumstances, the apostle shows that it is detrimental to the Christian community. "Without openness and truth, there can only be disunity, disorder and trouble" (Foulkes, p. 132).

4:26–27 / The second exhortation is directed toward controlling anger. The Greek imperative, "be angry" (*orgizesthe*), is probably a "concessive" or "permissive imperative" and may be translated appropriately "if you become angry" (GNB, cf. Ps. 4:4).

The important point is that anger is restricted by a series of negative admonitions:

In your anger do not sin. Believers must learn to keep their anger in check. If one is legitimately angry (righteous indignation?), caution must be taken that it does not become the cause for such sins as pride, hatred, or self-righteousness.

All anger is to be dealt with before the day is out. The translation **do not let the sun go down while you are still angry** suggests that there is no justification for carrying anger over into the next day; that surely would lead to sin.

No opportunity should be given to **the devil.** The apostle understands that anger that is unjustified, that promotes other sinful actions, and that is permitted to remain in one's life ultimately gives God's adversary access to the believer's heart, thus destroying the harmony of the church.

4:28 / The third exhortation seeks to terminate **stealing** (*kleptō*). Those who became Christians and continued their former practice of **stealing** are told to end this practice and **work.** Stealing is an attempt to get something for nothing. Thieves seek to enrich themselves at the expense of someone else's labors. Individuals practicing this sin are to **work, doing something useful with** their **own hands.**

Manual labor, however, is more than a cure for theft or a method of personal gain. The apostle raises the motive of work to a higher level and indicates that those who labor honestly will be able to fulfill their corporate duty to **share with those in need.** The biblical motive for possessions is not personal or selfish gain but the opportunity to assist others (for biblical injunctions on giving, see Matt. 19:21; Luke 14:13; John 13:29; Acts 2:44; 4:32–37; 6:1–4; Rom. 15:25–29; 2 Cor. 8 and 9). The ultimate goal for work is to have something to give away. The readers of Ephesians are to share in that concern for humanity.

4:29 / The fourth injunction deals with **unwholesome** speech—do not let any evil or rotten (*sapros*) word come out of your mouth. According to Mitton, this would include "words of a complaining, sneering, cynical, sarcastic type, all of which spread demoralisation in a community" (p. 171). In their place, use **only what is helpful.** Both individuals and the body of believers need words that build up, that will edify and **benefit those**

who listen. The Greek word translated **benefit** is *charis*, meaning grace. Thus, proper speech communicates something about God's grace. Although silence may be considered a virtue at times, the believer is encouraged to make a positive contribution to the life of the body by graceful speech. "Evil speech grieves the Holy Spirit, who works through good words" (Westcott, p. 80).

4:30 / It appears that the author refers to the **Holy Spirit** because of his connection with a person's speech. "The Spirit," states J. A. Robinson, "claims to find expression in the utterances of Christians . . . (cf. 5:18). The misuse of the organ of speech is accordingly a wrong done to, and felt by, the Spirit who claims to control it" (p. 113). Improper speech grieves (*lypeō*) **the Holy Spirit of God**. "The sins against the brotherhood are also an offense against the divine Spirit which inhabits the body of believers" (Beare, p. 701).

Once again, the readers are reminded that they have been sealed with the Holy Spirit—**with whom you were sealed for the day of redemption** (cf. 1:13). Since he is a seal or guarantee of the believers' destiny (**the day of redemption**), they are asked to revere him in their speech and thus be worthy of their inheritance.

4:31 / The presence of the Holy Spirit within the believer is sufficient reason to clean up one's speech by abolishing the following vices: **Bitterness** (*pikria*) comes from harboring resentful feelings; **rage** (*thymos*) is a bitter outburst of anger; **anger** (*orgē*) may be understood as resentment that lingers in one's life; **brawling**, or clamor (*kraugē*), is boisterous face-to-face confrontation; whereas **slander** (*blasphēmia*) can be abusive and slanderous words spoken about someone.

Lastly, there is **every form of malice**. This term may be considered a separate category or, as some commentators suggest, it may be a category that embodies all the previous vices (Mitton, p. 173; thus the NIV **every form of malice** and the NEB "bad feeling of every kind"). Any one or all of these vices grieve the Holy Spirit when they manifest themselves in the life of the believer.

4:32 / This verse provides a striking contrast to the previous one by emphasizing the virtues that should characterize believers in their interpersonal relationships. Instead of those negative and destructive qualities, believers are admonished to

be kind and compassionate to one another. Both of these virtues promote a spirit of acceptance, tolerance, and patience within the congregation.

Beyond that, the readers are to be continually **forgiving each other.** The word for forgiveness (*charizomai*) is also the word from which grace (*charis*) is derived. Within this context, believers are to respond to each other with the same grace, forgiveness, and generosity that they have experienced from God: hence **forgiving each other, just as in Christ God forgave you.** Christians have been forgiven by Christ (*echarisato*, past/aorist tense), but they are to go on forgiving (*charizomenoi*, present tense) one another on the strength of the example that Christ has provided.

5:1 / The thought of God's gracious activity in Christ leads the apostle to summon his readers (**dearly loved children**) to **be** (imperative, *ginesthe*) **imitators of God.** This is the only place in the NT where believers are called upon to imitate God. Elsewhere, Paul asks his converts to imitate him because they are his children (1 Cor. 4:14–16; 11:1; 1 Thess. 1:6; 2 Thess. 3:7, 9) and because he, himself, is an imitator of Christ. Here, the imitation of God is introduced within the context of forgiveness, and the apostle wants to use God's example in Christ as a pattern for personal relationships. It is doubtful that he would make a distinction between imitating Jesus and imitating God since one can only know God through Jesus.

5:2 / Since forgiveness and love are bound together, believers are admonished to **live a life of love.** That love finds its example in Christ who **gave himself up for us.** By implication, the Christian's love is to be expressed as a self-giving sacrifice (cf. 5:25). Love is the essence of God and is to be the main feature of the believer's walk (*peripateō*). By mentioning Christ's death, the apostle recalls words that were applicable to Jewish sacrifices— namely, **a fragrant offering and sacrifice to God.** The sacrifice of Jesus and the sacrificial life of love that believers live are pleasing to God.

§21 Living in the Light (Eph. 5:3–21)

In the previous section (4:25–5:2), the apostle concentrated on those vices disruptive to the unity of the Christian community. From there, he moved to the sins of immorality. In a sense, sexual sins also destroy the trust, unity, and respect that Christians have for each other and should, therefore, be banished. But in this case, the main point is that sexual sins are an offense to God, and they incur God's wrath because they are considered idolatrous. The new walk is explained further by the imagery of darkness and light. As the readers have been admonished to walk in "love" (5:1, 2), they are to walk in "the light" that they have received.

Given the general application of this epistle, it seems unlikely that these exhortations address anything specific that the readers faced. They resemble the denunciations elsewhere in the NT (Romans, 1 Corinthians, Gal. 5:19–21; Col. 3:5–8). But at the same time, a form of Gnostic teaching had possibly gained access to the Christian community. In some cases, for example, the heresy at Colossae (2:8–23), the teaching emphasized a rigid asceticism; but a variation of it tended toward libertinism, taking the attitude that those who had received spiritual knowledge (*gnōsis*) were free to participate in sexual indulgences. Those who separated body and spirit argued that it did not matter what one did with the body; they thus sinned with impunity. Perhaps these exhortations are addressing a situation in which such teachings were taking hold.

5:3 / The writer is emphatic in stating that, since his readers are **God's holy people**, the question is not only one of nonparticipation; rather, **there must not be even a hint** of these sins among them. When believers approach sin with an attitude of indifference (as in Gnostic libertinism), then it is not uncommon to discuss and to make light of one's personal sins or the sins of others. This is to be avoided in their fellowship.

Sexual immorality (*porneia*) covers a wide variety of unlawful sexual activity, such as prostitution, adultery, fornication, and promiscuity. **Impurity** (*akatharsia*) is tied to immorality and probably means sexual perversions of various kinds. **Greed**, or covetousness (*pleonexia*), in the context of immoral behavior would be the desire to engage in sexual activity solely for selfish reasons. Christians are to remove such evil from their lives as well as from their conversation. Such perversions are a contradiction to one who is called to imitate God and to walk in Christ's love (5:1, 2).

5:4 / The list of prohibitions goes on (in the Greek there is no new sentence) to include **obscenity** and **foolish talk or coarse joking.** Obscene words are ugly, base, shameful (*aischrotēs*); **foolish** words (*mōrologia*) are those uttered by a fool (*mōros*), words void of any decency or honor; *eutrapelia* (**coarse joking**) has a positive side meaning "wit" or "pleasantry." Here, however, it is used negatively in the sense of crude jesting, dirty insinuations, and so forth. All of these have no place in the life of a believer.

In place of foolish and shameful talk should be **thanksgiving.** Thankfulness, rather than indecency, should dominate one's speech. Though **thanksgiving** should be expressed to God for all things, the context may imply that **thanksgiving** be expressed to God for sexual activity and speech when it is proper to do so (cf. Mitton, p. 179).

5:5 / The emphatic **of this you can be sure** and the "let no one deceive you with empty words" (5:6) suggest that there was a serious moral threat at the time. Immorality, impurity, and greed exclude people from the inheritance that God has prepared for them. **Greed**, or covetousness (*pleonexia*), is equated with idolatry because sexual passions can become objects that dominate one's life and destroy one's relationship to God. A similar statement occurs in Colossians 3:5 in the context of "putting off" immoral practices.

Even though much is said about the "kingdom of God" in the NT, Galatians 5:21 is the only passage that specifically mentions this concept within the context of immoral behavior: Those who indulge in the "acts of the sinful nature" will not receive "the kingdom of God" (Gal. 5:19–21). But the phrase **kingdom of Christ and of God** is unique in the NT (unless "Lord" in Rev. 11:15 means God). The author of Ephesians makes no distinction between the two, because he understands the rule of Christ and God to be synonymous (cf. 1 Cor. 15:24–28). The main point, however, is that God's rule (**kingdom**) is denied to people who practice immoral behavior.

5:6–7 / There is no way of knowing specifically who was attempting to deceive these believers with **empty words**. Since Ephesians does not appear to have a local situation in mind, the **no one** could mean "everyone" who speaks empty or foolish words. Mitton refers to this as "arguments that sound plausible and attractive but which run counter to true reasoning and intuitive insights" (p. 181). This could be an amplification of the reference to the "men in their deceitful scheming" who teach by error and trickery (4:14).

The false teachers would want the Christians to believe that there is nothing wrong about participating in illicit sexual behavior and dirty talk. Such teaching, however, is deceptive; it leads people to believe something that is not true. The hard fact is that **God's wrath comes upon those who are disobedient**; eventually, wrongdoers will be punished for their sins.

Believers are admonished, **do not be partners with them**. The Greek term "partner" (*symmetochos*) indicates that they must not join in with these people and participate in their evil practices. This verse does not mean that believers should avoid all contact with immoral people; otherwise the exhortations that follow about light penetrating the darkness would have no purpose (cf. Col. 4:5, 6: "Be wise in the way you act toward outsiders"). Rather, they warn against participating in the vices of others.

5:8 / The apostle talks about the Christian life in 5:8–14 with the familiar imagery of darkness and light. Since they are **light in the Lord**, they are no longer **darkness**; nor do they participate in the unfruitful works of darkness. The life lived as children of light is characterized by goodness, righteousness, truth, and whatever is pleasing to the Lord. The section ends with the quotation of a saying that calls upon the spiritually dead to arise from their slumber and experience the light of the Lord (5:14).

The language, imagery, and theology of this section (5:8–14) strongly suggest that the author has baptism in mind. First of all, there is convincing evidence that the early church possessed a catechetical form that employed the motifs of darkness and light. These motifs play a crucial part in the passage, and it is quite likely that the author is borrowing thoughts from existing tradition.

Second, the contrast between the "then" and the "now," as has been noted on other occasions, relates to the concept of baptism as a change of status for the individual. Those who had been strangers, alienated from God (2:12–22), and subject to the powers of the world (2:1, 2) had also lived in darkness (5:8, 11). Now, however, in addition to having been brought near to God (2:13ff.), they are victorious and experience salvation in Christ (2:5–9). They are in the **light** and are admonished to **live as children of light** (5:8). This imagery reaches a climax in 5:14 with the affirmation that Christ is the instrument of light.

Earlier, the author contrasted the status of these believers in terms of being "dead" and "alive" (2:1–5) and "far away" and "near" (2:11–13). Here, as a continuation of darkened minds (4:18) and renewed hearts (4:23), darkness and light describe their moral condition. Darkness symbolizes their life of sin and participation in the evils just denounced; light is life in obedience to God.

You were once darkness (*ēte gar pote skotos*) means that they were identified as darkness, not just surrounded by it in their environment. Moule states it succinctly when he writes: "So had the night of spiritual ignorance and sin penetrated them that they were, as it were, night itself, night embodied" (Moule, p. 131). The same language applies to their new status as believers: **Now you are light** (*nyn de phōs*) **in the Lord**. Since they have become light (the indicative) the ethical charge that follows (the imperative) exhorts them to be what they are, that is, **live as children of light**. This change from darkness to light was, of course, due to their new relationship in the **Lord** through faith and baptism.

5:9 / Just as a seed, plant, or tree fulfills its true nature by producing **fruit**, a believer, who is light in the Lord, will produce the virtues of **goodness, righteousness and truth**—quite the opposite of the fruit of darkness in 5:3, 5. By insisting on the moral implications of light, the author would be opposing any false theories, such as those in the Gnostic system, that made enlightenment a mystical experience and viewed the ethical life with indifference and even disdain. To *be* light is to walk in the light (John 3:19, 20; 1 John 1:5–7; 2:8–11).

The fruit of light is similar to the fruit of the Spirit mentioned in Galatians 5:22, although **goodness** is the only concept that occurs there. The items on this list are probably selected for their relevance to the theme of unity within the body of Christ. The virtues of goodness, righteousness, and truth are essential to healthy personal and social relationships.

5:10 / Although part of the process of becoming a Christian is the acceptance of the truth as it is found in the gospel, the other part is learning by careful thought and experience what it means to be a Christian. Earlier, when the author was running through a list of pagan vices, he reminded the believers that they "did not come to know Christ that way" (4:20). Through instruction and guidance, probably in the form of a baptismal catechism, new converts were taught what to believe and how to act. Here they are exhorted to **find out what pleases the Lord**.

The word *dokimazō* means "putting to the test," "proving," "examining." The Christian life is not just a simple acceptance of doctrines and rules; believers exercise intelligent judgment as they relate their theology to specific moral situations. The things that **please** (*euarestos*) **the Lord** include the rich harvest of every kind of fruit mentioned in verse 9: **all goodness, righteousness, and truth.**

Both *dokimazō* and *euarestos* occur in Romans 12:2, where Paul writes that because of the inner transformation of their minds, believers "will be able to test and approve [*dokimazō*] what God's will is—his good, pleasing [*euarestos*] and perfect will." Beare notes that *euarestos* ("well-pleasing," "acceptable") nearly always concerns a sacrificial offering (Rom. 12:1; Phil. 4:18): "So here it suggests the thought that the life of the Christian is ever laid upon the altar. All of our actions are to be an offering to God . . . and we must therefore take care that they are *acceptable* to him" (p. 709).

5:11 / In contrast to the fruitful works of light (5:9), the works of darkness are unfruitful, or **fruitless.** Believers are admonished not to have anything to do with people who belong to the darkness. Again, as in 5:7, the apostle uses a *syn* noun (*synkoinōnos*), by which he means do not become a participant, a partner, in the unfruitful works of darkness. **Rather,** believers are to correct, convict, or reprove (*elenchō*) evil by exposing it to the light. The Christian life is not only the avoidance of evil; it is active participation in the things that expose evil.

5:12 / **For it is shameful even to mention what the disobedient do in secret** is a strong admonition against discussing the works of darkness in secrecy. This could be a veiled reference to the secret rites of the mystery religions or just a more general reminder that much of the evil that goes on is done in secret, under the cloak of darkness. Since the evil deeds are so shameful, it is wrong even to talk about them (cf. similar thoughts in John 3:19–21).

5:13 / Here the author returns to his thoughts in 5:10 by affirming that **everything exposed by the light becomes visible**. The repetition of *elenchō* (5:11) reaffirms the positive nature of light in exposing and reproving the works of darkness. In that process, people will come to see the true nature of evil and, it is hoped, turn to the light. As stated by Beare, "The power of light not only reveals, but penetrates and transforms into its own likeness whatever it illumines" (p. 711).

5:14 / The continuing emphasis in the first part of this verse is that darkness cannot exist in the presence of light. It appears that the most reasonable way to understand the imagery of darkness and light and the quotation that follows is in the context of baptism. Darkness, sleep, and death are striking figures symbolizing the condition of an individual apart from Christ. Baptism could be seen as the act by which a person awakens from sleep, rises from the dead, and responds to the light of Christ. Thus: **"Wake up, O sleeper, rise from the dead, and Christ will shine on you."**

There has been considerable speculation about the origin of this saying. Some scholars see it as a rather free synopsis from ideas in such OT passages as Isaiah 26:19 and 60:1, 2; others speculate that it may come from an apocryphal text or from some Hellenistic literature with a Gnostic or mystery religion's background; and others have found parallels and allusions to it in the Dead Sea Scrolls.

The introductory phrase, *dio legei* (cf. 4:18, where an OT citation is introduced), suggests that a written source is being quoted. But the failure to find such a literary formula opens the possibility that this was a well-known expression in the Christian community. The NIV **this is why it is said** leaves room for such a possibility.

Although the reconstruction of the setting of this quotation remains highly speculative, it may have been used by the church at a baptismal service as part of a hymn that was recited or sung. The early church created and used many songs in worship services (Eph. 5:19, 20; Phil. 2:6–11; Col. 3:16; 1 Tim. 3:16), and there is no reason to doubt that hymns could have been used on the occasion of baptism as a "call" to the candidate. It may have been sung when the candidate came out of the water after immersion. In the unbelieving state he or she has been regarded as asleep and dead; consequently, the believer is summoned to rise to a new life.

Another possibility is that the saying, together with the preceding discussion on darkness and light (5:8–13) and the following exhortations on Christian living (5:15ff.), belongs to the context of instruction (catechesis) just prior to baptism. Those being baptized would be reminded of their former life of darkness and then invited to **wake up** from their sleep and **rise from the dead**.

Although some of this is speculative, it does appear that the author is consciously alluding to baptism and that his readers would catch this allusion. His purpose, however, is neither to create nor to provide a baptismal liturgy for baptism, even though the material he utilizes is so oriented.

The exhortations of 5:8–14 fall within the context of a larger section (4:17–5:20) and illustrate the apostle's use of traditional catechetical material. His quotation from an existing baptismal hymn emphasizes that Christ is the source of all spiritual light. Now that Christians are light in the Lord, they are to walk (*peripateō*) as children of light. This, he goes on to say, includes wisdom (5:15), an understanding of God's will (5:17), fullness of the Spirit (5:18), as well as joyfulness and thanksgiving (5:19, 20).

5:15 / Within the context of Christian teaching, theology and ethics belong together: Behavior must be based upon correct doctrine; knowledge should not be regarded as a substitute for proper behavior. Basically, it is another way of reminding believers to be what they are. Consequently, they are to walk carefully and to live as **wise** rather than **unwise** people. Wisdom, here, has a practical dimension, that is, the ability to discern between right and wrong. For Mitton, "This means that the recognition that we live in a world where evil actions are followed by evil consequences is the first step toward wise conduct" (p. 187).

5:16 / The next exhortation advises the readers to make **the most of every opportunity.** Literally, the term *agorazō* comes from the language of the marketplace and means "to buy up" or "redeem." *Kairos* ("time") is the God-given opportunity that the believer has to walk in wisdom and to demonstrate the qualities of life that project light into darkness. Time is a precious commodity entrusted to believers for the purpose of doing good in a world in which **the days are evil.** Far too often Christians are so heavenly minded that they are no earthly good.

5:17 / In this brief exposition on Christian wisdom (5:15–17), the apostle has reminded his readers that wisdom has a practical dimension and that they are wise when they make good use of every opportunity. His final exhortation is that they **not be foolish** but discern God's will with respect to the course of their moral action.

5:18 / Ephesians 5:18–21 is an exhortation directed toward the worshiping community and stands in sharp contrast to the attitudes and actions of those who live in darkness (5:8–12). Instead of prohibiting certain conduct and conversation, the believers are encouraged to express their spiritual joy with song and thanksgiving. In 5:15–17, they are reminded to be wise and learn God's will; in 5:18–21 they are shown how that is accomplished.

These verses are adapted from Colossians 3:16, but here the main emphasis is upon the Spirit rather than on Christ's message (the word of Christ). The admonition—**do not get drunk on wine**—leads one to suspect that the author was thinking about religious cults, such as the worship of Dionysus, in which intoxication manifested itself in wild frenzies and ecstatic behavior that were interpreted in religious terms. Christians have a better way of experiencing spiritual elation—it is by being **filled with the Spirit.**

It should be noted that this is not a prohibition against the use of wine but against the excessive use of any alcoholic beverage leading to drunkenness (1 Tim. 3:3, 8; Titus 1:7; 2:3; *asōtia,* "debauchery," "profligacy," "waste") The contrast is not between

wine and the Spirit but between the two states that they produce: Intoxication with wine has a degrading effect; intoxication
with the Spirit (cf. Acts 2:13) can have an uplifting effect upon
the Christian community.

5:19 / This uplifting effect manifests itself in several ways.
One is in worship: This verse suggests that early Christian worship had a spontaneity about it and had not become fixed by liturgical order. **Psalms** (*psalmos*), **hymns** (*hymnos*) **and spiritual
songs** (*ōdais pneumatikais*) are listed as ways believers can praise
the Lord. Though it is impossible to make any real distinctions
between these categories (cf. disc. on Col. 3:16), some authors
think that **psalms** are OT musical pieces accompanied by the
plucking of strings, as on a harp; **hymns** are songs of praise to
God; and **spiritual songs** are more spontaneous pieces of inspired
music or words of exhortation. The important thing is that such
worship is a corporate, not an individual, experience. Believers
are to **speak to one another** as they praise the Lord.

5:20 / A second manifestation is in **giving thanks**:
Though thanksgiving undoubtedly is a component of worship,
it is another sign of being filled with the Spirit. Spirit-filled Christians live in a continual attitude of gratitude for everything. This,
as Stott wisely notes, should not be pressed too literally: "For we
cannot thank God for absolutely 'everything' including blatant
evil. . . . the 'everything' for which we are to give thanks to God
must be qualified by its context, namely *in the name of our Lord
Jesus Christ to God the Father*" (p. 207).

5:21 / The final manifestation noted is in submission:
Scholars, and consequently Bible translators, are divided on how
this verse fits into the context. Grammatically, it belongs to the
section on worship (5:18–21) and should be seen as another manifestation of the Spirit-filled believer. As singing and thanksgiving
are to be expressed corporately, members also must willingly submit to one another. Fullness of the Spirit leads to mutual subordination and unity, not to individual pride and disunity (cf. 1 Cor.
14:26–33; Phil. 2:1–5). At the same time, 5:21 is a transitional verse
from which the author proceeds to illustrate how that submission
is to be observed in specific domestic relationships (5:22–6:9).

If 5:21 is taken as an independent sentence then it serves
as a heading for the specific relationships that follow. Some trans-

lations, namely, GNB and RSV, use it this way. The NIV, however, lets it stand with the previous section. In either case, the position of the verse is not as important as its teaching—a teaching in which believers are exhorted to **submit** themselves **to one another out of reverence for Christ**. "We are not asked to yield to the wishes of others, no matter what they wish, but only when what they ask of us is in line with *reverence for Christ*" (Mitton, p. 196).

Additional Notes   §21

5:4 / P. W. van der Horst goes through a lengthy examination of the word *eutrapelia* and concludes that "the warning in Eph. v. 4 need not be read as a denouncement of humor and wittiness in the church" ("Is Wittiness Unchristian? A Note on *eutrapelia* in Eph. v. 4," in *Miscellanea Neotestamentica, Supplements to NovT*, vol. 48, ed. T. Baarda, A. F. J. Klijn, and W. C. van Unnik [Leiden: Brill, 1978], 163–77).

5:8 / Cf. disc. on Colossians 1:11–12, pp. 23–25. Extensive studies on the catechetical teaching in the early church can be found in P. Carrington, *The Primitive Christian Catechism*, and Selwyn's *I Peter*. Especially helpful is Selwyn's Table II, pp. 376–78, which he calls "Further Catechetical Material: The Children of Light (*Filii Lucis*)." Much of the language in Ephesians reminds one of the symbolism in the Fourth Gospel, where following Christ as the light of the world means to have the light of life and not to walk in darkness (8:12; cf. also, 3:19ff.; 9:5; 12:35, 36, 46).

5:14 / On the history of interpretation of this passage, see Barth, *Eph. 4–6*, pp. 573–77; R. Orlett, "Awake, Sleeper," *Worship* 35 (1961), pp. 102–5. Houlden, p. 185, lists parallels between this passage and Acts 12:7. Most scholars support some kind of association of this saying with a baptismal hymn, believing that it could have been used as an "awakening call" for the unbeliever to step out of his or her darkness into the light of Christ.

5:18 / C. E. Rogers believes that the wild, drunken practices connected with the worship of Dionysus form the general background for this command. See his "The Dionysian Background of Ephesians 5:18," *BibSac* 136 (1979), pp. 249–57; also, Beare, p. 714; Mitton, pp. 188–89.
In addition to the commentaries on the hymnody of the early church, cf. H. Schlier, "*ōdē*," *TDNT*, vol. 1, pp. 164–65; G. Delling, "*hymnos . . . psalmos*," *TDNT*, vol. 8, pp. 498–501.

§22   Wives and Husbands (Eph. 5:22–33)

What motivates the author to move from general admonitions on moral life and corporate worship to specific instructions regarding household relationships? Beare suggests that the arrangement of material follows the conventional pattern of Hellenistic philosophical literature, which concluded its doctrinal exposition with a brief presentation of the social code (p. 716). Another author places the code, particularly this section on husbands and wives, within the context of the ethical instructions that preceded it: "What," he asks, "was more necessary than to counter immorality with a true doctrine of man and wife?" (Houlden, p. 331).

A third suggestion comes from J. A. Robinson, who sees the code related structurally to the preceding instructions on worship (5:18–20). The church is not a fanatical and disorganized Spirit-filled community; rather, it is regulated by order and the principle of subjection of one member to another (p. 123).

A fourth theory explains the arrangement in Ephesians on the basis of Colossians, which, according to a number of commentators, the author was using as a model. Colossians, likewise, has a section on instruction and worship (3:16–17) before it moves on to discuss "Personal Relations in the New Life." The differences between the Colossian and Ephesian codes can be accounted for by the specific purpose they have in each epistle.

Finally, there is the principle of submission in 5:21. This statement relates to mutuality within the church but also forms a transition to the section on the household code. Thus, the author states a general principle; now he provides specific examples of how it is to be applied in relationships between husband and wife, parents and children, and masters and slaves.

Beyond these observations, one must rightfully question the purpose for the lengthy exposition on the relationship between husband and wife in this epistle (Ephesians has eleven verses, whereas Colossians has two). Is it the writer's primary intention to *(a)* offer domestic guidance regarding the husband-wife relationship (as is the case in 6:1–9 with child-parent and master-slave)? *(b)* Or is he using the example of husband and wife for an ecclesiological purpose, that is, to portray the nature of the relationship between Christ and the church? *(c)* Or is he using Christ's relationship to the church as a prototype for an ideal Christian marriage?

It appears that the author's primary intention is to emphasize the quality of relationship that should exist between husband and wife. In order to do this properly, and thus bring out the deepest implications of marriage, he resorts to the analogy of Christ and the church. And what could be a more fitting analogy! As Christ is head over the church, the husband is the head of his wife (5:23); as the church submits itself to Christ, wives submit themselves to their husbands (5:24); husbands are to love their wives with the same sacrificial love as Christ, who feeds and takes care of the church, his body (5:25, 29). The Lordship of Christ and his relation to the church epitomize the ideal union between husband and wife.

But though this appears to be the author's main purpose, the analogy works in the opposite direction as well. Throughout the epistle he has been expounding on the nature of the church and how Christ, the Head, is related to his body, the church. Marriage gives him an illustration—albeit imperfect—of how his readers can understand his ecclesiology. Thus, the church is under Christ's authority just as the wife is under the authority of her husband (5:23); Christ loves and cares for the church in the same way that a husband ought to love his wife (5:28). The analogy has both a domestic and an ecclesiological function.

Barth, although he agrees with these two foci of this section, does not think that either is foremost in the author's mind. Marriage, along with the other problems raised in Ephesians (e.g., sin, death, ethnic divisions, institutions), comes under the power and riches of God's grace. "The intention of Paul is to show that 'the grace of our Lord Jesus Christ' gives husband and wife the basis, the strength, and the example which they need in order to live in that 'peace to [or by] which God has called' them (1 Cor. 7:15). The 'peace' between God and man, Jews and Gentiles, of which Paul spoke in Eph. 2:14–16 shall be extended into every house and praised by the conduct of husband and wife" (*Eph.* 4–6, p. 655).

The subjects of husband-wife relationships, the equality of women, and the role of women in the church continue to be debated and controversial issues today. With respect to Ephesians, several things must be noted: First, the author is talking about husband-wife relationships, *not* male-female differences and the equality, rights, roles, and so on of women. Some of those issues are dealt with in other epistles, such as 1 Corinthians and 1 Timothy. Second, the relationship between husband and wife is not modified *or* qualified by arguments used elsewhere in Scripture, such as the order and glory of creation (1 Cor. 11:3–16) or the sin of Eve (1 Tim. 2:9–15). Neither is submission demonstrated by outward things such as women covering their heads in public worship (1 Cor. 11:3–16) or remaining silent in the presence of men during worship (1 Cor. 14:33–38). The submission taught in Ephesians is a *mutual subordination* between husband and wife that is *based on the prototype of Christ and his church*; Christ is the example who determines the qualities of headship and submission. Third, the teaching with respect to husband and wife—as well as the other categories in the code—must be seen within the larger context of the position of women and marriage in the first century (cf. disc. in chap. 18 on Colossians; Barth, *Eph.* 4–6, pp. 655–62).

The need for order lies behind all the instruction that encompasses the domestic code. The authors of the NT did not want Christianity to be misunderstood by society or to have new Christians feel that their freedom in Christ meant the abolition of current standards regulating domestic life. But in Ephesians the motive goes beyond "good order." The household rules illustrate the principle of subordination that is essential to the unity and harmony within the body of Christ. The church becomes a pattern for all social order.

5:22–24 / Colossians exhorts wives to be submissive (*hypotassō*) to their husbands because it is the proper thing for Christians to do (3:18). Submission is required on the basis of the socially acceptable norms of the day. In Ephesians, wives are called to submission for a different reason, namely, the divine order to creation that appears to be at the heart of the entire passage. This principle of "creationism" is assumed rather than explicitly stated, as it is, for example, in 1 Corinthians 11:3 ("the head [*kephalē*] of every man is Christ, and the head of the woman is man, and the head of Christ is God").

The husband is the head of the wife. What is significant in Ephesians is that the so-called hierarchical order of creation is qualified profoundly: First, the submission of the wife to her husband is exercised within the wider principle of mutual subordination. Members within the body of Christ are to "submit to one another out of reverence for Christ" (5:21). This, however, does not abolish the concept of authority: "The principle of mutual subordination is not applied so as to destroy the complementary principle of authority, without which there can be no ordered social life among men" (Beare, p. 717). Second, the *motive* for submission is placed within the context of the wife's relationship to the Lord—**wives, submit to your husbands as to the Lord**. Those who submit must do so as if they were submitting to Christ.

Third, submission is regulated by the divine pattern of Christ's relationship to the church. Those to whom submission is given likewise must find the pattern of their obedience and conduct in Christ. Hence the reciprocal exhortations: wives, submit **as to the Lord** . . . "just as Christ loved the church" (5:25).

From these principles it becomes obvious that a husband's authority is regulated by Christ's example and the principle of love. Authoritarianism, self-assertion, and self-centeredness have no place in a marriage based on these principles. Submission is not "obedience," for the word "obey" (*hypakouō*) is used only for children and slaves (6:1, 5). When a husband relates to his wife out of love (*agapē*), there will be no problems with respect to submission or obedience.

The author is aware of the limits of his analogy, because no human, fallible husband can even approximate the extent and quality of love that Christ has for the church. This seems to be the case when he states that Christ is **head of . . . his body, of which he is the Savior** (5:23). Only Christ can be considered the savior of the body because of his work for and relationship to it. Nevertheless, "The sacrificial concern of the Lord for the salvation of the Church should have a parallel, even if at a much lower level, in the loving and sacrificial concern of the husband for the welfare of his wife" (Foulkes, p. 156).

5:25 / Lest husbands come to believe that Ephesians 5:21–33 is a document legitimizing their authority to restrict the freedom of their wives, it should be noted that the admonition for husbands to love their wives puts a greater responsibility on them. *Agapē* means to subordinate one's own interests, pleasures, and personality for the benefit of someone else. In fact, Christ's love, which the husband is to model, was completely sacrificial—**Christ loved the church and gave himself up for her.** The **church** is considered as the sum total of persons for whom Christ died (Rom. 4:25; 8:32; Gal. 1:4; 2:20). **Loved** (past tense) refers to some definite action in the past, such as the cross.

5:26 / The sense of the corporate nature of the church is carried over into the two verses describing the **washing** of the church and its subsequent results. At first glance, 5:26, 27 appear as an interpolation, because the thoughts of 5:25 and 5:28 join so nicely together. Yet, there is no textual evidence that these verses are of questionable origin; nor is there any suggestion that they do not fit into the context of the writer's discussion on Christ and the church. It appears that the mention of Christ's death for the church (5:25) triggered thoughts the author had about baptism. Perhaps he was thinking of Jesus' death as a baptism in which his followers are to share (Mark 10:38, 39). Christian baptism is a baptism into Christ's death (Rom. 6:3; Gal. 3:27; Col. 2:11, 12, 20).

Beyond the relationship between Christ's death and baptism, another analogy appears to be at work, namely, the nuptial or ceremonial bath that a bride took before marriage. In the cultures of that day it was customary for a bride to take this bath before the marriage day. Following the bath, the bride, clad in her lovely garments, would present herself before the bridegroom. Does the author conceive of baptism as a bridal bath that sanctifies the church? Does Paul have this imagery in mind when he writes to the Corinthians, "I promised you to one husband, to Christ, so that I might present you as a pure virgin to him," (2 Cor. 11:2)? On the basis of context, it seems more probable that when the author speaks of Christ giving himself up for the church (5:25), he thinks of baptism as the rite that symbolizes this death and by which the church is made clean by the washing in water.

There are a number of reasons why the thoughts in verse 26 are associated with baptism: First, there is the imagery of washing and cleansing (**cleansing her by the washing with water**). The cleansing of the church, which here is viewed collectively or corporately, took place when its individual members were baptized.

The readers would have been aware of the baptismal teaching in the early church that conceived of baptism as a moral washing (John 13:10; Acts 2:38; 22:16; 1 Cor. 6:11; Titus 3:5; Heb. 10:22; 1 Pet. 3:20, 21).

Second is the relationship between baptism and the **word** (lit., "the washing of water by/in the word"). Baptism, in the context of the NT, was accompanied by a *spoken word*. Here it could mean either *(a)* some kind of gospel utterance; *(b)* a confession from the candidate in which he or she expresses faith in the Lord; *(c)* some prebaptismal words of instruction; or *(d)* a baptismal formula, such as baptism into the name of Christ (Acts 2:38; 8:16; 19:5; 22:16; 1 Cor. 6:11) or into the names of the Trinity (Matt. 28:19). In spite of all these possibilities, it would be safe to conclude that **word** refers to a confession or formula that accompanied baptism.

The new, or perhaps unusual, idea of Ephesians at this point is that the entire church receives this bath. This idea of a corporate baptism may have originated in the preceding discussion on the unifying elements of the Christian church (4:4–6) in which, among other things, the writer mentions the one body (4:4) and the one baptism (4:5). Although baptism ordinarily is received by the believer, its application to the whole church is justified on the basis of the church's corporate and unified nature.

5:27 / The reason or the ultimate purpose behind the baptism of the church is now stated: **to present her to himself as a radiant church, without stain or wrinkle or any other blemish, but holy and blameless**. This is where the analogy of the bride and the bridal bath—if it is implied—breaks down. In a marriage the bride presents herself to the bridegroom; it would be inappropriate for the bridegroom to present the bride to himself (Mitton, p. 201). Here Christ takes the initiative by cleansing the bride (church) through baptism and presenting it to himself "free from all disfigurements or deformities" (Mitton, p. 204; Mitton also draws attention to the parallel between individual and corporate holiness in 1:4 and 5:27). The husband is to love his wife "not just because of the beauty he finds in her, but to make her more beautiful. Christ sees the Church in all her weaknesses and failures, and yet loves her as His body and seeks her true sanctification" (Foulkes, p. 160).

Baptism has a three-dimensional focus: It is a past event grounded in the redemptive work of Christ ("he gave himself up for her," i.e., the church); it continues to be a present reality by which individuals are baptized into the body of Christ and by which they are cleansed. Moreover, it has an ethical and eschatological function (in order **to present**). Sanctification and cleansing lead to the church's ultimate glorification and splendor.

5:28 / Even though husbands cannot love their wives in the same way that Christ demonstrated his love for the church, the divine model is still in the author's mind: **Husbands ought to love their wives as their own bodies**. It appears that the husband, based on the principle that in marriage the two will become one (5:31), should regard his wife as his own body. He will, therefore, love his wife just as he loves his own body. Union and intimacy of this kind seem to agree with the phrase, **he who loves his wife loves himself**. Thus it is true that husband and wife are "complementary parts of one personality" (Beare, p. 725).

This interpretation fits the drift of the author's thought better than one that sees these statements as encountering "prudential" or "pragmatic self-interest," as Mitton, for example, suggests: "It is easier to do what is right and good if one can see at the same time that it will produce something beneficial to ourselves" (p. 205). What we have, instead, is a fusion of the bride image into the body image (Houlden, p. 334). Thus, "As the Church is Christ's body, so in a true sense the wife is the husband's body. Through her he extends his life" (Westcott, p. 85).

5:29 / By prefacing 5:29 and 30 with **After all**, the NIV understands these verses as a commentary on 5:28. The love that a husband has for his own body and, consequently, for his wife is illustrated in practical ways: First, **he feeds and cares for it**. Once a husband has come to think of his wife as his own flesh he will **feed** (lit., "nourish," *ektrephō* and **care for** (lit., "cherish," *thalpō*) her as Christ does with respect to his body, the church. On the human level this is true because **no one ever hated his own body**. (The Greek uses the term "flesh" rather than **body**, probably because it anticipates the quotation in 5:31 from Gen. 2:24, which states that the two shall become one "flesh.")

5:30 / The second illustration is through being **members of his body** (cf. 1 Cor. 6:15—"Do you not know that your bodies are members of Christ himself?"). The meaning of this phrase must be seen in relation to the previous statement on Christ's love and care for the church: **we are members of his body**; therefore, Christ "feeds" and "cares for" us. Although there does not appear to be any conscious application of this truth to the readers, it would remind them of Christ's concern for each one of them. Foulkes finds a helpful analogy from the vine and the branches in John 15: "As in the divine purpose the wife becomes part of the very life of her husband, and he nourishes and cherishes her, even so the Lord does to us as members of Himself, part of His own life that he has joined to Himself" (Foulkes, p. 161).

5:31 / The OT verse (Gen. 2:24) from which the author has been drawing his imagery is finally quoted. It confirms the thoughts that he has been expounding on the relationship between husband and wife in marriage. Prior to marriage, a man and a woman are bound in an intimate relationship with their parents; but the marriage bond transcends that former bond by uniting the two as one flesh. For the author, this verse appropriately expresses the intimacy, unity, and, according to his thoughts, the identity of the husband and wife within marriage— a condition undoubtedly created by their sexual union (cf. 1 Cor. 6:16, 17, where Gen. 2:24 is used with reference to an immoral relationship with a prostitute).

Some of the older commentaries suggest that this verse has a secondary reference to Christ and how he left his heavenly home in order to be joined with his bride, the church. Moule, for example, writes: "We may reverently infer that the Apostle was guided to see in that verse a divine parable of the Coming Forth of the Lord, the *Man* of Men, from the *Father*, and His present and eternal mystical union with the true Church, His Bride" (p. 143; cf. other examples in Abbott, pp. 173, 174). Such an interpretation, however, is highly speculative and presses the analogy beyond its intended purpose as an illustration of unity.

The significance of this quotation and the context from which it is taken cannot be overstated. In Scripture, it is used as the main argument against polygamy, sexual immorality, and divorce. No one verse speaks more strongly for the sacredness and permanency of the marriage bond and for fidelity within marriage.

5:32 / As appropriate as Genesis 2:24 is in describing the essence of marriage, and as overcome as the author is by the beauty of such a relationship, he still is preoccupied with thoughts about Christ and the church. Consequently, he sees in the one-ness of husband and wife a great revelation that, for him, applies to **Christ and the church**. "The husband's position as head and his duty of sacrificial love and devoted care for his wife are but pictures, imperfect, but the best that this life can offer, of Christ as Head, and of His love, self-sacrifice and concern for His church. The dependence of the wife on her husband and her duty of sub-mission are a picture of how the Church should live and act towards her divine Lord" (Foulkes, p. 162).

The phrase **this is a profound mystery** is a translation of the Greek *to mystērion touto mega estin* ("this mystery is great!"). Earlier in this epistle, **mystery** referred to God's plan for human-kind, which had been hidden but now has been revealed (1:9; 3:3–6, 9; cf. also 6:19). Here it refers to a deep insight or a **pro-found** truth that is revealed. A **mystery**, in this context, is not a secret but a revelation—the union between Christ and the church.

One cannot help but notice that the references to **mystery** in Ephesians have unity as a theme. The mystery revealed in 3:3–6 *unites* Jew and Gentile into the body of Christ; in 5:32, one ap-plication of the mystery is the *union* between Christ and the church. In the former case there is the creation of *one new people in union with himself* (Christ); in the latter, the *two become one*. Stott notes that in Ephesians the metaphors of the church—"the body, the building and the bride—all emphasize the reality of its unity on account of its union with Christ" (p. 231). The Latin render-ing of *sacramentum* for mystery does not legitimize viewing mar-riage as a sacrament (cf. Barth, *Eph. 4–6*, pp. 744–49).

The precise meaning of the author's thoughts is by no means easy to determine—as is obvious from the variety of trans-lations and interpretations (for a list, see Mitton, pp. 207, 8). Some commentators, in spite of the apostle's application of Genesis 2:24 to Christ and the church, believe that it refers primarily to human marriage as the great **mystery**. Others concede that though that may be true in itself, the phrase **but I am talking about** (*egō de legō*) or, "it also applies," indicates that the marriage union illus-trates something even more meaningful. Beare paraphrases such thinking in the following way: "The mystery of the union of man and wife into one flesh is of far-reaching importance and clearly points itself toward some transcendental, eternal reality. I for my part take it to be a symbol of the union of Christ and the church" (Beare, p. 727).

5:33 / Lest the readers be too caught up in the mystical aspects of these thoughts, and in spite of that application to Christ and the church in 5:32, the author brings them back to reality: **However, each one of you. . . .** By doing this, he returns to the more practical and human considerations that initiated the discussion about husband and wife (5:22ff.): **Each one of you also must love his wife as he loves himself, and the wife must respect her husband. Respect** is a translation of the Greek *phobeō*, which, as in 5:21, also has the meaning of reverence. It is best understood as "awe," such as an individual would show before God (cf. Barth, *Eph. 4–6*, pp. 662–68 for a detailed explanation). Barth protests the equation of "fear" with awe, reverence, or respect, insisting that it be given an eschatological meaning as well, that is, "conduct that heeds the crisis of the present, the last judgment, and the ultimate triumph of Christ" (*Eph. 4–6*, p. 667).

This section of the household code ends in much the same way as it began—submission, reverence, and love. Throughout, the author has fluctuated between two analogies: At times the husband-wife relationship served an ecclesiological function by illustrating Christ's relationship to the church; at other times, the Christ-church analogy illustrated a domestic ideal. The result is that one has a deeper appreciation and understanding of both relationships, even though the author's original intention was to enrich the understanding of marriage.

Additional Notes §22

In addition to the disc. and bibliography on the household codes in §§ 18–21 on Colossians 3:18–4:1, see F. Stagg, "The Domestic Code and Final Appeal: Ephesians 5:21–6:24," *RevExp* 75 (1979), pp. 541–52. On the use of traditional material in this section, P. Sampley, *And the Two Shall Become One Flesh: A Study of Traditions in Ephesians 5:21–33* (Cambridge: Cambridge University Press, 1971); Barth, *Eph. 4–6*, pp. 652–55; Mitton, pp. 208–10.

5:23 / For questions regarding the legitimacy of translating head (*kephalē*) as "authority," see the article by B. and A. Mickelsen, "Does

Male Dominance Tarnish Our Translations?" *Christianity Today,* October 5, 1979, pp. 23–29. The main point the Mickelsens make is that head "*does not* mean 'boss' or 'final authority' . . . but source or origin . . . or beginning."

5:26–27 / For arguments pro and con on the bridal bath, see R. Batey, "Jewish Gnosticism and the 'Hieros Gamos' of Eph. v.21–33," *NTS* 10 (1963), pp. 121–27; C. Chavasse, *The Bride of Christ* (London: Faber & Faber, 1939); Hanson, *The Unity of the Church in the New Testament.* Barth argues against a baptismal interpretation of 5:26, 27, in his *Eph. 4–6,* pp. 687–700.

5:31 / On the use of Gen. 2:24 in Eph. 5:31, 32, see A. T. Lincoln, "The Use of the OT in Ephesians," *JSNT* 14 (1982), pp. 16–57, esp. pp. 30–36. For additional thoughts on marriage, singleness, and individuality, Barth, *Eph. 4–6,* pp. 700–738; F. Stagg, "The Domestic Code and Final Appeal: Ephesians 5:21–6:24," *RevExp* 76 (4, 1979), pp. 547–48.

5:32 / Discussion on the concept of "sacred marriage" (*hieros gamos*) in Jewish and Hellenistic thought can be found in Barth, *Eph. 4–6,* pp. 738–44; Beare, pp. 726–28; and Batey, "Jewish Gnosticism and the 'Hieros Gamos' of Eph. v. 21–33."

§23 Children and Parents (Eph. 6:1–4)

A continuation of these rules of conduct as they apply to children and parents (6:1–4) and slaves and masters (6:5–9) appears in 6:1–9. As in the section on the husband-wife relationship, there is the specific emphasis that the ethical life of the Christian is both grounded in and directed toward the Lord.

The superscription of submission "out of reverence for Christ" in 5:21 serves the entire code. Wives are to submit to their husbands as to the Lord (5:22); children are to obey their parents "in the Lord"; fathers are to raise their children "in the training and instruction of the Lord" (6:4); slaves are to obey their earthly masters "just as you would obey Christ" (6:5) as his slaves (6:6). Masters, likewise, are to let Christ, the Master in heaven, govern their attitude and conduct toward their slaves (6:9).

It is possible that such rules of conduct were given as part of the catechetical instruction to newly baptized believers, but it is not necessary to conclude that the author is here addressing the congregation during a baptismal service. Nor does the inclusion of children in this instruction mean that infants were baptized. The primary concern is to demonstrate the kind of personal and domestic unity that should exist among Christians in the church.

6:1 / Although the author is following Colossians 3:20–21 rather closely, there are some significant differences in this epistle. Children are exhorted to **obey** their **parents** because **this is right**. Obedience to parents is considered to be a self-evident and morally acceptable thing to do.

Thus, obedience to parents is considered to be a self-evident and morally acceptable thing to do for all families (the statement does not specify that only Christian parents are meant). The NIV **in the Lord** is a disputed reading in the Greek text, probably copied later because of a similar phrase in 5:22 (*tō kyriō*) and/or because it is parallel to Col. 3:20. If retained, it makes obedience a Christian as well as a universal obligation.

In Colossians, children are to "obey in everything." Mitton suggests that the change in Ephesians would be appropriate "where the children addressed may have pagan parents," thus necessitating "an obedience which does not contravene a primary obedience 'to the Lord.' " (p. 210). Though obedience to parents is a universally acceptable principle, there are conflicts when Christian children are required to submit to parents who have no Christian commitment and whose moral standards run counter to Christ's.

6:2–3 / **"Honor your father and mother"**: Since this quotation from Exodus 20:12 (cf. Deut. 5:16) does not occur in the Colossians parallel, it is reasonable to assume that the author of Ephesians is either relying on a different tradition or making a point specifically appropriate to his audience. Obedience to this commandment carries the promise of prosperity and longevity. By **the first commandment with a promise** the author must mean first in importance with respect to children, because the second commandment, which prohibits idolatry, is followed by God's promise to show his steadfast love to those who love him and keep his commandments (Exod. 20:6).

Initially, Exodus 20:12 referred to the promised land that God was giving to the children of Israel. Also, it would have been older children who were called upon to honor their parents by obeying and exercising care and responsibility for them. Ephesians shortens the phrase "in the land the Lord your God is giving you" (Exod. 20:12) to "on the earth." The promised land is replaced by a more general or universal conception. God rewards a society or a community in which obedience and respect are practiced.

It is difficult to demonstrate the fulfillment of this promise in a society where a promise of reward does not always seem to hold true. Most commentators, therefore, interpret the author's intention in general rather than individual terms. "Then what is promised," claims Stott, "is not so much long life to each child who obeys his parents, as social stability to any community in which children honor their parents. Certainly a healthy society is inconceivable without a strong family life" (p. 241; cf. also Foulkes, p. 165; Mitton, p. 212, for similar applications).

6:4 / The change from "parents" (6:1) to **fathers** may or may not be significant. Does the author mean that whereas obedience is required toward both parents, it is the father's responsibility to administer discipline and nurture the child in spiritual things? This could attest to the strong patriarchal orientation of the first century in both Jewish and pagan society. A Roman father, for example (*pater familias*), exercised a rigid and sovereign control over his household (Stott, p. 245; Barclay, p. 208).

Negatively, **fathers** are exhorted **not** to **exasperate** (from *parorgizō*, "provoke to anger") their **children**. Obedience can be expected, but it cannot be demanded by provoking and irritating children, or causing them to be angry (Col. 3:21 adds "or they will become discouraged"). Positively, parents are urged to **bring them up in the training and instruction of the Lord**.

The verb for "raise" (*ektrephō*) has the meaning of nourish. Though it can be used for bodily nourishment and care (5:29), it applies also to the care given to the entire person. This nurture is given through Christian discipline (*paideia*) and instruction (*nouthesia*). These exhortations for catechetical instruction may be related to the baptismal nature of the epistle. This may be one reason why this verse is omitted in Colossians; another could be that Ephesians was written considerably later than Colossians and thus reflects an increasingly parental and church concern for children.

Some commentators draw a rather rigid distinction between the two categories of nurture that are employed, suggesting that *paideia* means training by disciplinary action and *nouthesia* refers to verbal instruction (Foulkes, p. 166; Stott, p. 248). Such distinctions, according to Mitton, are a little "strained," although "the words together suggest both the inculcation of patterns of behaviour worthy of a Christian and also verbal instruction about the contents of the faith" (p. 213).

§24 *Slaves and Masters (Eph. 6:5–9)*

Most of the things that were said about slavery in the exegesis of Colossians (Colossians § 21) and Philemon apply to Ephesians as well. But though the Colossian code was directed specifically toward the need for order in the church, the code in Ephesians appears to be more general in nature and to conform to the writer's concern that there be unity and understanding within the Christian community as believers seek to serve Christ within the guidelines of the principle of submission (5:21).

6:5 / The slaves who are being addressed are Christians. This means that their life has a new center of reference and that their ultimate loyalty is directed toward the Lord, who puts new meaning into their earthly responsibilities. Consequently, they are to **obey** their **earthly masters** as though they were serving Christ (6:5); they are to consider themselves as "slaves of Christ" (6:6) and perform their duties as though they served "the Lord, not men" (6:7).

Respect and fear appears to be a common expression in connection with obedience (2 Cor. 7:15; Phil. 2:12). To some, this may connote cowardice or submission occasioned by severe oppression. But more likely reverence and respect for those in authority is meant. Slaves, in spite of their newly found freedom in Christ, need to remember that they have not been freed socially from the institution of slavery. Disobedience to one's earthly masters could still result in severe punishment (cf. 6:9, "Do not threaten"). Service to earthly masters is to be rendered with the same kind of **sincerity of heart** that governs one's service to **Christ**.

6:6 / The previous idea is carried over into this verse, where sincerity is defined as enthusiastic behavior (**from your heart**) without any attempt to attract human attention (**not only . . . when their eye is on you**) or any desire for human **favor**. By serving in this way they do **the will of God**.

This, to be sure, is a revolutionary transformation of the work ethic and has many implications for labor relations today. For a Christian, there is no distinction between the secular and the sacred. "The Christian's ideal is for his daily work, seen or unseen by men, to be accepted as the *will of God*, rejoiced in and done not by constraint or carelessness but because it is his will" (Foulkes, p. 168).

6:7 / This verse essentially repeats—and thus re-emphasizes—the thought in the two preceding ones. Work that is done cheerfully (*eunoia* carries the idea of zeal and enthusiasm) has to come from the heart. That inner conviction brought about by a new relationship to Christ and new attitude toward work enables the slave to perform his or her responsibilities with enthusiasm.

6:8 / As in Colossians (3:24), the **reward** motif is introduced into the discussion as a reminder that there is more to life than poor working conditions or one's paycheck. In Colossians, there is a direct connection to the future inheritance that the faithful receive ("you will receive an inheritance from the Lord as a reward") because the problem of injustice seems to have been more pronounced (3:25). In Ephesians, the emphasis is upon the **good** that is performed by **slave or free**: Both will be rewarded by the Lord.

6:9 / **Masters** are exhorted to **treat** their **slaves in the same way**. This means that the Lord expects sincerity, cheerfulness, and a detachment from earthly attention and the need for approval; they are Christian masters and so their believing slaves share the same heavenly Lord (**you know that he who is both their Master and yours is in heaven**). "In civil law, the slave had no rights as against his master, but under Christianity the obligations are reciprocal" (Beare, p. 735). A higher social or economic status is of no advantage in the Christian community as far as one's relationship with the Lord is concerned. With Christ **there is no favoritism** (lit., "before him there is no partiality," *prosōpolēmpsia*).

Slave owners who became Christians had to make a radical change in their attitudes and behavior toward their slaves. One common way of controlling their labor force was by threats—threats of death, punishment, or sale. This practice, states the apostle, must be terminated (**do not threaten them**). Service must be earned; it should not come through the fear of reprisal.

Although the author does not abolish the institution of slavery, this new relationship between slave and master ultimately led to its demise. In connection with this, Stott notes that the gospel, with its teaching of equality, justice, and brotherhood, "lit a fuse which at long last led to the explosion which destroyed it" (p. 257).

Additional Notes   §24

6:9 / In line with this, Stagg prophetically observed: "Slavery sooner or later had to come under the judgment of the Christian conscience. What about male domination or any other denial of the full personhood of any person?" ("The Domestic Code and Final Appeal," p. 550).

§25 The Christian's Armor (Eph. 6:10–20)

Since the imagery of war and armor is quite prominent throughout the NT, this section in Ephesians does not specifically represent any new teaching. Paul, for example, speaks of his own Christian life as a spiritual fight (1 Cor. 9:24–27), and the author of the Pastorals encourages Timothy to "fight the good fight" (1 Tim. 1:18; 6:12) in an age of apostasy. On several occasions Paul even identifies the weapons that the Christian is to use. Because the battle is a spiritual one, he says, "the weapons we fight with are not the weapons of the world. On the contrary, they have divine power to demolish strongholds" (2 Cor. 10:4). He exhorts the Romans to "put on the armor of light" (Rom. 13:12), whereas his admonition to the Thessalonians is to be "putting on faith and love as a breastplate, and the hope of salvation as a helmet" (1 Thess. 5:8).

There are at least two possible sources for this kind of imagery. The original and most immediate source of inspiration may be the pieces of armor that the Roman armies used. Paul had sufficient opportunity to observe such armor on the soldiers who were guarding him in prison. But although the Roman military power is the nearest at hand, the author of Ephesians undoubtedly is working from concepts that had been fairly well established in the church.

The most obvious starting point for this biblical imagery lies in Isaiah 59:17, where God is pictured as the warrior who arms himself for battle: "He put on righteousness as his breastplate, and the helmet of salvation on his head; he put on the garments of vengeance and wrapped himself in zeal as in a cloak." In the prophecy of Isaiah 11:5, it is the Messiah who comes for war and judgment: "Righteousness shall be the girdle of his waist, and faithfulness the girdle of his loins" (RSV). This imagery is carried into the apocryphal literature, where it states that the coming of the Lord and even all of creation will be armed for battle (Wisdom of Solomon 5:17–20). The idea of the heavenly armor originates

in these OT sources and reaches its fully developed form in the
NT picture of the Christian warrior.

Apart from the idea that the Christian life can be considered as a battle or a fight, it is likely that these exhortations were
particularly useful when Christians were being persecuted. In
1 Peter 4:1, for example, the believers are exhorted to "arm themselves" spiritually for the suffering that awaits them.

In Ephesians, the Christian warrior is exhorted to "put on
the full armor of God" (6:11) for the battle against the forces of
wickedness. Here there is no indication of persecution or suffering. The exhortation clearly is intended for the present life of the
church, although mention of the coming evil day (6:13) brings
in an element of the future as well. The author indicates that this
is his final exhortation to the readers (6:10). Thus, they who are
already in Christ by virtue of their baptism are to continue to find
strength for their new life "in the Lord" (6:10).

The numerous references to "stand" (6:11, 13, 14) emphasize the theme of watchfulness and steadfastness that characterizes this early catechism (cf. 1 Cor. 16:13; Col. 4:12; James 4:7;
1 Pet. 5:8, 9). Although the NT often speaks about an inner warfare caused by the passions of the flesh (Rom. 7:23; Gal. 5:17;
James 4:1; 1 Pet. 2:11), the enemies that the readers of Ephesians
are to resist are spiritual in nature and include the devil and
"the rulers, . . . the authorities, . . . the powers of this dark
world" (6:12).

There is very little evidence to indicate whether such an exhortation was connected specifically with baptism. Although baptism would be a suitable occasion to remind new Christians that
they have spiritual armor to face the world, there is little to com-
mend this connection in Ephesians. The most tangible evidence
in this respect is found in Ignatius' letter to Polycarp: "Let your
baptism be your arms; your faith, your helmet; your love, your
spear; your endurance, your armor" (6.2).

The most that one can say about the author's final exhortation in the Epistle to the Ephesians is that it is built upon traditional imagery of the Christian warrior and early catechetical
material on steadfastness and watchfulness in the Christian life.
This section could, as Mitton suggests, pick up the warnings that
the author developed in 5:3–20, or even in 4:25–31, where the
readers are admonished not to give the devil a chance (4:27). The

exhortations in 6:10–20 provide specific ways in which evil can be thwarted (p. 219).

6:10 / **Finally,** that is, this is the last or concluding exhortation. The phrase **be strong in the Lord** is not a plea for self-effort. The present passive verb *endynamoō* literally means "be made strong in the Lord continually." The next phrase indicates that this empowerment is possible because of the resources that the Lord supplies—**in his mighty power.**

Within this verse there are three Greek words for power—*dynamis, kratos,* and *ischus.* Distinctions between these words are not always possible or necessary; the message that comes through is that God's resources enable the believer to face evil. These same words in 1:19 described the spiritual gifts of the believer (indicative); now believers are exhorted to experience the effect of that power in their daily life (imperative).

6:11 / **Put on** is a common expression in Ephesians and Colossians used, as has been seen, in the context of baptism (4:24; Col. 3:10, 12). The aorist tense indicates that the author is thinking of a specific time or situation when this took place in the believer's life. "This would fit a baptismal occasion when the new Christian is ready to step out in his new venture of Christian discipleship" (Mitton, p. 220). **Stand,** as noted above, was a common theme in the catechetical instruction of the early church.

The believer's equipment is **the full armor of God** (*tēn panoplian tou theou*)—**full** in the sense of adequacy and quality and not completeness, since there were other items that a "fully armed" person would require for combat. What is included here, however, is all that the believer needs to **stand against the devil's schemes.** *Methodeia,* from which we derive the English words *methodical, planning, inquiry,* and so on, also means "cunning, subtlety, and scheming cleverness"—hence **devil's schemes** or "wiles" of the devil (RSV). The language is quite similar to another exhortation in Scripture: "Be self-controlled and alert. Your enemy the devil prowls around like a roaring lion looking for someone to devour" (1 Pet. 5:8).

6:12 / In addition to the devil, believers face a host of wicked spiritual forces, described as **rulers** (*archōn*), **authorities** (*exousia*), and **powers** (*kosmokrator*) **of this dark world.** Stott gives a rather striking and complete picture of the evil forces that believers face: "The enemy," he states, is "powerful," "wicked," and "cunning," (pp. 263-67). No wonder, then, that believers are summoned to build up their strength and to "put on God's armor." "Only the power of God can defend and deliver us from the might, the evil and the craft of the devil" (Stott, p. 266).

By stating that the believer's warfare is not **against flesh and blood** but cosmic **powers**, the author is utilizing the same cosmic mythology that he used earlier (1:21; 3:10) and that is found in other parts of the NT (Rom. 8:38; Gal. 4:3; Col. 1:16; 2:15, 20; 1 Pet. 3:22). Basically, these classes of evil spirits are a comprehensive designation for the enemy that Christians face. By belonging to the **heavenly** order they are nonmaterial or superterrestrial: "Though their present domain extends over the earth, their origin and base of operations lie beyond this world" (Mitton, p. 222). Only Ephesians uses the term *kosmokrator* (a compound noun made up of *kosmos*, "world," and *kratos*, "rule"). It is a title that was applied to a number of pagan gods (Beare, p. 738). Here, it affirms that these evil powers exercise their authority in the world (*kosmos*) and thus over the believer.

This passage takes the reader back to Ephesians 1:21, which describes Christ's victory and exaltation over these evil forces. Believers "in Christ" through their faith and baptism share in that victory and exaltation (2:1-10). In Colossians, Christ's victory and authority over evil powers are stated even more emphatically (1:16; 2:15). The main point of the epistle is that, by virtue of Christ's work, these spirits no longer exercise any control over the believer—"You died with Christ to the basic principles of this world" (2:20). Nevertheless, believers are admonished continually to "become" what they "are" (the tension between the indicative and imperative).

The evil and cosmic powers are presented as still exercising power over the believer even though they have been defeated by Christ (6:12). They are still active; they continually attempt to regain their once-eminent position; they are a constant threat to the believer's spiritual welfare. This is why the readers are exhorted to utilize the armor that God has given to them.

6:13 / **Therefore put on the full armor of God**. The imagery of "putting on" the different pieces of armor may come from observing a soldier dressing himself or being dressed for battle.

But given the nature of the Christians' armor and their having received that armor when they became believers, it is unlikely that one should think of the Christian soldier as gradually dressing to face Satan. To "put on" (6:11, 13) is a call for believers to utilize what they already possess.

The coming **day of evil** commonly is interpreted to mean some future eschatological conflict (Mark 13; 2 Thess. 2:8–10; 1 John 2:18; 4:17) or the final battle of Armageddon (Rev. 16:12–16; 20:7, 8). True, believers are warned in Scripture to prepare themselves for eschatological judgment, but this is not what appears to be in the apostle's mind; he sees the conflict as a current crisis and so admonishes them to be ready. The coming **day of evil** is a reminder of the ever-present reality of wickedness and temptation. Those equipped with God's armor will **be able to stand** their **ground**.

When assaults come, believers are assured that the devil will not be able to move them—**and after you have done everything, to stand**. Though the context of the passage emphasizes "readiness" and "firmness," *katergazomai* has the meaning of combat leading to victory (contra Barth, *Eph. 4–6*, pp. 765, 766). The result of this combat, however, is not progress in conquest but the strengthening of one's position (**stand your ground**). Moule reminds readers that the picture of the battle in Ephesians is not a "march" but "the holding of the fortress of the soul" (p. 151). Here, "The scene is filled with the marshalled host of the Evil One, bent upon *dislodging* the soul, and the Church, from the one possible vantage-ground of life and power—union and communion with their Lord" (p. 154).

6:14 / Having discussed the benefits and the need for preparedness, the apostle finally describes the individual pieces of the believer's armor. Again, there is no attempt to be complete, since a number of items are omitted (cf. disc. on 6:11; also Beare, who quotes Polybius' account of the armor carried by the Roman spearman, p. 740). But this does not mean that the believer is inadequately equipped, since the author believes that the six items he lists are the essential ones: The **belt, breastplate**, shoes (**feet fitted**), shield, helmet, and sword picture truth, righteousness, the gospel of peace, faith, salvation, and the word of God.

In interpreting these items, it is wise to heed the advice of Mitton: "It is, however, a mistake to overelaborate the precise correspondence in each case. . . . The emphasis is rather on the total equipment. Just as the soldier in physical warfare needs all six items, if he is not to be needlessly vulnerable at some points, so the Christian needs each piece of spiritual equipment for his struggle" (p. 223). **Stand firm, then.**

First, stand ready **with the belt of truth buckled around your waist**: In a culture where the people wore long loose-fitting robes, garments were tied close to the body when quick action was required. Here, the believer is summoned to stand, therefore, literally, "having girded (*perizōnnymi*) your loins in truth" (cf. RSV; the meaning is the same as in 1 Pet. 1:13, where the phrase "loins of your mind" is used). "This means getting rid of anything which might be a hindrance in the struggle against evil, eliminating an easy-going casualness which might make him less than ready for the fray" (Mitton, p. 225).

Truth could carry two meanings: It may be a specific reference to the gospel that is the true message (Col. 1:5), or to the equivalent concepts of genuineness, faithfulness, reliability, and integrity. If the gospel or correct doctrine was intended, one would expect to see the article ("the truth"). This verse could be an allusion to the previous emphasis on truthfulness and integrity within the body of Christ (4:25ff.; 2 Cor. 6:7).

Second, stand **with the breastplate of righteousness**: Righteousness is one of the qualities of the divine warrior (Isa. 11:5; 59:17); in 1 Thessalonians, faith and love are the breastplate (5:8); as God's servants, writes Paul, "with weapons of righteousness in the right hand and in the left" (2 Cor. 6:7). In NT usage, righteousness (*dikaiosynē*) can mean the justification of the sinner as well as the moral quality of godliness (*dikaios*). Stott takes the expression to mean righteousness of character and conduct and quotes G. G. Findlay for support: " 'The completeness of pardon for past offence and integrity of character that belong to the justified life, are woven together into an impenetrable mail' " (p. 279). In either case, righteousness constitutes the breastplate that protects the heart.

6:15 / Third, the Christian warrior's feet have been **fitted with the readiness that comes from the gospel of peace**. With this equipment the believer is ready to bear the Good News. The imagery is similar to the description of God's servant, the Messiah, in Isaiah 52:7: "How beautiful on the mountains are the feet of those who bring good news, who proclaim peace" (also Rom. 10:15). Earlier in the epistle, the author stated that "he came and preached peace to you" (2:17).

In the context of Ephesians, peace was proclaimed to the Gentiles (those "far off") and the Jews (those "near"), and it became a reality when they were reconciled to each other through Christ (2:15). In this verse, the emphasis seems to be on the immediacy of the spiritual battle that all believers face and their readiness to proclaim the gospel that Christ has defeated these evil forces of darkness.

6:16 / Fourth, **take up the shield of faith**. According to ancient historians, the large door-shaped protective shield was composed of two layers of wood covered with a flame-resistant hide. The **flaming arrows** that the enemy shot would strike the shield and burn out without penetrating it. **Faith**, claims the author, acts like an impregnable shield and will extinguish all the **flaming arrows of the evil one**. Faith is complete confidence in and reliance upon God to give the victory.

6:17 / Fifth, **take the helmet of salvation** (cf. 1 Thess. 5:8). In the case of the divine warrior (Isa. 59:17), salvation is the helmet that God wears into battle. In that context, the helmet symbolized God's "power and readiness to save others," not protection, as in Ephesians (Beare, p. 743; also Moule, p. 157). As protective headgear, the helmet guards "the centre of life. The sense of salvation puts life beyond all danger" (Westcott, p. 97).

The use of **take** or "receive" (*dechomai*) is significant. Earlier, the writer used "put on" (*endyō, analambanō*) for the other pieces of armor. So far, one could picture the soldier dressing and attaching each piece of armor carefully. Beare suggests that once a soldier was fully clad, the helmet and sword would not be taken up from the ground by himself but would be handed to him by his attendant or armor bearer (Beare, p. 743). By analogy, **salvation** and **the word of God** are gifts that believers *receive*. Salvation is a gift of God, and "there is no doubt that God's saving power is our only defence against the enemy of our soul" (Stott, p. 282).

Sixth, and finally, **take . . . the sword of the Spirit, which is the word of God**. An issue related to this verse is how to interpret the phrase **the sword of the Spirit** (*tēn machairan tou pneumatos*). Is it "the sword which consists of the Spirit, or the sword which the Spirit provides?" (Mitton, p. 227). And how does this relate to the next phrase, **which is the word of God?**

The best explanations take the sword as given by the Spirit but identified as the word of God—the sword **which is the word of God** (for biblical examples comparing speech to a sword, cf. Ps. 57:4; 64:3; Isa. 49:2; Heb. 4:12; Rev. 1:16; 2:16; 19:15). The **word of God** is not only the gospel (1 Pet. 1:25) but all of the words of God that come from his Spirit. "Salvation *is* the Christian's helmet, the indwelling Spirit *is* his sword. The Spirit gives him the word to speak" (cf. Mark 13:11, and Isa. 51:16; Houlden, p. 339; also Mitton, p. 227).

6:18 / Although the military imagery continues into this verse—arm yourselves and **be alert**—the prayer to which the readers are summoned should not be taken as a seventh piece of the Christian's armor. God has given his splendid armor to the believer, but the "putting on" and the utilization of that armor in battle calls for discipline in prayer **in the Spirit**. According to Stott, "Equipping ourselves with God's armor is not a mechanical preparation; it is itself an expression of our dependence on God, in other words, of prayer" (p. 283).

The prayer that the believers are admonished to utter has some significant qualities about it. First, it is to be unceasing: **pray . . . on all occasions**. The Christian warrior, although heavily armed, can only stand firm against the enemy through the agency of prayer. Praying is done **in the Spirit**. To do so is not to be transposed into some ecstatic or euphoric condition beyond the senses but to live in the realization that the Spirit is the believer's helper (5:18) and intercessor (Rom. 8:15, 16, 26, 27). "It is an approach to God relying not on our own piety, but on the help which God in his Spirit offers to us" (Mitton, p. 228).

The Greek, and most English translations (RSV, NIV), employ the two expressions **prayers** (*proseuchē* and "supplication" or **requests** (*deēsis*). Most commentators feel that "prayer" always addresses God, whereas "supplication" may be used to address either God or humankind. The GNB "asking for God's help" takes the Greek as a request to God and not as intercession on behalf of human beings.

Second, prayer is to be intense. **Be alert and always keep on praying**. In other words, maintain a spirit of watchfulness and perseverance. A Christian warrior must not be caught off guard.

This exhortation toward constancy and watchfulness in prayer and the Christian life is common to the NT (Luke 18:1; Rom. 12:12; 1 Cor. 16:13; Phil. 4:6; Col. 4:2; 1 Thess. 5:17; 1 Pet. 5:8). But since this phrase falls between two other exhortations, it is not entirely clear where "perseverance" (**keep on praying**) belongs. Should it go with the idea of praying constantly with all alertness, or does it relate to the following phrase, in which believers are summoned to intercede for others? Beare suggests that alertness refers to the believer's spiritual conflict but that this, in turn, leads to "persevering intercession on behalf of all his comrades in the fight" (p. 746).

Third, prayer is unlimited. **Always keep on praying for all the saints.** Since all believers are involved in a spiritual battle, prayer must transcend its narrow individualism and encompass the entire body of Christ. As members of an army, believers must manifest a concern for all who are fighting along with them. Here the apostle's concerns are not unlike those in 1 Peter, where, in a similar context of warning his readers about the devil, Peter writes: "Resist him, standing firm in the faith, because you know that your brothers throughout the world are undergoing the same kind of sufferings" (5:9).

6:19–20 / The thought of Christians praying for one another leads the apostle to think of his needs for prayer as well. (Cf. this pattern in Col. 4:3; 1 Thess. 5:25; 2 Thess. 3:1. This verse is almost identical in substance with Colossians 4:3.) Basically, the apostle has two requests: First, **pray . . . that whenever I open my mouth, words may be given me.** Literally, the phrase reads, "Pray . . . so that a word (*logos*) may be given to me to open my mouth." According to Abbott, " 'Opening the mouth' is an expression used only when some grave utterance is in question" (p. 189). God is the giver of this special utterance, but the apostle knows that he is the bearer of it.

Second, he requests boldness to **make known the mystery of the gospel.** This concern is repeated in the next verse, thus indicating the burden that the apostle felt for a clear presentation of the gospel. The **mystery** refers elsewhere in Ephesians to the unity of Jews and Gentiles in the body of Christ (3:3–6, 9). Although he is an **ambassador in chains** (*hylasis*) because of the gospel, he envisions further opportunities to serve as the Lord's representative.

Additional Notes   §25

6:12 / In addition to disc. and bibliography on principalities, powers, etc. on 1:22; 3:10; and Col. 1:16; 2:15, 20, see D. E. H. Whiteley, "Ephesians vi. 12—Evil Powers," *ExpT* 68 (1956–57), pp. 100–103. Whiteley sums up the teaching of 6:12 this way: "Because Christ is One with God and because we are members of Christ, the whole power of God is behind us in our struggle with the Evil Powers" (p. 103). Another helpful source dealing with the struggle of believers with evil powers that have already been defeated by Christ is O. Cullmann's *Christ and Time* (London: SCM, 1951 ed.); Cullmann's analogy of "D" and "V" Day has become famous.

6:15 / Barth takes *en hetoimasia* to mean "steadfastness" rather than "readiness." Thus shoes are more of a defensive weapon enabling the believer to stand and resist the devil (*Eph. 4–6*, pp. 770–71; 797–99).

§26 Final Greetings (Eph. 6:21–22)

6:21–22 / Ephesians ends in a rather unexpected and uncharacteristic way: First, the personal references to Tychicus and a specific congregation(s) conflict with the impersonal and universal nature of the epistle. The most that one can say is that Tychicus, who is the bearer of Colossians and Philemon, may be taking Ephesians to the congregations in Asia Minor as well. Here Tychicus is considered a **dear brother and faithful servant**, who will give news of the apostle's situation in prison.

Second, there is the problem of verbal correspondence with Colossians. Mitton has noted that "thirty-two consecutive words in Ephesians are identical with a similar number of words from Col. 4:7–8" (p. 230). Although there are many other similarities between these two epistles, there is little doubt that in this section the author is copying verbatim from Colossians.

6:23–24 / These closing verses contain the familiar virtues of **peace, love, faith,** and **grace** that have occurred throughout the epistle. This benediction has a twofold application: First, **peace, love,** and **faith** are extended **to the brothers,** that is, members of a local Christian community; second, the benediction of **grace** is much more general, being extended to **all who love our Lord Jesus Christ,** that is, members of the universal church.

The benediction includes the unusual phrase **undying love.** *Aphtharsia,* which carries the meaning of immortal, incorruptible, or imperishable, may be just another way of saying forever. The NIV (as RSV, GNB) takes this word in connection with love, meaning that God's grace is for those who love the Lord forever. Some commentators, however, feel that this makes an unjustified distinction between two kinds of love—eternal versus transient— and connect it instead with God's grace. This has the effect of applying the word to God's unlimited grace rather than to human love (so NEB: "God's grace be with all who love our Lord Jesus Christ, grace and immortality"). As such, the epistle ends with the same theme with which it began—God's grace (1:1, 2).

For Further Reading

Abbott, T. K. *Epistles to the Ephesians and to the Colossians*. Edinburgh: T. & T. Clark, 1924.

Allan, J. A. *The Epistle to the Ephesians*. London: SCM, 1959.

Barclay, W. *The Letters to the Galatians and Ephesians*. Edinburgh: Saint Andrew, 1959.

_____. *The Letters to Philippians, Colossians, Thessalonians*. Edinburgh: Saint Andrew, 1959.

_____. *The All-Sufficient Christ*. Philadelphia: Westminster, 1963.

Barth, M. *The Broken Wall*. Philadelphia: Judson, 1959.

_____. *Ephesians 1–3*. Garden City, N.Y.: Doubleday, 1974.

_____. *Ephesians 4–6*. Garden City, N.Y.: Doubleday, 1974.

Beare, F. W. "The Epistle to the Ephesians." In *The Interpreter's Bible Commentary*, vol. 10. Nashville: Abingdon, 1953.

_____. "The Epistle to the Colossians." In *The Interpreter's Bible Commentary*, vol. 11. Nashville: Abingdon, 1953.

Bruce, F. F. "The Epistle to the Colossians." In *Commentary on the Epistles to the Ephesians and the Colossians*. London: Marshall, Morgan & Scott, 1957.

_____. *The Epistle to the Ephesians*. London: Pickering & Inglis, 1961

_____. *The Epistles to the Colossians, to Philemon, and to the Ephesians*. Grand Rapids: Eerdmans, 1984.

Caird, G. B. *Paul's Letters from Prison (Ephesians, Philippians, Colossians, Philemon)*. New Clarendon Bible. London: Oxford University Press, 1976.

Cannon, G. E. *The Use of Traditional Materials in Colossians*. Macon, Ga.: Mercer University Press, 1983.

Caragounis, C. C. *The Ephesian Mysterion*. Lund: C.W.K. Gleerup, 1977.

Cross, F. L., ed. *Studies in Ephesians*. London: Mowbray, 1956.

Foulkes, F. *The Epistle of Paul to the Ephesians*. Grand Rapids: Eerdmans, 1963.

Francis, F. O., and Meeks, W., eds. *Conflict at Colossae*. Sources for Biblical Study 4. Missoula, Mont.: Scholars Press, 1975.

Hanson, S. *The Unity of the Church in the New Testament*. Lexington: American Library Association, 1963.

Houlden, J. L. *Paul's Letters from Prison: Philippians, Colossians, Philemon, and Ephesians*. Philadelphia: Westminster, 1977.

Kirby, J. *Ephesians: Baptism and Pentecost*. Montreal: McGill University Press, 1968.

Knox, J. *Philemon Among the Letters of Paul*. New York: Abingdon, 1959.

Leaney, A. R. C. *Timothy, Titus and Philemon*. Torch Bible Commentaries. London: SCM, 1960.

Lloyd-Jones, D. M. *God's Way of Reconciliation* (Ephesians 2). Grand Rapids: Baker, 1972.

_____. *Life in the Spirit* (Ephesians 5:18–6:9). Grand Rapids: Baker, 1973.

_____. *The Christian Warfare* (Ephesians 6:10–13). Grand Rapids: Baker, 1976.

_____. *The Christian Soldier* (Ephesians 6:10–20). Grand Rapids: Baker, 1977.

_____. *God's Ultimate Purpose* (Ephesians 1:1–23). Grand Rapids: Baker, 1978.

_____. *The Unsearchable Riches of Christ* (Ephesians 3:1–21). Grand Rapids: Baker, 1979.

_____. *Christian Unity* (Ephesians 4:1–16). Grand Rapids: Baker, 1980.

_____. *Darkness and Light* (Ephesians 4:17–5:17). Grand Rapids: Baker, 1982.

Lohse, E. *Colossians and Philemon*. Hermeneia. Philadelphia: Fortress, 1971.

Mackay, J. *God's Order: The Ephesian Letter and This Present Time*. New York: Macmillan, 1953.

Martin, R. P. "Ephesians," *The Broadman Bible Commentary*, vol. 11. Nashville: Broadman, 1971.

_____. *Colossians and Philemon*. New Century Bible. Greenwood: Attic Press, 1974.

_____. *Reconciliation: A Study of Paul's Theology*. Atlanta: John Knox, 1981.

Mitton, C. L. *Ephesians*. New Century Bible. Greenwood: Attic Press, 1976.

Moody, D. *Christ and the Church*. Grand Rapids: Eerdmans, 1963.

Moule, C. F. D. *Ephesians*. Cambridge: Cambridge University Press, 1935.

_____. *The Epistles of Paul the Apostle to the Colossians and to Philemon*. Cambridge: Cambridge University Press, 1957.

O'Brien, P. T. *Colossians, Philemon*. Word Biblical Commentary, vol. 44. Waco, Tex.: Word, 1982.

Robinson, J. A. *St. Paul's Epistle to the Ephesians*. 2d ed. London: Macmillan, 1909.

Schweizer, E. *The Letter to the Colossians*. Minneapolis: Augsburg, 1982.

Scott, E. F. *The Epistles of Paul to the Colossians, to Philemon, and the Ephesians*. London: Hodder & Stoughton, 1958.

Simpson, E. K. "The Epistle to the Ephesians," in *Commentary on the Epistles to the Ephesians and the Colossians*. London: Marshall, Morgan & Scott, 1957.

Stott, J. *God's New Society: The Message of Ephesians*. Downers Grove: InterVarsity, 1979.

Strauss, L. *Galatians and Ephesians*. New York. Loizeaux Brothers, 1957.

Summers, R. *Ephesians: Patterns for Christian Living*. Nashville: Broadman, 1960.

Thompson, G. H. P. *The Letters of Paul to the Ephesians, to the Colossians and to Philemon*. Cambridge: Cambridge University Press, 1967.

Vaughan, C. *Ephesians*. A Study Guide Commentary. Grand Rapids: Zondervan, 1977.

_____. "Colossians." In *The Expositor's Bible Commentary*, vol. 11. Grand Rapids: Zondervan, 1978.

_____. *Colossians and Philemon*. Bible Study Commentary. Grand Rapids: Zondervan, 1980.

Westcott, B. F. *Saint Paul's Epistle to the Ephesians*. London: Macmillan, 1906.

White, R. E. O. *In Him the Fulness*. Old Tappan, N.J.: Revell, 1973.

Wood, A. S. "Ephesians." In *The Expositor's Bible Commentary*, vol. 2. Grand Rapids: Zondervan, 1978.

Subject Index

Abbott, T. K., 160, 192, 201, 203, 273, 291
Above, 70
Ages, the coming, 183
Alcoholic beverages, 263
Allan, J. A., 127, 137
Ambassador, Paul as, 110–11, 291
Aliens, 220
Amen, 227
Angels, worship of, 5, 62, 63
Anger: 74, checking of, 252, 253, 254; and children, 279
Antiochus III, 3
Apart from Christ, 189–92; from God, 36
Apostles and prophets, 201, 239, 240
Apostolic authority, 15
Appeal for unity, 228–34
Apphia, 106
Archippus, 101; and Philemon, 106, 107
Aristarchus, 99, 100
Armageddon, 287
Armor of Christians, 283–92; full, 285
Ascension, 236–38
Asceticism and Gnostics, 5–6
Assistance, 99
Astrology, 4–5
Attainment of unity, 243–47
Authoritarianism, 269
Authorities, 215

Baptism: and armor, 285; as circumcision of Christ, 55–57; as God's gift, 58–59; and living in light, 258–59; new life and, 250–51; one baptism, 233; suffering of Christ and, 41; the word and, 271; three-dimensional focus, 270–72; unity and, 139
Barclay, W., 279
Barnabas, 100
Barth, M., 125, 131, 137, 120, 171, 195, 203, 216, 236–37, 244, 267, 274, 275, 287
Baur, F. C., 8, 130

Beare, F., 129, 130, 213, 225, 236, 261, 266, 272, 275, 281, 289, 291
Beloved, the, 153–54
Benediction: in Colossians, 102; in Ephesians, 294
Bitterness, 254
Blessings and hope, 167
Blood of Christ, 193
Body: growth, 64; harsh treatment of, 66; love of, 272–73; members of one, 252; one, 232
Brawling, 254
Bridal bath, 270–71
Brother: dear, 99, 115; in the Lord, 113
Building on Christ, 49
Burial with Christ, 56

Caesarea, 11
Calvin, John, 128
Cannon, G., 9, 10
Ceremonial laws, 195
Chadwick, H., 135
Charismatic leadership, 238–39
Child-parent relationships: in Colossians, 90; in Ephesians, 277–79
Chosen people, 78, 156–57; Gentiles apart from, 190–91
Christ: alive with, 57; and the church, 274; in the church, 31–32; circumcision made by, 55–56; as dear Son, 25, 153–54; enthronement of, 70–71, 169–74, 180; Ephesian greetings, 146; fulness, 171–73; full nature of God and, 32–33; God's mystery and, 214; image of God, 29–30; as Lord, 17; preeminence, 29; raised with, 70; as Son of God, 243–44
Christ hymn, 27–35; application to Colossians, 36–38; author of, 28; of Colossians, 27–35; and heresy, 7; intercession prayer and, 21; on reconciliation, 33–35; structure of, 27–28
Christian liberty, 61–67

Christian tradition, 51–54
Christology of Ephesians, 126
Church: as body of Christ, 31–32, 171, 269; in Christ hymn, 31–32; concern of Paul for, 46–48; as fulness of Christ, 171–73; in Ephesians, 133–39; immaturity of, 244; leaders of, 238–41
Circumcision, 55–60; rite of, 190
Cleansing, 270–72
Clement of Alexandria, 121
Clothe yourselves, 78
Coarse joking, 257
Coleridge, Samuel Taylor, 128
Colossae, 3
Comfort, 99
Commandments and regulations, 193, 195
Commission of Paul, 43
Compassion, 78
Confidence, 218
Conzelmann, H., 130
Cornerstone, 201–2
Corporate Christ, 41
Cosmology, 215–16; in Ephesians, 125
Covenants, foreigners to, 190; promise of, 190–91
Covetousness, 257
Creation in Christ hymn, 30
Creationism, 268
Creator of all things, 214
Cross and reconciliation of Jew and Gentile, 196–97

Dahl, N. A., 129–30, 132
Dale, R. W., 230
Darkness: deliverance from, 24–25; as symbol, 258–59
Date of Ephesians, 140
Day of Atonement, 198
Dead Sea Scrolls, 124, 131, 261
Death: spiritual death, 177–78; of vices, 72–75
Deliverance from darkness, 24–25
Demas, 101
Descension, 236–38
Destination of Ephesians, 140
Deutero-Pauline, 122–25, 140
Devil. *See* Satan
Dibelius, M., 132
Dietary rules, 65, 195
Discouragement, 218
Divine enlightenment; prayer for,

163–68, 220–26
Dodd, C. H., 128
Doxology: praising through, 227; and theology, 154

Ecclesiology: in Ephesians, 125–26; Lohse's examination of, 9
Election, 151–53
Encouraged, 46
Encouragement and Philemon, 109
Endurance, 23
Enlightenment, prayer for, 163–68, 220–26
Enthronement of Christ, 169–74; 180
Epaphras, 19, 43, 100; as faithful worker of Christ, 19–20; report of, 7
Ephesians: authorship of, 123–25; destination of, 121–22; epistle to, 120–94; origin and date of, 139–41; summary of Paul's theology, 128; Reminder and Congratulation, 129–30
Ephesus, 3, 121; letter addressed to people of, 146; Paul writing in, 11–12
Eschatology: in Ephesians, 126; Lohse's examination of, 9; Paul's understanding of, 181
Ethics: of Christian life, 68–69; specific directions, 252–55; of unity, 248–51
Evangelists, 238, 240
Every family, 221
Evil day, 287
Evil desires, 73
Exaltation as power, 182–83
Exclusivism: 8; in early church, 134–35; Gentile, 136–37; Jewish, 134–35

Faith: indwelling of, 222; in the Lord, 108, 163, 233; one, 232; and salvation, 183–85; as a shield, 289; strengthened in, 49
Faithful brothers, 16
Faithfulness, 145
False teaching, 4; warning on, 51–54
Falsehood, 252
Family, whole, 221
Fatherhood of God, 207
Fellowship, 230; of churches, 101
Fellow soldier, 106
Filled with God, 225
Final greetings: in Colossians, 99–

102; in Ephesians, 293; in Philemon, 117
Findlay, G. G., 288
Firm and sure foundation, 37
First-born Son, 30
Fischer, K. M., 136
Foolish words, 258; talk, 257
Foreigners, 200
Forgiveness, 58, 255; in Ephesians, 154; of sins, 26,154
Foulkes, F., 203, 210, 252, 271, 273, 274, 278, 279, 281
Foundation, love as, 223
Fruitfulness in good works, 19, 22
Fulness: in Christ, 32–33; of Christ, 244; of him, 172; of God, 225

Galatians, 134
Gentiles: apart from Christ, 189–92; by birth, 189; in Christ, 193–99; exclusivism of, 136–37; heirs with Israel, 211; as inclusive term, 209; Paul's mission to, 205–8; preach to, 213
Gentleness, 79, 230
Gifts, spiritual, 235–42
Glorious: Father the, 164; inheritance, 167; riches, 222
Glory: Paul's ministry of, 219; in the church, 227
Gnosticism, 5–6; in Ephesians, 130–31, 224
God and Father, 150, 233
God: good pleasure of, 155; grace of, 209, 212; mystery of, 44, 155, 214–15; will of, 145
God's master plan, 214–15; workmanship, 185
God's New Society, (Stott), 133, 216
God's people. *See* People of God
Goodness, 259–66
Good works, life of, 185
Goodspeed, Edgar J., 129
Gospel, of peace, 288; of salvation, 157
Grace: appeal for, 16; benediction as, 102, 117; Christ apportioned as, 235; essence of, 183–85; as favor to humanity, 179–80; in Ephesians, 146; and peace, 146; and salvation, 179, 183–85
Greed, 73,257
Greetings: in Colossians, 15–16; in

Ephesians, 145–47; in Philemon, 106–7
Grundmann, W., 136
Guthrie, D., 124, 127

Hapax legomena, 8
Haustafeln, 83–87
Head-body imagery, 32, 63–64; in Ephesians, 171–73
Headship, Christ of, 63
Heart, eyes of, 165
Heavenly: beings, 170, 215–16; realms, 150–51, 180
Heavenly life, 70–71
Heavenly realms, 150–51, 180
Hellenistic Judaism, 6–7; and Christ hymn, 29
Heresy, 4; Ephesians as antiheretical tract, 130–31
Hierapolis, 3
Holy and blameless, 152, 271
Holy Spirit: as guarantee, 159–61; promised, 158; as seal, 159; in speech, 254
Honor, of parents, 278
Hope, 18, 157; to Gentiles, 191; goal of, 232; in prayer for enlightenment, 167
Houlden, J. L., 236, 237, 272, 292
Household of God, 200–201
Household rules, 83–87
Human commands, 65
Human tradition, 51–52
Humility, 78, 229; false, 66
Hunter, A. M., 128
Husband-wife relationships. *See* Wife-husband relationships
Hymns, 81, 264; of praise, 148–62; *see also* Christ hymn, 264

Identification of Colossians, 15–16
Idolatry, 73
Ignatius, 284
Immorality, sexual, 73, 257
Impurity, 73, 257
Inclusivism. *See* Exclusivism
Indulgence, sexual, 66
Inheritance, glorious, 167
Inner being, 222
Innitzer, T., 132
Instructions in Colossians, 99–102; in Ephesians, 279
Intercession prayer, 21–26

Irenaeus, 121
Israel, salvation of, 137; citizenship excluded, 191

Jesus. *See* Christ
Jewish believers, 156–57
Jewish exclusivism, 134–35
Jewish law, 193–95
Josephus, 194
Joy, 23; and Philemon, 109
Justus, 99

Käsemann, E., 126, 130, 135
Keystone, 202
Kindness, 78, 79
Kingdom of the Son, 25
Kingdom of God: and greed, 257–58; and missionary preaching, 99
Kingdom of light, 24
Kirby, J., 132, 148
Kneel, 221
Knowledge, 223; of God, 22; of the Son, 294; renewed in, 76; treasures of, 47
Knox, John, 106
Kuhn, K. G., 131
Kümmel, W. G., 127, 136

Language, filthy, 74
Laodicea, 3; epistle from 101
Libertinism of Gnostics, 6
Light: exposed by, 261; living in, 256–65
Logos. *See* Wisdom
Lohmeyer, E., 132
Lohse, E., 5, 9–10, 24, 40
Love: of Christ, 224; in church's life, 18, 245–46; as foundation, 223; and knowledge, 223–24; of Philemon, 108; for all saints, 108, 164; and sacrifice, 255; between spouses, 88; as virtue, 79, 230
Luke, 101, 123
Lust, 73
Lying, 74

Mackay, John, 128
Malice, 74, 254
Manual labor, 253
Marcion's canon, 121
Mark, 99
Marriage bond, 274–75
Martin, R. P., 11, 12, 123, 129, 132

Master-slave relationships. *See* Slave-master relationships
Mature people, 244
Meyerhoff, E., 8
Mission to Gentiles, 205–8
Mitton, C. L., 123, 129, 132, 148, 171, 172, 181, 184, 186, 197, 202, 214–15, 221–22, 224, 230, 236, 238, 244, 245, 249, 250, 257, 263, 271, 272, 274, 284, 285, 286, 293
Moffatt, J., 131–32
Monotheism, 233
Moses, 236
Moule, C. F. D., 202, 237, 259, 273, 287, 289
Muratorian canon, 121
Murphy-O'Connor, J., 131
Mussner, F., 130, 131
Mystery: administration of, 214; Christ of, 46–47, 96, 97; God of, 44, 207; gospel of the, 291; plan of his, 214; union between Christ and the church, 274; of his will, 155
Mystery religion, 6

New life, 248–51; virtues of, 76–80
New Man, 196
New Moon Celebration, 62
New self, 250

Obedience: of children, 90, 277–78; of Philemon, 115; of slaves, 280–81; of wives, 268–69
Obscene words, 257
Onesimus, 10, 105; Ephesian author, 123; Paul's request for, 110–16; and Philemon, 108–16
Origin of Ephesians, 140

Pagan way of life, 249
Paganism, 248–49
Parent-child relationships. *See* Child-parent relationships
Parousia, 180–81
Pastoral Epistles, the 238, 283
Pastors/teachers, 238
Patience, 79, 230
Pattern for unity, 228–34
Patzia, A., 12
Paul: authorship of, 8–10; and Christ hymn, 20; to Colossae, 3–4; eschatological understanding, 181–82; inferiority feelings, 212–13; ministry

as a gift of God, 212; and mission to the Gentiles, 205–8; old man, 110; personal suffering of, 39–42; Philemon, letter to, 105–17; prisoner, 209; summary of theology, 128–29

Peace: from Christ, 193; in Ephesians, 138; preached, 197; through his blood, 34; and unity, 230

Pentecost, 236

People: God's chosen, 78, 207, 212; God's, 243

Perfect Man, Christ as, 244

Perseverance, 291

Philemon, 105–17, 293

Philo, 31

Philosophy, 51

Phrygia, 4

Plan of God, 155

Plato, 31

Pokorný, P., 130

Polycarp, 284

Power: and authority, 52; of God, 23; prayer for, 167; resurrection and exaltation as, 182; to grasp, 224

Powers: authorities and, 59; cosmic, 286

Praise: doxology and, 227; glory of his, 157, 161; hymn of, 148–62; for Philemon, 108–9

Prayer: for enlightenment, 163–68; 220–26; exhortations to, 96–98; of intercession, 21–26; of thanksgiving, 17–20; of warrior Christian, 290–91

Predestination, 151–53

Principles, world of this, 51, 52

Prisoner of Christ Jesus, 209

Proclamation of mystery, 43–45

Profession of Christian, 22

Prophets, 201, 240

Psalms, 81, 264

Purpose of letter (Colossians), 7–8

Put off . . . on, 250

Qumran: community, 130–31; writings of, 124

Rabbinical Judaism, 28

Rage, 74, 254

Raised with Christ, 57

Reality and shadow, 62

Realms, heavenly, 150, 215

Received Christ, 49

Reconciliation, 33–35, 36–37; of Jew and Gentile, 197

Refresh, 115

Regulations, 58, 193

Reicke, Bo, 11,13

Respect: of spouse, 275; and fear, 280

Resurrection as power, 182–83

Reward to slaves, 93, 281

Riches, unsearchable, 213

Righteousness: 259, 260; as weapon, 287–88

Robinson, J. A., 170–71, 191, 194, 202–3, 254, 266

Roman armies, 283

Rome, Paul writing in, 10–11

Rooted: in Christ, 49; in love, 223

Rule of Christ, 180–81

Rules, 65

Rulers, 215

Sabbath day, 62

Sacramentalism, 9

Sacred temple of the Lord, 202

Saints, 15, 78, 24, 109, 145, 223, 224, 291

Salt, seasoned with, 98

Salvation: Christ and, 175–76; election for, 152–53; Gnosticism and, 5–6; as helmet, 289; from spiritual death, 177–78; to spiritual life, 178–86

Sanders, J. N. 128

Satan, 178; armor against, 283–92; no opportunity to, 253; resistance, 291

Schlier, H., 130

Seal, 158

Secret. *See* Mystery

Septuagint, 212

Sexual sins, 256–57

Shadow and reality, 62

Singing praise, 81–82, 264

Sins, forgiveness of, 25–26

Slander, 74

Slave-master relationships: in Colossians, 91–95; in Ephesians, 280–82; Philemon letter, 105–17; position of slaves, 85–87

Sleeper, 261

Sojourners, 200

Son: of God, 244; kingdom of, 25

Sonship, 153

Speech, unwholesome, 253–54
Spirit: with congregation, 47; filled
    with, 263; God's, 203; one, 232
Spiritual: forces, 31; gifts, 235–42; life,
    179–86; songs, 264; powers, 31
Stamp of ownership, 158
Steadfastness, 49–50
Stealing, 253
Stoics, the, 31
Stott, John, 152, 195, 202, 211, 213,
    216, 217, 224, 229, 234, 236, 239, 241,
    264, 279, 282, 285, 286, 289, 290
Strength: of God, 23; prayer for, 165
Submission, 264–65, 268; of children
    277–78; between husband and
    wife, 268–69
Sufferings of Paul, 39–42
Supremacy of Christ, 170
Sword, word of God as, 289–90
Syncretism, 4, 7
Syn words, 137–38

Teachers, 238, 239, 240–41
Temple area, 194
Temple in the Lord, 203
Tertullian, 121
Thankfulness, 50, 80
Thanksgiving: to the Father, 23; and
    fulness of spirit, 264; as gratitude,
    82, in hymn of praise, 148–62; and
    joy, 22; prayer, 17–20; singing in,
    82; and steadfastness, 49–50; as vir-
    tue, 80
Theology is doxology, 154
Threats to slaves, 281
Timothy: and Paul, 15; in Philemon
    greetings, 106
Title of Christ, 170
Titus, Roman general, 193
Tolerance, 230
Transforming power, 92
Transgressions, dead in, 179
Trinity in hymn of praise, 150
Trophimus, 193
Truth: and armor, 287–88; in church's
    life, 245–46; as fruit, 259; in Jesus,
    250
Truthfulness of gospel, 19

Tychicus, 11, 99, 293

Uncircumcised, 190
Understanding: in intercession
    prayer, 22–23; power for, 223–24
Unity: appeal for, 228–34; attainment
    of, 243–47; of believers, 187–88; of
    church, 133–39; and ethics, 248;
    new unity, 200–204; other terms
    for, 230–31
Universe in Christ hymn, 30–31
Usefulness of slave, 111–12

Vices, 248–49; of old life, 72–75
Von Soden, H., 138

Wall, dividing the, 194–95
Washing, 270–71
Weapons of Christians, 283–92
Westcott, B. F., 164, 202, 272, 289
Wife-husband relationships: in Colos-
    sians, 88–89; in Ephesians, 266–76
Wine, 263
Wisdom: church as manifestation,
    215; and understanding, 21, 154–
    55; and head-body imagery, 32; in
    intercession prayers, 22–23; practi-
    cal dimension, 262–63; prayer for,
    165; and proclamation of mystery,
    43–45; as Logos, 32; treasures of,
    47; spirit of, 164; of God, 216
Without God, Gentiles as, 191
Witness, exhortations to, 96–98
Woes, Messiah of the, 40
Women: in Colossians, 85–87; in
    Ephesians, 268; in Greek culture,
    85–87
Wood, A. S., 124, 140
Word: of Christ, 81; of God, 287; as
    sword, 289; of truth, 18, 157
Words: us of, 230; empty, 258
Work, of Archippus, 101–2
World, ways of, 177–78
Worship, 81–82
Wrath, of God, 73, 178
Written code, 58

Zealots, the, 115

Scripture Index

OLD TESTAMENT

Genesis 1:27, 76, 251; **2:24**, 272, 273, 274, 276; **12:1–3**, 211; **15:8–21**, 190; **17:1–21**, 190; **17:11**, 190

Exodus 6:8, 24; **19**, 236; **20:6**, 278; **20:12**, 278; **24:1–11**, 190

Deuteronomy 4:20, 157; **4:37**, 151; **5:16**, 278; **7:6**, 151; **7:7**, 151; **9:29**, 157; **10:16**, 190; **32:9**, 157

1 Kings 8:51, 157

Job 5:9, 213; **9:10**, 213

Psalms 4:4, 252; **33[32]:18**, 95; **57:4**, 290; **64:3**, 290; **67:19**, 241; **68:18**, 236, 238, 241; **103**, 225; **106:40**, 157; **110:1**, 171; **110:1ff.**, 169; **118:22**, 201; **119:18**, 165; **139**, 225

Isaiah 11:5, 283, 288; **11:10**, 211; **26:19**, 261; **28:16**, 201; **41:9**, 229; **42:6**, 211, 229; **43:1**, 229; **43:21**, 157; **44:1**, 151; **44:2**, 151, 229; **45:3**, 229; **45:4**, 229; **49:2**, 290; **49:6**, 211; **51:16**, 290; **52:7**, 197, 288; **55:3**, 190; **57:19**, 193, 197; **59:17**, 283, 288, 289; **60:1**, 261; **60:2**, 261; **60:3**, 211; **61:1**, 197; **61:2**, 197

Jeremiah 1:5, 151; **10:16**, 157; **13:11**, 157; **16:19**, 211; **31:31–34**, 190

Ezekiel 37:26, 190

Hosea 11:1, 229

Joel 2:28ff., 85

Micah 4:2, 211

Zephaniah 2:11, 211

Zechariah 2:12, 157; **8:16**, 252

NEW TESTAMENT

Matthew 3:13–17, 153; **5:3–11**, 72; **5:8**, 165; **5:10–12**, 39, 41; **5:11–12**, 23; **5:17–48**, 195; **5:22–30**, 74; **6:5**, 221; **6:12**, 58; **6:13**, 25; **6:19**, 150; **6:20**, 70, 150; **7:13**, 177; **7:14**, 177; **7:21**, 26, 186; **7:24–27**, 37; **10:19**, 97; **15:7–9**, 65; **15:19**, 72; **17:5**, 153; **18:12–14**, 241; **18:21–35**, 115; **19:21**, 253; **19:28**, 155, 181; **20:23**, 41; **24**, 40; **25:35–40**, 92; **28:5**, 197; **28:10**, 197; **28:19**, 271

Mark 1:9–11, 153; **1:11**, 25; **1:20**, 229; **4:1–20**, 19; **7:7**, 65; **7:19**, 61; **7:21**, 72; **7:22**, 72, 73; **9:1**, 84; **9:7**, 25, 153; **10:38**, 270; **10:39**, 270; **11:25**, 221; **13**, 287; **13:5–27**, 40; **13:11**, 97, 290; **13:30**, 84; **14:51**, 99; **16:16**, 184

Luke 2:14, 155; **2:21**, 55; **3:21**, 153; **3:22**, 153; **4:18**, 92, 197; **4:19**, 92, 197; **8:15**, 23; **9:35**, 153; **10:21**, 164; **11:14–26**, 178; **12:11**, 97; **12:12**, 97; **12:47**, 26; **14:13**, 253; **15:3–7**, 241; **16:2–4**, 155; **18:1**, 96, 291; **21:4**, 97; **22:30**, 181

John 1:1–3, 32; **1:9**, 165, 166; **3:5**, 57; **3:19**, 259; **3:19–21**, 261; **3:19ff.**, 265; **3:20**, 259; **8:12**, 265; **8:31**, 37; **9:5**, 265; **10:11–18**, 241; **10:30**, 30; **12:35**, 265; **12:36**, 265; **12:46**, 265; **13:2**, 178; **13:10**, 271; **13:16**, 240; **13:29**, 253; **14:6**, 177; **14:9**, 30; **14:16**, 99; **14:17**, 164; **14:26**, 99; **14:27**, 197; **14–17**, 164; **15**, 273; **15:4–7**, 37; **15:16**, 151; **15:20**, 41; **16:7**, 99; **17:1ff.**, 164; **20:17**, 164

Acts 1:1–11, 169; **1:14**, 96; **1:21**, 145; **1:21–23**, 240; **1:22**, 145; **1:24**, 96; **1–12**, 195; **2:13**, 264; **2:17–21**, 85; **2:32**, 169; **2:33**, 169, 237; **2:37ff.**, 157; **2:38**, 57, 158, 159, 162, 184, 271; **2:38ff.**,

159; **2:39**, 193; **2:41**, 158, 184; **2:44**, 253; **3:15**, 169; **4:10**, 169; **4:31**, 218; **4:32–37**, 253; **5:3**, 178; **5:30**, 169; **5:31**, 169; **6:1–4**, 253; **6:1–6**, 92; **6:4**, 96; **7**, 195; **8:12**, 158; **8:12–17**, 159; **8:16**, 271; **8:35–38**, 158; **9:2**, 177; **9:4**, 41; **9:16**, 41; **9:18**, 158; **10:1–43**, 196; **10:9–16**, 61; **10:40**, 169; **10:44–48**, 159; **10:47**, 158; **10:48**, 158; **11:27ff.**, 201; **12:7**, 265; **12:12**, 99, 101; **12:25**, 99; **13:2**, 145; **13:5**, 44; **13:13**, 99; **13:47**, 211; **14:22**, 37; **15**, 125; **15:1–35**, 134, 196; **15:19–29**, 61, 134; **15:23**, 146; **15:37**, 99; **15:39**, 99; **16:19–33**, 139; **16:30**, 184; **16:31**, 184; **16:40**, 101; **17:13**, 44; **17:16**, 191; **17:22–31**, 191; **18:23**, 3; **18:25**, 177; **18:26**, 177; **19**, 100; **19:1**, 3, **19:1–6**, 159; **19:5**, 158, 271; **19:8**, 99; **19:9**, 100, 123, 140; **19:10**, 4, 100, 121, 140; **19:18**, 184; **19:23–41**, 11; **19:26**, 191; **19:26–35**, 245; **19:29**, 99; **19–20**, 12; **20:4**, 11, 99; **20:19**, 229; **20:28**, 241; **20:31**, 100, 121, 163; **21:8**, 239; **21:17–34**, 206, 209; **21:27ff.**, 11, 194; **22:16**, 57, 159, 162, 184, 271; **22:21–24**, 206, 209; **23:6**, 191; **23:23–26:32**, 139; **23:26**, 146; **23:33–26:32**, 11; **24:23**, 11; **25:8**, 91; **26:12–23**, 206, 209; **26:17–18**, 25; **26:18**, 165; **27:2**, 99; **28:16–31**, 10, 139; **28:30**, 97, 99; **28:31**, 99

Romans **1:4**, 164, 244; **1:5**, 209; **1:7**, 146; **1:8**, 17; **1:8–10**, 164; **1:16**, 184; **1:18–23**, 249; **1:18–24**, 248; **1:18–32**, 73; **1:24**, 72; **1:26**, 72; **1:29**, 73; **1:29–32**, 72; **1–3**, 178; **2:4**, 78, 230; **2:25–29**, 77; **2:28**, 190; **2:29**, 190; **3:20**, 185; **3:22**, 184; **3:23**, 178; **3:27**, 184; **4:9–12**, 77; **4:11**, 184, 190; **4:24**, 169; **4:25**, 270; **5:1**, 80, 184; **5:1–5**, 17; **5:1ff.**, 34; **5:3**, 39, 219; **5:9**, 157; **5:10**, 197; **5:12–14**, 178; **5:12–21**, 76; **6:1–4**, 68; **6:1–10**, 41, 57; **6:1–11**, 18, 55, 56, 139, 180, 222, 233; **6:3**, 270; **6:3–11**, 41; **6:4**, 179, 182; **6:5**, 60; **6:6**, 55, 56, 179, 182; **6:8**, 179; **6:11**, 68; **6:12**, 68; **6:13**, 68, 72; **6:22**, 36; 7, 76; **7:4**, 22; **7:22**, 222; **7:23**, 284; **7:24**, 55; **8:3**, 194; **8:9**, 232; **8:9ff.**, 47, 222; **8:9–17**, 68; **8:11**, 169; **8:14–17**, 150; **8:15**, 153, 158, 233, 290; **8:16**, 158,

290; **8:17**, 41, 211; **8:18**, 182; **8:18–25**, 155; **8:19–21**, 212; **8:23**, 153, 161; **8:23a**, 182; **8:23b**, 182; **8:24**, 18; **8:25**, 18; **8:26**, 290; **8:27**, 290; **8:29**, 76, 151, 153; **8:31–39**, 225; **8:32**, 270; **8:34**, 169; **8:38**, 31, 170, 215, 286; **8:38ff.**, 39; **9:11**, 151; **9:22**, 78, 230; **9–11**, 136; **10:8–10**, 165; **10:9**, 158, 169, 184; **10:14**, 157; **10:15**, 193, 289; **10:17**, 157; **11**, 136; **11:4**, 221; **11:13–24**, 134, 135; **11:22**, 37, 78; **11:30**, 36; **11:33**, 213; **11:36**, 227, 233; **12:1**, 70, 78, 90, 260; **12:1–2**, 182; **12:1–8**, 32; **12:1ff.**, 68; **12:2**, 178, 260; **12:3**, 209; **12:4**, 133; **12:5**, 133; **12:12**, 96, 291; **12:13**, 116; **13:1–7**, 85, 91; **13:8–10**, 79; **13:9**, 156; **13:12**, 283; **13:12–14**, 74; **13:13**, 72; **13:14**, 68; **14:11**, 221; **14:17**, 62; **14:18**, 90; **14:21**, 62; **15:9–12**, 211; **15:14**, 45; **15:15–16**, 209; **15:19**, 43; **15:25–29**, 253; **15:28**, 11; **15:30**, 19; **16:1–24**, 98; **16:5**, 101; **16:7**, 145; **16:22**, 102; **16:25**, 210; **16:25–26**, 44; **16:26**, 210; **16:27**, 227

1 Corinthians, 9, 224; **1:1**, 229; **1:1–3**, 15; **1:2**, 15; **1:3**, 146; **1:4**, 17; **1:10–13**, 201; **1:13**, 233; **1:13ff.**, 139; **1:21**, 184; **1:22**, 223; **1–3**, 62; **3:3**, 182; **3:5–9**, 201; **3:9**, 203; **3:10–15**, 37; **3:11**, 201; **3:16ff.**, 203; **4:9**, 216; **4:9–13**, 11; **4:14–16**, 255; **4:15**, 111; **4:17**, 15, 111; **4:21**, 164; **5:1**, 73; **5:3**, 110; **5:10**, 73; **5:10–13**, 72; **5:11**, 73; **6:8–11**, 68; **6:9**, 25, 73, 100; **6:9–10**, 72; **6:10**, 73; **6:10–14**, 72; **6:11**, 36, 57, 159, 162, 184, 271; **6:14**, 169; **6:15**, 272; **6:16**, 273; **6:17**, 273; **6:19**, 68; **6:20**, 68; **7:6**, 110; **7:15**, 267; **7:19**, 190; **7:20–24**, 91; **8:1**, 65; **8:1–3**, 223, 225; **8:4**, 191; **8:5**, 191; **8:6**, 191, 231, 232, 233; **9:1**, 110, 145, 240; **9:2**, 240; **9:14**, 44; **9:17**, 43, 155; **9:24–27**, 283; **10:17**, 197; **11:1**, 255; **11:3**, 88, 268; **11:3–8**, 86; **11:3–16**, 268; **11:5–8**, 86; **11–14**, 85; **12**, 238; **12:3**, 232; **12:4–6**, 232; **12:4–13**, 224, 231; **12:4–31**, 32; **12:7**, 243; **12:7–13**, 235; **12:12**, 139, 171, 198; **12:12–26**, 133; **12:12–31**, 63; **12:13**, 18, 57, 77, 139, 159, 197, 198, 199, 232, 233; **12:14–26**, 32, 171; **12:28**, 127, 201, 239; **12:29**, 201; **13**, 143; **13:1–3**, 225; **13:4**, 230; **13:13**, 17;

14, 62; **14:1–5**, 201; **14:12**, 224; **14:16**, 81; **14:24ff.**, 201; **14:26**, 224, 243; **14:26–33**, 264; **14:31**, 243; **14:33–38**, 268; **15:2**, 184; **15:3ff.**, 182; **15:9**, 145, 212; **15:9–11**, 151; **15:10**, 145; **15:11**, 184; **15:15**, 169; **15:24**, 31, 170; **15:24–28**, 258; **15:28**, 88; **15:29**, 191; **15:32**, 11, 139, 191; **15:45–49**, 76; **15:50**, 25; **15:51–54**, 181; **15:51–58**, 84; **16:9**, 96; **16:13**, 284, 291; **16:19**, 101; **16:21**, 102

2 Corinthians **1:1**, 15; **1:1–2**, 15; **1:2**, 146; **1:3**, 78, 150; **1:4**, 39; **1:5**, 39, 41; **1:6**, 39, 42; **1:8**, 39; **1:8–10**, 11, 139; **1:22**, 158, 159; **2:4**, 39; **2:12**, 96; **3:18**, 76; **4:4**, 30, 166; **4:4–12**, 11; **4:6**, 24, 166; **4:10**, 41; **4:10–14**, 41; **4:13**, 164; **4:14**, 60, 169; **4:16**, 222; **4:17**, 39; **5:5**, 160; **5:9**, 90; **5:16ff.**, 187; **5:17**, 139, 182, 185, 196; **5:17–19**, 152; **5:17–21**, 68; **5:18**, 197; **6:4**, 11, 39, 41; **6:5**, 11, 139; **6:6**, 72; **6:7**, 72, 288; **6:16**, 203; **7:4**, 39, 109; **7:7**, 109; **7:10**, 184; **7:15**, 280; **8**, 253; **8:1–4**, 92; **8:2**, 39; **8:23**, 240; **9**, 253; **9:7**, 113; **9:8**, 22; **10:1**, 78, 209; **10:4**, 283; **11:2**, 270; **11:23**, 139; **11:23–25**, 11; **12:10**, 39, 219; **12:11**, 212; **12:12**, 110; **12:20**, 72; **12:21**, 73; **13:7ff.**, 17

Galatians, 9; **1:1**, 169; **1:3**, 146; **1:4**, 270; **1:5**, 227; **1:12**, 210; **1:13–15**, 212; **1:15**, 155; **1:16**, 210; **1:23**, 232; **1–3**, 136; **2**, 125, 134, 196; **2:2**, 210; **2:5**, 20; **2:14**, 20; **2:16**, 134; **2:19**, 56; **2:20**, 179, 222, 244, 270; **3:10**, 185; **3:26**, 222, 233; **3:26–27**, 18, 56, 154; **3:26–28**, 41, 77, 87; **3:27**, 74, 139, 198, 222, 233, 270; **3:27–28**, 55; **3:28**, 74, 134, 139, 194, 196, 198, 233; **3:29**, 211; **4:3**, 52, 54, 286; **4:4**, 194; **4:5**, 153; **4:6**, 150, 158, 233; **4:7**, 150, 211; **4:8**, 192; **4:9**, 54; **4:19**, 111; **5:1ff.**, 68; **5:2**, 209; **5:5**, 17; **5:6**, 17, 22, 77; **5:14**, 79; **5:16**, 73; **5:17**, 284; **5:19**, 73; **5:19–21**, 72, 178, 256, 257; **5:20**, 73; **5:21**, 25, 100, 257; **5:22**, 19, 72, 78, 230, 260; **5:22–23**, 23; **5:23**, 72, 78; **5:24**, 56, 68; **5:25**, 68; **5:26–6:6**, 98; **6:1**, 164; **6:11**, 102; **6:15**, 187, 196; **6:18**, 117

Ephesians **1**, 175, 220; **1:1**, 15, 121, 141, 145–46, 164, 168, 207, 294; **1:1–2**, 15, 145–47; **1:1–14**, 161; **1:2**, 138, 146–147, 154, 294; **1:3**, 70, 149–51, 161–62, 164, 180, 208; **1:3–6**, 149, 154; **1:3–8**, 146; **1:3–10**, 156, 1:3–11, 139, 144, 146, 148–62, 163, 168, 175, 205, 220; **1:3–2:10**, 189; **1:4**, 137, 147, 151–53, 156, 161, 185, 208, 217, 229, 230, 271; **1:5**, 137, 149, 150, 151, 153–54, 155, 156, 161, 229; **1:6**, 25, 153, 154, 161, 164, 185, 220; **1:7**, 149, 154, 162, 175; **1:7–11**, 161; **1:7–12**, 149; **1:8**, 154–55; **1:9**, 44, 154, 155, 156, 161, 207, 210, 274; **1:9–10**, 210; **1:10**, 133, 137, 138, 155–56, 161, 162, 172, 176, 187, 208, 210, 212, 215, 228, 229, 238; **1:11**, 157, 161; **1:11–12**, 156–57, 162; **1:12**, 154, 161, 164, 167, 185, 220, 229; **1:13**, 57, 125, 149, 156, 157–159, 161, 162, 163, 208, 211, 254; **1:13–14**, 149; **1:13–16**, 145; **1:14**, 154, 156, 159–61, 162, 163, 164, 167, 185, 207, 208, 220, 225, 232; **1:15**, 108, 125, 163–64, 168, 185, 207; **1:15–18**, 17; **1:15–19**, 163–68; **1:15–20**, 220; **1:15–22**, 147; **1:15–23**, 205; **1:15–2:10**, 163; **1:15–2:20**, 146; **1:16**, 163, 164; **1:17**, 164–65, 166, 168, 207, 208, 220; **1:17–19**, 163; **1:18**, 126, 164, 165–67, 168, 207, 220, 229, 232, 249; **1:18a**, 165, 175; **1:18b**, 165, 175; **1:18c**, 165; **1:18f.**, 220; **1:19**, 57, 165, 167, 172, 182, 208, 220, 285; **1:19–23**, 175; **1:20**, 70, 150, 151, 165, 169, 173, 180, 182, 238; **1:20–22**, 237; **1:20–23**, 163, 169–74; **1:20–3:13**, 163; **1:21**, 31, 151, 170, 178, 183, 215, 216, 219, 238, 286; **1:21–22**, 173, 219; **1:21–23**, 165; **1:22**, 32, 133, 138, 171, 202, 216, 219, 292; **1:23**, 32, 133, 138, 171–73, 173–74, 187, 208, 225, 238, 244; **1–3**, 132, 147, 171, 195, 203, 228; **2**, 156, 175; **2:1**, 57, 176, 177, 178, 179, 185, 190, 259; **2:1–3**, 74, 135, 176, 177–78, 189; **2:1–5**, 182, 259; **2:1–7**, 175; **2:1–10**, 56, 147, 163, 169, 175–76, 187, 189, 190, 217, 220, 222, 286; **2:1–22**, 205; **2:1ff.**, 139, 157; **2:1–3:13**, 220; **2:2**, 177–78, 185, 190, 229, 259; **2:3**, 74, 176, 178; **2:3–7**, 176; **2:4–5**, 179–80; **2:4–6**, 185; **2:4–10**, 176, 179–86, 189; **2:4ff.**, 139; **2:5**, 137, 146, 175, 177, 179, 181, 183, 184; **2:5–9**, 259; **2:5–**

10, 138–39; **2:6**, 70, 133, 137, 150, 151, 179, 180–82, 186; **2:7**, 78, 146, 182–83, 186, 208; **2:8**, 146, 176, 179, 184; **2:8–9**, 183–85; **2:9**, 172, 184, 185; **2:10**, 22, 147, 152, 176, 182, 184, 185–86, 229, 248; **2:11**, 57, 112, 135, 155, 163, 176, 187, 189–90, 193, 198, 203, 209; **2:11–12**, 189–192; **2:11–13**, 259; **2:11–18**, 198; **2:11–19**, 74; **2:11–22**, 44, 77, 125, 147, 175, 187–88, 189, 200, 203, 204, 205, 210, 217, 220; **2:11ff.**, 137, 139, 210; **2:12**, 38, 57, 135, 155, 163, 187, 189, 190–92, 193, 200, 208; **2:12–22**, 259; **2:13**, 112, 135, 189, 190, 193, 194, 197; **2:13–18**, 187, 193–99; **2:13ff.**, 139, 259; **2:14**, 80, 135, 137, 138, 146; **2:14–15**, 193–96, 199; **2:14–16**, 133, 193, 231, 267; **2:14–18**, 200; **2:15**, 135, 137, 138, 146, 189, 194, 289; **2:15–16**, 199; **2:16**, 33, 127, 133, 137, 196–97; **2:17**, 138, 146, 189, 193, 197, 199, 289; **2:18**, 137, 197–99; **2:19**, 137, 189, 200, 207; **2:19–21**, 188; **2:19–22**, 37, 188, 200–204, 205; **2:20**, 126, 145, 200–202, 204, 207, 211, 239; **2:20–22**, 133; **2:21**, 126, 138, 202–3, 221; **2:22**, 138, 203–4, 208; **3:1**, 100, 121, 125, 205, 206, 209, 218, 219, 221, 228; **3:1–9**, 121; **3:1–12**, 147; **3:1–13**, 163, 205, 209–19, 220; **3:1–21**, 205–8; **3:2**, 146, 206, 209, 212, 219, 235; **3:2–12**, 44; **3:2–13**, 205; **3:3**, 44, 206, 207, 211, 214, 215; **3:3–4**, 210; **3:3–6**, 96, 155, 274, 291; **3:4**, 44, 206, 210; **3:5**, 126, 201, 207, 208, 210–11, 214, 215, 239; **3:6**, 135, 137, 138, 152, 155, 205, 206, 207, 210, 211–12, 224, 229; **3:7**, 146, 208, 209, 212, 235; **3:8**, 206, 209, 212–13, 235; **3:9**, 44, 96, 206, 208, 214, 215, 217, 218, 274, 291; **3:10**, 70, 126, 133, 138, 150, 151, 162, 172, 173, 183, 206, 207, 208, 214–17, 218, 219, 238, 286, 292; **3:11**, 137, 208, 217–18; **3:12**, 198, 208, 218; **3:13**, 206, 218–19; **3:14**, 164, 207, 208, 221, 233; **3:14f.**, 220; **3:14–19**, 207, 220–26; **3:14–21**, 163, 220, 226; **3:14ff.**, 205; **3:15**, 208, 221–22, 226; **3:16**, 164, 207, 208, 220, 221, 222; **3:16–21**, 46; **3:17**, 153, 208, 222–23, 230, 247; **3:17a**, 207, 221; **3:17b**, 207, 221; **3:18**, 207, 221, 223–25, 226; **3:18–19a**, 207;

3:18f., 220; **3:18–20**, 198; **3:19**, 172, 208, 220, 221, 225–26; **3:19b**, 207; **3:20**, 167, 207, 208, 222, 227; **3:20–21**, 220, 227; **3:21**, 133, 164, 207, 220, 227; **4**, 228; **4:1**, 70, 100, 121, 182, 228–29, 248; **4:1–3**, 139, 228, 248; **4:1–6**, 68, 138, 198, 199, 228–34, 235; **4:1ff.**, 68; **4:2**, 63, 153, 229–30, 247; **4:2–3**, 79; **4:2–5**, 17; **4:3**, 138, 139, 146, 228, 230–32; **4:4**, 133, 137, 167, 197, 231, 232, 271; **4:4–6**, 228, 231, 271; **4:4–16**, 147, 248; **4:5**, 137, 139, 149, 232–33, 243, 271; **4:6**, 137, 233–34; **4:7**, 137, 146, 209, 235, 238; **4:7–11**, 235–42; **4:8**, 236–37, 241; **4:9**, 237, 241; **4:9–10**, 235; **4:10**, 237–38; **4:11**, 127, 201, 211, 235, 236, 238–41, 241–42; **4:11–16**, 126, 224; **4:12**, 133, 243; **4:12–16**, 235, 240, 243–47; **4:13**, 45, 126, 138, 172, 207, 225, 230, 235, 243–44; **4:14**, 45, 244–45, 246–247, 258; **4:15**, 22, 32, 139, 153, 202, 230, 245–46, 247, 248; **4:15–16**, 63, 79; **4:16**, 32, 64, 126, 133, 137, 138, 139, 153, 230, 246–47; **4:17**, 248–49, 251; **4:17–24**, 248–51; **4:17ff.**, 121; **4:17–5:20**, 139, 262; **4:17–5:21**, 248; **4:18**, 38, 249, 251, 259, 261; **4:19**, 249; **4:20**, 249–50, 251, 260; **4:21**, 125, 209, 250; **4:22**, 56, 68, 74, 250, 252; **4:22–24**, 250–51; **4:22–5:20**, 68; **4:23**, 259; **4:24**, 68, 74, 285; **4:25**, 138, 252; **4:25–31**, 284; **4:25–32**, 139; **4:25ff.**, 288; **4:25–5:2**, 248, 252–55, 256; **4:25–5:20**, 143; **4:26**, 252; **4:26–27**, 252–253; **4:27**, 252, 284; **4:28**, 253; **4:29**, 252, 253–54; **4:30**, 57, 159, 160, 182, 225, 254; **4:31**, 72, 254; **4:31–5:2**, 252; **4:32**, 254–55; **4–5**, 49; **4–6**, 147, 228, 275, 276; **5:1**, 255, 256, 257; **5:2**, 153, 255, 256, 257; **5:3**, 73, 256–57, 259; **5:3–5**, 72; **5:3–14**, 248; **5:3–20**, 284; **5:3–21**, 256–65; **5:4**, 257, 265; **5:5**, 73, 257–58, 259; **5:6**, 73, 257; **5:6–7**, 258; **5:7**, 138, 260; **5:8**, 24, 25, 112, 165, 166, 258–59, 265; **5:8a**, 139; **5:8bff.**, 139; **5:8–12**, 263; **5:8–13**, 262; **5:8–14**, 166, 203, 258, 262; **5:8ff.**, 139; **5:9**, 259–60; **5:10**, 90, 260, 261; **5:11**, 138, 259, 260–61; **5:12**, 261; **5:13**, 261; **5:14**, 258, 259, 261–62, 265; **5:15**, 262–63; **5:15–17**, 263; **5:15–20**, 138; **5:15–21**, 248;

5:15ff., 262; **5:16**, 97, 263; **5:17**, 262, 263; **5:18**, 254, 262, 263–64, 265, 290; **5:18–20**, 266; **5:18–21**, 263, 264; **5:19**, 27, 81, 82, 164, 262, 264; **5:20**, 164, 262, 264; **5:21**, 264–65, 266, 269, 275, 277, 280; **5:21–33**, 133, 269, 275, 276; **5:21ff.**, 88; **5:21–6:6**, 139; **5:21–6:9**, 83, 87, 138, 147; **5:21–6:24**, 275, 276; **5:22**, 275–276, 277; **5:22–24**, 268–69; **5:22–33**, 266–76; **5:22ff.**, 275; **5:22–6:9**, 264; **5:23**, 88, 133, 171, 267, 269; **5:24**, 133, 267; **5:25**, 133, 255, 267, 269–70; **5:26**, 270–71, 276; **5:26–27**, 276; **5:27**, 37, 126, 133, 153, 182, 270, 271–72, 276; **5:28**, 267, 270, 272; **5:29**, 133, 267, 272, 279; **5:30**, 133, 272–73; **5:31**, 272, 273, 276; **5:31–33**, 139; **5:32**, 133, 273–75, 276; **5:33**, 137, 275; **6:1**, 269, 277–78; **6:1–4**, 277–79; **6:1–9**, 267, 277; **6:2–3**, 278; **6:4**, 277, 278–79; **6:5**, 269, 277, 280; **6:5–8**, 91; **6:5–9**, 95, 277, 280–82; **6:6**, 277, 280–81; **6:7**, 280, 281; **6:8**, 281; **6:9**, 95, 277, 280, 281–82; **6:10**, 284, 285; **6:10–20**, 283–92; **6:11**, 178, 284, 285, 287; **6:12**, 31, 150, 151, 162, 170, 173, 178, 182, 215, 216, 219, 284, 285–86, 292; **6:13**, 284, 286–87; **6:14**, 284, 287–288; **6:14–17**, 72; **6:15**, 138, 146, 288–89, 292; **6:16**, 289; **6:17**, 289–90; **6:18**, 96, 207, 290–91; **6:18–20**, 96; **6:19**, 44, 274; **6:19–20**, 291; **6:20**, 209, 218; **6:21–22**, 293; **6:21ff.**, 124; **6:23**, 138; **6:23–24**, 294

Philippians, 9; **1:1**, 15; **1:1–2**, 15; **1:2**, 17, 26, 146; **1:3**, 164; **1:4**, 23, 26, 164; **1:7**, 209; **1:12**, 97; **1:17**, 39; **1:18**, 39; **1:20**, 218; **1:24**, 39; **1:26**, 26; **1:27**, 232; **1:29**, 39, 40, 41; **2:1–4**, 229; **2:1–5**, 264; **2:2–4**, 245; **2:3**, 63; **2:5–11**, 27, 78, 79, 229; **2:6–11**, 262; **2:9**, 169, 170; **2:9–11**, 70; **2:10**, 221; **2:11**, 232; **2:12**, 280; **2:19–24**, 15; **2:25**, 106, 240; **3:3**, 190; **3:10**, 39, 41, 179; **3:19**, 70; **3:20a**, 182; **3:20b**, 182; **4:1ff.**, 68; **4:4–6**, 23; **4:6**, 164, 291; **4:8**, 72; **4:8–13**, 98; **4:18**, 260; **4:19**, 182

Colossians **1:1**, 10, 15, 97, 105, 106, 145; **1:1–2**, 15–16; **1:2**, 15–16, 26, 78, 102, 107, 146, 168; **1:3**, 17, 20, 50, 96, 164; **1:3–8**, 17–20, 21, 26, 37, 96; **1:3–14**, 17, 108; **1:3–19**, 36; **1:4**, 15, 17–18, 26, 108, 164, 232; **1:5**, 7, 17, 18, 19, 20, 24, 157, 164, 167, 191, 232, 288; **1:5–7**, 51; **1:5–8**, 50; **1:6**, 7, 8, 17, 19, 20, 22, 38, 43, 45, 50; **1:6–8**, 17; **1:7**, 4, 18, 19, 37, 97, 100, 140, 164; **1:8**, 19; **1:9**, 7, 17, 21–22, 26, 45, 77, 101, 154, 164, 168; **1:9–11**, 21, 26; **1:9–14**, 21–26, 96; **1:9–15**, 68; **1:10**, 7, 16, 17, 22–23, 26, 36, 168; **1:10a**, 21; **1:10b**, 21; **1:10c**, 21; **1:11**, 21, 23, 79, 101; **1:11–12**, 23–25, 265; **1:12**, 7, 26, 33, 50, 80, 93, 96, 167, 203; **1:12–13**, 25; **1:12–14**, 24, 26; **1:12–20**, 23; **1:13**, 24, 25, 27, 59, 203; **1:14**, 25–26, 27, 55, 154; **1:15**, 27, 29–30, 32, 33, 34, 76; **1:15–16**, 38; **1:15–17**, 7, 29; **1:15–20**, 7, 17, 21, 24, 27–35, 38, 47, 52, 63, 92, 147, 170, 198; **1:15a**, 29; **1:15b**, 29; **1:16**, 27, 29, 30–31, 34, 53, 151, 170, 215, 219, 286, 292; **1:17**, 27, 29, 31; **1:17–18a**, 38; **1:18**, 29, 31–32, 34, 62, 171, 172, 173; **1:18–20**, 29; **1:18a**, 27, 29; **1:18b**, 28, 29; **1:18b–20**, 38; **1:19**, 28, 29, 32–33, 34–35, 52, 225; **1:20**, 8, 28, 29, 33–34, 35, 36, 80, 155; **1:21**, 36, 38, 127, 178; **1:21ff.**, 15; **1:21–23**, 27, 36–38; **1:22**, 33, 36–37, 38, 152; **1:23**, 7, 8, 16, 37, 38, 43, 44, 51, 101, 206, 209, 223; **1:23–27**, 205; **1:24**, 32, 39–42, 43, 44, 46, 171, 206, 219; **1:24–29**, 46; **1:25**, 43, 44, 51, 206, 209; **1:25–27**, 7; **1:25–29**, 8, 43–45, 46, 96, 155, 206, 210, 214; **1:26–27**, 45; **1:27**, 44, 155, 167, 191, 206, 207, 210; **1:28**, 8, 44–45, 81, 101, 206; **1:29**, 45, 46, 212; **2:1**, 4, 17, 46; **2:1–5**, 46–48; **2:1–8**, 15; **2:2**, 8, 44, 46, 47–48, 96, 101, 155, 206; **2:3**, 8, 46–47, 48; **2:4**, 18, 47, 51; **2:5**, 47; **2:5–7**, 8, 101; **2:6**, 16, 17, 29, 49, 50; **2:6–7**, 49–50; **2:6–10**, 64; **2:6–23**, 64; **2:7**, 16, 29, 49–50, 80, 96, 223; **2:8**, 4, 5, 6, 7, 18, 24, 25, 50, 51–52, 53–54, 65, 100; **2:8–10**, 51–54; **2:8–15**, 19; **2:8–23**, 12, 82, 195, 256; **2:9**, 6, 7, 32, 52, 225; **2:10**, 7, 31, 52, 53, 63, 225; **2:11**, 6, 8, 18, 41, 55–56, 57, 59, 64, 74, 190, 270; **2:11–12**, 57; **2:11–13**, 180, 198, 222, 233; **2:11–15**, 55–60, 64, 68, 69, 162; **2:12**, 7, 8, 18, 41, 56–57, 59, 60, 64, 69, 169, 179, 182, 270; **2:13**, 7, 57–

58, 74, 127; **2:14**, 7, 60, 65, 127; **2:14–15**, 19, 58–59; **2:15**, 5, 7, 31, 56, 59, 60, 151, 170, 196, 215, 219, 237, 286, 292; **2:16**, 5, 6, 61 62; **2:16–19**, 52; **2:16–23**, 6, 56, 61–67; **2:17**, 6, 62, 66; **2:17–18**, 65; **2:18**, 5, 6, 24, 53, 60, 62–63, 64, 65, 66–67, 223; **2:19**, 7, 19, 62, 63–64, 171, 246; **2:20**, 6, 7, 25, 52, 54, 62, 64–65, 67, 68, 69, 71, 74, 215, 216, 219, 270, 286, 292; **2:20f.**, 53; **2:20–22**, 5; **2:20–23**, 52, 64, 70; **2:21**, 65; **2:21–23**, 71; **2:22**, 6, 65; **2:23**, 5, 6, 65–66, 67, 223; **3:1**, 7, 68, 69, 70, 71, 101, 179, 180, 182; **3:1–2**, 72; **3:1–4**, 25, 68, 70–71, 180; **3:1–8**, 69; **3:1ff.**, 8, 49, 69, 228; **3:1–4:6**, 68–69; **3:2**, 70, 71, 101, 182; **3:2–4**, 70–71; **3:3**, 68, 69, 139; **3:3–4**, 71; **3:3a**, 182; **3:3b**, 182; **3:4**, 18; **3:5**, 68, 70, 72–73, 74–75, 78, 257; **3:5–8**, 74, 256; **3:5–9**, 70, 71, 72–75; **3:6**, 73; **3:7**, 36, 73–74, 112; **3:8**, 72, 74, 112; **3:8–12**, 250; **3:9**, 56, 68, 74, 252; **3:9–11**, 198; **3:9–17**, 69; **3:10**, 56, 68, 74, 76–77, 139, 196, 233, 251, 252, 285; **3:10–15**, 76–80; **3:11**, 8, 77, 87, 139, 196, 233; **3:12**, 26, 63, 72, 74, 77–79, 285; **3:12–15**, 229; **3:12–16**, 70; **3:12–17**, 77; **3:13**, 78, 79, 80; **3:14**, 78, 79, 230; **3:15**, 50, 78, 79–80, 81, 96, 197; **3:15–17**, 80, 164; **3:16**, 27, 78, 81, 84, 96, 198, 262, 263, 264; **3:16–17**, 81–82, 266; **3:16–18**, 96; **3:17**, 78, 82, 84, 96, 198; **3:18**, 88, 90, 268; **3:18–19**, 88; **3:18–21**, 69; **3:18–4:1**, 83–87, 90, 275; **3:19**, 88–89; **3:20**, 90, 277; **3:20–21**, 90, 277; **3:21**, 90, 279; **3:22**, 93, 94, 95; **3:22–4:1**, 69, 91–95, 113; **3:23**, 93, 94; **3:24**, 93, 94, 281; **3:25**, 94, 95, 281; **4:1**, 94; **4:2**, 50, 96, 164, 291; **4:2–4**, 84; **4:2–6**, 69, 96–98; **4:3**, 8, 102, 105, 106, 155, 210, 291; **4:3–4**, 96–97; **4:4**, 8; **4:5**, 258; **4:5–6**, 97; **4:6**, 97–98, 258; **4:7**, 37, 97; **4:7–8**, 99, 293; **4:7–14**, 11; **4:7–16**, 102; **4:7–17**, 4, 117; **4:7–18**, 97, 98, 99–102; **4:7ff.**, 124; **4:8**, 98; **4:9**, 10, 97, 99, 105; **4:10**, 10, 209; **4:10–11**, 99–100; **4:10–14**, 10; **4:12**, 4, 19, 21, 45 ,97, 140, 284; **4:12–13**, 100–101; **4:13**, 4, 19; **4:14**, 101; **4:15–16**, 101; **4:16**, 102, 106; **4:17**, 101–2, 105, 106; **4:18**, 39, 96, 102, 105, 106, 218

1 Thessalonians 1:1, 15, 146; **1:1–2**, 15; **1:2**, 17, 164; **1:3**, 17; **1:6**, 255; **2:13**, 17; **2:18**, 209; **2:19**, 191; **3:1ff.**, 15; **3:9**, 17; **4:3**, 73; **4:3–6**, 73; **4:12**, 97; **4:13**, 191; **4:13–5:11**, 84; **4:16**, 182; **4:17**, 181; **5:8**, 17, 283, 288, 289; **5:12**, 45; **5:12–22**, 98; **5:14**, 45; **5:16–18**, 23; **5:17**, 291; **5:18**, 164; **5:25**, 291; **5:27**, 101

2 Thessalonians 1:1–2, 15; **1:2**, 146; **1:3**, 17; **2:1–12**, 84; **2:8–10**, 287; **2:9**, 178; **2:13**, 17, 151; **2:17**, 22; **3:1**, 291; **3:7**, 255; **3:9**, 255; **3:17**, 102

1 Timothy 1:2, 146; **1:3**, 140; **1:4**, 223; **1:9**, 72, 73; **1:10**, 72, 73; **1:12–14**, 212; **1:16**, 230; **1:17**, 227; **1:18**, 283; **2:8–15**, 83; **2:9–15**, 268; **2:13**, 86; **2:14**, 86; **3:1–7**, 85; **3:2**, 72, 116; **3:3**, 72, 263; **3:8**, 263; **3:8–13**, 85; **3:9**, 232; **3:16**, 169, 262; **4:1**, 232; **4:3**, 62, 65; **4:6**, 232; **6:1**, 91; **6:1–10**, 83; **6:2**, 91; **6:4**, 223; **6:4–5**, 72; **6:11**, 72; **6:12**, 283; **6:18**, 186

2 Timothy 1:2, 146; **1:9**, 151; **1:10**, 166; **1:12**, 41; **1:18**, 140; **2:11**, 60; **2:12**, 181; **2:15**, 26; **2:18**, 60; **2:19**, 158; **3:2–5**, 72; **3:17**, 243; **4:1**, 25; **4:2**, 230, 240; **4:5**, 41, 239, 240; **4:10**, 101; **4:11**, 99, 101; **4:12**, 99, 140; **4:18**, 25

Titus 1:4, 146, 232; **1:5**, 85; **1:7**, 72, 85, 263; **1:8**, 72, 116; **1:13–14**, 65; **2:1–10**, 83; **2:3**, 263; **2:7**, 186; **2:13**, 167; **3:3**, 72; **3:5**, 57, 159, 162, 184, 271; **3:5–7**, 139; **3:12**, 99

Philemon, 4, 10, 92; **1**, 10, 15, 105, 106, 209; **1–3**, 106–7; **2**, 101, 106–7; **3**, 107, 117; **4–5**, 108–9; **4–7**, 108–9, 110, 114; **5**, 108, 109; **6**, 108, 109, 112, 114; **7**, 108, 109, 115; **8**, 111, 116; **8–9**, 110–11, 114; **8–22**, 110–16; **9**, 106, 108, 209; **10**, 106, 111; **10–13**, 114; **11**, 111–12; **12**, 112; **13**, 105, 112; **14**, 108, 109, 112–13, 114; **15**, 111, 113, 116; **15–16**, 114; **16**, 94, 108, 109, 113; **17**, 108, 111, 114; **18**, 114; **19**, 112, 114–15; **20**, 108, 109, 115; **21**, 115; **22**, 10, 97, 115–16; **23**, 10, 11, 19, 100; **23–25**, 117; **24**, 10, 11, 99

Hebrews **2:14**, 194, 196; **4:12**, 290; **4:14**, 238; **4:16**, 218; **5:12**, 51, 54; **6:2**, 166; **6:4**, 166; **6:10–12**, 17; **6:18**, 167; **7:26**, 238; **9:1–14**, 198; **9:14**, 36, 153; **10:19**, 218; **10:19ff.**, 198; **10:22**, 271; **10:22–24**, 17; **10:32**, 166; **10:36**, 26; **12:1**, 23; **13:2**, 116; **13:20**, 241

James **1:1**, 146; **1:2**, 41; **1:3**, 39; **1:4**, 39; **1:22**, 186; **2:14–26**, 186; **3:17**, 72; **4:1**, 284; **4:2**, 222; **4:3**, 222; **4:7**, 284

1 Peter, 72, 83, 92; **1:2**, 151; **1:3**, 150, 191; **1:3–8**, 17; **1:3–12**, 144, 161, 168; **1:6**, 39, 41; **1:7**, 39; **1:8**, 23; **1:12**, 216; **1:13**, 288; **1:19**, 36, 153; **1:21**, 17, 169; **1:22**, 17; **1:23–25**, 19; **1:25**, 290; **2:1**, 72; **2:2**, 22; **2:4–8**, 201; **2:4–10**, 37, 203, 204; **2:9**, 24, 25, 78, 160, 165, 166, 203; **2:10**, 203; **2:11**, 284; **2:12**, 186; **2:13–17**, 85, 91; **2:18–25**, 83, 91; **2:21**, 41; **2:25**, 241; **3:1–7**, 83; **3:5**, 191; **3:14**, 41; **3:15**, 97; **3:16a**, 97; **3:18–21**, 57, 162; **3:19**, 237; **3:20**, 230, 271; **3:21**, 184, 271; **3:22**, 31, 170, 215, 286; **4:1**, 41, 284; **4:3**, 72; **4:4**, 72; **4:6**, 237; **4:7**, 96; **4:9**, 116; **4:10**, 155; **4:11**, 23, 227; **4:13**, 23, 39, 41; **4:16**, 41; **5:2**, 241; **5:4**, 241; **5:5**, 63; **5:8**, 96, 284, 285, 291; **5:9**, 284, 291; **5:10**, 41; **5:11**, 23; **5:12**, 102

2 Peter **1:5–7**, 72; **3:8**, 84; **3:9**, 184; **3:10**, 54; **3:10–13**, 155; **3:12**, 54; **3:15**, 230; **3:18**, 22

1 John, 237; **1:5–7**, 25, 259; **1:7**, 165; **2:7–11**, 62; **2:8–11**, 259; **2:8ff.**, 165; **2:9**, 224; **2:15–17**, 177; **2:18**, 287;

3:11–19, 224; **4:1**, 19; **4:8**, 224; **4:13–21**, 224; **4:17**, 287

2 John **9**, 37

Jude **3**, 232; **8**, 72; **16**, 72; **24**, 37, 153, 227; **25**, 23, 227

Revelation, 92; **1:6**, 23; **1:11**, 140; **1:16**, 290; **1–3**, 140; **2:1–7**, 140; **2:10**, 41; **2:16**, 290; **3:14–22**, 101; **3:21**, 181; **5:13**, 23; **7:2–8**, 158; **9:4**, 158; **9:20**, 72; **9:21**, 72; **11:15**, 257; **16:12–16**, 287; **19:15**, 290; **20:4**, 181; **20:7**, 287; **20:8**, 287; **21:8**, 72; **22:4**, 158; **22:5**, 181; **22:15**, 72

APOCRYPHA

Wisdom of Solomon **5:17–20**, 283

EARLY CHRISTIAN LITERATURE

2 Clement **7.6**, 159; **8.6**, 159

Eusebius, *Ecclesiastical History* **11.22.1**, 10

Ignatius, *Letter to Polycarp* **6.2**, 284

Justin Martyr, *Apology* **I, 61**, 168; **I, 65**, 168

OTHER EARLY WRITINGS

Cicero, *Pro Flacco* **28**, 12

Josephus, *Antiquities* **15.11**, 194